# TEACHING THE SEVERELY HANDICAPPED,
## VOLUME I

*edited by*

## NORRIS G. HARING, ED.D.

*Director, Experimental Education Unit*
*Child Development and Mental Retardation Center*
*University of Washington*
*Seattle, Washington*

## LOUIS J. BROWN, PH.D.

*School of Education*
*Department of Studies in Behavioral Disabilities*
*University of Wisconsin*
*Madison, Wisconsin*

GRUNE & STRATTON
*A Subsidiary of Harcourt Brace Jovanovich, Publishers*
New York   San Francisco   London

**Library of Congress Cataloging in Publication Data**

Main entry under title:

Teaching the severely handicapped.

"The papers . . . are outgrowths of presentations made at a
seminar in Kansas City in November 1974."
Includes bibliographies and index.
1. Mentally handicapped children—Education—
Congresses.  I.  Haring, Norris Grover, 1923-  III.  Brown,
Louis J.
LC4601.T43      371.9 '284      76-25992
ISBN 0-8089-0945-2 (v. 1)
ISBN 0-8089-0980-0 (v. 2)

*Grune & Stratton, Inc.*
*111 Fifth Avenue*
*New York, New York 10003*

Library of Congress Catalog Number 76-25992
International Standard Book Number 0-8089-0945-2
Printed in the United States of America

# CONTENTS

Preface                                                                    vii
Contributors                                                                ix

I.   Introduction                                                           1

     A.   Future Directions in Work with Severely and Profoundly
          Handicapped Persons: An Overview                                  3
          *Norris G. Haring and Connie Pious*

     B.   Overview of Comprehensive Services for the
          Severely/Profoundly Handicapped                                  17
          *Norris G. Haring and Diane Bricker*

II.  Developmental Sequence and Curricula                                  33

     A.   Developmental Pinpoints                                          35
          *Marilyn Cohen, Pam Gross, and Norris G. Haring*

     B.   Educational Programming for the Severely/Profoundly
          Mentally Retarded                                               111
          *Ellen Somerton and Donald G. Meyers*

     C.   Prototypic Model for the Development of
          Instructional Materials                                         155
          *Debby D. Smith, James O. Smith,*
          *and Eugene B. Edgar*

III. Assessment and Performance Measurement                               177

     A.   Educational and Assessment Strategies for the
          Severely Handicapped                                            179
          *Wayne Sailor and R. Don Horner*

B.   Essentials of Performance Measurement            209
     *Dale Gentry and Norris G. Haring*

IV.  Intervention Strategies                            237

A.   Early and Continuous Intervention Strategies for
     Severely Handicapped Infants and Very
     Young Children                                     239
     *Alice H. Hayden, Gael McGinness,
     and Valentine Dmitriev*

B.   Intervention Strategies for the Severely and Profoundly
     Handicapped Child                                  277
     *Diane Bricker, William Bricker, Richard Iacino,
     and Laura Dennison*

C.   Language Development Programs for Severely
     Handicapped Children                               301
     *Doug Guess, Wayne Sailor, Bill Keogh,
     and Donald M. Baer*

     Index                                              327

# PREFACE

The papers collected in this book are outgrowths of presentations made at a seminar in Kansas City in November 1974. At that time, a number of people involved in training personnel to educate severely and profoundly handicapped children met for an informal information exchange. The group included professors from universities that have personnel preparation programs, graduate students, representatives of the Bureau of Education for the Handicapped, pediatricians, businessmen, parents of handicapped children, public school teachers and administrators, and state directors of special education. As the presentations and discussions concerning topics of mutual interest continued, this remarkably diverse group decided that they would form an organization devoted to improving the quality of life for severely handicapped persons. Since that time, their organization—The American Association for the Education of the Severely/Profoundly Handicapped—has been legally incorporated as a nonprofit organization.

The group recognized that there was an urgent need to provide instructional materials—guidelines, procedures, curricula—so that teachers and others on the front line could have something useful to work with as many of them met for the first time, in their classrooms, their new clientele: severely and profoundly handicapped children. We were extremely fortunate when Drs. Lester Mann and Robert Kalapos offered their assistance in disseminating materials that originated at the Kansas conference, and when Grune and Stratton agreed to publish the volume.

This volume, then, is the first product in what we hope will be a continuing series of materials from annual meetings of the Association, one of whose goals is to become an advocate group on behalf of the severely and profoundly handicapped. This is how that goal is spelled out in the Association's Articles of Incorporation:

The purposes for which the corporation is organized are as follows:

A. To function as an advocate organization for the development and implementation of comprehensive, high-quality educational services for severely and profoundly handicapped individuals from birth through early adulthood in the public school sector.

B. To serve as a separate entity in advocating the development of relevant and efficient pre-service and in-service teacher-training programs; and the development of highly specialized doctoral level, teacher training, research, and instructional design personnel.

C. To develop, refine, and disseminate inexpensive training packages, instructional programs, and materials pertinent to educational programs for the severely and profoundly handicapped.

D. To facilitate parent involvement in all program services for the severely and profoundly handicapped.

We can't say enough in praise of the response we received from this volume's authors. We presented them with something of a dilemma: we asked them to send us their manuscripts in less than four months, but at the same time we demanded quality, well-written material that would work in practical settings such as classrooms. Of course, the only way editors can make such demands and not risk questions about their sanity is to make them of people who know what they are doing. The authors of the chapters in this volume work daily and directly with severely handicapped children and they speak from first-hand experience. They have developed and refined the materials described, now presented for your consideration and use. There is very little in the volume that does not reflect direct acquaintance with the challenges we all face as we try to meet the needs of severely handicapped children.

Several Experimental Education Unit staff members have made major editing and writing contributions to some of these chapters, and for these efforts we would like to thank Gael McGinness, Connie Pious, John Bush, and Tracy Singer. Frances Anderson served as an executive assistant throughout all of the work associated with the first Kansas conference, and she has been responsible for coordinating our efforts to prepare this volume. The proof of her effectiveness is that we did get the manuscripts to the publisher by his deadline, and that the volume is now in your hands.

*NORRIS G. HARING*
*LOU BROWN*

# TEACHING THE SEVERELY HANDICAPPED
## VOLUME I

# Introduction

Norris G. Haring and
Connie Pious

**A**

# Future Directions in Work with Severely and Profoundly Handicapped Persons: An Overview

Most readers would expect that the logical place for a chapter about future needs is at the end of a volume. The final chapter in a book that describes current activities might begin, "You've just read about what we're doing now; here's what we still have to do." At the risk of seeming illogical, however, I have chosen to introduce this volume with a discussion about the future, for the following reason. I take very seriously the remark whose variations have been attributed to everyone from Hegel to Santayana: "If we ignore the past, we are condemned to repeat it." Since it is no secret that our history of serving severely handicapped citizens in our society is anything but distinguished, we dare not repeat our old mistakes. I want to emphasize how serious the contributors to this volume (and its companion volumes) are about developing new programs and new options that represent significant departures from old practices. The programs you will read about in subsequent chapters offer many creative responses to identified problems, and they represent the basis for future activities. Therefore, by identifying some of the most glaring mistakes we have made in the past and by outlining the directions we need to take in the future, I hope to establish a context in which the significance of this volume's contents can be appreciated. I would like to begin by discussing our reasons for preparing this volume.

## WHY IS THIS BOOK NECESSARY?

### The Need To Change Attitudes

The most generous word that can be used to describe traditional public attitudes toward handicapped persons is "apathetic." For the most part, people not directly involved in the life of a severely handicapped person have preferred to maintain a distance between themselves and the handicapped. Over the years, people have frequently done more than play ostrich—they have balked at providing the public funds required for adequate services to this segment of the population. The corollary to both ostrich behavior and fiscal narrow-mindedness in our society has been a system in which we put our severely handicapped persons into storage. We removed them to institutions that were conveniently isolated from population centers. Having done that much, we saw no reason to do more, and we turned our attention to more comfortable, or at least less intractable, problems. Putting "difficult" citizens into storage turned out to be the cheapest, least bothersome way of coping with them. Moreover, since the public view of a segment of the population permitted their dismissal from ordinary life, it followed that the public holding that view was equally apathetic about providing care at anything more than the custodial level. At least one of the arguments stated: There is nothing you can do for these people; why bother?

Occasionally, however, jolts to our apathy were provided by media exposures of some of the "storage" conditions. Burton Blatt's *Christmas in Purgatory* (1966) brought the public a shocking view of the dismal conditions in the locked back wards of state institutions for the severely handicapped—forgotten children, young adults, and others living in filth and degradation. The public was outraged. Although the reasons for these conditions were "explainable"—the institutions were overpopulated and understaffed—it was clear that more acceptable standards of care had to be achieved. Frederick Wiseman's 1967 film, "Titicut Follies," was a savage indictment of conditions in a state mental institution. Once again, there was an appalling picture of filth, degradation, and inhumane treatment of patients. Once again, there was public outrage and revulsion that any human beings should be treated this way. By the time Geraldo Rivera produced his film and book *Willowbrook* (1972), it was apparent that public pressure to upgrade standards had had at least some impact. Some amenities had been added to storage; the children were clean and their rooms were clean. But physical amenities are only one part of the picture, and *Willowbrook* documented other conditions of storage that were unchanged. For here, too, there were back wards, locked doors, and abandoned people. The gloom that hung over these institutions matched perfectly the psychological condition of the patients. Improving the living conditions of institutionalized persons is simply not enough. To be stored, even in a lush environment, is nevertheless to be stored. So long as we focus our moral outrage and public pressure on physical improvements only, we are simply begging the question.

Fortunately, public attitudes about handicapped citizens are beginning to undergo fundamental change, attributable to several factors. Out of the turmoil and stress of the 1960s came a legacy of concern for the civil and constitutional rights of people routinely denied these rights in the past—minority persons, prisoners, institutionalized populations, and children. This period also marked the culmination of many years' struggle by parents of handicapped children to achieve a fair share of public services for their children. The legislative and judicial mandates which resulted from parents' legal and civic activities require that we educate our handicapped citizens, not merely give them custodial care. Finally, we have looked at technology developed over the last two decades in work with moderately handicapped people, and we have had to ask ourselves whether the "surprising" progress that so many of them have made in response to systematic intervention might not also be possible for their more severely involved peers.

In fact, the most promising aspect of the changing public views is that we are asking questions that were rarely expressed before. Is storage in fact the most economical "treatment" for severely handicapped persons? Can we find the means to teach skills that will enable these people to do more than busy work? Can we help them to become at least semi-independent financially through meaningful occupational activity? Can we find alternate living arrangements that accord these people the dignity they deserve? Can we impart self-help skills and other skills that permit handicapped persons to express their individuality and to meet their social needs? Notice that the questions we ask are directed exactly where they should be—to those of us who are responsible for educating severely handicapped persons, for that is really the crux of the matter. In order to reverse completely the prevailing view of severely handicapped persons—that "nothing can be done for them, so why bother"—it is our responsibility as educators to *teach* and to demonstrate unmistakably to the public that severely handicapped persons *can* learn.

### The Need To Develop Systematic Instruction

We are beginning to recognize some of the instructional components necessary for the undertaking of educational responsibilities mentioned earlier. The skills that special educators need in order to educate their handicapped pupils are of a very high level, in part because of one of the educational differences between handicapped and nonhandicapped children. Normal children usually have little difficulty in learning how to learn; to some extent, they teach themselves. But children who have handicapping conditions that interfere with learning obviously require interventions that teach these learning skills as well as more conventional topics. Moreover, these interventions must be systematic and precise. Special educators have had to focus so much of their effort on *how* to teach that they have developed some fairly sophisticated task-analysis skills, beginning with analysis of the first step in the teaching process: attracting and keeping their pupils' attention.

Nevertheless, the procedures that educators have developed in their work with moderately handicapped children will have to take a quantum leap; what we now consider sophisticated skills may well seem primitive as we develop the instructional competencies necessary to teach our new educational clientele, the severely/profoundly handicapped. Because these children have traditionally been dismissed as uneducable, we have little reliable information about what they can, in fact, accomplish. We do know, however, that the few earlier attempts to teach this population began with instructional steps that were far too broadly defined. Expectations were too high at the beginning of the instructional sequence, and there was inevitable disappointment in the children's progress, disappointment that bolstered the prevailing view that "nothing can be done." We know that we need to slice the learning steps into much finer increments. What were formerly considered beginning competencies may, in fact, be the end product of many prerequisite competencies. We also know that under the most ideal conditions for learning, the instructional cues are arranged to elicit responses that reveal progress. The cues we will need and the responses we seek may seem microscopic compared to those in earlier efforts. What this suggests, of course, is that we will need to build much more systematization into our instruction of the severely handicapped than has been necessary in our instruction of mild-to-moderately handicapped children.

We will also need to pay far more attention to those stages in the learning process that go beyond mere acquisition of skills. In the past, work with severely handicapped children has focused almost exclusively on skill acquisition at the expense of later phases in the learning sequence, such as proficiency building, maintenance, generalization, and application of learned skills in new and broader contexts. We have learned in our work with moderately handicapped children that the instructional procedures required for pupils to develop skills through these different stages vary according to the phase of learning that the child is experiencing. For instance, those procedures or tactics we use to enable a child to *acquire* the skill of shoe-tying will change somewhat when our instructional goal is for the child to *master* that skill to some criterion such as ten errorless trials; and they will change again when the goal is for the child to use that same shoe-tying skill with different shoes, or to employ the tying skills to tie string around a package or a sash around the child's waist.

As children advance from skill acquisition to the point where they can perform tasks appropriately and at a rate tolerable to parents, teachers, peers, and others in their environment, they will be involved in practicing these skills continuously and across situations. Work with moderately handicapped children suggests that without such practice, they will not be able to maintain or use the skills appropriately. Research findings indicate that demonstration and modeling have been useful instructional procedures in promoting skill acquisition; drill helps to promote proficiency; practice of various kinds promotes generalization; problem solving *may* be the most useful tactic for promoting appropriate application of learned skills, although not enough work has been undertaken in this area to permit unequivocal statements about this procedure. The problem, of course, is that most research findings derive from work with *moderately* handicapped children. We know all too little about how their counterparts in the severely handicapped population move through the various stages of learning, and, as a result, we know correspondingly little about instructional procedures to match this progression. Moreover, the research has been somewhat fragmentary and some of the "answers" to instructional questions are ambiguous. The challenge we face as educators is to find these answers as they relate to severely handicapped children and to refine and systematize our instructional procedures sufficiently to make transitions from skill acquisition to application as efficient and satisfying as possible.

Educators could improve the efficiency of their planning and instruction if they had systematic guidelines to use in selecting instructional procedures. Such selection has often been either haphazard or defeatingly rigid. Selecting procedures at random reduces teachers' efficacy in working with individual pupils, but worse, it virtually eliminates the possibility of evaluating children's performance changes in relation to instructional methods. At the other extreme, when procedures are rigidly prescribed (as with adherence to certain teaching "fads" or theories), it is difficult to alter instructional tactics to accommodate learning idiosyncrasies or individual differences in pupil performance. Guidelines for selecting procedures should avoid both pitfalls and should enable teachers to select child-appropriate, phase-appropriate, and task-appropriate instructional tactics. The basic requirements are that teachers have alternate tactics (procedures that are flexible enough to permit individualized programs) and that the procedures permit evaluation of pupil performance. Through the use of developmental pinpoints and task analysis, the teacher can determine and sequence curriculum activities based on typical development. With guidelines for selecting instructional procedures, he can also match his teaching tactics to his pupils' actual movement through the various stages of learning a given skill.

Moreover, as suggested in the contribution to this volume by Smith, Smith, and Edgar, instructors are going to have to apply their task analyses to a wide variety of skills to be imparted. Unfortunately, because severely handicapped persons have been presumed to be uneducable, there are few curriculum materials that teach the skills they need. The available commercial materials tend to teach skills which the commercial developer wants to teach, and which may have limited application to the real-world needs of these children and young adults. For instance, fitting together the pieces of a puzzle may promote some cognitive and fine-motor development but have minor utility if the specific skills do not generalize. Those fine-motor and cognitive exercises might be more appropriate if they were organized around a self-help task, such as dressing or feeding oneself. The most urgent need is for curriculum materials with built-in measurement components so that we can adequately assess the progress of children in our charge.

In order to meet the responsibilities spelled out in legislative and judicial mandates regarding education of severely handicapped children and youth, we have to seek a much higher level of precision than we have customarily brought to the instructional scene. We may need a laboratory environment where all aspects of the environment are arranged and re-arranged until we find out what works best to meet the individual needs of our pupils. Only through uniform and systematic procedures can this challenge be met.

### The Need for Coordinated Efforts

Thinking about the magnitude of the task ahead, it is not hard to be overcome by frustration at one's own limited ability to undertake such a complex and challenging responsibility. But perhaps that is the main point. One lesson we must learn from the mistakes of the past is that this work should not be undertaken by anyone alone. The comprehensive and lifelong management of severely handicapped persons—a theme throughout this volume—requires the coordinated effort of many professionals, community persons, agencies, and parents. If anyone thinks this is an exaggeration, I suggest reading the May 1975 issue of *Exceptional Children*, an issue devoted to "The Parent–Professional Partnership." That is, of course, a somewhat ironic title, since so many of the articles document the appalling struggle that parents of severely handicapped children have had as they tried to make their way through bureaucratic mazes in an attempt to find services that usually turned out to be unavailable for their children. The frustration and psychological isolation of parents of severely handicapped children are simply magnified versions of the frustration and psychological isolation that threaten professionals who attempt to provide services without coordinated effort.

Yet a look at the present picture tells us that we have a long way to go in coordinating the work of all people and agencies involved. For instance, the U.S. General Accounting Office's *Report to the Congress* (1974) describes fragmented, duplicative, and thoroughly inadequate service delivery to handicapped persons. Therefore, a first step in improving the efficiency and the comprehensiveness of our services is to develop procedures for insuring, at local, state, regional, and national levels, that the work of different agencies is coordinated. There are several promising precedents for this, such as the Office of Child Development/Bureau of Education for the Handicapped Collaborative Projects, aimed at integrating handicapped children in Head Start; and collaboration among state agencies in many areas, such as Washington State, to insure the delivery of necessary services without duplication.

Any plans for educating severely/profoundly handicapped persons must address not only the future welfare of the persons served, but also improvements in the field and in service delivery. These issues are, of course, interrelated. A second step, then, in our efforts to avoid the mistakes of the past is to insure that training provided for those who will work with the severely handicapped is oriented towards coordinated approaches to management.

If we are to develop an adequate supply of well-trained professionals who will participate in long-term management of the severely/profoundly handicapped, and if we are to develop programs that address the complicated questions involved in such management, the most efficient means for achieving these goals is to establish comprehensive centers for training, service, and research. We would expect that, in such centers, professionals from many different disciplines would pool their expertise to develop appropriate programs and to train new generations of experts in various aspects of management. Dr. George Tarjan (1975) has made an interesting distinction between multidisciplinary and interdisciplinary work. He suggests that multidisciplinary efforts are usually akin to "parallel play," in that the various professionals work on problems from their separate vantage points, even though they may work in the same building or center. On the other hand, the end product of interdisciplinary work is greater than the sum of its parts—the interactive learning and give-and-take among the professionals yield something new and different that reflects more than one particular approach to problems. If we are, in fact, to provide more than the custodial care that has traditionally been offered our new educational clientele, anything less than an interdisciplinary assault on the many problems would be decidedly unsatisfactory. No single profession has arrived at workable solutions to these problems, and only concerted effort will lead to comprehensive solutions. If a network of such interdisciplinary centers were located strategically across this country, their staffs would contribute significantly toward providing appropriate education for all severely handicapped children, and they would be important sources of research in the areas of education and management. They might also contribute to efforts to standardize procedures.

But it is extremely expensive to train professionals. Moreover, the service these professionals provide after they have been trained is costly to consumers. One means of making service delivery more efficient and cost-effective is to share our professional expertise—for instance, by drawing paraprofessionals, community volunteers, and parents (or other caregivers) into our management strategies. We serve more than economic ends by extending the pool of trained management personnel; by increasing the skills and confidence of those who work directly with severely handicapped children, we do much to insure continuity in appropriate care for the children. Active participants in the centers just mentioned would, therefore, need to include the children's parents or surrogate parents, paraprofessional trainees, and community volunteers, as well as those undergraduate and graduate students training for professional careers in the social or health sciences. Trainees in such centers would benefit from extensive practicum training supervised by those at the postdoctoral level who have strong basic competencies and experience in interdisciplinary work. At least part of the training time should be devoted to developing the skills necessary for working on an interdisciplinary team.

It may be that one means of insuring adequate assessment of service needs and appropriate delivery of service would be a registry system maintained either by the regional centers just proposed or by an agency within the catchment area of the centers. Although there are some risks involved in maintaining registries of any sort, such as invasion of privacy, the benefits to be derived from tracking and identifying individual and community service needs should outweigh those risks. There are precautions that can be taken to protect the privacy of anyone listed in the registry.

Coordinated efforts of agencies and truly interdisciplinary work among professionals and trainees should improve the welfare of severely handicapped persons and the services delivered to them. First, through coordinated efforts, local services would be available to families—a particularly important factor for families of handicapped infants and young children. If we accept that the earliest possible intervention is necessary and can, in fact, prevent a handicapped child from developing secondary or associated handicaps, then it is vitally important that services be accessible, so that families are not disrupted by long-distance travel for appropriate care. Such local services should also increase the support necessary for parents in the crucial early stages of accepting their child's handicapping condition—the kind of support that encourages them to look positively at what they can do for their child. Alice H. Hayden and Valentine Dmitriev address this topic in their contribution to Volume II of this series. Second, it is likely that management procedures could more readily be standardized through coordinated efforts, thus insuring continuity of service. Another important outcome of coordination would be better dissemination of relevant information; easier access by professionals to the work of their peers in other centers; more information available to parents and families concerning existing or proposed services in their area (the nationally distributed newsletter, *Closer Look Report,* is a superb example of this kind of information dissemination); and better communication among staffs of agencies so that their deployment of resources is efficient and nonduplicative.

Through interdisciplinary work, it should be possible for professionals from allied health disciplines to improve their early diagnostic and assessment measures, another step necessary in insuring early intervention for handicapped infants. Although one must make the case for lifelong interdisciplinary management of severely handicapped persons, it is in early infancy and at the level of identification that we need to take immediate steps. With the cooperation of obstetricians, pediatricians, nurses, educators, developmental specialists, and parents, it should be possible to identify and accurately assess every severely handicapped child soon enough after birth to permit effective intervention. It is here that one has the most dramatic illustration of just how necessary everyone's skills are—the overall quality of management and the probability of its success are diminished if any part of the equation is missing. Robin Beck, Georgia Adams, Sandra Livingston, and Lynn Chandler discuss this topic in Volume II, and they describe a new infant program that is attempting to bring together the many disciplines in comprehensive management.

Finally, a more coordinated approach to management of severely handicapped persons should address one of the critical needs of our society—the need for acceptance of the handicapped.

## The Need for Community Acceptance of Handicapped Persons

Any consideration of future directions in work with severely handicapped persons must address large societal issues which are not often thought to be within the province of educators. Special educators, who will no doubt comprise a large part of the audience for this volume, have also stayed outside the struggle on these issues, perhaps, as one educator has suggested, because they are too "special" and too removed from the mainstream not only of education, but also of community life. I would suggest, however, that because the educational community has day-to-day responsibility for the welfare of handicapped persons from infancy or early childhood through an extended period of their lives, educators should be involved in planning and coordinating the lifelong services that will be available after their pupils leave the strictly educational setting. The issue is not restricted to those services provided by agencies, however. The more fundamental concern is the immense and complicated issue of the community's acceptance of and attitude towards its handicapped citizens, particularly now that the old practice of storing these citizens is changing.

How many accommodations will a community make to enable handicapped persons to participate as fully in community life as they choose? How many options are there within society for utilizing the skills that handicapped persons have acquired during their education? What recreational facilities exist for older handicapped persons who may no longer have access to recreational activities provided by schools? And, now that the health and social sciences have improved conditions enough to lengthen the life expectancy of handicapped persons, do we know enough about their aging process to meet their changing needs? We do know that aging in our society is no joyous process and that "senior citizens" do not enjoy the respect accorded their peers in other societies—witness organizations like the Grey Panthers, whose main objective is to increase the possibilities and options for aging citizens and to make their lives more meaningful. The lead article in the June 2, 1975, issue of *Time* magazine reveals the enormous blank spaces in our culture reserved for the aging; yet the only mention of "the handicapped" in the six-page article refers to a program whereby older persons can visit and serve handicapped persons as a means of doing meaningful work.

Interestingly, the discussions now concerning senior citizens sound very much like discussions we should be having about handicapped citizens: how to integrate them successfully into community life; how to provide the social and health services they need but can rarely afford; how to house them in dwellings that accommodate their handicapping conditions but are not social ghettos; how to insure that their care is not a staggering burden for their families. Perhaps our newly-awakened concern for our aging citizens can generalize to others exiled from our society. The record so far is a sorry one. (For an interesting review of attitude studies, see *Attitudes Towards the Retarded*, 1973.)

Yet it is fair to say that, without community support systems, any work by educators to meet congressional and judicial mandates for educating handicapped persons will be wasted effort. Now that our society has agreed to provide at least one kind of care for handicapped citizens through the educational system, we look forward to abolishing institutions. But it is sobering to examine at least one of the reasons why institutions were started in the first place: because families and communities could not provide adequate care, let alone education, for severely handicapped persons. This is one egregious mistake of the past that cannot be permitted to recur; if handicapped persons are to live in communities, the communities must find the means of making life tolerable and enjoyable for them and their families.

I will give only a few examples of the kinds of services that need to be established and developed. First, we need to provide opportunities for respite for families of handicapped children. We need trained persons who can take over for families at reasonable prices, whether they come to the family home or work in a center where children can be left for an evening, a vacation, or other needed respite. We need to consider adoptions or foster parenting for children whose natural parents cannot cope with the burdens of lifelong care. We need to do some creative thinking about living arrangements, such as group homes or other communal systems that enable handicapped persons to live in the community but in a semisheltered environment, if necessary. We need to insure that everyone within the community whose work impinges on the life of a handicapped person will perform that work kindly and intelligently. This includes barbers and hairdressers, bus drivers, supermarket employees, insurance agents, shop clerks, dentists, and physicians. The community's meeting places—churches, cinemas, restaurants, social organizations, recreational facilities—must keep their doors open to severely handicapped persons, so that they can participate in activities of their choice without feeling that they are only grudgingly admitted. Perhaps we need some "desegregation" laws to achieve this admittance into society. Laws will not insure acceptance, but enforced custom may eventually do so. In any case, I believe that educators have a critical role to perform in educating the larger community to its responsibilities toward handicapped persons and in coordinating the work of social and health service agencies to bring about fundamental social change.

## FOR WHOM WAS THIS BOOK WRITTEN?

This book is addressed to everyone involved with severely/ profoundly handicapped citizens: parents, professionals, trainees, bus drivers, grocery store clerks—anyone who has frequent contact with severely handicapped citizens and who cares enough to want to interact with them as meaningfully and helpfully as possible. As a result of recent legislative and judicial mandates for educating the severely handicapped, the number of professionals and nonprofessionals interacting with these citizens will necessarily increase. Yet, if the past has taught us anything, it has made us sensitive to the isolation and frustration that result from trying to serve this population without coordinated effort. I hope that the diversity of topics covered in this book will point the way to coordinated approaches to management and to meeting the challenge faced by all of us.

## WHY WERE THESE AUTHORS SELECTED?

Dr. Edward Sontag, of the Personnel Preparation Division of the Bureau of Education for the Handicapped, has identified and worked with some of the key personnel in preparation centers throughout the country. Through his encouragement to establish the competencies needed by teachers of the severely handicapped, and with his leadership in all inservice training matters, he has involved the contributing authors of this volume in the most relevant, active advancement of this technology. The authors, in turn, are disseminating this information to teachers and other interested personnel who are involved with the severely handicapped. This chapter has been concerned with the future and its challenges to develop approaches to serving the severely handicapped which radically depart from the custodial approach of ''storing'' these citizens in the back wards of institutions. Authors contributing to this volume are committed to exploring new ways of serving handicapped populations, of providing new directions for the development of community support services, and of enabling our severely handicapped citizens to live as independently as possible.

### REFERENCES

Attitudes Towards the Retarded: A Summary of Studies to 1972. Washington, D.C., The President's Committee on Mental Retardation, 1973, DHEW Publication No. (OS) 73–82
Blatt B: Christmas in Purgatory: A Photographic Essay on Mental Retardation. Boston, Allyn & Bacon, 1966
Closer Look Report. Periodic publication of the National Information Center for the Handicapped
Comptroller General of the United States. Report to the Congress. Federal Programs for Education of the Handicapped: Issues and Problems. Washington, D.C. United States General Accounting Office, December, 1974 [GAO Report No. B-164031(1)]

New outlook for the aged. Time, June 2, 1975, pp 44–51
*The* "Parent–Professional Partnership" *issue* of Exceptl Child, 41 (May): 8, 1975
Rivera G: Willowbrook. New York, Vantage, 1972
Tarjan G: Critical issues in interdisciplinary research. Paper presented at the Charles C.
    Strother—Child Development and Mental Retardation Center Seminar, The Interdisci-
    plinary Team in Health: Critical Issues in Education, Leadership, Clinical Practice, and
    Research. Child Development and Mental Retardation Center, University of
    Washington, Seattle, Washington, May 27, 1975
Wiseman F, Bridgewater Film Company (producers). Titicut Follies [film]. Directed by
    Frederick Wiseman and presented by Titicut Follies Film Distributing Company, 1967

Norris G. Haring and
Diane Bricker

**B**

# Overview of Comprehensive Services for the Severely/Profoundly Handicapped

One hundred years ago, Itard and Séguin, usually considered the founding fathers of special education, had just begun to acquire a mild notoriety in Western Europe. These two men were among the first to propose that training in appropriate ways of behaving might enable the severely handicapped (then called "natural idiots") to lead more normal lives. Special education as a discipline has had a number of birthdays since the work of these early pioneers, and has progressed far from such appalling terminology as "natural idiots"; nevertheless, the idea that severely handicapped individuals can be helped by training and can approach normalized living has not been fully accepted.

This nation's continued practice of placing severely and profoundly handicapped children in state residential institutions has for years precluded the development of effective community programs that provide identification, early intervention, and long-term community integration. Recently, however, several excellent, comprehensive programs have been developed which have allowed such children to remain in their natural home environments. But even these few comprehensive community programs for severely handicapped children are providing only a rough approximation of the ideal educational model.

Severely handicapped persons are difficult to teach; they present the parent and professional with the most challenging problems in intervention, instruction, and daily management. In fact, the problems are so numerous and complex that many educators have concluded that severely handicapped children do not or cannot learn. This is a prime example of self-fulfilling prophesies: certainly these individuals will not learn if their teachers assume that they cannot learn. Moreover, this damaging attitude has resulted in placing limits on instructional goals for this population. The view that the profoundly handicapped person needs to be hospitalized, kept in a crib or bed, fed, toileted, and supervised 24 hours a day is outdated. For example, at the Yakima Valley School, where the superintendent would not accept the view that profoundly handicapped children should be kept in cribs and constantly supervised, a teaching program based on behavioral principals was initiated. In less than a year the children were out of the cribs during the day, ambulating in some form on their own, and almost all were feeding and dressing themselves unaided.

Our own conceptual limitations about the learning capacity of these children no doubt contribute significantly to our failure to develop effective instructional plans and curricula. This is especially true when an early diagnosis of a severely handicapping condition is accompanied by a prognosis of minimal learning potential. Certainly, in some diseases diagnosis may lead to accurate prognosis; however, in most cases, the diagnosis of a severely handicapping condition should not be treated as an accurate prognosis used for excluding children from educational services.

Another rationale for withholding effective instruction from severely handicapped persons derives from the philosophy that, in the face of limited resources, these resources should go to those who will gain the most from them. This philosophy is based on at least two spurious assumptions. The first is that the severely handicapped make fewer gains than other individuals; however, when these children receive systematic instruction, their proportional behavioral gains may approximate the gains of other children (Hamblin, 1971). The second assumption is that resources are conserved by withholding costly educational services; yet, in the birth-through-adult perspective, the state uses far greater resources to maintain severely handicapped persons when they have not had early, effective instruction. Furthermore, the cost of lifelong institutionalization is not trivial.

"Trainable" and "educable" are terms still in use, even though these terms rest on definitions which set preconceived limits on what a handicapped individual will be able to learn; however, research is demonstrating that the severely involved individual can reach levels of performance beyond that predicted by such traditional terms. Prehm and Mayfield (1959) and Zeaman and House (1958) were among the first researchers to demonstrate that methods found successful in educating the mildly or moderately handicapped would work with the severely handicapped. This work, conducted 15 years ago, primarily involved laboratory tasks such as paired-associate learning. Today, our task is to extend those efforts to skill areas critical to the achievement of semi-independent living in a complex society. We can look forward to success in this endeavor, partly because we have at last achieved a technology of instruction which will allow us to effect meaningful levels of behavioral change even in the most handicapped pupil.

## THE TECHNOLOGY OF BEHAVIORAL CHANGE

The technology of behavioral change did not exist when special education was born; it has grown up over the last 25 to 50 years, and has revolutionized special education, as well as other behavioral disciplines. Without this technology, the effort to improve the functioning of the severely handicapped would have been almost impossible.

The 13 principles of behavioral technology defined by Krumboltz and Krumboltz (1972) can be divided into five areas: developing new behavior; strengthening new behavior; maintaining new behavior; eliminating inappropriate behavior; and modifying emotional behavior. These behavioral principles allow for a functional analysis of behavior and furnish intervention agents with a powerful means of producing and maintaining positive changes in human behavior. This technology allows us to target the exact behavior of concern; to observe reinforcing events that can be used contingently to maintain, increase, or decrease behavior; and, finally, to measure objectively the implementation of an effective intervention, using the environment/behavior relationships to promote substantial behavioral change.

If we look closely at the application of behavioral technology to the education of the severely handicapped, we see that most special educators have not been trained to teach or shape such skills as self-feeding, toileting, dressing, or walking. Even skilled behavioral technologists have a difficult task applying their technology to an area which, as far as curriculum is concerned, is an uncharted wilderness. The need for developing curricula to teach the severely handicapped is acute.

Anyone who has faced a "normal" classroom should know that teaching is a process which begins with two basic questions: "What am I going to teach?" and "How am I going to teach it?" These questions become crucial when applied to the special education classroom for severely handicapped individuals. We know some of the answers to the second question. Teaching methods are becoming more sophisticated each day, as research identifies more and more instructional tactics appropriate to the various stages of learning: acquisition, proficiency, maintenance, generalization, and application to novel problems (Haring, 1974). However, the question of what to teach is more complicated, and it includes academic skills and preacademic and self-help skills ranging from learning to read a stop sign to appropriate tracking behavior. Moreover, "What am I going to teach?" may be different for each individual in each community across the country. What is an essential skill in rural Kansas may be an unnecessary skill in New York City. Skills once considered highly survival-related, such as cloth-making, are now valued mainly by hobbyists or artisans. Over time and geography, skills keep changing. Therefore, it is of the utmost necessity that teachers of the severely handicapped perfect methods of changing behavior which lead not only to specific skill acquisition, but to generalization of these skills across tasks, settings, and people.

If we cannot predict in advance what specific skills are likely to be needed in a given situation, we must provide teachers with the behavioral technology to analyze novel skills or tasks in order to deal with the criteria, behavioral objectives, and the sequencing of behavioral components.

We must also provide instructors with step-by-step procedures for teaching any skill or task. Inevitably, the day will come when comprehensive curricula for teaching essential life skills will be available for the severely handicapped individual. For this population in particular, it should not be utopian to expect some degree of uniformity in a curriculum to impart the foundation skills. Systematic procedures and comprehensive curricula are essential in providing individualized programs to teach the severely handicapped. Little room for error exists in our instructional strategies and tactics for severely involved pupils. The normal or gifted child seems to learn as he lives, without the benefit of systematic instruction. The more handicapped the child, the less able he is to use the "natural cues" in the everyday environment to teach himself.

### Model Community Programs for the Severely/Profoundly Handicapped

Special educators have evolved from the more general class of educators, and this "ancestry" has clear implications in terms of their skills. The training given to most special educators has concentrated on refining their skills for teaching primarily school-age children rather traditional academic subjects. Recently, however, the discipline of special education has found itself in a whole new realm, confronted with teaching children from the first days after birth through adulthood and concerned with subject matter such as self-feeding, toileting, sitting without support, or walking with prosthetic devices.

Many local, state, federal, and private agencies have indicated intense interest in obtaining appropriate services for severely handicapped persons, suggesting that we have already evolved beyond questioning whether we should serve this population. Consequently, the primary goal of this book is to offer a variety of strategies for meeting the service needs of the severely handicapped. Although the contributors have attempted to provide a variety of specific curriculum approaches and methods for meeting this challenge, the purpose of this chapter is to articulate the need for a comprehensive system to serve this population adequately. We believe the success of the movement depends on the formulation, dissemination, and implementation of such a comprehensive approach.

In traditional educational settings, the classroom teacher has been the sole agent responsible for implementing an intervention program. This strategy is unrealistic when the pupils are multiply handicapped, since a teacher, no matter how well trained, is only one of several professionals needed to generate the required programs. Faced with a group of children and adults who are multiply handicapped, difficult to manage, and at risk of needing special services for most of their lives, no single intervention agent, whether a teacher, physician, speech therapist, or vocational rehabilitation specialist, could be expected to solve the problems single-handedly. Indeed, we believe that in order to provide adequate, comprehensive intervention programs for the profoundly handicapped person, interventionists from a number of disciplines are needed to help structure and apply the resulting program.

By comprehensive intervention, we mean a system which can be activated when the problem is detected (at birth in the case of most profoundly impaired individuals) and continued until the individual has become at least semi-independent. In addition to this longitudinal breadth, a comprehensive system must provide service in depth. It must include components that cover all important aspects of the individual's life. We have isolated six basic interactive components that we believe are necessary for comprehensive intervention: (1) a developmental framework; (2) early and continuous intervention; (3) systematic instructional procedures; (4) appropriate curricula; (5) adjunctive services from professionals in medicine, occupational therapy, physical therapy, speech pathology and audiology, nutrition, social work, and parent training; and (6) objective evaluation. An implicit consideration is that these interventions must continue throughout the life of the handicapped person and include long-range planning for integrating the person into his home community.

## NECESSARY COMPONENTS
## OF A COMPREHENSIVE SYSTEM

### A Developmental Framework

One of the primary weaknesses in the field of special education is the lack of models or comprehensive systems that provide structure and guidance for determining what to teach and criteria for subsequent evaluation of that material (Hobbs, 1975). Working from a model or theoretical base is useful because one can focus on generative response forms which transcend specific situations, materials, and organisms. In more cases than we care to document, decisions are made about the futures of children in the absence of any systematic framework. Although a number of psychologists have spent considerable time and effort generating theories or models to explain behavior (Bruner, 1966a; Hull, 1951; Osgood, 1967), the field of special education has no corollary model building effort (Bricker, 1972). The few models that exist are relatively circumscribed in their application (e.g., ITPA is concerned only with linguistic behavior). A few comprehensive models have direct application to the field of special education, such as Tharp and Wetzel (1969), Bruner (1966b), and, of course, Piaget (1970).

We believe that future progress may be heavily dependent on the creation and implementation of general systems which can offer a systematic basis for decision-making. The model which currently holds the greatest promise for building and implementing a comprehensive approach to profoundly handicapped persons is the developmental model, which accepts three basic tenets. First, growth or changes in behavior follow a developmental hierarchy. For example, children generally learn to vocalize before uttering words, they are able to hold their heads up before bilateral crawling, and they must be able to grasp before picking up objects. Second, behavior acquisition moves from simple to more complex responses (e.g., the child learns to focus his eyes before he learns to read). Third, more complex behavior is the result of coordinating or modifying simpler component response forms. For example, the hand-eye coordination scheme is the result of coordination of two primary circular reactions: visual tracking and grasping (Bricker, Bricker, Iacino, and Dennison, this volume).

Several chapters in this book discuss the application of the developmental model to severely/profoundly handicapped children. The constructive interaction adaptation approach described by Bricker, Bricker, Iacino, and Dennison is based on a developmental model; while the chapter by Cohen, Gross, and Haring is an excellent example of incorporating developmental sequences as training guides. Applying the developmental model to special children seems to be particularly appropriate, since most of the information to date on young community-based handicapped children suggests that differences between these children and their normal counterparts are quantitative rather than qualitative (Bricker, Vincent-Smith, Bricker, 1973; Bricker and Bricker, 1974; Miller and Yoder, 1974; Hayden and Dmitriev, 1975; and Hayden and Haring, 1975).

We believe that the developmental model should serve as the basis for designing curriculum materials, structuring the input from adjunctive services, and organizing the educational intervention system. These in turn should help to refine the developmental model.

## Early and Continuous Intervention

Although it is still difficult to point to hard data supporting the position that early intervention does make a difference in the developmental progress of severely handicapped children, there are data to support the efficacy of early intervention with mildly to moderately handicapped children (Heber, et al., 1972; Skeels, 1966; Kirk, 1972; Caldwell and Richmond, 1968; Hayden and Haring, 1975; Hayden and Dmitriev, 1975; Stedman and Eichorn, 1964). Because the developmental model suggests that differences between children are quantitative rather than qualitative, it seems reasonable to assume that early intervention would produce positive effects with the more significantly impaired child as well. The basic rationale for early intervention can be divided into three areas. First, the developmental model states that simple forms of behavior serve as the building blocks for more complex responses; therefore, in order to develop important cognitive and linguistic responses, prerequisites to these behaviors must be shaped into the child's repertoire. Early intervention increases the probability that the child will develop prerequisite building blocks. Second, it is important to intervene early in order to reduce the likelihood of a child developing inappropriate responses. Most of us are aware of the difficulties encountered in working with a large child who engages in self-abusive, aggressive, or stereotypic behavior. Clearly, one solution to this difficulty is to provide the necessary input to the child and his family so that these inappropriate forms of behavior are not allowed to develop. Third, by intervening early, one can support the primary caregiver in the tremendous responsibility of providing adequate care for a child who is severely/multiply handicapped. Providing a support system for the family early in the child's life should help reduce negative interactions and family stress, as well as to assist the family in developing realistic expectations (Berger, 1974; Farber 1968; Gorham et al., 1975). Again, better data are needed before we arrive at a firm conclusion, but there are strong indications that comprehensive support for the primary caregivers decreases family stress and increases the probability that the child can be maintained in the community. If this turns out to be the case, early intervention will become economically more feasible when compared to the cost of lifelong institutionalization. Finally, common sense suggests that it is logical to maximize the educational input offered the handicapped child. The term "profoundly handicapped" implies that the person has, for any number of reasons, a significant impairment in acquiring new information or modifying his current behavior. Populations with the most severe learning problems should be exposed to an educational system at the earliest possible time and, if the initial diagnosis is correct, should be maintained in such systems longer than those with few or no learning problems.

We believe that it is not only important to intervene early, but to continue the individual in some form of educational program until the terminal goals or criteria have been met. For the majority of the target population, a goal of independence within the community may be unrealistic. However, other goals should be established, and the individual should be maintained in an appropriate program for as long as necessary. Some individuals may have to spend their entire adulthood in a sheltered workshop. Providing the handicapped individual with a protected environment does not have to result in his becoming a drain on community resources; rather, he can use his training to make usable products, payment for which might offset the cost of operating the workshop.

### Systematic Instructional Procedures

In dealing with the various skill levels of the severely handicapped individual, developmental pinpoints or targets can be used to determine which behavior should be taught and in what sequence. Once the training content is determined, bracketing the child's stage of learning as he begins working on new skills is necessary. This bracketing permits teachers of the severely handicapped to employ precise instructional procedures that match the stages of learning which can be divided into five "classic" phases: (1) acquiring, (2) strengthening, (3) maintaining, (4) generalizing, and (5) applying the new skill. These learning phases have been discussed in the previous chapter; here, the discussion will focus on instructional procedures that can be used to help the learner during the different phases.

Helping a child acquire a new skill can be facilitated by several instructional procedures, such as shaping, imitation, and cueing. *Shaping*, which entails reinforcing successive approximations to the target skill, is often the first strategy a teacher uses. For example, teaching the child to localize sound might begin with reinforcing even the slightest movement toward the sound. *Imitation* is another instructional procedure useful in teaching the acquisition of a new response. This procedure requires that the teacher actually perform the activity that he or she wishes the child to reproduce. For example, the teacher may clap his or her hands while saying, "Bobby, clap your hands." If modeling does not elicit the appropriate response from the child, an additional procedure, such as prompting, may be necessary. *Prompting* involves providing the child with extra "physical" assistance to help him complete the targeted skill. *Cueing* is used to teach the child to remember a response at a specific time. The child receives a "cue" to elicit the correct performance just prior to the expected action. For instance, "Bobby, it is time for lunch" might be employed as a cue for moving toward the table.

Once the pupil has acquired a skill, he or she must build proficiency in using the skill if it is to be functional in his/her environment. It is not sufficient simply to perform a skill; one must be able to perform it repeatedly under the appropriate conditions. Strengthening a new skill or building proficiency requires reinforcing the targeted skills for being produced at the appropriate time. When a new skill is being taught, the criterion level is often defined as the child's ability to complete the skill independently. Once the response is established, it is necessary to increase the child's initial rate of performance. To do this, one must reinforce each response produced under the appropriate conditions. Further, providing a variety of reinforcing stimuli for the child's newly developed skill should result in strengthening that skill. For example, if food has been used as the primary reinforcer during the acquisition stage, the use of social stimuli, such as hugging, verbal feedback, or permitting the child to play with a special toy, should be initiated.

Once the rate of the newly developed skill has been strengthened, the next phase in learning is for the child to maintain that skill in his/her repertoire as long as it is appropriate and necessary. Intermittent reinforcement is a useful instructional procedure for promoting maintenance of a new skill; it involves reinforcing the child on a variable schedule for producing the skill. In strengthening the new skill, reinforcement should be given continuously; that is, each time the child demonstrates the skill, he/she receives immediate reinforcement. During maintenance training, reinforcement should not be provided continuously; rather, it should be given intermittently, such as every two or three times the response is produced by the child.

Another strategy for helping a child maintain a new skill involves pairing a primary reinforcer with a secondary reinforcer, if the primary reinforcer was used to establish the response. The primary reinforcer, often a bite of the child's favorite food, can be paired with a secondary reinforcer, such as verbal praise, and then faded out across training sessions until the behavior is maintained through secondary reinforcement only. Although shifting to the use of a secondary reinforcer is important, our terminal goal is for the child to be motivated by intrinsic—rather than external—stimuli. For example, a young child learning to sit up should engage in the behavior not because he is given bites of food for doing so, but because sitting up allows him to see his surroundings more adequately. Categories of reinforcers can be seen as a hierarchy with highly personal, nontangible reinforcers, such as satisfaction through achievement, at the top and reinforcers of basic human needs at the bottom. As skill maintenance is taught, the reinforcers used will progress to the top of the hierarchy. This should allow the child to develop and maintain as many independent skills as possible.

Generalization of the skill is the next learning phase and can be defined as producing the learned response in the presence of similar but novel stimuli. The actual response remains the same, but the stimulus or antecedent event changes. The instructional procedure most often recommended to foster skill generalization is *practice*. One type of practice, called discrimination training, concentrates on the child's learning a specific response in the presence of certain stimuli, but not in the presence of others (Catania, 1968). For example, the child is taught to add when he sees a "+" but not when he sees a "−."

Research on a second type of practice, called differentiation, suggests that response generalization can be facilitated by reinforcing responses to stimuli while varying one essential aspect of those stimuli, such as duration or intensity. The results indicate that practice of this type should focus on that particular aspect of the stimulus which is important. This is the basis of Engelmann's (1969) approach to teaching concepts. An example of this strategy might involve repeated presentation of items that have "corners" with those that do not, as the child responds orally to questions about corners.

A skill must not only be useful to the individual in response to environmental stimuli similar to those under which it was learned, it must also be useful or applicable in modified forms in response to new problems or in new situations. Application, then, is the next learning phase. Educators cannot teach specific behaviors for each environmental event or problem the child is likely to encounter. The child must retrieve and apply responses that are appropriate in a variety of settings. He must be able to discriminate both the key elements in a situation and the consequent appropriate response. Without application skills, an individual has only the most limited control of his or her behavior and environment. Educators, therefore, need to insure that their pupils learn how to apply each learned skill.

Training for application is probably the educator's biggest challenge, perhaps because in the acquisition, strengthening, maintenance, and generalization stages of a child's skill development, the educator can focus on relatively discrete tasks. But to apply skills in wide and even unpredictable contexts means to move away from the discrete and the specific. This complicates the task greatly, since it is clearly more difficult to establish generative behavioral repertoires than to train specific responses to specific stimuli. In facilitating skill application, one procedure is to provide the child with the opportunity to meet as many new and different situations as possible. In these varied situations, the child is confronted with novel conditions which will demand modifications of his newly acquired skill. Offering these opportunities under careful supervision should result in the child's developing a far more flexible repertoire, which should always be a primary goal of education.

### Appropriate Curricula

The structure of an intervention component is provided from the developmental framework, the methodology from systematic instructional procedures, and the content from the curriculum and adjunctive services components. Intervening early and for extended periods is only defensible if desired changes in behavior occur within the target population. Once a program is operational, the progress made by the students may depend heavily on the effectiveness of the daily curriculum. By curriculum, we refer not only to the programmatic steps moving along a developmental hierarchy, but the use of materials by the teaching staff. The training personnel are critical. Curriculum materials, no matter how excellent, cannot completely counter the effects of poor presentation by instructors who do not use behavioral principles.

Developing and disseminating curriculum materials for our target population is a substantial problem which deserves attention. Our experience has indicated that the development of educational programs or curricula in a specific area, such as language, is a difficult, time-consuming endeavor for which most teachers are not trained. Furthermore, teachers may not have the necessary scholarship to build an approach encompassing the best available information. Consequently, we believe the task of curriculum development should fall to those who have been trained to produce such materials. The job of teachers and parents is to adapt and modify the basic curriculum suggestions to meet the specific needs of their children, their physical settings, and their behavioral targets. The teaching personnel should be the environmental engineers employing the principles and programs developed by specialists in critical domains of behavior.

Several criteria must be met in structuring curriculum materials. First, materials should be developed which are flexible and which can be used in a variety of settings. We are not interested in adding to a child's repertoire specific responses which can only be elicited in special training sessions by selected trainers. Rather, we are interested in helping children acquire generative response forms that can be adapted to a variety of materials, settings, and individuals. Second, the training materials must include precise behavioral descriptions of target objectives, procedures for reaching these objectives, and criteria for determining when the objectives have been met. Third, there must be a direct link between the curriculum material and objective measures of progress; for example, a systematic probe system can be constructed as an integral part of the training program (Bricker, Dennison, and Bricker, 1975). Fourth, the training steps must be systematically sequenced, beginning with the most primitive response form and moving to subsequent developmental stages until the terminal level is reached. Developmental sequencing demands that the curriculum developer place great emphasis on the antecedent event and be less concerned with the consequation. Finally, training materials must be disseminable at low cost. Since our knowledge base is currently limited, it would seem inappropriate to develop and package elaborate and expensive curriculum materials that will become obsolete as more relevant information is acquired on the target population. Consequently, low-cost materials should be developed which are easily modifiable or disposable as more appropriate training materials are created.

### Adjunctive Services

The problems presented by severely and profoundly handicapped persons are, by definition, significant and multiple. Most members of this population have physical, sensory, and medical, as well as educational, problems. No teacher or parent alone can possibly be equipped to diagnose difficulties or to develop appropriate, effective interventions for a population containing so many significant and different problems. For this reason, we believe an effective approach must include individuals representing a variety of disciplines and various kinds of expertise.

Children with chronic health problems (e.g., respiratory difficulties, seizures, shunts) need consultative medical supervision by professionals who are sensitive to the problems of the profoundly handicapped person. Children and adults with significant health problems cannot be placed in public schools or other intervention programs without adequate medical supervision. It is possible that the role of the nurse practitioner can be expanded to provide the necessary medical monitoring.

Many of the children included in this category have physical disabilities that demand the attention of physical or occupational therapists. Children who have muscular problems which interfere with vital functions, such as swallowing, must have attention from specially trained individuals who can work directly with teachers and parents so that they, too, can acquire the necessary skills for assisting the children.

Severely and profoundly handicapped children may also develop dietary problems which require the consultation of a nutrition specialist. Equally likely is the need for speech and hearing specialists who are trained to cope with a population of significantly impaired individuals. Also, the problems inherent in having a profoundly handicapped person in the family often demand the attention of a variety of individuals trained in the delivery of social welfare services.

Perhaps the most important adjunctive personnel are the parents and/or family. We believe the parent must be included as an integral part of any intervention team for several reasons. Very often, the family members are the most reinforcing agents for the handicapped child. Secondly, the parent may have the most contact with the handicapped person, especially a child—which makes the parent the logical choice as the primary change agent. Finally, our experience suggests that parents, when given the opportunity, are valuable participants in devising and implementing plans to assist the handicapped individual.

Given the importance of adjunctive services, an effective means for delivery of these services becomes necessary. If one evaluates the number of professionals currently available for working with severely handicapped persons, it becomes clear that the traditional "therapy" model, in which children or clients are removed from the home or classroom setting for their half-hour interaction session with a specialist, is not feasible. A model described in detail by Tharp and Wetzel (1969) offers a viable alternative. In this model, the trained specialist acts in a consultative capacity to the primary change agent. For example, if a child needed special leg exercises, the physical therapist would teach both the classroom teacher and the parent the appropriate exercise. Once the parent and teacher learned the correct procedure, the physical therapist would be needed only for periodic evaluations of progress, freeing his professional time to be spent with additional clients. This model has appeal for two basic reasons. First, by teaching others the appropriate therapeutic skills, the highly skilled professional can reach many more handicapped individuals. Second, if several persons are trained to provide the appropriate therapy, the handicapped individual will be exposed to many more training sessions, which should enhance the probability that appropriate changes in behavior will occur.

The delivery of adjunctive services is necessary in a comprehensive approach to the severely and profoundly handicapped person. Consequently, the remaining task is to train professionals from allied fields and then to develop efficient and effective strategies for disseminating these skills to parents and others.

**Objective Evaluation**

The sixth component necessary to providing a comprehensive serv-ice system is the development and implementation of objective measures for evaluation. Curriculum, adjunctive services, and intervention compo-nents should be directly linked to a mechanism for providing feedback on how adequately these three components are functioning. Several systems for providing such an objective base have already been developed—for example, precision teaching (Lindsley, 1964); however, we still lack coordinated procedures for assessing variables at a variety of levels for a variety of reasons. One of the most difficult jobs facing educators is the development of evaluation systems that will allow for the assessment of programmatic variables on a daily, weekly, and yearly basis. One partial answer is the development of curricula with the assessment built directly into the program.

## SUMMARY

The intent of this chapter has been to point out the need for develop-ing comprehensive services if we are to serve our target population adequately. We have identified six necessary components of such serv-ices and have tried to present a rationale for including each component. During the next few years, the systematic building of information pools concerning the severely/profoundly handicapped individual should shape the crude beginning outlined in this chapter into an efficient, effective system of service delivery, training, and research. It is our belief that the programs throughout the country that will make a major contribution to the welfare of severely handicapped persons are those committed to de-veloping comprehensive services in tandem with field-training bases and research centers. Information generated from these centers will then be used to upgrade and support the numerous smaller programs which will eventually be located throughout the country. The challenge is to build comprehensive service, training, and research programs that are directly linked to other satellite projects at the local, state, and national levels.

## REFERENCES

Berger MI: Stress, family competence and family response to stress. Unpublished doctoral dissertation, Nashville, George Peabody College for Teachers, 1974
Bricker D, Dennison L, Bricker W: Constructive-interaction-adaptation approach to lan-guage training. Mailman Center for Child Development, Monograph Series, No. 1, 1975

Bricker DD, Vincent-Smith L, Bricker WA: Receptive vocabulary: Performances and selection strategies of delayed and nondelayed toddlers. Am J Ment Defic 77:579–584, 1973

Bricker WA: A systems approach to theory building in special education, in Walker DL, Howard DP (eds): Special Education: Instrument of Change in Education for the 70s. Charlottesville, Univ. of Virginia Pr 1972

Bricker WA, Bricker DD: An early language training strategy. *In* Schiefelbusch R, Lloyd L (eds): Language Perspectives: Acquisition, Retardation, and Intervention. Baltimore, University Park Press, 1974

Bruner JS: Toward a Theory of Instruction. Cambridge, Mass., Harvard Univ Pr, 1966a

Bruner JS: Studies in Cognitive Growth. New York, Wiley, 1966b

Caldwell BM, Richmond JB: The children's center in Syracuse, New York. *In* Dittman L (ed): Early Child Care: The New Perspectives. New York, Atherton, 1968

Catania CA (ed): Contemporary Research in Operant Behavior. Glenview, Ill., Scott, Foresman, 1968

Engelmann S: Conceptual Learning. San Rafael, Calif., Dimensions, 1969

Farber B: Mental Retardation: Its Social Context and Social Consequences. Boston, Houghton Mifflin, 1968

Gorham KA, Jardins CD, Page R, et al: Effect on parents. *In* Hobbs N (ed): Issues in the Classification of Children (vol 2). San Francisco, Jossey-Bass, 1975

Hamblin RL: The Humanization Process: A Social, Behavioral Analysis of Children's Problems. New York, Wiley-Interscience, 1971

Haring NG: Systematic instructional procedures: An instructional hierarchy. Paper presented at the Conference on Learning Disabilities and Behavior Problems, June 27–28, 1974, Washington, D. C., sponsored by the National Institute of Education

Hayden AH, Dmitriev V: Early developmental and educational problems for the child with Down's syndrome. *In* Friedlander BZ, Kirk G, Sterritt G (eds): The Exceptional Infant (vol III). New York, Brunner/Mazel, 1975, pp. 193–221

Hayden AH, Haring NG: Programs for Down's syndrome children at the University of Washington. *In* Tjossem T (ed): Intervention Strategies for Risk Infants and Young Children. Baltimore, University Park Pr, 1975 (in press)

Heber R, Garber H, Harrington S, et al: Rehabilitation of Families at Risk for Mental Retardation. Madison, Wis., Rehabilitation Research and Training Center in Mental Retardation, University of Wisconsin, 1972

Hobbs N: The Futures of Children: Categories, Labels, and their Consequences. San Francisco, Jossey-Bass, 1975

Hull CL: Essentials of Behavior. New Haven, Yale Univ Pr, 1951

Kirk SA: Educating Exceptional Children (ed 2). Boston, Houghton Mifflin, 1972

Krumboltz JD, Krumboltz HB: Changing Children's Behavior. Englewood Cliffs, N.J., Prentice-Hall, 1972

Lindsley OR: Direct measurement and prothesis of retarded behavior. J Educ 147:62–81, 1964

Miller, JF, Yoder DE: Language intervention for the mentally retarded. *In* Schiefelbusch RL, Lloyd LL (eds): Language Perspectives—Acquisition, Retardation, and Intervention. Baltimore, University Park Pr, 1974

Osgood CE: Behavior theory and the social sciences. *In* Jakobovits L, Miron M (eds): Readings in the Psychology of Language. Englewood Cliffs, NJ, Prentice-Hall, 1967

Piaget J: Piaget's theory. *In* Mussen PH (ed): Carmichael's Manual of Child Psychology (vol 1). New York, Wiley, 1970

Prehm HF, Mayfield S: Paired-associate learning and retention in retarded and non-retarded children. Am J Ment Defic 74:5, 622–625, 1959

Skeels, HM: Adult status of children with contrasting early life experiences. Monographs of the Society for Research in Child Development 31 (3, Serial No. 105), 1966

Stedman DJ, Eichorn DH: A comparative study of the growth and development trends of institutionalized and noninstitutionalized mongoloid children. Am J Ment Defic 69:391–401, 1964

Tharp RG, Wetzel RJ: Behavior Modification in the Natural Environment. New York, Academic, 1969

Zeaman D, House BJ: Use of special training conditions in visual discrimination learning with imbeciles. Am J Ment Defic 73:2, 453–459, 1958

# Developmental Sequence and Curricula

Marilyn A. Cohen,
Pamela J. Gross,
and Norris G. Haring

# A

# Developmental Pinpoints

### RATIONALE

The teacher working with a severely handicapped population today confronts tremendous programming problems. While much literature exists concerning many other areas in special education, little has been written for the teacher working with these youngsters. What behaviors the child might be expected to have when he enters the classroom, where the teacher should begin her programming efforts, and what types of terminal objectives would be reasonable for a given individual appear to be issues about which little information exists. Since it must certainly be acknowledged that severely handicapped persons represent an extremely heterogeneous population, the teacher may discover a desperate need for some programming guidelines.

In the search for such guidelines, it would appear crucial that the teacher of the severely handicapped have an excellent knowledge of normal developmental patterns. Without such knowledge, it becomes extremely difficult to determine where a given child is functioning. While the severely handicapped child may be expected to have many deficit areas, through knowledge of normal development, the teacher will be able to identify those few behaviors in which the child may demonstrate some approximation toward the normal growth patterns. For the severely

---

Sequences in this chapter were adapted by the authors from selected sources. All references consulted as sources in this project are listed in the Source Key on pages 109–110; a discussion of the adaptations made from these sources is contained in the *Rationale* section.

handicapped youngster, it is not uncommon to find extremely uneven development across areas. Therefore, identifying areas of potential strength, as well as those in which performance is extremely deficient, has tremendous implications for all programming efforts. For those areas in which the child is found to be extremely deficit, knowledge of normal development becomes even more critical, for, without such knowledge, it becomes most difficult to identify the behaviors which should become the focus for educational objectives.

## CURRENT CHECKLISTS AND INVENTORIES

### Problems and Needs

There is fairly universal agreement about the sequence in which various skills appear in the developing child; a review of the developmental checklists and sequential inventories currently available shows that identical skills listed as appearing in a child's repertoire at a given age are frequently included in the majority of comparable scales. However, skills or abilities are often described in ambiguous terms which offer teachers little help when they are confronted with a need to evaluate a given child's performance. Since the available sequences are the result of fairly comprehensive cross-sectional studies of large populations, and since so many of these scales exist, there seemed to be little need to duplicate the effort to sequence developmental "milestones"; however, there did seem to be a great need to translate the descriptors offered in available scales into unambiguous, measurable terms that could be of practical classroom value to teachers.

There also exists a need to offer a sequence which follows a single skill as it develops in a child's performance repertoire. While a developmental psychologist, for example, might be interested in a list of all the skills a child possesses at 1 month or 1 year, a teacher working on developing one skill at a time in a classroom setting would find a different sort of format more useful. In order to find the next step in the sequence of development for each particular behavior in available lists, one must scan other long lists of behavior for each of the many age groups considered. For example, a teacher who wished to set up a program for a child deficient in communication skills, using currently available scales, would have to extract the particular communication skill, as it appeared at each age, from a list of many other skills.

## A SET OF PINPOINTS SPECIFICALLY DESIGNED FOR EDUCATORS

### Guidelines in the Organization of the Developmental Pinpoints

The term "pinpoint" is one that has been taken from a set of procedures called precision teaching (Haring, 1970; Lindsley, 1970). In precision teaching, the precise specification of behavior in measurable terms, or pinpointing, is an essential first step in program development. The use of the term is quite appropriate here, for the authors have made every effort, whenever possible, to clearly specify in measurable terms the specific behavior of interest. Our principal effort in this project, therefore, was to adapt the developmental skills listed in existing scales by making them specific enough to be useful in the classroom and, by arranging them in a format which tracks each skill over time, rather than following the chronological appearance of skill clusters.

As the term "pinpoint" refers to a measurable behavior, it follows that emphasis throughout the listing would be that which is observable. It appeared highly incompatible, therefore, to include one area, which appears in many developmental checklists consulted, the area of cognition. Our belief that description of observable behavior results in more useful programming for children led us to include various skills often placed in the "cognition" category under fine-motor or gross-motor skills. Previous scales have provided some precedent for this decision, since often a skill reported by one sequence under the heading of cognition occurred under fine-motor skills or gross-motor skills in other researchers' lists.

### Format of the Developmental Pinpoints

Throughout the listings in each major developmental area, "large N" studies, screening batteries, and developmental checklists are cited. Generally, the pinpoints have been compiled from a standard group of sources. Beside each pinpoint listed, both an age and an abbreviation are given. The abbreviation represents the source from which this pinpoint and the age guideline listed were drawn. For some pinpoints, rather general agreement has been noted concerning the age of occurrence, while for others there may be several months discrepancy between sources. All abbreviations given across developmental areas are explained in the Source Key found at the end of the sequence. For those few areas in which the standard pool of sources offered few pinpoints, other "large N" studies were consulted for additional information.

Before each of the major pinpoint listings, the authors have provided an introductory section. These discussions are designed to provide a brief background regarding a few of the major concerns confronting an educator attempting to program in that particular area.

## GUIDELINES FOR USING THE DEVELOPMENTAL PINPOINTS

### Suggestions for Classroom Implementation

Pinpointing is an essential first step in program development. As the teacher views the large set of pinpoints provided here, it is important to be aware that the authors are not implying that the severely handicapped youngster develops in this way. Obviously, there have been many deviations from the normal course of development for these youngsters. While there remain many unanswered questions about the particular course of development for each individual included in this population, there is considerable data upon which guidelines for normal development have been based. This information has important implications for programs for severely handicapped, and cannot be ignored.

For some, this chapter might be useful in providing a quick overview of developmental sequences. Rather than having to devote hours to seeking out information concerning specific skill sequences, teachers are provided here with ready reference material.

For those teachers seeking to provide youngsters with a well-rounded curriculum, the Developmental Pinpoints may also be of interest. Comparing classroom objectives to all developmental areas presented, the teacher may note a heavy emphasis upon the fine-motor and self-help skills, for example, but few in the area of communication. Through a more careful scrutiny of the communication pinpoints, new program objectives may be specified.

It must be emphasized, once again, that pinpointing is a first step in the development of programs. Through careful pinpointing, the teacher may begin to formulate both short- and long-term objectives. When establishing meaningful objectives, the teacher will want to utilize the pinpoints listed in assessing the child's behavior. Careful examination of the pinpoint sequences shown will suggest ways in which to proceed in assessing behavior. For each sequence of behavior listed, the teacher would first want to consider the terminal behavior. If the child were able to perform the terminal behavior, there would be no need to further examine this skill sequence. If, on the other hand, the child is unable to perform the terminal behavior, the teacher will want to assess whether or not he has the behavior listed one step earlier in the sequence. If the answer is no, the teacher proceeds to assess other items listed in the sequence to identify which of the behaviors listed the child might have already. Whenever possible, the teacher will want to start programming with the closest approximation to the terminal behavior. Certainly, the teacher would hesitate to begin instruction in a given area at the developmental level beyond that indicated by the child's performance. Through implementation of the procedures listed, the Developmental Pinpoints can become the basis for an assessment sequence and the subsequent establishment of educational objectives.

The pinpoints offered here may provide guidelines for programming. Certainly, they do specify those behaviors which the child should possess. They cannot, however, determine programming strategies or program materials; these must be determined by each teacher in relation to the needs of the individual handicapped child. One suggestion for using the Developmental Pinpoints for programming purposes, however, is that the teacher carefully consider the amount of time involved in teaching any particular skill to a child, and the ultimate contribution of that skill to the child's total functioning. Through careful consideration and selection of program pinpoints, it may be possible to design programs which will allow many youngsters to one day rid themselves of their present labels of severely/profoundly handicapped.

## MOTOR SKILLS

Some sources (Gesell, 1947,1952) have identified motor activity as the basis and origin for all "mental life." Kephart (1964) stresses that motor activity is the first interaction between the child and its environment, and as such, provides foundations for later cognitive development. While some might argue with conclusions identifying motor activity as the "basis" or "origin" for all mental life and cognitive development, certainly the importance of motor development and coordination is evident in all major developmental areas.

Under normal circumstances, we are often not aware of the way in which the muscles work to maintain balance and facilitate motion. Muscles normally make automatic changes in tension, allowing the individual to maintain balance and posture, while hands and arms are free to use in any number of activities. The severely handicapped child, however, suffers some degree of fine- or gross-motor involvement, which substantially impairs balance, posture, or movement, and which will increase if early intervention does not occur. Cooperation among therapists, parents, and teachers is necessary in order to establish and maintain an effective program of remediation.

Nancy Finnie (1968), in a book designed to help parents deal with their cerebral palsied children, stresses that, while contractures and deformities are usually not apparent in the handicapped infant, early treatment and correct handling of the baby are necessary if later development of abnormal posture is to be avoided. Parents are encouraged to examine posture and motor patterns in all areas of function (e.g., mothers are asked to specify in what position they find it easiest to place the infant in order to dress it; if there are feeding difficulties such as tongue thrust, gagging, or inability to close the mouth; in what position can the child play; in what position does the infant find it easiest to sleep? etc.)

It is extremely important, then, that parents and teachers of the severely handicapped be familiar with the sequence of normal motor development, in order to recognize in what areas or activities the child is deficient and learn both what types of procedures will improve muscle control and what kind of activities or postures might be undesirable.

The pinpoints presented in the following fine- and gross-motor sequences represent the entire range of motor activities in the developing child. The classroom teacher attempting to apply these pinpoints in an assessment of motor development may not want to include all of the pinpoints within a movement area in that assessment. The teacher may, instead, wish to select a few of the major pinpointed behaviors which precede attainment of the final balance or movement objective. Take, for example, *standing*, a major skill within the gross-motor sequence. Rather than attempting to determine whether or not the child exhibits each of the behaviors listed, the teacher might plan an assessment in terms of a smaller number of pinpoints. The following are nine behavioral manifestations crucial to the development of the ability to maintain balance on both feet while standing: (1) bears weight on one extremity only (4 mo); (2) bears weight on both extremities (7 mo); (3) stands holding rail when placed in position and maintains for 5 sec (8 mo); (4) stands holding rail when placed in position and maintains for more than 5 sec (specify) (9 mo); (5) stands briefly, hands held (9.8 mo); (6) stands with minimal support (9.8–10.2 mo); (7) stands without support for 1 min (11–11.5 mo); (8) lowers to floor from standing without falling (12 mo); (9) pulls up to stand (12 mo).

By beginning assessment with the terminal behavior—pulling self to stand—and working backward toward the earliest behavior—bearing weight on extremities—the teacher is able to determine at what developmental level programming should begin. Which specific pinpoints or areas are surveyed for each child must be determined by the teacher in view of the individual handicaps each child presents.

## REFERENCES

Finnie N: Handling the Young Cerebral Palsied Child at Home. London, Heinemann, 1968

Gesell A, Armatruda E: Developmental Diagnosis (ed 2). New York, Hoeber, Harper, 1947

Gesell A: Infant Development: The Embryology of Early Human Behavior. New York Harper, 1952

Kephart N: Perceptual Motor Aspects of Learning Disabilities. Exceptl Child 31 (Dec):201–206, 1964

### DEFINITION OF TERMS IN MOTOR SEQUENCE

The following are terms commonly used in the motor pinpoint sequence. A brief definition of each term has, therefore, been provided:

Flexion: movement of body parts inward or toward each other; bending; or the state of tone that would tend to cause such movements

Extension: the opposite of flexion; outward movements or the tone necessary for such movements

Reflex: a movement response of a part or parts of the body which *always* occurs in a stereotyped manner when preceded by the appropriate inducing agent

Proximal: refers to the joints or other parts of the body which are closer to the trunk

Distal: refers to the joints or other parts of the body which are further away from the trunk; the periphery

Supine: refers to the back-lying position

Prone: refers to the front-lying position

### FINE MOTOR OVERVIEW

#### Eye Readiness

Sources often describe the sequential development of eye–hand coordination. While it is not always possible to determine whether a child actually "coordinates" eye and hand movements, the authors of this sequence have traced the development of numerous "eye-readiness" pinpoints prerequisite to tasks which might demand such coordination.

I. Moves eyes toward stationary objects, light source

II. Moves eyes to follow moving objects

III. Closes eyes in response to lights, objects

IV. Fixes gaze on object and reaches

#### Movements Involving Hands

I. General hand and wrist movement

   A. Hand movement
   B. Finger movement
   C. Wrist movement

II. General hand movements in relation to objects

   A. Holds, grasps, and/or manipulates objects
   B. Releases objects
   C. Picks up objects
   D. Uses hands with banging motion
   E. Pulls objects
   F. Transfers objects from hand to hand
   G. Uses hands with raking motion
   H. Shakes objects
   I. Pushes objects
   J. Pokes objects
   K. Retrieves objects
   L. Dumps objects
   M. Closes boxes
   N. Uses implements to obtain toys

III. Specific hand movements in relation to objects; often used as part of a preacademic program

   A.  Places objects
      1.  Cubes in containers
      2.  Pegs in holes
      3.  Pellets in containers
      4.  Blocks in structures
      5.  Forms in formboards
      6.  Pieces in puzzles

   B.  Takes objects apart; puts objects back together

   C.  Strings beads

## Eye Readiness

I. Moves eyes toward stationary objects, light

   A.  Moves eyes toward stationary objects

| | | |
|---|---|---|
| Moves eye toward ring | 0.1 mo. | Bay |
| | 1 mo. | Sher |
| | 1 mo. | Ges |
| | 2.5 mo. | Slos |
| | 3 mo. | C |
| Moves eye toward ring and holds eye on it | 0.4 mo | Bay |
| | 1.3 mo | Den |
| | 2 mo | Ges |
| Turns eyes to ring (at least 30°, Bay; past midline, Den) | 1.3 mo | Den |
| | 1.6 mo | Bay |
| | 2 mo | Ges |
| Moves eye toward cup or cube and holds eye there | 2.5 mo | Bay |
| | 3 mo | Ges |
| | 3 mo | C |
| | 3.3 mo | Den |
| Moves gaze from one object to another | 2.6 mo | Bay |
| Moves gaze to rattle in hand | 3 mo | Ges |
| Moves eyes to stationary objects within 6–10 inches for more than a second or 2, seldom fixates continuously | 3 mo | Sher |
| | 3.3 mo | Den |
| Moves eyes toward ring for sustained length of time (a few seconds) | 5.4 mo | Bay |
| Moves eyes in unison; (squint now abnormal) | 6 mo | Sher |
| Moves eyes toward third cube immediately | 6 mo | Ges |
| Moves eyes to inspect details of bell | 8 mo | C |
| Moves eyes to inspect contents of box | 9.5 mo | Bay |
| | 11 mo | C |

   B.  Moves eyes toward light source

| | | |
|---|---|---|
| Fixes gaze on brightness of window or blank wall | 1 mo | Sher |
| Turns eyes and head towards light | 1 mo | Sher |
| | 1.6 mo | Bay |

II. Moves eyes to follow moving objects

| | | |
|---|---|---|
| Moves eyes following ring (in horizontal direction | 0.5 mo | Bay |
| | 2 mo | C |
| Moves eyes following vertical light | 0.7 mo | Bay |
| Moves eyes following ring in vertical direction | 1 mo | Bay |
| | 2 mo | C |
| Moves eyes, following circular path of light | 1.2 mo | Bay |
| Moves eyes following ring in circular path (rattle for 10 sec— Slos; 180°—Den, Ges, Sher) | 1.2 mo | Bay |
| | 2.4 mo | Den |
| | 3 mo | Sher/Ges/C |
| | 3.5 mo | Slos |
| Follows pencil flashlamp briefly with eyes; flashlight at one foot | 2 mo | C |
| Converges eyes as dangling toy is moved toward face | 3 mo | Sher |
| Move eyes following movement of own hands (fingers—C) | 3 mo | Sher/LAP/Ges |
| | 3.8 mo | Bay |
| | 4 mo | LAP |
| Moves eyes to follow ball across table | 3.1 mo | Bay |
| | 4 mo | C |
| Moves eyes toward rattle in hand | 4 mo | Ges/Slos |

| | | |
|---|---|---|
| Moves eyes toward rolling balls of 2, 1, and ½ inch diameter at 10 ft | 6 mo | Sher |
| Moves eyes toward adult movement across room, follows movement | 6 mo | Sher |
| Manipulates bell, moving eyes to inspect detail | 6.5 mo | Bay |
| Moves eyes to correct place where toys dropped within reach of hands | 9 mo | Sher |
| Moves eyes after toys falling over edge of surface (carriage or table) | 9 mo | Sher |
| Moves eyes to correct place for toys that fall out of sight | 12 mo | Sher/LAP |
| Moves eyes to follow small toy pulled across floor up to 12 ft | 15 mo | Sher |
| Moves eyes to follow path of small toy swept vigorously from table | 15 mo | Sher |
| Fixes eye on small dangling toy at 10 ft | 18–23 mo | Sher |

III. Closes eyes in response to movement of lights and objects

| | | |
|---|---|---|
| Closes lids tightly when pencil light shone directly into them at 1–2 inches | 1 mo | Sher |
| Blinks at shadow of hand, delayed midline regard; blinks at ring | 2 mo | Ges |
| Blinks at toy moved toward face | 3 mo | Sher |

IV. Fixes gaze on object and reaches

| | | |
|---|---|---|
| Moves eyes toward raisin; reaches for raisin | 4 mo | Ges |
| | 4.4–5.5 mo | Bay |
| | 5 mo | C |
| Fixes gaze on small objects and reaches for them | 4.4 mo | Bay |
| | 6 mo | Ges/Sher |
| Fixes eyes on and retrieves rolling ball 2½ inches, at 10 ft | 18–23 mo | Sher |

## Movement Involving Hands

I. General hand and wrist movements

A. Hand movement

| | | |
|---|---|---|
| Holds hands open | 3 mo | Ges/C |

B. Finger movement

| | | |
|---|---|---|
| Clasps and unclasps hands in finger play | 3 mo | Sher/C |
| | 3.2 mo | Bay |
| Manipulates fingers | 4 mo | C |
| Closes fist and moves thumb | 34.5 mo | MPS |
| Closes fist and wiggles thumb in imitation, right and left | 36–48 mo | LAP/Sher |
| Touches thumb to two of four fingers on same hand | 36–48 mo | MPS/F |
| Moves fingers with agility | 36–42 mo | MPS |
| Brings thumb into opposition with each finger, right and left | 42–48 mo | MPS |
| | 48–54 mo | Sher |
| Spreads hand and brings thumb into opposition with each finger in imitation | 48–60 mo | Sher |

C. Wrists

| | | |
|---|---|---|
| Rotates wrist | 5.7 mo | Bay |

II. General hand movements in relation to objects

A. Holds, grasps, and/or manipulates objects

*Grasps*

| | | |
|---|---|---|
| Grasps handle of spoon, rattle, or like object when fingers are pried open, but may quickly let go | 0.7 mo | Bay |
| | 1 mo | Sher |
| Grasps rattle briefly | 2 mo | Ges |
| | 3 mo | LAP |
| Grasps rattle actively | 3 mo | C |
| | 3.3 mo | Den |
| Grasps with near hand only for rattle, ring | 5 mo | Ges |
| Grasps one cube on contact | 5 mo | Ges |
| Uses whole hand in palmar grasp (cube—Ges) | 6 mo | Sher |
| Grasps with thumb and finger | 7.8 mo | Vin |
| | 8.3 mo | Den |
| Grasps at pellet with unsuccessful inferior scissor grasp | 8 mo | Ges |
| Grasps between finger and thumb in scissor fashion | 9 mo | Sher/Ges |
| Grasps third cube | 9 mo | Ges |
| | 10 mo | C |

| | | |
|---|---|---|
| Grasps pellet or raisin in neat pincer grasp | 10    mo | Ges/LAP |
| | 10.7 mo | Den |
| | 11    mo | C |
| Grasps object by handle | 10    mo | Ges |
| Grasps object by top of handle | 11    mo | Ges |
| Grasps and holds two small objects in one hand | 14    mo | Slos |
| Grasps and holds third cube | 14    mo | C |
| | 15    mo | Sher |

*Holds*

| | | |
|---|---|---|
| Holds ring when placed in hand | 1    mo | LAP |
| Holds cube with ulnar–palmar prehension | 3.7 mo | C |
| Holds two cubes in hand | 4.7 mo | Bay |
| Holds one cube in hand, approaches another | 6    mo | Ges |
| Holds two of three cubes offered | 6.1 mo | Den |
| | 6.3 mo | Bay |
| Holds cube with radial palmar grasp | 7    mo | Ges |
| Holds one cube, grasps another | 7    mo | Ges |
| Holds two cubes more than momentarily | 7    mo | Ges |
| Holds rattle for at least 3-minute period | 7    mo | Slos |
| Holds second and third cube presented | 7.6 mo | Bay |
| | 8    mo | Ges |
| Holds two cubes | 8    mo | Ges |
| Holds pellet in neat pincer (thumb and forefinger) | 8.9 mo | Bay |
| Holds cube with radial digital grasp | 9    mo | Ges |
| Holds pellet in inferior pincer grasp | 10    mo | Ges |

*Manipulates*

| | | |
|---|---|---|
| Manipulates ring | 2.6 mo | Bay |
| Manipulates rattle in simple way | 2.8 mo | Bay |
| | 4    mo | Ges |
| Moves ring to mouth with hand | 3.8 mo | Bay |
| | 4    mo | Ges |
| Manipulates string (objects—Sher) | 8    mo | C |
| | 9    mo | Sher |
| Manipulates string on ring | 9    mo | Ges |
| Manipulates string with plucking movement | 10    mo | Ges |
| Dangles ring by string | 12.4 mo | Bay |
| | 13    mo | Ges |

B.  Releases objects

| | | |
|---|---|---|
| Drops rattle immediately when placed in hand | 1    mo | Ges |
| Releases toy by pressing against firm surface but cannot yet | 9    mo | Sher |
|     put down voluntarily | 10    mo | Ges |

C.  Picks up objects

| | | |
|---|---|---|
| Takes rattle placed on chest | 4    mo | LAP/C |
| | 4.9 mo | Bay |
| Picks up cube | 4.6 mo | Bay |
| | 6    mo | LAP |
| Takes rattle from shoulder | 5    mo | C |
| Picks up inverted cup | 5.2 mo | Bay |
| Picks up cup, grasping handle | 6    mo | LAP |
| Picks up cube from cup in imitation | 10.5 mo | Slos |
| | 11    mo | LAP/Ges |
| Picks up cube concealed by cup | 12    mo | LAP |
| Picks up small objects with precise pincer grasp | 12    mo | Sher/Ges |
| Picks up objects one by one, drops, picks up again | 12    mo | Ges |
| Picks up and holds two small objects in one hand | 14    mo | LAP |
| Picks up string, small objects, neatly between thumb and finger | 15    mo | Sher |
| Picks up small beads, threads, etc., Immediately on sight with delicate | | |
|     pincer grasp | 18–23 mo | Sher |
| Picks up pins and thread neatly and quickly | 24–29 mo | Sher |
| Picks up pins, thread, etc., with each eye separately covered | 36–48 mo | LAP |
| Picks up minute objects when each eye is covered separately | 60–72 mo | Sher |

D. Uses hands with banging motion

| | | |
|---|---|---|
| Bangs objects together in play | 5 mo | LAP |
| | 5.4 mo | Bay |
| Bangs bell | 7 mo | Ges |
| Bangs spoon | 8 mo | LAP/C |
| | 8.6 mo | Bay |
| Hits two objects together spontaneously | 9 mo | Slos |
| Hits cup with spoon | 10 mo | C/LAP |
| Rattles spoon in cup | 12 mo | C/Sher |
| Beats two spoons together | 12 mo | C |

E. Pulls objects

| | | |
|---|---|---|
| Pulls down suspended ring | 5 mo | C |
| | 5.6 mo | Den |
| | 5.7 mo | Bay |
| Pulls string and secures ring | 7.1 mo | Bay |
| | 8 mo | C |

F. Transfers objects from hand to hand

| | | |
|---|---|---|
| Transfers object from hand to hand | 5 mo | C/Slos |
| | 5.5 mo | Bay |
| Transfers cube hand to hand | 6 mo | LAP |
| Shifts brush from one hand to another in painting | 18–23 mo | Ges |

G. Uses hands with raking motion

| | | |
|---|---|---|
| Rakes and obtains small objects (raisins, beads) | 5.6 mo | Den |
| | 5.8 mo | Bay |
| | 6 mo | LAP |
| Attempts to pick up small objects (rakes, contacts—Ges, Bay) | 6.8 mo | Bay |
| | 7 mo | C/Ges |
| Rakes small object radially and holds | 8 mo | Ges |

H. Shakes objects

| | | |
|---|---|---|
| Shakes bell | 7 mo | LAP/Ges |

I. Pokes objects

| | | |
|---|---|---|
| Pokes at holes in pegboard | 8.9 mo | Bay |
| Pokes at small object with index finger | 9 mo | Sher |

J. Pushes objects

| | | |
|---|---|---|
| Pushes cube with cube | 9 mo | Ges |

K. Retrieves objects

| | | |
|---|---|---|
| Removes round block easily from formboard | 12 mo | Ges |
| Retrieves rolling ball with hand | 18–24 mo | Ges |

L. Dumps objects

| | | |
|---|---|---|
| Dumps raisins, beads from bottle spontaneously | 13.3 mo | Den |
| Dumps raisin from bottle (in imitation) | 14.8 mo | Den |
| Dumps raisins from bottle (spontaneously) | 18 mo | LAP |
| Fills and dumps containers with sand | 24–29 mo | LAP |

M. Closes boxes

| | | |
|---|---|---|
| Closes round box | 14.6 mo | Bay |
| | 16 mo | C |
| Closes oblong box | 20 mo | C |

N. Uses implements to obtain toys

| | | |
|---|---|---|
| Obtains toy with implement (i.e., stick) | 17 mo | Bay/LAP |
| | 20 mo | C |
| Uses string to draw toy closer | 27.6 mo | MPS |

III. Specific hand movements in relation to objects; often used as part of a preacademic program

A. Places objects

*Cubes in containers*

| | | |
|---|---|---|
| Places cube in cup | 9 mo | Bay |
| | 10 mo | C |

| | | |
|---|---|---|
| Places cube in cup on command | 9.4 mo | Bay |
| | 11  mo | C |
| Puts three or more cubes in cup | 11.8 mo | Bay |
| | 12  mo | LAP |
| Places one cube in cup and takes it out (on command—Ges) | 12  mo | C/Sher |
| | 13  mo | Ges |
| Places nine cubes in cup | 14.3 mo | Bay |
| Places six cubes in and out of cup with demonstration | 15  mo | Ges |
| Places 10 blocks in cup | 18  mo | C |
| Places 13 of 16 cubes in box | 21.6 mo | MPS |
| Places 12 cubes in box (12 of 12) | 24  mo | C |
| Places 16 cubes in box in 125 seconds | 26.3 mo | MPS |
| Nests four cubes in 250 sec | 27.6 mo | MPS |
| Places 16 cubes in box in 100 sec | 32.3 mo | MPS |
| Nests four cubes in 30 sec | 33  mo | MPS |

*Pegs in holes*

| | | |
|---|---|---|
| Touches holes in pegboard | 8.9 mo | Bay |
| | 10  mo | C |
| Places one peg repeatedly | 13  mo | Bay |
| Pulls out and replaces peg in Wallin Peg Board A | 14  mo | C |
| Puts all pegs in Wallin Peg Board (6 pegs in holes) when used—C; in 70 sec—Bay) | 16  mo | C |
| Puts pegs (six) in holes in 70 sec | 16.4 mo | Bay |
| Puts pegs (six) in holes in 42 sec | 16.4 mo | Bay |
| Puts six round pegs in holes in 30 sec (in 38 sec—MPS) | 17.6 mo | Bay |
| | 18  mo | C |
| | 20  mo | Bay |
| | 21  mo | MPS |
| Place six square pegs in square holes | 20  mo | C |
| Puts six round pegs in pegboard in 25 sec | 26.5 mo | MPS |
| Places six round pegs in holes on pegboard in 22 sec | 26.6 mo | MPS |
| Puts six square pegs in square holes in 41 sec | 27  mo | MPS |
| Places six square pegs in square holes on pegboard in 27 sec | 32.6 mo | MPS |
| Places six round pegs in round holes (in 20 sec—MPS) | 33–38.4 mo | MPS |
| | 36–48 mo | LAP |
| Puts six square pegs in square holes in pegboard | 40  mo | MPS |

*Pellets in containers*

| | | |
|---|---|---|
| Points at pellet released into bottle | 11  mo | Ges |
| Tries to put pellet in bottle; fails | 13  mo | Ges |
| Takes pellet out of bottle | 13.4 mo | Bay |
| Takes pellet out of bottle in imitation | 14  mo | C |
| Puts pellet in and takes it out to solve pellet and bottle problem | 16  mo | C |
| Puts 10 pellets in box in 25 sec | 48–60 mo | Ges |
| Puts 10 pellets into a box in 20 sec | 60–72 mo | Ges |

*Blocks in structures*
*Vertical structures*

| | | |
|---|---|---|
| Builds tower of two cubes | 13  mo | LAP |
| | 13.4 mo | Bay |
| | 15  mo | Ges/Sher |
| | 15.5 mo | Slos |
| Places blocks to make tower of three small blocks or spools | 16  mo | Slos |
| | 16.7 mo | Bay |
| Places blocks to make tower of four small blocks or spools | 17  mo | Slos |
| | 18–24 mo | Den |
| | 30–36 mo | Bay/C/Ges MPS/Minn/Sher |
| Places blocks to make tower of three cubes, | 20  mo | Sher/Ges/C |
| | 21  mo | MPS |
| Places blocks to make tower of five to six cubes | 21  mo | LAP |
| | 23  mo | Slos/Bay |
| Places cubes to form bridge or tower (in imitation) | 30  mo | C |
| | 32  mo | Den |
| | 36–38 mo | LAP |

| | | |
|---|---|---|
| Places cubes to form tower of seven cubes (8—Ges, Bay) | 30+ mo | Sher/Ges |
| Makes tower with nine cubes | 36–48 mo | Sher/Ges |
| | | LAP |
| Makes tower of five blocks graduated in size (Montessori Little Pink Tower—33 sec—38.6 mo, 22 sec—44.5 mo) | 36–48 mo | MPS |
| Places 10 or more cubes in tower | 48–60 mo | LAP/Sher |
| Places five blocks graduated in size, in a stack within 14 sec (in 17 sec—53.6 mo) | 50.6 mo | MPS |
| Stacks five blocks, graduated in size, within 10 sec | 63.0 mo | MPS |

*Horizontal structures*

| | | |
|---|---|---|
| Makes train of cubes, in imitation (places cubes horizontally) | 26.1 mo | Bay |
| | 27 mo | C |
| Lines up blocks to form "train" (spontaneously) | 30–35 mo | Sher |

*Combination, vertical-horizontal*

| | | |
|---|---|---|
| Moves blocks to build vertically and horizontally with beginning of symmetry | 30–35 mo | Ges |
| Puts chimney on train | 30–35 mo | Ges |
| Places blocks to make bridge (spontaneously) | 30–36 mo | Den/MPS |
| | 36–42 mo | Bay/C/Ges |
| | | H/Sher |
| | 48–54 mo | DL |
| Makes bridge of three from model | 32 mo | 'Den/C/H/ |
| | | MPS |
| | 42 mo | Sher/Ges |
| Makes gate from model (54 mo—Ges) | 48–60 mo | Ges |
| Builds bridge from model—three cubes (7 sec—48.7 mo—MPS) | 48–60 mo | Ges/MPS |

*Pyramids*

| | | |
|---|---|---|
| Makes three-cube pyramid in 17 sec | 33 mo | MPS |
| Places six blocks in pyramid | 36–42 mo | QSS |
| | 42–48 mo | Kuhl |
| | 48–54 mo | Sher |
| Builds three steps with six cubes after demonstration (Pyramid—35 sec—51 mo, 30 sec—57 mo—MPS) | 48–60 mo | Sher/MPS |
| Places 10 blocks in pyramid | No norms | |
| Places six cubes to form three steps, from a model (two steps—Ges) | 60–72 mo | Sher/Ges |

*Forms in formboards*

| | | |
|---|---|---|
| Places one round block in formboard (two each, three geometric shapes) | 13.6 mo | Bay |
| Places one round block in formboard (one each, three geometric shapes) | 15 mo | Ges |
| | 16 mo | C |
| Places circle in rotated formboard | 18 mo | C |
| Places two round and two square blocks on formboard | 19.3 mo | Bay |
| Places square in three-hole formboard | 20 mo | C |
| Places three blocks correctly on formboard (triangle, square, circle) | 21.2 mo | Bay |
| | 22 mo | C |
| | 24–29 mo | H/Ges |
| Places six blocks correctly on formboard (circle, square, triangle) | 22.4 mo | Bay |
| Places blocks correctly after four trials | 24 mo | LAP |
| Places three blocks (square, circle, triangle) on rotated formboard | 25.4 mo | Bay |
| | 30 mo | C |
| Puts six blocks on formboard in 150 sec | 30 mo | Bay |
| Places six round and square blocks in formboard in 90 sec | 30 mo | Bay |
| Places six round and square blocks on formboard in 60 sec | 30+ mo | Bay |
| Places two of three color forms, all one color | 30–35 mo | Ges |
| Places forms correctly and repeatedly when formboard is rotated or reversed | 30–35 mo | Bay |
| Places two of ten blocks in correct place on formboard (Séquin) | 31.5 mo | MPS |
| Places ten shapes on formboard in 222 sec (Séguin) | 33 mo | MPS |
| Places forms immediately when formboard is rotated or reversed | 36–38 mo | Bay/C |
| Places ten shapes in place, two of three trials 109 sec—37 mo, 73 sec—44 mo, 63 sec—48 mo | 36–48 mo | MPS |
| Forms rectangle of two triangular cards | 60–72 mo | C/LAP |
| Places ten forms out of ten correctly on formboard in 39 sec | 62.3 mo | MPS |

| | | |
|---|---|---|
| Places ten forms out of 10 on board in 35 sec | 69   mo | MPS |
| | | |
| *Pieces in puzzles* | | |
| Complete two-piece puzzle, 14 sec—4 sec | 42   mo | C/MPS |
| Completes two-piece puzzle, 3 sec | 50.1 mo | MPS |
| Completes three-piece puzzle, 46 sec | 50.2 mo | MPS |
| Completes four-piece puzzle | 51.4 mo | MPS |
| Completes seven-piece puzzle (317 sec—36–38 mo—LAP, MPS, 150 sec—50.6 mo. MPS) | 51   mo | LAP |
| Completes ten-piece puzzle | 65.6 mo | MPS |

B.  Takes objects apart; puts objects together

| | | |
|---|---|---|
| Takes things apart and puts them together | 24–29 mo | Ges |

C.  Strings beads

| | | |
|---|---|---|
| Strings four beads—two sec | 36–48 mo | C/H/LAP |

## GROSS-MOTOR OVERVIEW

I.  Maintains static balance

   A.  Supports head
   B.  Thrusts, waves arms
   C.  Thrusts legs
   D.  Sits
   E.  Stands
   F.  Bends from waist
   G.  Squats

II  Maintains dynamic balance, using basic movement patterns

   A.  Crawls and creeps
   B.  Takes steps
   C.  Rolls body
   D.  Runs
   E.  Climbs
   F.  Jumps
   G.  Hops
   H.  Skips

III.  Maintains general coordinated movement patterns

   A.  Reaches with arm
   B.  Kicks
   C.  Bounces
   D.  Pushes objects; pulls objects
   E.  Throws objects
   F.  Rolls objects
   G.  Kneels
   H.  Carries objects
   I.  Pedals
   J.  Swings
   K.  Catches objects
   L.  Turns
   M.  Moves with pounding motion
   N.  Skates
   O.  Dances

## GROSS-MOTOR PINPOINTS

I.  Static balance

   A.  Supports head
      1.  Moves head

| | | |
|---|---|---|
| Makes lateral head movements | 0.1 mo | Bay |
| | 1   mo | LAP |
| ʾMoves head following dangling ring | 3.2 mo | Bay |
| | 5   mo | Ges |

| | | |
|---|---|---|
| Moves head and eyes in every direction | 6    mo | Sher |
| Lifts head for five-sec interval when supine | 7.5 mo | Slos |
| 2. Lifts head | | |
| Lifts head when held at shoulder | 0.1 mo | Bay |
| | 1    mo | LAP |
| Lifts head momentarily when prone | 1    mo | LAP |
| | 1    mo | Ges |
| Lifts head from dorsal suspension | 1.7 mo | Bay |
| Lifts head up when prone (90°—Den; for several sec—C) | 2    mo | C |
| | 2.2 mo | Ges/Den |
| | 2.5 mo | Sher |
| Lifts head and upper chest well up in midline using forearms | 2.1 mo | Day |
| as support, legs straight out, buttocks flat when prone | 2.5 mo | Slos |
| (for 10 sec—Slos) | 3    mo | C/Den/Sher |
| | 4    mo | Ges |
| Lifts head and chest well up supporting himself on extended arms, when prone | 6    mo | Sher |
| Raises head from pillow when lying on back | 6    mo | Sher |
| | 7    mo | Ges |
| 3. Holds head | | |
| Holds head erect when held at shoulder for 3 sec | 0.8 mo | Bay |
| | 1    mo | Sher |
| Turns head immediately to sides when prone; arms and legs flexed under body, buttocks humped up | 1    mo | Sher/Ges |
| Lets head fall forward, with back in one complete curve when held sitting (marked head lay—Ges) | | |
| Holds head to one side when supine; with arms and legs on same side outstretched, or both arms flexed, knees apart, soles of feet turned inward, lifted head falls loosely | 1    mo | Sher/Ges |
| Holds head predominately erect when held sitting | 2    mo | Ges |
| | 3    mo | Vin |
| Holds head in midposition when prone | 2    mo | Ges |
| | 3    mo | Sher |
| Holds head steady, set forward when held sitting | 2.3 mo | Bay |
| | 2.9 mo | Den |
| | 3    mo | Vin/C |
| | 4    mo | Ges |
| Holds head in midposition when supine | 3    mo | Sher/Ges |
| Balances head when body is tilted | 4.2 mo | Bay |
| Holds head firmly erect, back straight when sitting | 6    mo | Sher/Ges |
| B. Thrusts, waves arms | | |
| Thrusts arm in play when supine | 0.8 mo | Bay |
| | 1    mo | Sher |
| Waves arm symmetrically | 3    mo | Sher |
| Moves arms briskly and holds them up to be lifted | 6    mo | Sher |
| Moves arms very actively in carriage, bath, and crib | 9    mo | Sher |
| C. Thrusts legs | | |
| Thrusts leg in play when supine | 0.8 mo | Bay |
| | 1    mo | Sher |
| Lifts legs into vertical position and grasps foot | 6    mo | Sher/Ges |
| Brings feet to mouth when supine | 7    mo | Slos |
| D. Sits | | |
| Holds back straight, except in lumbar region, with head erect and steady for several seconds, when held sitting | 3    mo | Sher/C |
| | 4    mo | Ges |
| | 4.5 mo | Slos |
| Pulls to sit, with no head lag | 4.2 mo | Den |
| | 4.8 mo. | Bay |
| | 5    mo | Ges |
| Sits without support (head erect, steady—Ges) | 5    mo | Ges/LAP |
| | 5.3 mo | Bay |
| | 5.4 mo | Vin |
| | 5.5 mo | Den |

| | | |
|---|---|---|
| Sits and turns from side to side to look around him | 6 mo | Sher |
| Sits propped 30 min | 6 mo | Ges |
| Sits briefly, leans forward on hands | 6.6 mo | Day |
| | 7 mo | Ges |
| Sits erect without support momentarily | 7 mo | Ges |
| Pulls self up to sitting position | 7.6 mo | Den |
| | 8.3 mo | Bay |
| Sits by self, 1 min erect, unsteady | 8 mo | Ges |
| Sits erect without support for 10 min | 8.5 mo | Slos |
| | 9 mo | Ges |
| Sits, leans forward, erect | 9 mo | Ges |
| Sits steady and indefinitely | 9.6 mo | Bay |
| | 9.5 mo | Slos |
| | 10 mo | Ges |
| Sits, goes over to prone | 10 mo | Ges |
| Attains sitting position unaided | 12 mo | Ges/LAP/Sher |
| Rises to sitting position from lying down | 12 mo | Sher |
| Sits well and for indefinite time | 12 mo | Sher |
| Lets himself down from standing or sitting by collapsing backwards with bump, or occasionally by falling forward on hands and then back to sitting | 15 mo | Sher/LAP |
| Sits with feet crossed at ankles | 36–48 mo | Sher |
| Sits for longer period of time | 60–72 mo | Ges |

E. Stands

On broad surface

| | | |
|---|---|---|
| Sags at knees when held standing with feet on hard surface | 3 mo | Sher |
| Bears some weight on legs when held standing | 3 mo | Ges |
| | 4.2 mo | Den |
| Lifts one foot when held standing | 4 mo | Ges |
| Stands while holding on | 5.8 mo | Den |
| | 6 mo | LAP |
| Pulls self upright | 6.6 mo | Vin |
| Stands, maintaining large fraction of weight | 7 mo | Ges |
| Pulls self to stand | 7.6 mo | Den |
| | 8.1 mo | Bay |
| | 8 mo | LAP |
| Stands, maintains briefly, when hands held | 8 mo | Ges |
| Stands holding on to support himself, but cannot lower self | 9 mo | Ges/Sher/Slos |
| Stands momentarily | 9.8 mo | Den |
| | 10.2 mo | Vin |
| Stands alone well | 11 mo | LAP/Bay |
| | 11.5 mo | Den |
| Pulls self to standing and lets self down again holding onto furniture (with support, cruises at rail—Ges) | 12 mo | Sher/Ges |
| May stand alone for a few moments (seconds—Slos) | 12 mo | Sher |
| | 13 mo | Slos |
| Stands up (from supine position) | 12.6 mo | Bay |
| Stands on right foot with help | 16.1 mo | Bay/LAP |
| Stands up on request; turns to side first | 21.9 | Bay |
| Stands on left foot alone | 22 mo | LAP |
| | 22.7 mo | Bay |
| | 23.2 mo | MPS |
| Stands with abdomen protruding less than at 18 mo | 24–29 mo | Ges |
| Stands up on request; pulls self to sitting position first | 30+ mo | Bay |
| Stands on tiptoe if shown | 30–35 mo | Sher |
| Attempts to stand on one foot | 30–35 mo | Ges |
| Stands on one foot for 1 sec | 30 mo | Den |
| Stands on one foot, 5 sec | 36 mo | LAP |
| Stands on one foot for 4–8 sec | 36–48 mo | LAP |
| | 54 mo | Den |
| Stands with shoulders erect | 36–48 mo | F/Sher |
| Stands on one foot with momentary balance (5 sec—Den, 2 sec—42 mo—Ges) | 38 mo | Sher/Ges H/Den |

On walking board

| | | |
|---|---|---|
| Tries to stand on walking board | 17 mo | LAP |
| | 17.5 mo | Slos |
| | 17.8 mo | Bay |
| Stands with both feet on walking board | 24.5 mo | Bay |
| | 24–30 mo | Bay |
| Balances on walking board | 48–60 mo | Ges |
| Balances on a narrow plank or on a chalk mark on floor (on 6-cm board—no step off—Ges) | 60–72 mo | H/Ges |

F. Bends from waist

| | | |
|---|---|---|
| Stoops and recovers | 11.5 mo | Den |
| Stoops to pick up toys from floor | 15 mo | Sher/LAP |
| Picks up toy from floor without falling | 18–23 mo | Sher |
| | 18–24 mo | LAP |
| Bends at waist to pick up something from floor | 24–29 mo | Ges |

G. Squats

| | | |
|---|---|---|
| Squats to rest or to play with object on ground and rises to feet without using hands | 24–29 mo | Sher |
| | 36–48 mo | Ges |

II. Maintains dynamic balance, using basic movement patterns

A. Creeps and crawls

| | | |
|---|---|---|
| Makes crawling movements when prone | 0.1 mo | Bay |
| Moves body more smoothly and continuously, with more pliable limbs | 3 mo | Sher |
| Attempts to crawl on all fours | 9 mo | Sher |
| Moves about on floor | 10 mo | Slos/Ges |
| Crawls rapidly on all fours | 12 mo | Sher/LAP |
| Crawls upstairs (creeps up—Ges) | 15 mo | Sher/Ges |
| Creeps backwards downstairs. Bumps down a few steps on buttocks, facing forward occasionally | 18–23 mo | Sher |
| | 18–24 mo | LAP |

B. Takes steps

On level ground

| | | |
|---|---|---|
| Presses down feet, straightens body, and often makes reflex stepping movements when held standing on hard surface | 1 mo | Sher |
| Lifts foot when held standing | 3 mo | Ges/LAP |
| Steps on alternate feet when held standing | 9 mo | Sher |
| Takes steps while holding onto furniture | 9.2 mo | Den |
| Takes steps but needs both hands held (with help—Bay) | 9.6 mo | Ges |
| | 11 mo | Slos |
| Takes steps with assistance | 11 mo | LAP |
| Takes steps with one or both hands held (five steps—Slos) | 12 mo | Sher/Slos |
| | 13 mo | Ges |
| Takes steps alone | 12 mo | LAP |
| | 17 mo | Den |
| Takes steps around furniture, stepping sideways | 12 mo | Sher |
| Walks well (without help, may fall—Slos) (unsteadily, with feet wide apart, arm flexed and held slightly above head or at shoulder level to balance—Sher; few steps, falls by collapsing; creeping discarded—Ges) | 12.1 mo | Den |
| | 13 mo. | Ges |
| | 15 mo | Slos/Sher/Ges |
| Takes steps sideways | 14.1 mo | Bay |
| Takes steps backward | 14.3 mo | Den |
| | 14.6 mo | Bay |
| Starts and stops walking without falling | 18–23 mo | Sher |
| Walks well, takes steps with feet only slightly apart | 18 mo | Sher/Ges/Slos |
| Walks with knees and elbows slightly bent, shoulders hunched, holds arms out and backward | 24–29 mo | Ges |
| Walks, taking steps on tiptoe | 25.7 mo | Bay |
| | 30 mo | F/Sher/H/Ges/LAP |
| Walks; takes steps heel-to-toe | 43 mo | F/Den |
| Walks backward; takes steps heel-to-toe | 56 mo | Den/LAP |
| Upstairs, downstairs | | |
| Takes steps upstairs with help | 16.1 mo | Bay |
| | 18–23 mo. | Sher |
| Takes steps downstairs with help | 16.4 mo | Bay |

| | | |
|---|---|---|
| Takes steps upstairs unassisted | 21 mo | Vin |
| Takes steps downstairs when one hand is held | 21 mo | LAP |
| | 21.5 mo | Slos |
| Takes steps up and down stairs, without assistance | 21 mo | LAP |
| Takes steps upstairs and down holding on to rail or wall, two feet to a step | 24–29 mo | Ges/Sher |
| Takes steps upstairs alone, with both feet on each step | 25.1 mo | Bay |
| Takes steps downstairs alone, with both feet on each step | 25.8 mo | Bay |
| Takes steps downstairs with alternating forward foot | 30+ mo | Bay |
| Takes steps upstairs with alternating forward foot | 30+ mo | Bay |
| Takes steps upstairs alone, but downstairs holding rail, two feet to a step | 30–35 mo | Sher |
| Takes steps upstairs using alternating feet | 36–48 mo | LAP/SHER/F/Ges/II |
| Takes steps downstairs one step per tread | 39 mo | Ges/Sher/H/Vin |
| Takes steps alone up and down stairs, one foot per step | 48–60 mo | Sher/Ges |
| *On walking board, line* | | |
| Takes steps with one foot on walking board | 20 mo | LAP |
| | 20.6 mo | Bay |
| Takes steps on a line, general direction | 23 mo | LAP |
| | 23.9 mo | Bay |
| Attempts step on walking board | 24–30 mo | Bay |
| Attempts step on walking board | 27.6 mo | Bay |
| Takes steps backward for 10 feet | 27.8 mo | Bay |
| Alternates steps part way on walking board | 30+ mo | Bay |
| Takes steps with feet on line for 10 feet | 30+ mo | Bay |
| | 30–36 mo | Bay |
| Takes steps part way on walking board | 30–36 mo | Bay |
| Takes steps between two parallel lines, 8 inches apart on the floor, without stepping on the lines for 8–10 ft | 30–36 mo | H |
| Takes steps on a line | 36–48 mo | LAP/Ges |
| Takes steps on walking board with both feet | 42–48 mo | Ges |
| Takes steps forward perfectly on walking board | 60–66 mo | Ges |
| Takes steps forward, backward, sideways on walking board | 60–66 mo | Kep |
| Takes steps on walking board (6-cm board) without stepping off for full length | 60 mo | LAP |
| C. Rolls body | | |
| Rolls partway to side when supine | 1 mo | Ges |
| | 1.5 mo | Slos |
| Turns to same side when cheek touched; turns away when ear rubbed | 1 mo | Sher |
| Turns from side to back | 1.8 mo | Bay |
| | 2 mo | LAP |
| Rolls over | 2.8 mo | Den |
| | 3.8 mo | Vin |
| | 3 mo | Lap |
| Turns from back to side | 4 mo | LAP |
| | 4.4 mo | Bay |
| Verges on rolling when prone | 5 mo | Ges |
| Rolls over front to back | 6 mo | Sher |
| Rolls from back to stomach | 6 mo | Slos/Ges |
| | 6.4 mo | Bay |
| Pivots 180° in order to obtain toy which is kept just out of reach | 6.5 mo | Slos |
| Pivots body when prone | 8 mo | Ges |
| Turns body to look sideways while stretching out to grasp toy | 9 mo | Sher |
| Progresses on floor by rolling or squirming | 9 mo | Sher |
| D. Runs | | |
| Runs stiffly upright, with eyes fixed on ground 1–2 yd ahead, but cannot continue around obstacles | 18 mo | Sher/Slos |
| Runs on whole foot, stopping and starting with ease and avoiding obstacles | 24–29 mo | Ges |
| Runs leaning forward | 24–29 mo | Sher |
| Runs well straight forward | 30–35 mo | Sher |
| Runs around obstacles; turns corners while running | 36–48 mo | Sher |

| | | |
|---|---|---|
| Runs on tiptoe | 48–60 mo | Sher |
| Runs lightly on toes | 60–72 mo | LAP/Sher |
| Runs with few falls; plays game while running | 60–72 mo | H |

E. Climbs

| | | |
|---|---|---|
| Climbs forward into adult's chair then turns around and sits | 18–23 mo | Sher |
| Climbs down from adult chair without assistance | 21   mo | LAP |
| Climbs on furniture to look out of window, and climbs down again without assistance | 24–29 mo | Ges/Sher |
| Climbs easy nursery apparatus | 30–35 mo | Sher |
| Climbs ladders and trees | 48–60 mo | LAP/Sher/Ges |
| Climbs on overhead ladder | 60–72 mo | LAP/Ges |
| Climbs actively and skillfully | 60–72 mo | Sher |

F. Jumps

| | | |
|---|---|---|
| Jumps (general activities requiring jumping skills) | 18–24 mo | Bay/DDST |
| | 30–36 mo | DL/Sher/Des |
| | 60–66 mo | Kep |
| | 66–72 mo | QSS/PAR |
| Vertically | | |
| Jumps in place | 23.5 mo | Bay |
| | 24   mo | LAP |
| Jumps from bottom step | 24.8 mo | Bay |
| Jumps from second step | 28.1 mo | Bay |
| Jumps distance of 4–14 inches | 29.1 mo | Bay |
| Jumps with two feet together | 30–35 mo | Sher/Ges |
| Jumps over string 2 inches high | 30+ mo | Bay |
| Jumps over string 8 inches high | 30+ mo | Bay |
| Jumps from bottom step (6–8 inches—Ges) | 36–48 mo | Ges/F/Sher |
| Jumps from height of 12 inches, landing on toes only | 60–72 mo | LAP, H |
| Jumps ropes | 60–72 mo | LAP/H |
| Horizontally | | |
| Makes broad jump (14–24 inches—Bay) | 30+ mo | Bay |
| | 34   mo | Den |
| Broad jumps, 24–34 inches | 30+ mo | Bay |
| | 34   mo | F/Den |
| Jumps, running or standing broad jump (23–33 inches—H) | 48–60 mo | Ges/H |

G. Hops

| | | |
|---|---|---|
| Hops on one foot (two or more hops—Bay) | 30+ mo | Bay |
| | 36–48 mo | LAP |
| | 41   mo | Den |
| | 42–48 mo | Den/Par/Sher |
| | 48   mo | Sher |
| Hops 2–3 yd on each foot separately | 54–60 mo | Ges/F |
| | 60–66 mo | Kep/DL |
| | | Sher/LAP |

II. Skips

| | | |
|---|---|---|
| Skips on one foot | 36–48 mo | F/Ges/LAP |
| Skips, using both feet | 60–66 mo | QSS/Ges/Kep |
| | | PAR/Sher |

III. Maintains other general coordinated movement patterns

A. Reaches with arm

| | | |
|---|---|---|
| Reaches for dangling ring | 3   mo | LAP |
| | 3.1 mo | Bay |
| | 3.6 mo | Den |
| | 4.2 mo | Vin |
| Reaches for cube | 4.1 mo | Bay |
| Holds arms extended when prone | 5   mo | Ges |
| Reaches with two hands to approach rattle, bell | 5   mo | Ges |
| Reaches unilaterally | 5.4 mo | Bay |
| | 6.0 mo | C |
| Reaches for second cube | 5.4 mo | Bay |

| | | |
|---|---|---|
| Reaches for rattle held in front of him with one hand, grabs, and shakes it | 6.5 mo | Slos |
| Reaches for and holds two cubes | 7   mo | C |
| Reaches for toy out of reach on table | 8   mo | Slos |
| | 9   mo | Sher |
| Reaches around object for toy | 14 mo | C |

B.  Kicks

| | | |
|---|---|---|
| Kicks vigorously, legs alternating or occasionally together | 3   mo | Sher |
| Kicks strongly, legs alternating | 6   mo | Sher |
| Kicks ball forward | 20–22.3 mo | Den |
| | 23.4 mo | Bay |
| Kicks large ball | 21   mo | LAP |
| | 24–29 mo | Ges |
| | 30–35 mo | Sher |
| Kicks | 48–60 mo | F |

C   Bounces

| | | |
|---|---|---|
| Bears weight on feet and bounces up and down actively when | 6   mo | Sher |
| held standing with feet touching hard surface | 7   mo | Ges |

D   Pushes objects; pulls objects

| | | |
|---|---|---|
| Pushes small toy (pulls car) | 11   mo | LAP |
| | 11.3 mo | Bay |
| Pushes large wheeled toy with handle on level ground | 15   mo | Sher |
| Pushes and pulls large toys, boxes, etc., around floor | 18–23 mo | Sher/Ges |
| Pushes and pulls large toys, boxes, etc., around floor without falling | 18–24 mo | LAP |
| Pulls wheeled toy by cord | 24–29 mo | Sher |
| Pushes and pulls large toys skillfully, but has difficulty steering them | | |
| around obstacles | 30–35 mo | Sher/Ges |
| Pushes and pulls large toys around large obstacles | 36–48 mo | Sher/Ges |

E.  Throws objects

| | | |
|---|---|---|
| Throws ball with examiner | 11.6 mo | Den |
| | 13   mo | LAP |
| Throws ball, releasing with slight cast forward (Ges) | 13.6 mo | Bay |
| | 14   mo | Ges |
| Casts objects in play | 15   mo | Ges |
| Throws small rubber ball | 20   mo | LAP/Slos |
| | 21   mo | MPS |
| Throws ball overhand | 18–24 mo | Den |
| | 48–54 mo | QSS/Ges/H |
| Throws ball overhead | 19   mo | LAP |
| Throws small ball without falling | 24–29 mo | Sher |
| Throws ball underhand | 30–36 mo | DL |
| | 36–42 mo | PAR |
| Throws using shoulder and elbow | 36–48 mo | F |
| Throws, guiding course of the ball with fingers | 36–48 mo | F |
| Throws ball overhead (9½-inch ball—12 ft—H) | 48–60 mo | Ges/H |

F   Rolls objects

| | | |
|---|---|---|
| Rolls ball back and forth in game | 12   mo | Ges |

G   Kneels

| | | |
|---|---|---|
| Kneels unaided or with slight support on floor and in carriage, crib, and | | |
| bath | 15   mo | Sher/LAP |

H   Carries objects

| | | |
|---|---|---|
| Carries large objects while walking | 18–24 mo | LAP |
| | 18–23 mo | Sher |

I   Pedals tricycle

| | | |
|---|---|---|
| | 23.9 mo | Sher/Ges/H/Den |
| | 24   mo | LAP |
| Turns wide corners on tricycle | 36–48 mo | Sher |
| Rides tricycle expertly | 50–60 mo | Sher |

J   Swings

| | | |
|---|---|---|
| Swings | 36–48 mo | Ges |

K   Catches objects

| | | |
|---|---|---|
| Catches bounced ball | 36–48 mo | LAP |
| | 42–48 mo | PAR/QSS/Den |
| | 46  mo | Den |
| | 60–66 mo | DL |
| Catches a ball 5 inches in diameter | 60–72 mo | H |
| L.. Moves arm with pounding motion | | |
|    Drives nails and pegs | 36–48 mo | F/LAP |
| M. Turns | | |
|    Turns sharp corners, running, pushing, pulling | 48–60 mo | Sher |
| N. Skates | | |
|    Roller-skates ("skates"—Vin) | 60–72 mo | H/Vin/LAP |
| O. Dances | | |
|    Makes dancing movements | 60–72 mo | LAP |

## COMMUNICATION

While remediation of speech and language deficiencies is a major area of concern for teachers of the severely handicapped, specification of the goals and procedures of language intervention presents an enduring problem. Conflicting opinion about the relationship of communication deficits to retardation, which elements of language to emphasize in programming for severely handicapped individuals, and the nature of the language acquisition process itself have slowed progress in defining appropriate objectives and strategies. A review of the literature in the areas of language development and language intervention for handicapped populations makes clear the need for a collection of language pinpoints, clearly specified in terms of observable behavior, which will facilitate assessment of developmental deficits and encourage teachers and clinicians to implement programs aimed at development of language behaviors, rather than at remediation of phenomena specific to the handicapping condition.

### The Relationship of Language Deficits to a Severely Handicapped Population

There can be little argument with the statement that remediation of language deficits represents a major concern for teachers of the severely handicapped. In an extensive review of the literature dealing with language and mental retardation, Thomas E. Jordan (1967) finds that language deficiencies in the form of speech deficits are associated with between 40 and 79 percent of the populations studied. The ratio of deficiencies was reported to increase with the degree of retardation. Jordan suggests that the prevalent view of retardation and language defects as independent entities connected by a causal relation is supported by a number of factors:

1. Delay in speech consistently reported in populations of retarded individuals.

2. The accuracy of mental age as a predictor of articulation proficiency in retarded persons.

3. The relationship between language disorders and developmental disorders of early origin.

4. The consistently infirm quality of language exhibited by retarded individuals.

If Jordan's evidence may be extended to the severely handicapped population as a whole, a high incidence of language and speech deficiencies is to be expected. Confronted with this evidence, the teacher or clinician has traditionally possessed a limited number of alternatives:

1. Spending long hours drilling imitation of "vocabulary" and "useful phrases."

2. Attempting "therapy" in a round-about fashion, directed toward the behavioral dimensions of the handicapped: short attention span, short memory span, perceptual deficiencies, and bizarre social responses.

3. Arriving at the conclusion that there was no truly successful remedy unless one could alleviate the retardation.

These alternatives provide only partial treatment, as in the case of vocabulary drill which deals with only a small part of the language process, or no treatment at all. If the teacher were also to adopt the theory of Lenneburg (1967) that the development of language in human beings is an innate capacity, the dilemma would only be further compounded. The teacher might then assume that, since the child's development was inhibited, no attempts at treatment should be made until the individual had reached the proper stage of development.

In fact, the language "readiness" of individuals has played a large part in the selection of candidates for language training programs. General I.Q. has been used as an indicator of a child's ability to achieve a desired educational level. Often, according to Sylvia Richardson (1967, p. 152), a minimum mental age of between 4 and 6 years of age is suggested as the optimal time to begin therapy. Richardson, however, suggests that since the normal child begins to talk between 12–18 months, during what Piaget defines as the "height of the period of sensory–motor learning," remedy for handicapped children might prove more fruitful if intervention began as early as possible.

It is understandable, then, that Jordan, concluding his review, should recommend that the teacher treat language deficiencies as only one dimension of the handicapping condition, rather than as a correlate or consequence. McLean (1972), in his discussion of this issue, suggests that only by examining the demands of the language system itself, in terms of clearly observable behaviors, and by assessing the child's behavior in terms of those demands, can teachers avoid the tendency to provide partial or misdirected programs. If severely handicapped individuals are to be allowed any chance at effective participation within their communities and cultures, then they must receive a language program designed to meet individual needs, regardless of intelligence score or handicapping condition.

## A Description of Language Structures and Their Relationship to Language Acquisition by Severely Handicapped Individuals

In addition to arguments concerning the nature of the relationship between language deficits and severe handicapping conditions, such as retardation, another basic question exists. How does the language development of "normal" children relate to the development process in children labeled as severely handicapped? Can a model of normal development be used as a basis for pinpointing behaviors and developing programs for a profoundly handicapped individual? David E. Yoder and Jon F. Miller (1972), in a review of language studies involving mentally retarded populations, some of them severely handicapped, conclude that enough data exist to justify the clinician's or teacher's "selective use of the data available on normal language acquisition" (1972, p. 100).

Yoder and Miller find, as have others, that one problem in assessing studies concerning language development of the retarded is the great variety of definitions of language behavior which exist. While a number of studies have chosen to evaluate language acquisition in terms of mean length of response, vocabulary size, and abstract versus concrete word usage, the description of achievement in terms of structural levels— phonology, morphology, syntax, and semantics—has received minimal attention. A brief description of the elements analyzed within each of the structural levels follows.

PHONOLOGICAL LEVEL

At the phonological level, attention is given to articulation of sounds which make up a language; discrimination of phonemic distinctions in expressive and receptive activities (phonemes constitute the minimum sound features which correlate with changes of meaning in words, as in bin and pin); and aspects of voicing such as pitch, stress, and intonation.

MORPHOLOGICAL LEVEL

The morphological level involves the combination of sounds into sound segments which have a particular meaning. These segments may exist independently as words, or as bound morphemes such as inflectional endings. For example, the word "cat" is an independent utterance which cannot be further reduced without losing its meaning. In the word "cats," however, the *s* at the end of the word exists as a bound morpheme. It produces a crucial change in the meaning of the word, but can appear only as an addition to other morphemes.

## SYNTACTIC LEVEL

The syntax of a language specifies those patterns in which linguistic forms, such as words and phrases, may be arranged. It describes word order.

## SEMANTIC LEVEL

At the semantic level, meaning is the most important aspect. Dale (1972, p. 131), discussing semantic development in normal children, concedes that "in the competition for least understood aspect of language acquisition, semantic development is surely the winner." Research concerning acquisition of meaning has dealt primarily with vocabulary growth. However, dissatisfaction with vocabulary size as an accurate measure of meaning acquisition has increased as researchers consider more complex questions. According to Dale, compiling lists of words as they are acquired by children fails to give observers information about specific meanings words may have for a child, ignores "important relationships" between word meanings, and provides little information concerning the process by which word meanings are combined to provide larger sentence meanings. Dale postulates that because the more complex elements of language acquisition have been so closely associated with cognitive development, advances in the study of semantic growth have been slowed.

Until only recently, much research and programming emphasis has been placed upon the phonological aspects of language in severely handicapped populations (Yoder and Miller, p. 90). While the process by which the developing infant learns to discriminate distinctive phonemic elements may be no less complex than those used to formulate later language rules, there are, in any language, only between 15 and 60 phonemes to master. Perhaps, since many programs have stressed intensive imitative drill, the phonological level with its relatively restricted number of elements has seemed a logical place to devote training efforts.

Current efforts are being made to provide information and programs at the other levels, however. Newfield and Schlanger (1968) examined the acquisition of English morphology by normal and retarded children, using lists devised by Jean Burko in 1958. The results of their study indicated that the order of acquisition of inflectional forms was the same for both groups, but retarded children demonstrated less success in generalizing inflection to nonsense "words." Lovell and Bradbury implemented a similar experiment in 1967, testing a population of 160 retarded individuals. Research involving use of a cloze-test procedure with retarded and nonretarded individuals, by Semmel et al. (1967), studied the application of syntactic rules by these populations and found the retarded population particularly weak.

According to Yoder and Miller (1972), research efforts have provided little conclusive information about the quality of rule acquisition and application by retarded individuals, but even less information about language acquisition by the more severely retarded at any of the structural levels. However, while these authors, in summarizing studies of structural competence, stress that much more information is needed, they do find enough similarity in patterns of growth in retarded and nonretarded individuals to justify the "selective use" (1972, p. 100) of data describing normal languate acquisition.

### Descriptions of Normal Language Development

Description of that sequence of "normal language acquisition" has itself become a controversial issue. Until the publication of Chomsky's works on language theory in the late 1950s and early 1960s, linguists used a descriptive model. This model emphasized contrasts between adult language and that produced by the child (deviations from adult structures constituted errors); vocabularly size, categorized according to adult usage regardless of the child's usage patterns; and production of sounds. While many well-known sources faithfully recorded the age of appearance of each new receptive and expressive element, those elements were categorized without reference to language patterns peculiar to the child. Chomsky's (1965) work suggested that the child speaks his own language, that that language contains its own consistent patterns, and that the child, rather than merely imitating or attempting to match each utterance he hears, engages in active hypothesis formation and testing. Language development, then, becomes a productive process, involving active formulation and application of rules. These rules derive not from the surface phrase structure emphasized by descriptive linguists, but from the deep structure or semantic intent of utterances.

According to this generative theory of language acquisition, the child develops linguistic competence. That competence encompasses all the rules of grammar which he is able to employ. What he actually does with this competence is called his performance, which is subject to variables such as interest, or motivation, attention, understanding, memory span, concept knowledge, and task complexity or novelty. Competence cannot be measured; it can only be inferred from a child's performance.

Researchers such as Braine (1963), Brown (1964), Bloom (1970), and Klima and Bellugi (1966) documented early utterances in an attempt to formulate a new model for language usage, which would more accurately describe developing language structures not in contrast to an adult system, but as they are used by children. By systematically recording linguistic utterances and the nonlinguistic environments in which they occurred, these authors have arrived at a new picture of developing language which seems to say that children do systematically use at least two functional word classes in early utterances, but that these classes do not necessarily correspond to traditional noun/verb usage, and that a child's sentences develop a consistent hierarchical structure over time as the child approaches adult production.

While a generative view of language development does find support in the works of these authors, application of that view to a severely handicapped population presents some problems. It is difficult to deny that language is a complex symbolic process whose observable performance is only a surface representation of the internal behavior which enables the child to construct and specify language output. However, Braine, Brown, and Bloom themselves acknowledge inconsistencies within the developmental sequences observed. And, unfortunately, most of their analysis deals with the performance of very small populations (sometimes restricted to three children) who often come from upper middle-class homes which emphasize intellectual achievement. Generalization of their hypotheses to a broad "normal" population on the basis of so little data presents a problem in itself. Application of these descriptions to a population whose general functional level, let alone "competence" level, is notoriously difficult to assess, compounds the problem.

### The Developmental Pinpoints

James McLean (1972), in his introduction to a text on language intervention with the retarded, offers some hope of compromise between demands for an empirically substantiated list of language objectives and a description/ of language development which recognizes the performance/ competence dichotomy, as well as generative aspects of child-language. He states that "regardless of conflicting theories which describe the development of language behavior, the behaviors remain quantifiable and they are, therefore, the goal of intervention." (1972, p. 10). The following collection of language pinpoints is an attempt to describe such behaviors. The reader will notice that where possible, utterances are categorized according to nonlinguistic setting or inferred intent. When intent cannot be extrapolated from the information available, behaviors are categorized according to traditional descriptive headings. In accordance with the selection of pinpoints for other developmental areas, pinpoints here come from sources which have tested or described "large-N" populations. Recent studies of linguistic competencies in areas such as "interrogatives" and use of "negatives" may, therefore, not been included.

The language pinpoints are divided into two major categories: those requiring receptive or decoding skills, and those requiring expressive or encoding behaviors. Successful performance in each category depends upon certain motor and sensory capabilities which may be substantially impaired in a severely handicapped population. Additional information regarding hearing acuity, motor capacities, and unusual sensitivity, is, therefore, prerequisite to efficient use of the pinpoints for assessment and programming purposes.

Although receptive skills precede expressive skills in this checklist, there is some question as to whether reception precedes production in actual performance. Further research is needed in this area. The behaviors signifying communication reception which have been listed here fall, for the most part, into fine-motor categories, but Bernard Friedlander (1970), in a fascinating review of studies on receptive language development in infancy, suggests some novel ways of measuring early receptive abilities. Infant heart rate has provided one measure of the infant's discrimination of phonemic differences and sentence complexity. In a population such as the severely handicapped, in which fine-motor responses may be very poorly developed, such a measure could prove extremely valuable.

While most descriptions of expressive language deal with verbalization, gesture has been included in this sequence. Although speech as a vehicle for communication is a desirable goal, much information is communicated in everyday conversation by the use of facial and other gestures. Gesture can be developed as an effective communicative tool and represents a mode which must be explored when dealing with a population for whom intelligible verbal behavior may be a long-range or impossible objective.

Language is perhaps the most complex skill in the human behavioral repertoire. It is, certainly, an important prerequisite to integration of the severely handicapped individual within his community. The teacher attempting to remediate the language deficiencies of the severely handicapped child, must, therefore, have precise knowledge of both the communication demands made by the child's culture or community, and the child's position in relation to development of those communication skills. It is hoped that this list will provide a comprehensive and accurate description of language development from which the teacher can assess a child's skills and develop programs to meet developmental deficiencies.

## REFERENCES

Bloom L: Language Development: Form and Function in Emerging Grammars. Cambridge, Mass., Massachusetts Institutes of Technology Pr, 1970

Braine M: The ontology of English phrase structure: The first phase. Language 39:1–14, 1963

Brown R, Fraser C: The acquisition of syntax. in Coper CN, Musgrave BS (eds): Verbal Behavior and Learning: Problems and Processes. New York, McGraw Hill, 1963

Chomsky N: Aspects of the Theory of Syntax. Cambridge, Mass., Massachusetts Institute of Technology Pr, 1965

Dale P: Language Development: Structure and Function. Hinsdale, Ill., Dryden, 1972

Friedlander B: Receptive language development in infancy: Issues and problems. Merrill-Palmer Quart, 6:1, 7–49,

Jordan T: Language and mental retardation: A review of the literature. In Schiefelbusch R, Copeland R, Smith J (eds): Language and Mental Retardation. New York, Holt, Rinehart and Winston, 1967

Klima E, Bellugi-Klima U: Syntactic regularities in the speech of children. In Lyons J, Wales RJ (eds): Psycholinguistics Papers. Edinburgh, Edinburgh Univ Pr, 1966

Lenneburg E: Biological Foundations of Language. New York, Wiley, 1967

Lovell K, Bradbury B: The learning of English morphology in educationally subnormal special school children. Am J Men Defic, 71:609–615, 1967

McLean J, Yoder, D, Schiefelbusch, R (eds): Language Intervention with the Retarded. Baltimore, University Park, 1972

Newfield M, Schlanger B: The acquisition of English morphology by normals and educable mentally retarded children. J Speech Hear Res, 11:693–706, 1968

Richardson, S: Language training for mentally retarded children. In Schiefelbusch R, Copeland R, Smith J (eds): Language and Mental Retardation. New York, Holt, Rinehart and Winston, 146–162, 1967

Sander, E: When are speech sounds learned? J Speech Hear Disord, 37:1, 55–66, 1972

Semmel M, Barritt L, Bennett S, et al: The performance of educable mentally retarded and normal children on a modified cloze task. Stud Lang Behav 5:326–346, 1967

Yoder D, Miller J: What we know and what we can do: Input toward a system. In Schiefelbusch R, Copeland R, Smith J (eds): Language Intervention with the Retarded. Baltimore, University Park, 1972

## RECEPTIVE LANGUAGE PINPOINTS

I. Response to sounds
    A. Stops movement in response to sounds
    B. Stops whimpering in response to sounds
    C. Makes "startle" movement in response to sounds
    D. Turns toward source of sound
        1. Random sound
        2. Human voice

II. Response to verbal requests (following directions)
    A. Makes directional body movements
    B. Gives objects in response to request
    C. Points to objects, body parts, pictures
    D. Places objects in response to request
    E. Matches objects, pictures, colors in response to request

## RECEPTIVE LANGUAGE OVERVIEW

I. Responds to sounds
    A. Stops movement in response to sounds

| | | |
|---|---|---|
| Stops movement at sound of bell | 0.1 mo | Bay |
| | 1 mo | Sher |
| | 2 mo | LAP |
| Stops movement at sound of rattle | 0.1 mo | Bay |
| | 1 mo | LAP |
| Stops movement in response to sharp sound | 0.1 mo | Bay |
| Stops movement in response to voice | 0.7 mo | Bay |
| | 1 mo | LAP |
| | 2 mo | C |
| Stops movement or lessens it at the sound from a piece of paper when it is crumpled up close to ear, or two blocks gently knocked together | 1 mo | Slos |

B. Stops whimpering in response to sounds

| | | |
|---|---|---|
| Stops whimpering in response to sound of nearby soothing human voice, but not when infant is screaming for feeding | 1 mo | Sher |
| Stops whimpering or smiles to sound of mother's voice before she touches him, except when infant is screaming | 3 mo | Sher |
| Quiets to rattle of spoon or sound of bell rung out of sight for 3–5 sec at 6–12 inches from ear | 3 mo | Sher |

C. Makes "startle" movement in response to sounds

| | | |
|---|---|---|
| Stiffens, quivers, blinks, screws eyes up, extends limbs, fans out fingers and toes, and may cry when startled by sudden loud noises | 1–3 mo | Sher |

D. Turns toward source of sound
1. Random sounds

| | | |
|---|---|---|
| Moves eyes toward sound source | 2.2 mo | Bay |
| | 3 mo | Sher |
| Turns head to sound of bell | 3.8 mo | Bay |
| | 5 mo | C |
| | 6 mo | Ges |
| Turns head to sound of rattle (crumpling of paper—Slos) | 3.9 mo | Bay |
| | 5.5 mo | Slos |
| Turns head after fallen spoon | 5.2 mo | Bay |
| Turns head to sounds such as bells, whistles, clock | 18–23 mo | Ges |

2. Human voice

| | | |
|---|---|---|
| Turns head to voice | 3 mo | C |
| | 4 mo | LAP |
| | 5.6 mo | Den |
| Stops movement, turns head to familiar words | 7.9 mo | Bay |
| Responds by turning head, stopping movement to name, "no-no" | 9 mo | Ges |
| | 10.1 mo | Bay |
| | 9–12 mo | LAP |
| Turns immediately to own name | 12 mo | Sher |

II. Responds to verbal requests

A. Makes directional body movements in response to requests

| | | |
|---|---|---|
| Moves body to follow simple directions, adjust to gestures (pat-a-cake, bye-bye) | 9 mo | C |
| | 9.1 mo | Bay |
| | 9.5 mo | Slos |
| | 10 mo | Ges |
| | 11–16 mo | Vin |
| Unwraps cube: upon question, "Where's the block?" | 10.5 mo | Bay |
| Moves body appropriately to show that he understands several words in usual context (e.g., own and family names, bye-bye, walk, dinner, kitty, cup, spoon, ball, car) | 12 mo | Sher/LAP |
| Moves body in response to two of the following prepositions; on, in, under, behind, in front of | 28.2 mo | Bay |

B. Gives objects upon request

| | | |
|---|---|---|
| Gives several common objects on request | 12 mo | Sher |
| | 15 mo | LAP |
| | 15.3 mo | Bay |
| Follows command to give pencil, paper to examiner; choice of pencil, paper, book | 26–27 mo | Slos |

C. Points to objects, body parts, and pictures on request

Objects

| | | |
|---|---|---|
| Points to familiar persons, animals, toys, etc., when requested | 15   mo | Sher |
| Points to objects showing discrimination of two—cup, plate, box | 22   mo | LAP |
| Points to two of six objects (kitty, button, thimble, cup, engine, spoon) | 22   mo | LAP |
| Points to four of six of the following objects: cat, button, thimble, cup, spoon, engine | 24–29 mo | C |
| Points to three—cup, plate, box (third—C) | 25.6 mo | Bay |
| Points upon request to floor, window, door | 31   mo | Slos |

Body parts

| | | |
|---|---|---|
| Points to one named body part | 17   mo | LAP/Den/Sher |
| | 19.1 mo | Bay |
| Points to three body parts of self or doll (hair, eyes, nose—Sher) | 18   mo | LAP |
| | 18–23 mo | C |
| | 20   mo | C |
| Points to five body parts of self or doll | 22   mo | C/LAP |
| Points to fingers, shoes | 30   mo | Slos |
| Points to six body parts of self or doll | 30–35 mo | LAP/C |
| Points to teeth and chin on request | 34   mo | LAP |
| Points to tongue, neck on request | 43–48 mo | LAP |
| Points to tongue, neck, arm, knee, thumb on request | 43–48 mo | Slos |
| Points correctly to answer question "Where is your head?" | 51   mo | Slos |

Pictures

| | | |
|---|---|---|
| Points to three pictures upon request | 19.7 mo | Bay |
| Points to five of six pictures of common objects (two of six—clock, basket, book, flag, leaf, star—C) | 21.6 mo | Bay/Vin |
| | 22   mo | C |
| Points to 7 of 10 pictures of common objects | 24.7 mo | Bay |
| | 30   mo | C |
| Points to 6 of 10 pictures by name | 27   mo | C |
| Points to pictures described, three of six (four of six—54 mo) | 48–60 mo | C |

Other (size, part-whole)

| | | |
|---|---|---|
| Can indicate correctly when asked to point to chair and leg of chair | 25   mo | Slos |

D. Places objects in response to request

One-step directions

| | | |
|---|---|---|
| Follows direction to put doll in chair | 17.8 mo | Bay |
| Follows one-step direction | 18   mo | LAP |
| Follows two of three directions, i.e., "put the doll in the chair," "put the spoon in the cup," etc. | 19.8 mo | Den |
| | 20   mo | C |
| | 24   mo | LAP |

Complex directions

| | | |
|---|---|---|
| Carries out two-step directions with ball | 18   mo | LAP |
| Follows three directions with object | 21   mo | LAP |
| Follows a two-stage command | 30–36 mo | LAP |
| Follows four-step command using prepositions | 48   mo | LAP |
| Follows commands using four prepositions, ball and chair | 48–60 mo | LAP |
| Follows three commands in proper order | 54   mo | LAP/C |
| | 60–72 mo | Ges |

E. Matches objects, pictures, and colors in response to requests

*Objects, pictures*

| | | |
|---|---|---|
| Matches familiar objects | 24   mo | LAP |
| Matches pictures of animals that are alike (lotto—Choose one from several animals—four animals selected) | 42   mo | C/LAP |
| Matches 3 of 16 silhouette pictures (Decroly matching game) | 45   mo | MPS |
| Matches 4 of 16 silhouettes in 160 sec | 63   mo | MPS |
| Matches 12 pictured silhouettes (of 12) in 133 sec | 69   mo | MPS |

*Colors*

| | | |
|---|---|---|
| Matches colored blocks | 30–35 mo | LAP |
| Matches blocks of four colors (red, green, yellow, blue) | 30.8 mo | MPS |
| Matches two of three primary colors | 36–48 mo | Sher/LAP |

| | | |
|---|---|---|
| Places (matches) three color forms (all red, different shapes) on shape board | 36–48 mo | Ges |
| Matches and names four primary colors | 48–60 mo | LAP/Sher/H |
| Matches 10 of 12 colors | 60–72 mo | LAP |
| Names four primary colors and matches 10 of 12 colors | 60–72 mo | Sher/Ges |

## EXPRESSIVE LANGUAGE OVERVIEW

I. Nonverbal
   A. Makes eye contact
   B. Makes gestures
   C. Imitates motor activities

II. Verbal
   A. Makes early sounds
     1. Emits sounds with a potential relationship to specific situations
     2. Vocalizes in relation to specific primary needs

   B. Establishes control of potential speech sounds
     1. Phonological development
       Differentiated speech sounds
       Expanded control of intonation, pitch, stress
     2. Imitates sounds
     3. "Masters" consonants

   C. Says words
     1. Says words in response to environmental cues
     2. Says words in imitation, spontaneously
     3. Says words labeling objects, pictures, colors (in response to verbal cue)
     4. Says words imitatively in response to verbal cue

   D. Uses words in sentences—"grammar" rules
   E. Says phrases
     1. Makes statements
     2. Asks questions
     3. Gives descriptions, definitions, or information about function

## EXPRESSIVE LANGUAGE PINPOINTS

I. Nonverbal
   A. Makes eye contact

| | | |
|---|---|---|
| Turns eyes to fix vision on person temporarily | 0.1 mo | Bay |
| Fixes eyes on examiner's face; ceases activity | 1 mo | Ges |
| Fixes eyes directly on examiner's face | 3 mo | LAP |

   B. Makes gestures

| | | |
|---|---|---|
| Smiles as examiner talks and smiles | 1.5 mo | Bay |
| Smiles (spontaneously—Den) | 1.9 mo | Den |
| | 2 mo | Ges |
| | 2.1 mo | Bay |
| Waves "bye-bye" | 6–12 mo | LAP |
| Offers objects, such as small toy, to another person | 12 mo | Sher |
| Gestures to make wants known | 14.6 mo | Bay |
| Combines gestures and utterances to make wants known | 18–23 mo | LAP |

   C. Imitates motor activities

| | | |
|---|---|---|
| Plays peek-a-boo | 6 mo | LAP |
| Plays pat-a-cake | 9 mo | LAP |
| Seizes bell in hand, imitates ringing action | 9 mo | C |
| | | Sher |
| | 10 mo | Ges |
| Imitates putting beads in box | 12.9 mo | Bay |

II. Verbal
   A. Makes early sounds
     1. Emits sounds with a potential relationship to specific situations

| | | |
|---|---|---|
| Vocalizes once or twice (small throaty voices other | 0.9 mo | Bay |
| than crying—Slos, Ges; babbles—C) | 1 mo | Slos/Ges/ |
| | | Sher/LAP |
| | 2 mo | C |
| Vocalizes at least four times | 1.6 mo | Bay |
| Vocalizes—not crying | 2 mo | LAP |
| Squeals | 2.2 mo | Den |
| | 5 mo | Ges |
| Laughs | 2 mo | Den |
| | 3 mo | Vin |
| Coos | 3 mo | Slos |
| Chuckles | 3 mo | Slos/Ges/LAP |
| Laughs aloud | 4 mo | Ges |
| Cries (m-m-m-sound) | 7 mo | Ges |

2. Vocalizes in relation to specific primary needs

| | | |
|---|---|---|
| Cries when hungry or uncomfortable | 1 mo | Sher |
| Vocalizes—babbles or coos in play when alone or when talked to | 2 mo | LAP |
| Cries when uncomfortable or annoyed | 3 mo | Sher |
| Vocalizes when spoken to or pleased | 3 mo | Sher/Ges |
| Grunts, growls spontaneous vocal sounds (social) | 6 mo | Ges |
| Vocalizes deliberately as means of interpersonal relationship | 9 mo | Sher |
| Shouts to attract attention, listens, then shouts again | 9 mo | Sher |
| Indicates wants by gesture and vocalization | 12 mo | LAP |

B. Establishes control of potential speech sounds
  1. Phonological development

  *Differentiated speech sounds*

| | | |
|---|---|---|
| Makes single vowel sounds—ah, eh, uh | 2 mo | Ges/LAP |
| Vocalizes two different sounds | 2.3 mo | Bay |
| Babbles, using series of syllables | 4 mo | LAP |
| Vocalizes four different syllables | 7 mo | Bay |
| Makes polysyllabic vowel sounds | 7 mo | Ges |
| | 7.8 mo | Bay |
| Says "da-da" or equivalent | 7.9 mo | Bay |
| | 8 mo | Slos/C |
| | 9 mo | Ges |
| | 10 mo | Den |
| Vocalizes single syllable as da, ba, ka | 8 mo | Ges |
| Babbles tunefully, repeating syllables in string (mam-mam) | 9 mo | Sher |
| Jabbers loudly using wide range of inflections and phonetic | 12 mo | LAP |
| units | 15 mo | Sher |
| Uses jargon | 15 mo | Sher |
| On one word responses, often uses initial consonant with a vowel, but | | |
| seldom the final consonant | 18 mo | LAP |
| Speaks intelligibly but shows many infantile phonetic substitutions | 36–48 mo | Sher |
| Verbalizes sounds—b, p, m, w, h | 36–48 mo | LAP |
| Uses perfected sounds—b, p, n, h | 36–48 mo | F |
| Makes only a few infantile substitutions in speech | 48–60 mo | Sher |
| Articulates, not in infantile style | 54 mo | LAP/Ges |

  *Expanded control of intonation, pitch, stress*

| | | |
|---|---|---|
| Jabbers tunefully to self at play | 18–23 mo | Sher |
| Changes voice to a faster rate when necessary | 36–48 mo | LAP |
| Increases volume of voice | 36–48 mo | LAP |

  2. Imitates sounds

| | | |
|---|---|---|
| Imitates sounds | 6.6 mo | Vin |
| Imitates speech sounds | 7 mo | LAP |
| Imitates sounds such as cough, tongue click, smacking lips, brrr, etc. | 9 mo | Sher/Ges |

  3. "Masters" consonants

  The information below represents the average age at which correct
    consonant production first occurs and the upper age limit of
    customary production. At the upper age limit, according to sources
    consulted (Sanders, 1972), 90% of the population tested could

produce the required consonants in two out of three positions in
words.

| | | |
|---|---|---|
| p, m, h, w, b | 18–36 mo | |
| k, g, d | 24–48 mo | |
| t, ng | 24–72 mo | |
| f, y | 30–48 mo | |
| r, l, s | 36–72 mo | |
| ch, sh, z | 42–84 mo | |
| j | 48–84 mo | |
| v | 48–96 mo | |
| th (*th*ink) | 52–84 mo | |
| th (*th*en) | 60–96 mo | |
| zh | 72–96+ mo | |

C.  Says words
1.  Says words in response to environmental cues; expands vocabulary
    (although not specifically stated by sources consulted, one suspects
    that imitation plays an important part)

| | | |
|---|---|---|
| Says one word other than mama or dada, this one word can be short syllable child uses consistently to designate an object | 10   mo<br>11   mo | Slos/Ges<br>C |
| Uses two words in speaking vocabulary besides "ma-ma" or "da-da" (including "da-da"—Bay, says "ta-ta" or equivalent—Ges) | 12   mo | C |
| | 12.5 mo | Slos |
| | 13–15 mo | Ges |
| | 14.2 mo | Bay |
| Says three words other than ma-ma and da-da | 12.3 mo | Den |
| | 12.5 mo | Slos |
| | 14   mo | Ges/LAP/C |
| Says four or five words including names | 15   mo | LAP |
| Says vocabulary of four to six words (including names—Ges; five words—C, Slos) | 15   mo | Ges |
| | 16   mo | C/Slos |
| Says six words (besides mama and dada) | 17   mo | LAP/Slos |
| Uses 6–20 recognizable words and understands many more | 18–23 mo | Sher |
| Uses expressive vocabulary of at least 15 words (25—Vin) | 20.5 mo | Vin/Slos |
| Says 20 words | 21   mo | LAP |
| | 24–29 mo | Sher/Slos |
| Uses expressive vocabulary of 50 or more words (average vocabulary—272 words—H) | 24–29 mo | LAP |
| Uses 200 or more recognizable words (speech shows numerous "infantilisms") | 30–35 mo | LAP/Sher |
| Uses 900-word vocabulary | 36–48 mo | MPS |

2.  Says words in imitation

| | | |
|---|---|---|
| Imitates words | 12   mo | Sher |
| | 12.5 mo | Bay |
| Echoes prominent or last words addressed to him | 18–23 mo | Sher |
| Says words; echolalia almost constant, with one or more stressed words repeated | 24–29 mo | Sher |
| Repeats self in speech activity (echolalia) | 30–325 mo | Sher/Ges |

3.  Says words, labeling objects, pictures, colors
    *Objects*

| | | |
|---|---|---|
| Labels one object (When asked "What is this?") | 17.8 mo | Bay |
| Labels two of five objects (ball, watch, pencil, scissors, cup) | 21.4 mo | Bay |
| Labels three of four objects of following: ball, watch, pencil, scissors, and cup | 24   mo | Bay |
| Labels three of the following objects: chair, automobile, box, key, fork (four at 27 mo—C) | 24   mo | C |
| Names special miniature toys at distance of 10 ft | 24–29 mo | Sher |
| Names four of five common objects: chair, auto, box, key, fork | 27   mo | C/LAP |
| Labels own mud and clay products as pies, cakes | 30–35 mo | Ges/LAP |
| Names six of six common objects: flag, chair, car, box, key, fork | 30–35 mo | LAP |
| Names block structure as a bridge, bed, track | 30–35 mo | Ges |
| Names agent of six of 20 actions (What cuts?—knife) | 34.4 mo | MPS |

*Pictures*

| | | |
|---|---|---|
| Names one of five pictures of common objects (cat, bird, dog, | 19.3 mo | Bay |
| horse, man) | 20.3 mo | Den |
| Names three of four pictures of common objects | 22  mo | LAP |
| | 22.1 mo | Bay |
| Names 3 of 18 pictures of common objects | 24  mo | C |
| Names familiar picture cards | 24  mo | LAP |
| Names 5 of 10 pictures | 25  mo | Bay |
| Identifies 6 of 10 pictures of common objects | 27  mo | C |
| Names 8 of 18 pictures of common objects (most of Golden ABC | | |
| pictures—Vin) | 30–35 mo | C/Vin |
| Names own drawing | 36–48 mo | MPS/LAP |
| Names one pictured animal from memory | 36–48 mo | LAP/C |
| Names 10 of 18 pictures of common objects | 36–48 mo | LAP |
| Says phrases telling about pictures (names three objects, describes | | |
| one object, interprets one element correctly or incorrectly) | 42  mo | C |
| Names 14 of 18 pictures of common objects | 48–60 mo | LAP/C |
| Names objects (pictured) removed, from memory (one of three | | |
| objects, two or three trials) | 48–60 mo | C |

*Colors*

| | | |
|---|---|---|
| Names one color | 30–35 mo | Vin |
| Names all colors | 36–48 mo | LAP/Vin/Den |

4. Says words imitatively in response to verbal cue (i.e., "say 'kitty' ")

| | | |
|---|---|---|
| Imitates two of four words (ball, kitty, bird, dinner) | 22.4 mo | MPS |
| | 24  mo | LAP |
| Imitates four of four words (ball, kitty, bird, dinner) | 24.4 mo | MPS |
| Imitates names for hair, hands, feet, nose, eyes, mouth, shoes | 24–29 mo | LAP |
| Shows correctly and imitates words for hair, hands, feet, nose, eyes, | | |
| mouth, shoes—on request | 24–29 mo | Sher |
| Imitates a six-word sentence | 36–48 mo | LAP/Ges |
| | 41  mo | Slos |
| Imitates words together: "I have fun playing with my friends." | 53  mo | Slos |
| Imitates correctly "I go to the store to buy bread, butter, and milk." | | |
| (one of three trials—Ges) | 58  mo | Slos |
| Repeats one of two sentences correctly: "We are going to buy some | | |
| candy for mother." "Jack likes to feed the puppies in the barn." | | |
| (one of three—12 to 13 syllables—Ges) | 48–60 mo | C |

D. Uses words in sentences—words categorized according to "parts of
   speech." While the generative linguistics model attempts to avoid
   using this type of categorization, it may yet be of interest to note when
   these "parts of speech" are first used according to adult rules, and
   which constructions seem to present more problems.

*Nouns and verbs*

Nouns and verbs appear to be among the first words acquired and are still
used most frequently even between the third and fourth year.

| | | |
|---|---|---|
| Uses nouns and verbs most frequently | 36–48 mo | LAP |

*Pronouns*

| | | |
|---|---|---|
| Uses "me," "you," and refers to self by name | 23.5 mo | Slos |
| Uses "I," "me," "you," etc., in speech, not always correctly | 24–29 mo | Vin |
| | 24  mo | LAP |
| | 30–35 mo | Sher/Ges |
| Uses pronoun to refer to self | 36–48 mo | Sher/Ges |
| Uses frequently words "I," "it," "you," "that," "a," "do," "this," | | |
| "not," "the" | 36–48 mo | Vin/LAP |

*Plural and tense inflections*

| | | |
|---|---|---|
| Uses plural inflections | 28  mo | Vin/C/Den/ |
| | | Ges/Sher |
| | 36–48 mo | LAP |
| Uses inflections to indicate past, present | 36–48 mo | Sher |
| Uses inflections indicating future | 48–60 mo | Sher |

*Adjectives and adverbs*

| | | |
|---|---|---|
| Says words, verbalizing opposites | 30 mo | LAP |
| Says words verbalizing opposite analogies | 36–48 mo | LAP |
| | 38 mo | Den |
| Says words telling which of two pictured balls is bigger | 42 mo | C |
| Says words telling which of two sticks is longer | 35 mo | Den |
| | 42 mo | C |
| Makes opposite analogies, two of five (three of five—54 mo—C; three of three—50–54 mo—Slos) | 48–60 mo | C/Slos |
| Makes opposite analogies | 48–60 mo | LAP |
| Compares three pictures (which one is prettier) | 54 mo | C/LAP |
| Tells pictorial likeness and differences (on three of six pictures) | 54 mo | C/LAP |
| Responds correctly to "milk is white, butter is_____." (yellow or yellowish) | 59 mo | Slos |
| Tells similarities or differences in 9 of 12 pictures | 60–72 mo | C/LAP |
| Gives descriptive comment of one element with enumeration (names three objects spontaneously) | 60–72 mo | Ges |

E. Says phrases
1. Makes statements

| | | |
|---|---|---|
| Combines two different words in speech | 18 mo | LAP |
| | 20.6 mo | Bay |
| | 21 mo | Slos |
| Demands desired objects by pointing, accompanied by loud, urgent vocalization or single words (uses words to make wants known—C, Bay, Ges) | 18 mo | C |
| | 19 mo | Slos |
| Asks for water when thirsty | 23 mo | LAP |
| Asks for food when hungry | 23 mo | LAP |
| Talks to self continually during play | 24–29 mo | Sher |
| Combines two or more words to form simple sentences (three—Slos) | 24–29 mo | Sher/Slos/LAP |
| Says 10 words in a group | 30.5 mo | MPS |
| Utters negative statement | 30–36 mo | LAP |
| Talks intelligibly to self at play concerning events happening here and now | 30–35 mo | Sher/Ges |
| Says 13 words in a group | 34.0 mo | MPS |
| Talks to self in long monologue, mostly concerning the present, including make-believe activities | 36–48 mo | Sher |
| Says words relating experiences; describes activities | 38 mo | Sher/Vin |
| Speaks in nearly complete sentences | 48–60 mo | H |

2. Asks questions

| | | |
|---|---|---|
| Constantly asking names of objects | 24–29 mo | Sher |
| Asks for "another" | 24–29 mo | Vin |
| Forms a verbal unsolicited question | 30–36 mo | LAP |
| Asks many questions beginning what, where, who | 36–48 mo | Sher/LAP |
| Asks meaning of words | 60–72 mo | Sher |
| Asks meaning of abstract words | 60–72 mo | LAP/Sher |

3. Gives description, definition, or information about functions of objects, pictures, words

| | | |
|---|---|---|
| Answers 1 of 10 questions (e.g., "What is this?" "chair") | 21 mo | MPS |
| Answers 6 of 10 questions | 28.5 mo | MPS |
| Answers correctly "What do you hear with?" (pointing or saying "ear") | 29 mo | Slos/LAP |
| Identifies three of following six objects by use: cup, shoe, penny, knife, auto, iron | 30 mo | C |
| Identifies six objects by use. Points to cup, shoe, penny, knife, auto, iron. When asked a question such as "What do you drink out of?" | 30 mo | C/LAP |
| Says phrase giving use of test object | 30–35 mo | Ges/LAP |
| Says words identifying action in pictures | 30–35 mo | Vin |
| | 36–48 mo | LAP/Ges/MPS |
| Uses nouns and verbs most frequently | 36–48 mo | LAP/F |
| Answers questions: "Why do we have to take a bath?" "Why do we have stoves?" "What must we do when we are thirsty?" | 42 mo | C |
| | 47 mo | Slos/LAP |
| Says phrase defining words | 48–60 mo | LAP |

| Responds correctly to "A hat goes on your head. Shoes go on | | |
|---|---|---|
| your____." | 49   mo | LAP/Slos |
| Says words defining four words in terms of use | 54   mo | LAP/Ges |
| Names materials objects are made of (two of three, chair, | 54   mo | LAP/C |
| dress, shoe, etc.) | 59   mo | Den |
| Answers questions: "Why do we have houses, books, clocks, eyes, | | |
| ears?" | 55   mo | C/Slos |
| Says words defining concrete nouns by use | 60–72 mo | Sher |
| Says words defining two of three of the following objects (i.e., house, | | |
| book, shoes) | 60–72 mo | Sher |
| Tells source of 15 of 20 actions: "What bounces?" | 60–72 mo | LAP |
| Tells agent (producer) of 15 of 20 actions: "What skates?" | 60–72 mo | Ges |
| Tells agent (producer) of 16 of 20 actions in 86 sec | 62.4 mo | MPS |
| Tells how a crayon and pencil are the same and how they are different | 70   mo | Sher/LAP |

## SELF-HELP SKILLS

With the integration of the severely handicapped youngster into our nation's classrooms has come the need to reassess educational priorities. There are those within as well as outside the profession who might question the meaning of "education" for these youngsters. To many who raise this question, the term education connotes academic priorities in the classroom. Yet let us further examine the definition of "education" as it is offered by Webster. A crucial portion of that definition is the following: "the act or process of providing with knowledge, skill, competence, or desirable qualities of behavior or character, or of being so provided, especially by a formal course of study, instruction, or training." The definition here has immediate implications for the severely handicapped population, as nowhere is there mention of usage of this term only in relationship to certain content areas. Knowledge, skill, or competence may be needed across a number of areas; where such needs have been identified for a particular child, a "formal course of study, instruction, or training" should be initiated.

As one applies the definition to the severely handicapped child, it becomes quite apparent that needs exist across areas that were previously not of concern to teachers working with very different populations. For children who may not have yet acquired basic self-help skills such as toileting, dressing, and feeding, these skills must receive top priority consideration among the educational objectives which are to be established. Without basic self-help skills, survival in any but the most sheltered of environments will not be possible. It is hoped, therefore, that the reader will carefully consider all pinpoints listed in this section, as he establishes a relevant educational program for the severely or profoundly handicapped youngster.

## REFERENCE

Gove PB (ed): Webster's Third New International Dictionary. Springfield, Ill., Merriam, 1969, p 723

## SELF-HELP SKILLS OVERVIEW

I. Eating
  A. Establishes general feeding schedule
  B. Makes body movements anticipating feeding
  C. Takes liquids
  D. Takes solids
    1. Establishes chewing behavior
    2. Takes finger food
    3. Uses implements

II. Dressing
  A. Establishes general dressing skills
    1. Dressing
    2. Undressing

  B. Puts on clothing
    1. Coat, dress, shirt
    2. Pants
    3. Socks
    4. Shoes
    5. Hats, mittens

  C. Manipulates zipper, buttons

III. Toileting
  A. Establishes general toileting schedule, habits
  B. Carries out toileting routine

IV. Personal grooming
  A. Washes self
  B. Dries self
  C. Brushes teeth
  D. Brushes hair

V. Keeping house in order
  A. Imitates activities
  B. Performs activities independently

VI. Manipulates household fixtures
  A. Turns handles
  B. Turns knobs

VII. Gives general information about self

## SELF-HELP SKILLS PINPOINTS

I. Eating
  A. Establishes general feeding schedule, habits

| | | |
|---|---|---|
| Requires two night-feedings | 1–2 mo | Ges |
| Requires only one night-feeding | | |
| Takes solids well | 7 mo | Ges |
| Feeds self for at least first half of meal; insists on being independent | 30–35 mo | Ges |
| Feeds self with little spilling | 36–48 mo | Ges/H/LAP |

  B. Makes body movements anticipating feeding

| | | |
|---|---|---|
| Makes body movements anticipating feeding | 3 mo | C |
| | 4 mo | Ges |
| Licks lips in response to sounds of preparations for feeding | 3 mo | Sher |
| Discriminates edible substances (say, do) | 12–24 mo | LAP |
| Asks for food when hungry | 22.5 mo | Slos |
| Asks for drink when thirsty | 22.5 mo | Slos |
| Asks for food and drink | 24–29 mo | Sher/H |

  C. Takes liquids
    1. Establishes sucking behavior

| | | |
|---|---|---|
| Sucks well with inner mouth parts and lips | 1 mo | Sher |
| Closes mouth without drooling | 10.8 mo | Vin |
| | 11 mo | LAP |

    2. Uses bottle

| | | |
|---|---|---|
| Takes fluid from a dropper or bottle | No norms | |

| | | |
|---|---|---|
| Pats bottle during feeding | 5 mo | Ges |
| Puts hands around bottle or cup when feeding | 9 mo | Sher |
| Holds bottle to feed self | 9 mo | Ges |
| Discards bottle in feeding | 15 mo | Ges |

3. Uses cup

| | | |
|---|---|---|
| Opens mouth for cup with some prodding | No norms | |
| Opens mouth when sees cup approaching | No norms | |
| Reaches for cup | No norms | |
| Lifts inverted cup | 5.2 mo | Bay |
| Lifts cup with handle | 5.8 mo | Bay |
| | 6 mo | LAP/C |
| Drinks from cup when cup is held (some spilling) | 10.5 mo | Slos |
| | 11 mo | LAP/Ges |
| | 11.7 mo | Den |
| Drinks from cup with little assistance | 12 mo | Sher/Ges |
| Holds cup when adult gives and takes | 15 mo | Sher |
| Drinks from cup or glass unassisted | 16.6 mo | Vin |
| | 17 mo | LAP |
| Drinks without much spilling | 18–23 mo | Sher/Ges |
| Lifts and holds cup between both hands | 18–23 mo | LAP |
| | 20.5 mo | Sher/Ges/Slos |
| Hands cup back to adult | 18–23 mo | Sher/Ges |
| Lifts and drinks from cup and replaces on table | 24–29 mo | LAP/Sher Ges/H |
| Gets drink unassisted | 24–29 mo | LAP |
| | 29 mo | Vin |

D. Takes solids

1. Establishes chewing behavior

| | | |
|---|---|---|
| Chews and swallows without spilling | 12–24 mo | LAP/Sher |
| | 13.2 mo | Slos |
| Chews well | 18–23 mo | Sher/Ges |
| Chews competently | 24–29 mo | Sher/Ges |

2. Takes finger food

| | | |
|---|---|---|
| Feeds self cracker | 5.3 mo | Den |
| Holds, bites, and chews biscuit | 9 mo | LAP/Sher/Ges |
| Reaches for food | No norms | |
| Grasps finger food and brings toward mouth | No norms | |
| Puts finger food into mouth | 12 mo | Ges/LAP |

3. Uses implements

*Spoon*

| | | |
|---|---|---|
| Fixes gaze on spoon during feeding | 3 mo | C |
| Picks up spoon | 5 mo | C/LAP |
| Looks for fallen spoon, moves eyes toward fallen spoon | 6 mo | Bay |
| Reaches for spoon when being fed | 9 mo | Bay |
| Stirs with spoon in imitation | 9.7 mo | Ges |
| Holds spoon but cannot use it alone | 12 mo | Ges/Sher |
| Dips spoon in cup, releases it | 12 mo | Ges |
| Holds spoon, brings it to mouth and licks it but cannot | 14 mo | LAP |
| prevent it turning over (uses spoon, spilling little—Den) | 14.4 mo | Den |
| | 15 mo | Sher |
| | 16 mo | LAP |
| | 20 mo | Slos |
| Spoon-feeds without spilling | 24–29 mo | Sher/H/LAP |
| Takes bites from spoon (low error rate) | 30–35 mo | Sher |

*Fork*

| | | |
|---|---|---|
| Puts fork in mouth, eats | 28 mo | LAP/Vin |
| Eats with fork and spoon | 36–48 mo | LAP/Sher |
| East skillfully with spoon and fork | 48–60 mo | Sher |

*Knife*

| | | |
|---|---|---|
| Spreads butter on bread with knife | 36–48 mo | H/LAP |
| Cuts with a knife | 48–60 mo | LAP/H |

Pitcher
| | | |
|---|---|---|
| Pours well from pitcher | 36–48 mo | Ges/LAP |

II. Dressing
A. Establishes general dressing behavior
1. Dressing

| | | |
|---|---|---|
| Mother supports at shoulders when dressing | 3 mo | Sher |
| Mother supports at lower spine when dressing | 9 mo | Sher |
| Helps more constructively with dressing | 15 mo | Sher |
| Pulls on simple garment | 24 mo | LAP |
| Has to be helped during whole process of dressing, can sometimes put on socks | 30–35 mo | Ges |
| Dresses with supervision | 32 mo | Den/LAP |
| Dresses without supervision | 42 mo | Den/LAP |
| Points to front and back of clothing—puts clothing on body correctly | 48–60 mo | LAP/Ges |
| Discriminates left from right | 60–72 mo | LAP |
| Dresses and undresses alone | 60–72 mo | LAP/Ges |

2. Undressing
| | | |
|---|---|---|
| Removes garment | 15.8 mo | Den |
| Undresses completely | 21 mo | Ges |
| Undresses self | 36–48 mo | H/LAP |

B. Puts on, removes clothing
1. Coat, dress, shirt
| | | |
|---|---|---|
| Cooperates by putting arm into armhole | 12–13 mo | Kep |
| Puts on coat or dress unassisted | 34 mo | LAP/Vin |

2. Pants
| | | |
|---|---|---|
| Cooperates in dressing by putting arm in armhole or extending leg to have pants put on | 12 mo<br>13 mo | Sher<br>Ges |
| Pulls pants down and up, but needs help with buttons | 36–48 mo | Sher |

3. Socks
| | | |
|---|---|---|
| Enjoys having socks removed (smiles, giggles) | 12–13 mo | LAP |
| Pulls off socks | 12–24 mo | LAP |
| Takes off socks | 18–23 mo | LAP |
| Puts on socks, some errors still | 30–35 mo | Kep |

4. Shoes
| | | |
|---|---|---|
| Enjoys having shoes removed | 12 mo<br>12–13 mo | LAP<br>Kep |
| Pulls shoes off | 18–23 mo<br>24–29 mo | Kep<br>LAP |
| Attempts to pull shoes on | 22.3 mo | Den/Ges |
| Pulls shoes on | 22.3 mo<br>24–29 mo<br>36–48 mo | Den/Ges<br>Kep<br>LAP |
| Laces shoes | 48–60 mo | Ges/LAP |
| Ties single knot with lace around pencil (with model) | 60–72 mo | C/H/LAP |
| Ties shoe lace | 72 mo | LAP |

5. Hats, mittens
| | | |
|---|---|---|
| Enjoys taking off hat, shoes, and pants (socks—Slos) | 12 mo<br>13–56 mo | Ges/LAP<br>Slos |
| Takes off shoes, socks, hat (mittens—Ges) | 18–23 mo<br>24–29 mo | Sher/Ges<br>LAP |
| Puts on shoes, hat (mittens—Ges) | 24–29 mo | Sher/Ges |

C. Manipulates zippers, buttons
1. Zippers
| | | |
|---|---|---|
| Can unzip zipper | 18–29 mo<br>18–23 mo | LAP<br>Ges |

2. Buttons
| | | |
|---|---|---|
| Buttons one button | 30.5 mo<br>31 mo | MPS<br>LAP |
| Buttons two buttons (170 sec two-button strip)<br>(30 sec—49.5 mo) (23 sec—54.7 mo) | 33 mo | LAP/MPS |

| | | |
|---|---|---|
| two buttons in 19 sec | 61.4 mo | MPS |
| Buttons coat or dress | 40　mo | LAP/F/Den |
| (two—50 sec—38.8 mo—MPS) | | MPS/Ges/Vin |
| (two—34 sec—44.6 mo—MPS) | | |
| (four—76 sec—45 mo—MPS) | | |
| Buttons four buttons | 48–60 mo | MPS |
| (51 sec—50 mo) | 50　mo | LAP |
| (42 sec—57.9 mo) | | |

3. Unbuttons

| | | |
|---|---|---|
| Unbuttons accessible buttons | 36–48 mo | LAP/Ges |

III. Toileting
  A. Establishes general toileting schedule, habits

| | | |
|---|---|---|
| Usually dry after nap | 12　mo | LAP/Ges |
| Fusses to be changed after having bowel movement | 12　mo | Ges/LAP |
| Indicates wet pants | 15　mo | LAP/Sher/Ges |
| Has bowel control | 15　mo | LAP/Ges |
| Bowel control usually attained | 18–23 mo | Sher |
| Bladder control in transitional stage (usually wet after naps) | 18–23 mo | Ges |
| Indicates toilet needs by restlessness and vocalization (or fetches the pot—Ges) | 22.5 mo | Sher/Ges/Slos |
| Verbalizes toilet needs fairly consistently | 24　mo | LAP/Sher/Vin |
| Dry at night if taken up | 24　mo | LAP |
| | 24–29 mo | Ges |
| | 30–35 mo | Sher |
| Wakes wet but tolerates condition | 24–29 mo | Ges |
| Dry during day; muscles of bladder coming under control | 24–29 mo | Sher/Ges |
| Usually dry all night (no accidents) | 36–48 mo | Ges/Sher/LAP |
| Dry through night | 48–60 mo | Sher |

  B. Carries out toileting routine

| | | |
|---|---|---|
| Pulls down pants at toilet, but seldom able to replace | 24–29 mo | LAP |
| | 30–35 mo | Sher |
| Cares for self at toilet; pulls down clothing and can replace | 45　mo | Vin/H |
| Sits down on toilet without reminder, or moves to face toilet without reminder | 45　mo | LAP |
| Wipes self with toilet paper | 45　mo | LAP |
| Flushes toilet by self | 45　mo | LAP |
| Cares for self at toilet (pulls down clothing, sits, wipes, flushes) | 45　mo | LAP |
| Goes into bathroom by self and does all of the above | 60–72 mo | Ges/LAP |

IV. Grooming
  A. Washes self

| | | |
|---|---|---|
| Presents hands to be washed; stands quietly while face washed | No norms | |
| Washes hands and face unaided | 36–48 mo | LAP |
| | 42　mo | Ges/Vin |
| | 54　mo | LAP/Vin |
| Needs help and supervision washing other than hands and feet; washes only hands and feet alone | 60–72 mo | Sher |
| Washes face and hands without getting clothes wet | 60–72 mo | Sher/H |

  B. Dries self

| | | |
|---|---|---|
| Dries face, hands (with supervision) | 23　mo | Sher/Den |
| | 31　mo | Vin |
| | 42　mo | Ges/LAP |
| | 48–60 mo | LAP |
| Dries hands | 24–36 mo | LAP |
| | 31　mo | Vin |
| Washes and dries face and hands without getting clothes wet | 60–72 mo | Sher/H |

  C. Brushes teeth

| | | |
|---|---|---|
| Brushes teeth | 42　mo | H/LAP |
| | 48–60 mo | Sher/Ges |

  D. Brushes hair

| | | |
|---|---|---|
| Brushes and combs hair unassisted | 60–72 mo | LAP/H |

V. Keeping house in order
  A. Imitates activities

| | | |
|---|---|---|
| Imitates housework | 13.8 mo | Den |
| Follows mother around house and copies domestic activities in simultaneous play | 24–29 mo | Sher |

  B. Performs activities independently

| | | |
|---|---|---|
| Picks up toys and puts them away | 18–23 mo | LAP/Den |
| Helps put things away | 30–48 mo | LAP/Ges/F |
| Helps with adult activities in house and garden | 36–48 mo | Sher/LAP |
| Helps at household tasks (dusting, drying, dishes) | 36–48 mo | LAP |
| Makes effort to keep surroundings tidy | 36–48 mo | Sher/LAP |
| Carries breakable objects | 36–48 mo | LAP/Ges |
| Carries water without spilling while walking | 36–48 mo | F |
| Carries a tray | 36–48 mo | H/LAP |
| Performs simple errands | 60–72 mo | LAP |
| Puts toys away neatly in box | 60–72 mo | H/LAP |

VI. Manipulates household fixtures
  A. Turns handles

| | | |
|---|---|---|
| Turns door handles | 24–29 mo | LAP/Sher/Ges |
| Manipulates egg beater (one of three trials) | 28 mo | C/LAP |

  B. Turns knobs

| | | |
|---|---|---|
| Turns knob (radio) | 18–23 mo | LAP/Ges |

VII. Giving general information about self

| | | |
|---|---|---|
| Refers to self by name | 24–29 mo | Sher |
| Gives full name on request | 30–35 mo | Sher/Ges |
| | 30 mo | LAP |
| | 31–32 mo | Vin/Den |
| Gives home address | 48–60 mo | LAP |
| Gives home address and usually age | 48–60 mo | Sher |
| Gives age and birthday | 48–60 mo | LAP |
| | 60–72 mo | Sher |

## SOCIAL INTERACTION SKILLS

"Social adjustment" represents a major goal for the severely handicapped individual who must live and work outside the institutional setting. Kirk (1972), in a discussion of curriculum goals for the retarded, stresses the importance of that adjustment: "It is not expected that the child will become independent in the community. . . He is, however, expected to *get along* in the home and in his immediate neighborhood." In an extensive review of the literature concerning the successful integration of previously institutionalized individuals, Herbert Goldstein (1964) reports repeatedly that the ability to form "adequate personal relationships" and demonstrate appropriate social behavior is more important to steady employment and a position in the community than are other variables, such as I.Q. Recently, researchers (Koegel et al. 1974) have attempted to demonstrate the inverse relationship between appropriate play behaviors and self-stimulatory behaviors often associated with severely handicapped individuals.

In spite of this emphasis upon the development of social behaviors, a precise definition of what is meant by "social adjustment" or "social development" is lacking. Kirk (1972, p. 231) gives one description: "Social adjustment is not a subject which is taught like chemistry or physics—it is an *intangible* type of development which comes through recreation and play, singing, dramatics, and working and living with others." Rather than specifying a program whose goal is the development of social skills, authorities often prefer to assume that other programs will produce these skills as a secondary aspect.

The content of an area such as social development may not lend itself to the same precise descriptions accorded areas such as chemistry or physics. But teachers of individuals who are deficit in as many areas as are the severely handicapped cannot afford to merely "hope" that social adjustment will be the natural by-product of programming in other areas. They must assess behavioral repertoires and plan programs aimed at development of skills in the social area, just as in any other.

The pinpoints offered in the following section provide some precise measure of the behaviors which make up that complex goal known as "social adjustment." The severely handicapped child may not be able to participate in all those activities which normally allow the child to explore his immediate surroundings, and, as he grows older, to engage in more complex interactions. It is hoped, however, that the behavioral pinpoints will be adapted by teachers of the severely handicapped, in order to provide those individuals with a chance to acquire, first-hand, the skills which will make possible their successful participation in a world whose rapid technological and social change now demands major adjustment on the part of all individuals.

### REFERENCES

Goldstein H: Social and occupational adjustment, in Stevens HA, Heber R (eds): Mental Retardation: A Review of Research. Chicago, Univ Chicago Pr, 1964, pp 214–258

Kirk S: Educating Exceptional Children. Boston, Houghton Mifflin, 1972

Koegel R, Firestone P, Kramme K, et al: Increasing spontaneous play by suppressing self-stimulation in austistic children. J Appl Behav Anal 7:521–528, 1974

#### SOCIAL INTERACTION OVERVIEW

I. Establishes self–other discrimination
  A. Identifies self
  B. Identifies other

II. Establishes dependence, independence
  A. Maintains dependence
  B. Establishes independence

III. Establishes play activities
  A. Establishes manner and type of activity
    1. Manner of playing
      Potentially positive aspects of play
      Negative behaviors exhibited while playing
    2. Type of play activity

B. Establishes interaction patterns
   Isolate play
   Parallel play
   Cooperative play

## SOCIAL INTERACTION PINPOINTS

I. Establishes self–other discrimination
   A. Identifies self

| | | |
|---|---|---|
| Reacts to paper on face | 1.7 mo | Bay |
| Fingers mirror image | 4.4 mo | Bay |
| | 6 mo | C |
| Smiles at mirror image | 5 mo | Ges |
| | 5.4 mo | Bay |
| Smiles and vocalizes at image in mirror | 6 mo | Ges/LAP |
| | 6.2 mo | Bay |
| Pats and smiles at reflection in mirror | 7 mo | C |
| Reaches for image of ball in hand, reflected in mirror | 11 mo | Ges |
| Plays with or reaches for mirror image | 12 mo | Ges |
| Refers to self by name | 18–24 mo | LAP |
| Identifies self in mirror | 24.4 mo | MPS |
| Recognizes self in photographs when once shown | 30–35 mo | Sher/LAP |
| Answers correctly question "Are you a boy or a girl?" | 35 mo | Slos |
| | 36–48 mo | Sher/Ges/LAP |

   B. Identifies others

| | | |
|---|---|---|
| Visually recognizes mother | 2 mo | Bay |
| Reaches for familiar persons | 3.6 mo | Vin |
| | 4 mo | LAP |
| Discriminates strangers | 4.8 mo | Bay |
| | 5 mo | LAP |
| | 6 mo | Ges |
| Clearly distinguishes strangers from familiars; requires assurance before accepting their advances; clings to known adult and hides face | 9 mo | Sher |
| | 9.5 mo | Den |
| Recognizes familiars approaching from 20 ft or more away | 12 mo | Sher |
| Names possessions of others and tells to whom they belong | 24–29 mo | Ges |

II. Establishes dependence, independence
    A. Maintains dependence

| | | |
|---|---|---|
| Reaches for familiar persons | 12–24 mo | LAP |
| Demands personal attention | 12–24 mo | LAP |
| Demands proximity of familiar adult | 18–23 mo | Sher |
| Alternates between clinging and resistance to familiar adult | 18–23 mo | Sher |
| Plays contentedly alone, but likes to be near adult | 18–23 mo | Sher |
| Clings tightly in affection, fatigue, or fear | 24–29 mo | Sher |
| Constantly demands mother's attention | 24–29 mo | Sher |
| Cries, pouts when attention shown to other children | 24–29 mo | Sher |
| Performs for others, shows off | 44–54 mo | LAP |
| Calls attention to own performance | 54 mo | LAP/Ges |
| Performs in conformity to adult ideas | 60–74 mo | LAP |

    B. Establishes independence

| | | |
|---|---|---|
| Walks about room unattended | 12–36 mo | Vin |
| Constantly explores and exploits environment | 15 mo | Sher |
| Gives up baby carriage | 16–17 mo | Vin |
| Plays contentedly alone if near adults | 18–23 mo | LAP |
| Explores environment energetically | 18–23 mo | Sher/Ges |
| Goes about house, yard, causing little concern | 19 mo | Vin |
| Separates from mother without crying | 36–48 mo | Den |
| | 42 mo | LAP |
| Goes about neighborhood unattended | 48–60 mo | LAP |
| | 56 mo | Ges/Sher/Vin |
| Goes on errands outside home | 48–60 mo | Ges |
| Goes outside prescribed bounds | 48–60 mo | Ges |
| Asks adult help only as needed | 60–72 mo | Ges |

| | | |
|---|---|---|
| Crosses street safely | 60–72 mo | Ges |
| Explores neighborhood | 60–74 mo | Ges |
| Chooses own friends | 60–74 mo | LAP |
| Goes to school unattended | 60–74 mo | LAP |

III. Establishes play routines

    A. Establishes manner and type of activity
        1. Manner of playing

*Potentially positive aspects of play*

| | | |
|---|---|---|
| Plays, sits propped in play area 10–15 min | 4   mo | Ges |
| Plays by pulling dress over face | 4   mo | Ges |
| Plays actively with small toy, such as rattle—shakes rattle | 4   mo | C |
| Works for toy out of reach | 5.8 mo | Den |
| | 8   mo | Ges |
| Cooperates in games with adult | 7.6 mo | Bay |
| Handles everything within reach | 15   mo | Sher |
| Fills pots and dishes with sand, dumps, throws | 24–29 mo | Ges |
| Initiates own play activities | 24   mo | Vin |

*Negative behaviors exhibited while playing*

| | | |
|---|---|---|
| Throws self to floor in tantrum | 18–23 mo | Ges |
| Casts objects to floor in play or anger, but less often | 18–23 mo | LAP |
| Does opposite of what is asked | 21   mo | Ges |
| Throws violent tantrums when thwarted or is unable to express urgent needs and less easily distracted | 24–29 mo | Ges/Sher |
| Brings favorite toy to school to show but refuses to share it | 24–29 mo | Ges |
| Snatches and grabs toys | 30–35 mo | Ges |
| Clings to favorite possession when insecure | 30–35 mo | Ges |
| Has interest in acquiring possessions of others, but seldom plays with them | 30–35 mo | Ges |
| Demands independence and complete help (on things he can do) alternately | 30–35 mo | Ges |
| Has more disputes with others than at any other age | 30–35 mo | Ges |
| Yells, cries, whines when frustrated | 48–60 mo | LAP |
| Bosses and criticizes | 54   mo | Ges/LAP |

        2. Type of play activity

| | | |
|---|---|---|
| Bites, chews toys | 8   mo | Ges |
| Still takes everything into mouth | 9   mo | Sher |
| Takes objects to mouth less often | 12   mo | Sher |
| Seldom takes toys to mouth | 15   mo | Sher |
| No longer takes toys to mouth | 18–25 mo | Sher |
| Engages in simple make-believe activities | 24–29 mo | Sher |
| Engages in prolonged domestic make-believe play (putting dolls to bed, washing clothes, driving cars) but with frequent references to friendly adult | 30–35 mo | Sher |
| Invents people and objects—imaginative, pretend play | 36–48 mo | Sher/LAP |
| Enjoys dressing up in adult clothes | 48–60 mo | Sher/LAP/Ges |
| Shows off dramatically | 54   mo | Sher/Ges |
| Likes to play house and baby | 60–72 mo | Ges |
| Plays simple table games | 60–74 mo | LAP |
| Plays complicated floor games | 60–74 mo | LAP |
| Plays very complicated floor games | 60–72 mo | Sher |

    B. Establishes interaction pattern

*Isolate play*

| | | |
|---|---|---|
| Initiates own play activities | 24   mo | LAP |
| Prefers solitary play | 24–29 mo | Ges |

*Parallel play*

| | | |
|---|---|---|
| Parallel play predominates | 24   mo | LAP |
| Does little sharing of toys (has difficulty sharing—Ges) | 24–29 mo | Sher/Ges |
| Plays near other children but not with them | 24–29 mo | Sher |
| Enjoys using identical equipment as child next to him (clay, paints, beads) | 30–35 mo | Ges |

| | | |
|---|---|---|
| Enjoys going to park to see other children or to play with equipment | 30–35 mo | Ges |
| *Cooperative play* | | |
| Plays with other children | 18   mo | Vin/LAP |
| Plays interactive games, e.g., tag | 24   mo | Den |
| Has little notion of sharing | 30–35 mo | Sher |
| Domestic make-believe play | 30–35 mo | LAP |
| Plays simple group games as "Ring Around the Rosy" | 30–35 mo | Sher |
| Observes other children at play and joins in for a few minutes | 30–35 mo | LAP/Sher |
| Shares play things, sweets, etc. | 36–48 mo | Sher |
| Shows affection for younger siblings (hugs, kisses) | 36–45 mo | Sher/LAP |
| Takes turns | 36–48 mo | Ges/LAP |
| Shares toys | 36–48 mo | LAP |
| Joins in play with other children | 36–48 mo | Sher |
| Plays cooperatively at kindergarten level | 39   mo | Vin |
| Associative group play takes place of parallel play | 42   mo | LAP |
| Plays interactive games (tag, housekeeping, etc.) (replaces parallel play) | 42   mo | Den/Ges |
| Shows concern for younger siblings and sympathy for playmates in distress | 48–60 mo | Sher/LAP |
| Cooperates with children in play | 48–60 mo | Ges |
| Needs other children to play with, and is alternately cooperative and aggressive with them as with adults | 48–60 mo | Sher |
| Tender and protective toward younger children and pets | 60–72 mo | Sher |
| Plays according to rules of fair play | 60–72 mo | Sher |
| Comforts playmates in distress | 60–72 mo | Sher/LAP |
| Chooses own friends | 60–72 mo | Sher |
| Gets along well in small groups | 60–72 mo | Ges |
| | 60–74 mo | LAP |
| Cooperates with companions | 60–72 mo | Sher/Ges |

## LEISURE TIME ACTIVITIES

The utilization of free time is a major concern for all individuals in today's rapidly changing world. It should be considered an area of special concern, however, for the handicapped population. While there may be some activities to occupy the individual's day, there will still remain many hours to be spent outside an organized social or work situation. The problem then becomes: does this individual have any way in which to utilize his or her extra hours? Unfortunately, for too many, the solution to this problem will be that one-eyed monster, the television. For hours upon end, many of the children currently enrolled in our nation's special education programs may sit staring at this one option for leisure time activity. To some, it has become the only option available.

This section of the Developmental Pinpoints is offered in the hope of raising some questions about a crucial area which cannot be ignored for a group who will have a great deal of leisure time. It is hoped that as curriculum guides and instructional materials are developed for the severely handicapped, this area will receive the attention it merits.

The term "leisure time" does suggest that the individual will spend his or her time in a way he or she finds enjoyable. Through observation, the teacher may discover that certain activities lend themselves to this utilization far more easily than those offered in this section. Because, however, both music and arts and crafts are generally considered as major components within the area of leisure time, they were selected for presentation here.

## MUSIC OVERVIEW

I. Uses instruments
II. Says or sings rhymes and songs
III. Moves body to music

## MUSIC PINPOINTS

I. Uses instruments

| | | |
|---|---|---|
| Rings bell and smiles at sound | 7.8 mo | Bay |
| Approaches and chooses musical instruments, including record player | 30–35 mo | LAP/Ges |

II. Says or sings rhymes and songs

| | | |
|---|---|---|
| Enjoys (smiles, claps at) nursery rhymes and tries to join in | 18–23 mo | Sher/Ges |
| Attempts to sing (and hum—Ges) | 18–23 mo | Sher/Ges/LAP |
| Chooses to have short rhymes sung to him | 18–23 mo | Ges |
| Sings phrases of songs | 24–29 mo | LAP |
| Joins in nursery rhymes and songs | 24–29 mo | Sher/Ges/LAP |
| Says a few nursery rhymes | 30–35 mo | LAP |
| Asks for repetition of old familiar tunes | 30–35 mo | Ges |
| May know all or parts of songs which he produces at home or spontaneously at school, but often hesitates to sing with others at school | 30–35 mo | Ges |

III. Moves body to music

| | | |
|---|---|---|
| Moves whole body rhythmically to music | 18–23 mo | Ges |
| Joins in simple group activity as "Ring Around the Rosy" | 30–35 mo | Ges |
| Skips to music | | F |
| Makes dancing movements | 60–72 mo | LAP |

## ART OVERVIEW

I. Paints strokes
II. Folds paper
III. Manipulates clay
IV. Uses scissors
V. Draws figures

## ART PINPOINTS

I. Paints strokes

| | | |
|---|---|---|
| Moves whole arm in painting | 18–23 mo | Ges |
| Makes painting strokes on a page, often as an arc | 18–23 mo | Ges |
| Moves arm in "scrubbing" motion when painting with little regard for color | 24–29 mo | Ges |
| Moves paint randomly | 24–29 mo | Ges |
| Moves arm to paint strokes, dots, and circular shapes on easel | 30–35 mo | Sher/LAP |
| Moves arm to paint many pages that have similar content | 30–35 mo | Ges |
| Moves arm to paint, with good form at beginning but generally quick to deteriorate | 30–35 mo | Ges |
| Uses large brush to paint pictures on easel | 36–48 mo | Sher/H |

II. Folds paper

| | | |
|---|---|---|
| Folds paper once imitatively | 21   mo | LAP |
| | 24   mo | C |
| | 27.9 mo | Bay |
| Folds paper three times in imitation | 48–60 mo | LAP/Ges |
| Folds triangle from 6-inch paper square in imitation of model | 60–72 mo | H/C |

III. Manipulates clay

| | | |
|---|---|---|
| Rolls, pounds, squeezes, pulls clay | 24–29 mo | LAP/Ges/H |

IV. Uses scissors

| | | |
|---|---|---|
| Cuts with scissors | 24–30 mo | H/MPS |
| | 30–36 mo | Vin |
| | 35  mo | LAP |
| | 36–42 mo | Sher |
| | 42–48 mo | PAR |
| | 48–54 mo | Kuhl |
| | 60–72 mo | F |
| | 66–72 mo | Ges |

V. Draws figures

| | | |
|---|---|---|
| Draws head of person and usually one other part | 36–48 mo | Sher |
| Draws with pencil or crayon | 48–60 mo | Vin/LAP |
| Draws very simple house | 48–60 mo | Sher/LAP |
| Draws person with two parts (three parts—Den, six parts—58 mo—Den) | 48  mo | LAP/Sher/Ges/Den |
| Adds three parts to incomplete person | 48  mo | LAP |
| | 48–60 mo | GES/MPS |
| Draws three bubble shapes correctly | 54  mo | Sher/Ges/F/LAP |
| Draws four bubble shapes correctly | 60–72 mo | Ges |
| Adds seven parts to incomplete person (three parts—C) | 60–72 mo | Ges/C |
| Draws recognizable person with head, trunk, legs | 60–72 mo | Sher/H |
| Draws recognizable person with head, trunk, legs, arms, and features | 60–72 mo | LAP |
| Draws simple house with door, window, roof, and chimney | 60–72 mo | Sher |
| Draws dot configuration | 60–66 mo | Ben |
| | 66–72 mo | Kuhl |

## PREREADING

Certain readers may question the inclusion of a preacademic section in a set of pinpoints designed primarily for use by teachers of the severely handicapped. These readers may argue that individuals who demonstrate readiness for the academic areas would no longer be considered severely handicapped. It is precisely for this reason that a section concerning academic readiness is included in the Developmental Pinpoints. Through giving a child the opportunity to pursue maximum growth in each major developmental area as he becomes ready for such experiences, it may be possible to help him to rid himself of his previously assigned label.

For the teacher of the severely handicapped, then, the issue of academic readiness assumes a special importance. "When might I introduce some initial instruction?" "How will I know that the child is ready?" "What kinds of readiness experiences should I provide?" These are but a few of the many questions teachers ask as they consider some of the youngsters in their classrooms. Response to these questions requires further consideration of the term "readiness."

### History of the Reading Readiness Concept

In tracing through history, one finds that the concept of "readiness" is one which has been heavily influenced by contemporary thought. Dolores Durkin, a noted researcher in the area of reading, provides in her writings (1966, 1968, 1970, 1972) a fascinating review of the influences affecting views concerning reading readiness. Because this review has special implications for the teacher of the severely handicapped as he or she examines the readiness issue, Durkin's review must be given careful consideration.

Durkin notes that the term "reading readiness" first appeared in the professional literature in the 1920s. At this time, the influence of G. Stanley Hall, Arnold Gesell (his student) and Gesell's many followers was extremely strong. The view adopted here was, of course, that development occurs through stages whose sequence is predetermined and inevitable. Concurrent with this trend of thought, there was also the influence provided by the earlier development of group intelligence tests. With their development had come many reports about the relationship between a child's intelligence and his reading achievement. It followed that the concern was often for his achievements in reading—frequently, reading in the first grade. Durkin (1972, p. 39) notes that some authors of the 1920s began moving toward proposals that would establish a certain mental age level as a requirement for starting school instruction in reading. She further reports that this trend in thought regarding the relation between mental age and readiness would appear "to have been crystalized in an article which was published in 1931 and which became widely known and uncommonly influencial for a long period of time." (Durkin, 1972, p. 39). The article to which she refers was written by Morphett and Washburne. After describing the leading achievements of first grade children when one particular method was used in one particular school system, the authors concluded that by postponing the teaching of reading until children reach a mental age of 6.5 years, teachers could greatly decrease chances of failure. When considering how influential and long-lasting the mental age concept of readiness has been, it is amazing to note how readily the findings from a study of one teaching method in one school system were accepted as applicable to all children. Durkin suggests many reasons for this phenomenon, including the fact that the proposal here fit perfectly with the mood of the period. In addition to supporting the notion that development proceeds in stages, and therefore postponing instruction until the child reaches an appropriate stage in which he is ready to read, it also offered support for the importance of the measurement and testing movement which was gaining increased popularity at this time. How seriously the suggestion made here was taken is reflected quite clearly in the reading methodology textbooks which appeared not only immediately after the publication of this study but also as late as the 1960s (Durkin, 1972, p. 40). The rationale suggested by this study was presented in arguments designed to keep reading out of the kindergartens.

While the mental age concept was widely accepted, it is important to note that there were objections being raised. One researcher presenting an opposing view was Arthur Gates. Although Gates' research provided evidence which should have raised serious doubts among those advocating the mental age concept of readiness, his reports went seemingly unnoticed. His views concerning the need to examine the reading program being presented as it relates to the child's limitations and needs would appear to have been contrary to the popular beliefs held when his studies were published in 1936 and 1937.

The late 1950s were, however, to bring major changes in education. In the post-Sputnik era, Durkin reports (1972) that the young child received unprecedented attention. The emphasis on reading was to change. Future texts, she writes (1972), "recording the history of educational thought will surely describe positive and even enthusiastic reactions to preschool reading as a phenomenon of the 1960s. What they will also have to record, however, is that these reactions were hardly bolstered by research data; that, in fact, preschool reading was an aspect of development that remained practically untouched by researchers. It may be that these historians will record, too, that it was this very lack of facts which promoted myth-making, first in the form of exaggerated fears and then in the form of wishful expectations." (1968, p. 63).

Among the changes of emphasis in thought affecting education of the young in the post-Sputnik era was an emphasis upon environment, rather than hereditary factors. Growth and development now began to be explained more in terms of *learning and practice* than in relation to *maturation*. Therefore, learning opportunities were considered especially important to the young child's development. In response to these changes in emphasis, there arose much dissatisfaction with the traditional interpretation of reading readiness (Durkin, 1968). As a result, the schools altered the timing of their reading instruction. Readiness activities found their way into kindergartens, and, gradually, reading instruction, too, began to take place earlier. The research concerning actual readiness for reading activity has not been enriched by such activities, however, and, to date, there still exists meager information about readiness.

## A Definition of Readiness

A review of reading readiness research would suggest, then, that arbitrary decisions have affected the definition of readiness. When viewing a child's readiness for a task, what might be some basic considerations? Drawing upon definitions articulated earlier by Gates in the 1930s and others since that time, Durkin proposes that one carefully consider Ausubel's (1959) definition of readiness. Readiness, he suggested, is the "adequacy of existing capacity in relation to the demands of a given learning task." This definition, as well as Durkin's consideration of it, has tremendous implications for the teacher of the severely handicapped.

Let us first consider the term "existing capacity." Durkin suggests that it is important for the teacher to remember that each child's capacity at any given time is the product of an "interplay among genetic endowments, maturation, experience, and learnings." (1968, p. 51). It is essential that the teacher of a handicapped child remember the importance of this interplay. To overlook, for example, the fact that the child has a vision or hearing problem in approaching the teaching of reading would be a gross error. Special consideration must be given to these factors in the teacher's programming efforts. On the other hand, to deprive the child of all opportunities for reading readiness experiences with the assumption that his inherited capacities cannot cope with experiences of this type, no matter in what form they are offered, is equally a problem. The point concerning the interplay of factors cannot be too strongly made.

Next, Durkin (1972) suggests the term "demands of the task" be considered. What the task will demand of the child should not be considered as a single collection of abilities. As Durkin so clearly articulates, many factors account for the variation in demands; these would include most certainly the teaching method selected. A method which requires the child to memorize every word he is to read, for example, places somewhat different demands upon the child than the method emphasizing an exclusively phonic approach. It must also be remembered that different teachers will use various approaches differently. While one may require, for example, that the child work with a word list of five new words until he demonstrates mastery of all of them, another teacher may introduce 15 new words for him to memorize each day.

Durkin stresses that the consideration of a relation between demands of the task and the capacity of the child is one of the most important features of Ausubel's definition. The child who has an extreme problem with auditory discrimination tasks, for example, may not meet with success in reading should the teacher select to utilize a totally rigid phonics program. Conversely, the child with visual memory and visual discrimination problems may have limited success in a totally sight approach to reading. The teacher must consider the child's special strengths, and also any special modality problems as reading approaches are selected. The teacher must not "assume that certain deficiencies make children *un*ready for every type of teaching." (Durkin, 1972, p. 51). It does become extremely important, however, that the teacher be continually mindful of the child's special problems as she designs a program to allow him to have some success.

## Factors Relating to Reading Readiness

While the authors of this article present only those reading readiness pinpoints drawn from the selected pool of sources utilized in compiling this entire set of pinpoints, they wish to alert the reader to the fact that the pinpoints in the reading listing should not be viewed in isolation. There is a widely scattered body of research currently developing which examines the relationship of language to reading, for example. While the results of these studies would not lend themselves to a set of guidelines, one must be cognizant of the information they offer (Hodges and Rudorf, 1972). To date, no statement can be made regarding the level of language development necessary for initial reading readiness experience, as this remains a controversial point. Some teachers might feel, according to Durkin, that only after ability in oral language is an "accomplished fact" (1972, p. 67) may attention be turned to reading. Durkin reminds her audience that oral language is never an accomplished fact, and that while it is developing, one should give attention to matters such as reading and writing. While Durkin is attending primarily to the normal child, her concern in using reading as language skill is developing should be kept in mind by the teacher of the handicapped child. (It must be noted here that teachers of the handicapped, as those in the area of deaf education, may attempt to utilize the written word to stimulate language development.)

Still another reason for consulting language pinpoints would be to consider the child's ability to use and discriminate sounds. Auditory memory and auditory discrimination skills may be considered an important in achieving success in reading, especially should a phonic approach be selected (Durkin, 1972).

Visual memory and discrimination of letters is also an important skill related to reading, yet there are few developmental guidelines available on this subject. For the teacher of handicapped children who might devote hours to instruction in the discrimination of forms and shapes as reading readiness exercises, it is important that research in this area be carefully considered. As Helen Robinson (1972) notes, after an extensive review of the literature, the value of such training as it relates to reading remains extremely questionable. Teacher and pupil time might be better spent in working with tasks involving letters, syllables, and words, the symbols with which reading actually concerns itself. For this reason, the reader will find that, while behaviors relating to forms and shapes have been placed on the pinpoint listings in other areas, they have not been considered for inclusion on the reading readiness listing.

## Other Readiness Pinpoints Suggested by
## Research

Unfortunately, few researchers have explored the area of reading readiness. Dolores Durkin is one of the only researchers who may be found to have devoted considerable effort here. Durkin has devoted many years to exhaustive study of this problem. The findings from her longitudinal studies conducted over several years with a group of youngsters who were identified to have begun reading before receiving any classroom instruction will prove interesting for those concerned with readiness skills. The youngsters in Durkin's longitudinal studies were reported to be demonstrating some reading skills between the ages of approximately 3.0 and 5.5.

Through extensive home interviews of the parents of these pre–first grade readers, Durkin discovered some common factors which may be extremely worthwhile to consider as readiness pinpoints are explored. One of the most significant of her findings was the importance of writing skills to these youngsters. For more than half the youngsters in her New York and California studies, interest in learning to print developed prior to, or simultaneously with, an interest in learning to read. For many of those youngsters, she states that "ability to read seemed almost like a by-product of ability to print and spell." A sequence which might be generalized across many of these children would appear to resemble the following:

1. The child would start by scribbling.
2. Gradually the child began copying objects.
3. The child began copying letters of the alphabet.
4. One consequence of learning to print was the asking of many questions about the spelling of certain words. (Repeatedly, home interviews revealed that an inevitable initial request here was "Show me my name.") (1966, p. 137).

The interest in spelling words sometimes led to help by a parent or older sibling with letter sounds. Interest in printing may also have led the child to certain project binges of copying—for example, names and addresses or making calendars.

Of course, the interest in printing led to the reading of certain words. However, it is also interesting to note certain materials which held great interest for the child and often led him to question what a word said.

1. Alphabet books played an especially important role in stimulating early interest in letter names and, sometimes, letter sounds (1966, p. 108).
2. Picture dictionaries were also considered to have a high interest value.
3. The experience of being read to was identified as another important source of curiosity. (It is crucial to note here that Durkin states,

"Stories that were read and reread seemed more influential than those which were read only once or twice" (1966, p. 108).

4. Television programs, especially commercials, quiz programs, and weather reports, often elicited questions about words.

5. Also important were words found on places such as outdoor signs, food packages, menus, phonograph records, and cars and trucks.

When viewing Durkin's findings, it is important to remember that: (a) Durkin's studies concern themselves with early readers, a special group of children, all of whom were accelerated in their reading skill beyond the first grade entrant. The studies do, however, suggest further pinpoints which may have implications for other children; (b) All the children had received experiences in this area outside the classroom; (c) The normal or so-called "average" child, given equal or enriched experiences, may demonstrate behaviors similar to Durkin's subjects. While, admittedly, much more data must be obtained on this subject, present information certainly cannot be overlooked.

To the teacher of handicapped children who may spend much time in readiness activities, Durkin's pinpoints may be of special interest. With those children for whom writing is a possibility, Durkin's data would suggest a closer look at the writing readiness pinpoints which are included in this preacademic section. Concentration on writing skills could, it is suggested, be related to reading readiness activities. Also worthy of recognition is attention to the types of materials found important in early reading activity. Some of the sources mentioned offer basic survival vocabulary and suggest possibilities for ways to establish initial word recognition skills.

## REFERENCES

Ausubel D: Viewpoints from related disciplines: Human growth and developments. Teach Coll Rec 50:245–254, 1959

Durkin, D: Children Who Read Early. New York, Teacher's College Pr, 1966

Durkin, D: Teaching Them to Read. Boston, Allyn & Bacon, 1970

Durkin D: Teaching Young Children to Read. Boston, Allyn & Bacon, 1972

Durkin D: When should children begin to read. *In* Innovation and Change in Reading Instruction: The Sixty-seventh Yearbook of the National Society for the Study of Education, Part II. Chicago, University of Chicago Pr, 1968, pp 30–71

Hodges R, Rudorf E (ed): Language and Learning to Read. Boston, Houghton Mifflin, 1972.

Robinson H: Perceptual training—does it result in reading improvement? *In* Aukerman R (ed): Some Persistent Questions on Beginning Reading. Newark, International Reading Association, 1972, pp 135–150

### PREREADING OVERVIEW

I. Establishes book and story preferences.

II. Performs movements in relation to books and pictures.

III. Says words in relation to books, stories.

## PREREADING PINPOINTS

I. Establishes book and story preferences

| | | |
|---|---|---|
| Chooses tactile books such as *Pat the Bunny* | 18–23 mo | Ges |
| Chooses picture books; points to fine detail in favorite picture | 24–29 mo | Sher/Ges |
| Chooses books with sound repetition, rhymes | 24–29 mo | Ges |
| Asks to have stories simplified by interpreting them to him using his vocabulary, people and experiences he knows, especially his own name | 24–29 mo | Ges |
| Asks adult to "tell story" about himself; fills in phrases he knows | 30–35 mo | Ges |
| Asks for same stories from day to day | 30–35 mo | Sher/Ges |
| Listens attentively to stories | 36–48 mo | LAP/Sher |

II. Performs movements in relation to books and pictures

| | | |
|---|---|---|
| Fixes gaze on pictures in book | 10  mo | LAP/Bay |
| | 15  mo | Sher |
| Turns pages of book | 12  mo | Bay |
| | 15  mo | Ges |
| | 16.5 mo | Slos |
| Pats pictures in book (shows interest—Slos) | 15  mo | Ges |
| | 16.5 mo | Slos |
| Points to pictures in book (find ball) | 18  mo | LAP |
| | 18–23 mo | Sher/Vin/Ges/C/Bay |
| | 21  mo | LAP |
| Turns pages of book two or three at a time | 18–23 mo | LAP/Sher |
| | 24  mo | LAP |
| Turns pages singly | 24–29 mo | Sher/H |
| Picks up book on request | 28  mo | Slos |
| Makes gestures pretending to pick up objects from pictures | 30–35 mo | Ges |

III. Says words in relation to books, pictures

| | | |
|---|---|---|
| Says at least one nursery rhyme | 36–48 mo | Vin/Ges/Sher |
| Recites poem from memory or sings a song | 36–48 mo | Vin |
| "Reads" by way of pictures; says words about pictures | 48–60 mo | Vin |
| Listens to and tells long stories, sometimes confusing fact and fantasy | 54  mo | Sher/Ges |
| Acts out stories | 60–72 mo | LAP |

## PREWRITING

While the data available in the area of writing readiness is limited, the reader is encouraged to review the pinpoints evolving from Durkin's (1966) longitudinal studies of early readers. It is suggested from these studies that not only is writing a significant activity in itself, but it also may have an important relationship to reading and reading readiness activities. Although the teacher may find it necessary to substitute other modes of responding for some severely handicapped youngsters, writing, for those with certain readiness skills, may provide the basis for activity in other academic areas.

### PREWRITING OVERVIEW

I. Shows hand preference

II. Holds writing implements
  A. Holds with fist
  B. Holds with fingers

III. Makes marks
  A. Scribbles

B.  Makes controlled strokes
C.  Writes letters
D.  Writes numbers

## PREWRITING PINPOINTS

I.  Shows hand preference
   Uses one hand consistently for holding, grasping           8   mo       C
   Uses both hands freely but may have a preference for one    12  mo      Sher/Ges
   Uses hands with definite preference    18–23 mo   Sher/LAP
   Uses one hand consistently in most activities   24–29 mo   Ges/Sher/LAP

II.  Holds writing implements
   Holds crayon (adaptively)       11  mo     LAP
                    11.2 mo   Bay
   Holds crayon by fingers rather than fist   30  mo     LAP
                    30–35 mo   Ges
                    36–48 mo   F/Ges/LAP

III.  Makes marks
  A.  Scribbles
     Imitates scribble        10.4 mo   Bay
                    13.4 mo   Slos
                    14  mo     Ges
                    16  mo     C
     Makes marks with pencil   12  mo     LAP/C
     Scribbles spontaneously (marks with pencil or crayon—Vin)   13  mo     LAP
                    13.2 mo   Vin
                    13.3 mo   Den
                    14  mo     Bay
     Makes spontaneous scribble when given pencil and paper, using
       preferred hand       18  mo     Sher/V/C

  B.  Makes controlled strokes
     Makes incipient drawing stroke in imitation (straight   15  mo     Ges
       vertical line—Bay)       17.8 mo   Bay
     Makes vertical line in imitation   18.5 mo   Slos
                    21.7 mo   Den
                    24  mo     Sher/Bay
                    27  mo     LAP/C
     Makes V strokes in imitation   24  mo     LAP
     Makes horizontal line in imitation   24  mo     Slos/Bay/LAP
     Makes circle in imitation   24–29 mo   LAP/Ges
                    30  mo     Sher/C
                    33.5 mo   Slos
     Makes spontaneous circular scribble and dots when given paper and
       pencil         24–39 mo   Sher/H
     Makes vertical and horizontal lines, dots, and circular movements   30–35 mo   Ges
     Draws two or more strokes for cross   30–35 mo   Ges
     Draws circles       30–35 mo   C/Den/Sher
                    36–42 mo   Bay/Ges/I&A
                                  MPS/Minn/Slos
                    48–54 mo   DL
     Copies circle       31  mo     Den
                    36  mo     LAP
                    38.2 mo   Sher/H/Slos/
                                  Ges/C/MPS
     Draws cross in imitation   36–48 mo   Ges/Sher
                    36  mo     LAP
     Draws cross       36–42 mo   Ges/I&A/Minn
                    42–48 mo   Bay/Den/MPS
                    48–54 mo   DL
     Traces around diamond drawn on paper   42  mo     LAP
                    60–72 mo   H
     Copies cross       41  mo     Den
                    48–60 mo   Sher/Ges/F/LAP

|  | | | |
|---|---|---|---|
| Draws square | | 42–48 mo | I & A |
| | | 54–60 mo | Den |
| | | 60–66 mo | Bay/C/Ges/ |
| | | | Kuhl/Slos/Sher |
| | | 62  mo | PAR |
| | | 72–78 mo | DL |
| Copies star (three of three trials, MPS) | | 48–60 mo | LAP |
| | | 57  mo | MPS |
| Traces cross | | 54  mo | Ges |
| Copies square | | 56  mo | Den/LAP/F |
| Copies rectangle with diagonal | | 60–72 mo | Ges/LAP |
| Copies triangle | | 60–72 mo | LAP |
| Draws a triangle (copies—Ges) | | 60–72 mo | Ges/H |
| | | 60–66 mo | Ges/I&A/Minn/PAR |
| Draws a diagonal | | 60–72 mo | H |
| Copies diamond | | 72  mo | LAP |
| C. | Writes letters | | |
| | Copies V, H | 30–35 mo | Ges |
| | | 48–60 mo | LAP |
| | Copies V, H, T | 36–48 mo | LAP/Sher/Ges |
| | Prints a few capital letters, large, single letters anywhere on a page | 36–48 mo | H |
| | Draws letters | 42–48 mo | Ges/Sher |
| | Copies V, H, T, O | 48–60 mo | Sher |
| | Prints a few capitals, usually the initial capital of first name | 48–60 mo | H/LAP |
| | Prints capital initials of own name | 48–60 mo | LAP |
| | Prints simple words | 48–60 mo | F/Vin/LAP |
| | Writes a few letters spontaneously | 60–72 mo | LAP/Sher |
| | Prints first name in large and irregular letters, getting larger toward | | |
| | middle or end of name (prints a few letters—Ges) | 60–72 mo | H/Ges/LAP |
| | Reverses letters frequently, especially S | 60–72 mo | H/LAP |
| D. | Writes numbers | | |
| | Prints numbers 1–5, uneven and medium-sized | 60–72 mo | LAP/H |

## PREMATH

In organizing this section concerning math pinpoints, the authors found that their standard pool of developmental sources offered few guidelines. It then became necessary for them to explore other resources which might provide information about readiness pinpoints. In keeping with the attempt to cite "large-N" research studies, the authors, after conducting an extensive search of the literature, offer here only those sources which provide data gathered on at least 100 individuals. Unfortunately, a search of the literature revealed that, while there exists much speculation on the topic of math readiness, there exist few "large-N" research studies which could offer precise pinpoints in keeping with the format of the other sections of the Developmental Pinpoints. Those studies, which have been uncovered after an extensive search, may be in themselves subject to some design questions; however, when summarizing their results, one begins to note some rather interesting groupings into which the pinpoints explored may be categorized. In viewing the resulting list of pinpoints, the reader is encouraged to keep in mind that the precise ordering of topics from rote counting to related areas remains questionable. Within our outline, many major research questions concerning order remain; for example, the issue regarding placement of ordinal versus cardinal number. There are those researchers who would argue that ordination precedes cardination (Brainerd, 1973), still others arguing that these concepts develop concurrently (Copeland, 1970) and that the reverse order, cardinal before ordinal, exists (Brace and Nelson, 1965, Rea and Reys, 1971). The authors have placed ordination following cardination in their skill sequence here, based upon the resources that were finally, after careful deliberation, chosen to serve as the bases for these pinpoints. The general trend in the data utilized would indicate that ordination should follow cardination.

When viewing this set of pinpoints, the reader will note that the authors have taken particular care to note, whenever possible, the context in which a particular pinpoint has occurred. If the child's ability to judge the term "biggest" was to be pinpointed, for example, the authors have indicated, when possible, the context of the situation in which the child responded and the type of movement that was used to indicate his answer. That is, if the child were to say his answer rather than to point to the correct option, this would be carefully noted. The rationale behind the provision of such detail is that mode of responding may be a critical variable in the level of success an investigator achieved. As Brace and Nelson (1965) pointed out, there may be tremendous differences in data concerning a child's number knowledge, when manipulations of objects rather than verbalizations are used as dependent variables. Whenever possible, therefore, the authors have attempted to precisely identify the mode of responding used to indicate understanding, since making a mark, pointing or saying an answer must be considered very different modes, and can be responsible for producing very different results among investigators when viewing the results of the various studies reported. In the pinpoints offered, the reader is, therefore, reminded to consider the conditions under which the children were able to perform.

## SELECTED STUDIES

Wang, Resnick, and Boozer (1971) stated that studies concerning the very early aspects of a developing concept of number have been relatively rare. Rea and Reys (1971) concluded, after their review of the literature, that much of the information available on this topic "was generated prior to the mid-century mark." (p. 389). When considering that children today live in an environment vastly changed from that of prior generations, it seems inappropriate in a listing attempting to pinpoint behaviors of normal children today to rely upon data generated several decades ago. As

Callahan and Glennon (1968), in their review of the research, point out, there is evidence that many of today's kindergartners know as much about arithmetic as first grade youngsters did a few decades ago. It was the authors' decision, therefore, that the criteria for study selection would include not only the fact that a study involved more than 100 individuals, but also that it was a relatively recent study.

A review of the literature reveals that few studies meet both the author's criteria. Those articles which did provide data meeting the criteria mentioned were the following:

**REFERENCES**

Brace A, Nelson L: The Preschool Child's Concept of Number. 1965
Bjonerud C: Arithmetic Concepts Possessed by the Preschool Child. 1960
Holmes E: What do pre-first-grade children know about numbers? 1963
McDowell L: Number concepts and preschool children. 1962
Rea R, Reys R: Competencies of entering kindergartners in geometry, number, money and
   measurement. 1971
Schwartz A: Assessment of mathematical concepts of five-year old children. 1969
Williams A: Mathematical concepts, skills and abilities of kindergarten entrants. 1965
Wang M: Psychometric studies on the validation of an early learning curriculum. 1973

---

*An additional study (McDowell, 1962), while it fails to meet criteria involving number of subjects, having 58 subjects, does seem appropriate for consideration here. This study concerns itself with the very same pinpoints as the other studies, and has the added advantage of being one which allows an age breakout for 3, 4, and 5-year-olds.

## GENERAL OVERVIEW OF THE STUDIES

### Some Factors Worthy of Consideration

GEOGRAPHIC LOCATIONS

While the listing which follows utilizes study data offering precise pinpoints in the area of math readiness, the reader may be interested in an overview of the studies utilized and some of the general conclusions drawn by researchers regarding the categories found in our listing. The studies were conducted throughout the country to include California (Williams, 1965), Iowa (Holmes, 1963; McDowell, 1962), Missouri (Rea and Reys, 1971), Michigan (Bjonerud, 1960), Pennsylvania (Wang, 1973), and Georgia (Schwartz, 1969). One other study meeting the authors' criteria was conducted in Canada (Edmonton, Alberta) by Brace and Nelson (1965).

## SOCIOECONOMIC STATUS

The Brace and Nelson (1965), Schwartz (1969), and Williams (1965) studies made effort to control for the variable of socioeconomic grouping in their populations. It is interesting, then, to note that, when analyzing their data, both Brace and Nelson and Williams, in an attempt to determine the possible effect of this factor, conclude that children of high socioeconomic groups attain superior performances compared to those of the lower socioeconomic group. Schwartz does not discuss this aspect of his data. While there may be many factors contributing to this result, it is interesting to keep in mind as one views the results of the other studies. Holmes (1963) states that she used children from middle and upper socioeconomic groups. Wang (1973) states only that her subjects were from an "urban" elementary school in Pittsburgh. When discussing the composition of the population, she adds that approximately 90% of the children were black. On the other hand, Rea and Reys' (1971) youngsters were "carefully selected to be broadly representative of subpopulations found in modern urban areas." (p. 380). Bjonerud (1960) and McDowell (1962) offer little information in their brief descriptions of their populations.

## AGE

Age is another important variable in these studies. A majority of the studies offer data concerning the entering kindergartner, a child generally ranging in age from 5.0 – 6.5. Only three of the studies included younger children. Holmes (1963) sampled children ranging in age from 3.0–6.4; McDowell's (1962) sample concerned 3 through 5-year-olds, and Wang (1973) included 3-year-olds through entering first graders. While the resulting pinpoints offer, then, considerable information concerning expected behavior for the entering kindergartner, they do not provide a great deal of information regarding developmental sequences within skill areas. Yet, even within the limited age range which many choose to explore, the authors generally conclude that age seems to be a factor in performance. Brace and Nelson (1965), for example, found highly significant differences in performance of children 6 years and over and 6 years and below. Rea and Reys (1970) conclude that, in all cases, kindergartners in the oldest groups (older than 68 months) were significantly higher in achievement than children in the youngest groups (less than 62 months. One example here would be that, although 37% of the entire sample of 727 youngsters could rote count to 20, over twice as many children in the oldest groups, compared to the youngest, successfully demonstrated this behavior. While performance was also influenced, Rea and Reys (1970) point out, by other factors as parents' education and occupation, it is important to consider age as one views the data. Williams, (1965) data, too, confirmed the importance of chronological age.

Holmes (1963), one of the few researchers examining children younger than 5 years old, discovered that the prenursery (3.0–3.7) and nursery-age (3.8–4.7) children in her sample showed little understanding of number, as measured by the test she devised. Further, she discovered that the percentage of preschool age youngsters (4.8–5.7) who performed on any of her subtests was small. In comparing the performances of the preschool youngsters to those of the kindergarten group, Holmes (1963) concluded that the differences between percent correct on the following subtests were all significant at the 0.05 level: rational counting, equality, locating ordinal number, and seriation and correspondence.

McDowell (1962) discovered interesting differences in her 3, 4, and 5-year-olds. In examining correct performance of greater than 50% of the youngsters across the 12 items given, one finds only three tasks which would qualify for her 3-year-olds (median age 3,4), while eight meet this criterion for the 4-year-olds (median age 4–6) and nine meet the criterion for the 5-year-olds (median age 5.4). Using a criterion of correct performance by greater than 80% of each grouping, the results reveal that the 3-year-olds achieved this criterion on only one task, the 4-year-olds on four tasks, and the 5-year-olds on six tasks. Across all tasks given, the highest percentage responding correctly was always achieved by the 5-year-old group. In addition, when comparing the performances of the 3-year-olds to that of the 4-year-olds, one finds that, on all but one task where both groups were unable to perform, the percentage correct is always greater, often significantly so, for the 4-year-olds.

BACKGROUND OF RESEARCH

In their reviews of the literature, several of the researchers acknowledge the work of Piaget. As Brace and Nelson (1965) point out, Piaget has probably conducted the most extensive investigation into the preschool child's concept of number. There has been, however, some criticism of Piaget's sampling and statistical procedures. Some aspects of Piaget's work have been replicated as both Brace and Nelson (1965), and Schwartz (1969) state. While many of these studies have tended to support his findings, some have refuted them. Investigators, such as Lovell (1965), can be consulted for more extensive overviews of Piagetian research.

The Piagetian influence is quite clear as certain researchers examine the young child's concept of number. The purpose of Holmes' research, for example, was to investigate the nature of young children's concepts of cardinal and ordinal number. As she states, "The tests I used to measure concepts of cardinal and ordinal number were adapted from those described by Piaget." (1963, p. 398). The influence of Piaget is quite evident in the work of other researchers such as Brace and Nelson (1965), as one examines the test which they devised to "measure the underlying concepts of number as distinct from the ability to remember number names." (p. 128). Among the tasks selected one finds, for example, a subtest designed to examine conservation of number.

Other researchers, while certainly cognizant of Piaget, have not designed their studies specifically as replications or further explorations of his work. Many researchers (Bjonerud, 1960, McDowell, 1962, Rea and Reys, 1971, Schwartz, 1969, Williams, 1965) express their primary interests in the further assessment of mathematical skills of the young child. Schwartz, (1969) for example, is primarily interested in developing an assessment instrument which can be used to examine the mathematical achievements of youngsters ages 3 through 5. The Schwartz work reported in 1969 concerns itself with data gathered during the first stages of that developmental process. Rea and Reys' work (1971) also develops an assessment tool, primarily to explore the young child's general knowledge in the specific areas of measurement, money, number, and geometry. Their choice of these areas is a result of a survey of contemporary mathematics programs in the kindergarten curriculum. They attempt, then, to determine what knowledge the child brings to those specific areas where he will actually be asked to perform. Williams (1965), too, is interested in the assessment of an entering kindergartener's mathematics understandings. Validity for items used in the assessment instrument in his study were determined by textbook analysis and opinions of a jury of experts, as well as actual child performance during a pilot study.

Wang (1973), unlike the researchers interested primarily in assessment, is concerned with the development of "empirically validated hierarchical curriculum sequences in several basic skill areas appropriate to an early learning curriculum." (p. 54). The curriculum sequences discussed in this article are a part of a research and development project called the Primary Education Project (PEP). The research reported here is a part of an ongoing research program. The purpose of this study was to examine one learning sequence questioning the hierarchical order between units of instruction as well as within each individual unit.

### General Findings Concerning Major Pinpointed Areas

ROTE COUNTING

As one views the general conclusions across areas, it becomes immediately apparent that there is not general agreement concerning the importance of any of the major pinpointed areas listed. When considering the importance of rote counting, for example, some, as Rea and Reys (1971), conclude that there is a strong relationship between the abilities of rote and rational counting. Williams (1965), from his data, goes even further in concluding that there is a "substantial relationship" (p. 267) between rote counting ability and mathematical achievement. One is cautioned, of course, that a relationship does not mean a cause–effect situation exists. Wang, Resnick, and Boozer (1971) offer evidence that counting skills may be developed independently of such skills as 1:1 correspondence. A teacher, following their data, would not assume proficiency in counting necessarily insured development of other skills. The teacher, in consulting the Wang (1973) data, would furthermore cease to emphasize rote counting until the child could count competently through 10, for example. He would instead stress counting successfully to five, and follow that experience by insuring that the child could then rationally count small groupings to five, that is, insuring that the child could make the correct association between objects and the names of the corresponding cardinal numbers. Later in the program sequence, there would be a concern that the child gain proficiency in rote counting to 10.

COMPARISON OF SET SIZE

The placement of this topic within the sequence of skill development is not clear. Brace and Nelson (1965) find that comparison of two groups of objects to determine whether one group was either equivalent to, more than, or fewer than the other is superior to any other concept tested. The researchers state that this is "actually a more immature process than rational counting, since it enables the child to talk about equality or inequality of groups without actually using the number names." (p. 128). McDowell (1962) offers further information in support of Brace and Nelson. She concludes that, according to the results of her particular test, the earliest number ideas which appear are the general comparison ideas of "more" and "enough" (a. 1:1 correspondence task). In testing 3, 4, and 5-year-olds, she discovered the items concerning general comparisons using the words "more" and "enough" were the only ones in the test where over 50% of the 3-year-olds responded. On these items, in fact, 71% responded correctly. There would appear to be, then, some limited evidence that comparison of set size is a relatively early task. However, as one carefully examines the Brace and Nelson article, a question arises concerning those variables which may affect successful performance in this area.

Brace and Nelson have chosen to examine separately another topic which also requires comparison of set size—the topic of conservation. Here, they attempt to determine whether their subjects are able to grasp the idea of the invariance of a given number or of a total quantity. For example, given changes in spatial arrangements of a set of objects previously determined as equal, the child was once again asked to consider the issue of equality. The researchers discovered that approximately four-fifths of their children showed "an almost complete lack of knowledge of the invariance of number." (p. 131).

With conservation as an issue to be considered in comparison of sets, it seems likely that Brace and Nelson's view concerning the placement of this skill in a developmental sequence might be altered. McDowell's (1962) article would indicate that conservation was not a factor in her task requirements, accounting for her conclusion concerning relative ease of performance. If conservation is to be considered an issue, research according to Callahan and Glennon (1968) would seem to indicate that youngsters up to 5 years of age do not demonstrate this skill. In those from 5 to 6, it remains an unstable notion. For those between 6 and 7½, it appears that a logical and axiomatic certainty of conservation develops. When viewing the math readiness pinpoints, the reader is encouraged to remember these findings.

Still another finding which would appear to throw question on the notion that 1:1 correspondence and other means of comparing set size enter the developmental sequence fairly early is the data offered by Williams (1965). In a study involving a much larger sample than Brace and Nelson or McDowell, Williams discovered that only approximately 34% of his children could perform a 1:1 correspondence task correctly when asked to match items of equivalent sets. Matching elements in subsets was performed correctly by only 21 percent, and matching elements in nonequivalent sets reduced the number correct to 8 percent.

After considering the Brace and Nelson (1965) data concerning conservation and the Williams (1965) data, Wang's (1973) findings would appear much more understandable. Wang, in her empirically determined hierarchical learning sequence, reports that comparison of set size (involving determinations of "more," "less," and "equal") occurs later in the sequence after a series of tasks involving rote and rational counting with groupings of up to five objects. (It is important to note that Wang approaches comparisons initially using groupings only to five, and only later, after dealing with rote and rational counting to 10, does she introduce comparisons involving groupings to 10. Rea and Reys (1971) would appear to support, as they state, that most children are able to make small group comparisons, starting first with smaller groupings. Wang's data also offers some information about the relation of the terms "more," "less," and "equal" in comparisons. The concepts of "more" and "less" would appear before that of "equal."

CARDINATION

"Cardinal number is generally considered as embracing the quantitative aspect of number." (Holmes, 1963, p. 399.). When considering the concept of cardination, it appears to be important to consider the size of the grouping with which the child is presented. Wang, Resnick, and Boozer (1971), in a study which provided preliminary data for the Wang (1973) research, concluded that counting and numeration for small sets, up to five, are acquired before counting of large sets is learned. The 1973 data supported this conclusion. Brace and Nelson's (1965) conclusion would also tend to support Wang's information. They state that the "knowledge required to recognize groups of up to five in pattern arrangement without counting and up to four in random arrangement was different from that required to recognize groups of larger size." (p. 131). Their observations led them to conclude that much practice in the recognition of groups of up to four or five should precede work with larger groupings.

There has been much controversy over the placement in the developmental sequence of ordinal versus cardinal number. The data offered used in formulating pinpoints concerning this issue would generally conclude that cardinal concepts were developmentally earlier in the sequence than ordinal. (Brace and Nelson, 1965; Bjonerud, 1960; Holmes, 1963; Rea and Reys, 1971).

ORDINATION

"Ordinal number has been defined as referring to the serial order of number names, the positional phase of number, or the relational phase of number." (Holmes, 1965, p. 399). Brace and Nelson (1965) offer some of the most interesting data on this topic. They conclude that knowledge of ordinal number was the one factor that contributed most to the total common variance in their sample: "Wherever significant differences were found to exist among the various age levels compared, it was this factor that contributed most to these differences." (p. 131). Holmes (1973) found that the percent differences between kindergarten (5.4–6.4) and preschool-age (4.8–5.7) children were significant at the 0.05 level for two ordination tasks, one involving locating ordinal number and the other involving seriation and correspondence. In the latter task, the child was first to order correctly by size a set of objects, as dolls, and then he was required to order a second set, hats, so that the two sets were in correspondence, that is, each doll would have her own hat. When examining the ordination tasks Holmes presents to the children, it is also interesting to note the differences in performance of the kindergarten group across tasks. Approximately 66 percent of the children were able to locate the ordinal number named, while only 29 percent were able to perform the seriation and correspondence task. In still another task involving ordinal correspondence, only 1 percent of the children were able to perform. In this task, the children were required to match a designated element in one seriated set with its corresponding element in a second seriated set, when the second set was not in direct visual correspondence with the first.

The data concerning the location of the correct ordinal number varied across studies. For example, both Williams (1965) and Bjonerud (1960) reported their greatest success with the identification of the "first" number in a series. Approximately 95 percent of Bjonerud's kindergarten children were able to perform correctly here, while 68 percent of Williams' children were accurate. Approximately 50 percent of Bjonerud's sample were able to locate "second," while 37 percent of Williams could perform on a similar task.

SEQUENCES

Rea and Reys (1971) found, when giving a sequence as 1,2,3,—and requiring the child to provide the missing number, approximately 90 percent of the children could answer correctly. However, giving only a single number cue, and asking what number came before or after, decreased the child's success considerably. They also found that the percent able to answer correctly decreased as the size of the number cue increased.

Schwartz (1969) considered the most difficult items on his test to be those answered by less than 30 percent of the children. Among these items were some backward chaining items requiring that the child "mark the numeral" that should be said next. An example here would be 5,4,3,2,—.

NUMERAL IDENTIFICATION

While both Williams (1965) and Rea and Reys (1971) found their children to have great difficulty in identifying two-digit numerals, both found some indications that environmental influences were affecting two-digit numeral recognition. Those numerals which represented television channel indicators, for example, were more easily recognized.

Although children experienced far more success with one digit than two-digit numerals, certain one-digit numerals were also found to create difficulty. In the Williams (1965) sample, 50 to 75 percent of the children could not identify 6, 9, and 0.

MATH RELATED TOPICS

Rea and Reys were able to pinpoint many areas where youngsters were demonstrating important initial skills. The identification of money, for example, was found to be one of the easiest portions of their test. Many children also had some important initial skills in the area of geometry. Correct identification of measuring devices such as the thermometer was also noted by Williams (1965). Rea and Reyes (1971) found the calendar to be one of the most difficult areas of measurement. This is an interesting point, as the calendar so often becomes an integral part of the young child's opening exercises at school. Much instruction is indicated for this area when returning to Rea and Reys' data.

While the clock may be identified and the child may be able to verbalize its function, both Rea and Reys (1971) and Williams (1965) present data indicating that the kindergarten entrant has problems successfully identifying time as indicated by the clock. Bjonerud (1960) reports that about 50 percent of his 5-year-olds could recognize time on the full hour; however, only about one-third were able to recognize time on the half-hour.

Schwartz (1969) and Williams (1965) also find among their difficult items those concerning fractions. To identify one-half of a grouping or mark the frame showing one fourth of a jar or one-third of a pie are sample items with which their youngsters had difficulty. Bjonerud (1960), however, reports greater success in the identification of fractional concepts. About 50 percent of his youngsters were able to recognize the identification of fractional concepts. About 50 percent of his youngsters were able to recognize one-half of one item, 89 percent recognized an item divided into thirds, and 66 percent responded accurately to one-fourth of an item.

**OTHER FACTORS ASSOCIATED WITH READINESS—
SELECTED HOME INFLUENCES (WILLIAMS STUDY)**

As the Durkin study regarding home influence was cited during the discussion of reading readiness, it seemed appropriate to include here some of the factors which emerged in Williams' exploration of this topic as it related to math. Small but significant relationships emerged between math achievements and knowledge of television channel numbers and frequency of playing counting games with cards. Other relationships were indicated between math achievements and knowledge of house number, knowledge of telephone number, knowledge of telephone dialing, interest in counting, and frequency of playing counting games using spinners and dice. It is interesting to note that many of these activities, as knowledge of house and telephone numbers have become important program activities in special education classes for youngsters who may not demonstrate competency in these areas.

## FORMAT OF THE READINESS PINPOINTS

In organizing the pinpoints, the authors have attempted to present only those areas where children achieved success. Success, where researchers did define it, was sometimes noted in terms of 80 percent of the children passing (Schwartz, 1969). Rea and Reys (1971) not only note the 80 percent success criterion but also, in their final summary, specifically attend to those items passed by 50 percent. Williams (1965) not only utilizes the 50 percent criterion in his discussions, but also a 75 percent criterion. In an attempt to compromise here, the authors utilize all three criteria in their presentation, 50 percent, 75 percent, 80 percent, so that the reader may have some idea as to the proportion of a study population involved. In some special cases, if a percentage is a borderline case, the authors offer the precise figure.

Because the pool of resources in this listing is different, for the most part, from those utilized throughout the other areas, the source key followed here is presented below.

B     Bjonerud C: Arithmetic concepts possessed by the preschool child. *The Arithmetic Teacher* 7:347–350, 1960
B&N   Brace A, Nelson L: The preschool child's concept of number. *The Arithmetic Teacher* 12:126–133, 1965
Ho    Holmes E: What do pre-first-grade children know about number? *Elementary School Journal*
McD   McDowell L: Number concepts and preschool children. 1962
R&R   Rea R, Reys R: Competencies of entering kindergarteners in geometry, number, money and measurement. *Social Science and Mathematics* 71:389–402, 1971
S     Schwartz A: Assessment of mathematical concepts of five-year-old children. *Journal of Exceptional Education* 37:67–74, 1969
Wa    Wang M: Psychometric studies in the validation of an early learning curriculum. *Child Development* 44:54–60, 1973
Wil   Williams A: Mathematical concepts, skills and abilities of kindergarten entrants. *The Arithmetic Teacher* 12:261–268, 1965

## REFERENCES

Bjonerud C: Arithmetic concepts possessed by the preschool child. Arith Teach 1:347–350, 1960
Brace A, Nelson L: The preschool child's concept of number. Arith Teach 12:126–133, 1965
Brainerd C: The origins of number concepts. Sci Am 101–109, March 1973
Callahan L, Glennon V: Elementary School Mathematics. Washington, Association for Supervision & Curriculum Development, NEA, 1968
Copeland R: How Children Learn Mathematics. London, Macmillan, 1970
Holmes E: What do pre-first-grade children know about number? Elemen Sch J 63:397–403, 1963

Lovell K: The Growth of Basic Mathematical & Scientific Concepts in Children. London, Univ London Pr, 1965

McDowell L: Number concepts and preschool children. Arith Teach 9:433–435, 1962

Rea R, Reys R: Competencies of entering kindergarteners in geometry, number, money and measurement. Sch Sci Math 71:389–402, 1971

Rea R, Reys R: Mathematical competencies of entering kindergartners. Arith Teach 17:65–74, 1970

Schwartz A: Assessment of mathematical concepts of five-year-old children. J Exp Educ 37:67–74, 1969

Wang, M, Resnick, L, Boozer R: The sequence of development of some early mathematical behaviors. Child Develop 42:1767–1778, 1971

Wang, M: Psychometric studies in the validation of an early learning curriculum. Child Develop 44:54–60, 1973

Williams A: Mathematical concepts, skills and abilities of kindergarten entrants. Arith Teach 12:261–68, 1965

## PREMATH OVERVIEW

I. Sort objects using form and discrimination vocabulary

II. Counts by rote (says numbers without reference to objects)
   A. Repeats digits, 1–10
   B. Repeats digits beyond 10

III. Performs cardination tasks
   A. Forms 1:1 correspondence

   B. Counts rationally
      1. Counts fixed, ordered sets of objects
      2. Counts movable objects
      3. Counts fixed, unordered sets of objects
      4. Identifies, among several sets, the set which has a stated number of objects
      5. Counts out a specified subset from a larger set of objects

   C. Compares set size (after pairing objects (such as chips of two colors))
      1. Identifies set with *more*
      2. Identifies set with *less*
      3. Compares set of *same* size

IV. Performs ordination tasks
   A. Places concrete objects in order, shortest to tallest, smallest to largest, etc.
   B. Orders semiabstract objects
   C. Begins ordering set according to size

V. Identifies numerals
   A. Matches numerals
   B. Identifies numbers when named
   C. Names numerals
   D. Matches numerals with sets
   E. Seriates numerals
   F. Provides missing numerals
   G. Compares numerals (more, less)
   H. Writes numerals 1–5

VI. Uses numbers in related math areas
   A. Money
   B. Time
   C. Calendar
   D. Ruler
   E. Thermometer
   F. Geometric shapes
   G. Fractions

VII. Uses numbers in number stories

## PREMATH PINPOINTS

I. Sorts objects using form and discrimination vocabulary such as big, little; large, small; larger, smaller; heavy, light

| | | |
|---|---|---|
| Points to smaller of two squares | 42 mo | Slos |
| Responds accurately to situations requiring an understanding of largest, smallest, tallest, longest, most, inside, beside, closest, farthest (80%) | 60 mo | Bj |
| Recognized situations describing terms: shortest, underneath, few, some (approx. 50%) | 60 mo | Bj |
| Finds longest (>80%) | 60–72 mo | Wil |
| Finds shortest (>50%) | 60–72 mo | Wil |
| Shown golf ball and marble; tells which is biggest (99%) | 60–68 mo | R & R |
| Shown golf ball and marble; tells which is heaviest (94%) | 60–68 mo | R & R |
| Shown pictures of a book, feather, pencil; tells which is heaviest (94%) | 60–68 mo | R & R |
| Shown pictures of a book, feather, and pencil; tells which is lightest (80%) | 60–68 mo | R & R |
| Frame of sticks or heavy lines; marks the stick that does not fit (>75%) | 60 mo | Sch |
| Frame of circles; marks the circle that does not fit (>50%) | 60 mo | Sch |
| Marks the largest dog (>80%) | 60 mo | Sch |
| Marks the shortest pencil (>80%) | 60 mo | Sch |
| Frame of alternate circles–squares as beads; marks circle or square which will make look right (>50%) | 60 mo | Sch |
| Frame of square, two circles, square, etc. as beads; marks circle or square which when added looks right (>50%) | 60 mo | Sch |

II. Counts rotely (says numbers without reference to objects)

A. Repeats digits, 1–10

| | | |
|---|---|---|
| Repeats digits rotely, 0–5 | 40 mo | McD |
| Repeats digits rotely, 6–10 | 54 mo | McD |
| Says numbers in order, 1–10 | 60–66 mo | Ges |

B. Repeats digits rotely beyond 10

| | | |
|---|---|---|
| Counts rotely beyond 10 (>75%) | 60–68 mo | R & R |
| Counts rotely beyond 14 (>50%) | 60–68 mo | R & R |
| Counts rotely to 19 (mean for group) | 60 mo | Bj |
| Counts rotely beyond 20 | 64 mo | McD/B & N |

III. Performs cardination tasks

A. Forms 1:1 correspondence

| | | |
|---|---|---|
| Answers correctly "Do we have enough straws for the cups?" (>50%) | 40 mo | McD |
| (>80%) | 54 mo | McD |
| (96%) | 64 mo | McD |
| Answers correctly when shown two sets and asked "Is there a disk for each child?" (sets with four objects each) (80%) | 60–68 mo | R & R |
| Makes the same number of marks as circles (2) (>50%) | | Sch |
| Draws a line from dot to dot (dots 7 inches apart) (>80%) | | Sch |
| Makes one less mark than circles: two circles (>50%) | | Sch |
| Four frames: marks the two frames that have the same number of squares: three squares (>50%) | | Sch |

B. Counts *rationally* (synchronizes *touches* with *objects*)

1. Counts fixed, ordered set of objects

| | | |
|---|---|---|
| Counts fixed, ordered set of objects | 36–72 mo | Wa |
| Rational counting to 10 | 36–72 mo | Wa |
| Counts objects to 19 (mean for entire group) | 60 mo | Bj |

2. Counts movable objects

| | | |
|---|---|---|
| Counts movable objects | 36–72 mo | Wa |
| Counts two blocks | 36–48 mo | LAP/MPS |
| Counts three objects | 42–48 mo | PAR |
| Counts six pennies (>70%) | 54–64 mo | McD |
| Says correct number when shown two to six objects and asked "How many?" | 54 mo | LAP |
| Given 20 chips, correctly associates between chip and corresponding cardinal number, beyond 10 (>75%), beyond 15 (>50%) | 60–68 mo | R & R |

3. Counts fixed, unordered sets of objects

| | | |
|---|---|---|
| Counts fixed, unordered sets of objects | 36–72 mo | Wa |
| Counts five tractors (pictures mounted on paper) (>70%) | 54 mo | McD |
| (>80%) | 64 mo | McD |
| Counts sets containing one, two, three objects (>90%) | 60–68 mo | R & R |
| Counts sets containing four, five objects | 60–68 mo | R & R |

4. Identifies, among several sets, the set which has a stated number of
   objects                                36–72 mo    Wa

| | | |
|---|---|---|
| 4. Identifies, among several sets, the set which has a stated number of objects | 36–72 mo | Wa |
| Recognizes two pictured items when flashed on cards (93%) | 60 mo | Bj |
| Marks box with three dots (>80%) | 60–72 mo | Wil |
| Marks box with five dots (>50%) | 60–72 mo | Wil |
| Marks box with nine dots (>50%) | 60–72 mo | Wil |
| Marks frame that has three squares (>80%) | 60 mo | Sch |
| Marks frame that has five squares (>70%) | 60 mo | Sch |
| 5. Counts out a specified subset from a larger set of objects | 36–72 mo | Wa |
| Counts out 10 objects | 36–72 mo | Ho |
| Selects quantities of three or less (100%) | 60 mo | Bj |
| Forms a group of three disks (>80%) | 60–68 mo | R & R |
| Marks three of the squares in the frame (>70%) | 60 mo | Sch |
| Marks four of the circles in the frame (>70%) | 60 mo | Sch |
| Forms groups of three and seven objects (>50%) | 60–68 mo | R & R |
| Marks three dots (>50%) | 60–78 mo | Wil |
| Marks seven dots (48%) | 60–78 mo | Wil |
| C. Compares set size (after pairing objects, such as chips of two colors) | 36–72 mo | Wa |
|   1. Identifies set with *more* | | |
|     Two sheets of paper, one with four cars one with six: Which picture has *more* cars? (>70%) | 40 mo | McD |
|     (>80%) | 54 mo | McD |
|     (96%) | 64 mo | McD |
|     Three pictures, 1–10 houses (>80%) | 54 mo | McD |
|     Which frame has more buttons? (>80%) | 60 mo | Sch |
|     Two frames, if one more than other mark it. If same number of circles in both frames mark each frame (>70%) | 60 mo | Sch |
|     Which frame has the most pictures? (>70%) | 60 mo | Sch |
|     Mark frame with set greater than three (>70%) | 60 mo | Sch |
|     Frame has more squares than circles, mark extra squares (>50%) | 60 mo | Sch |
|     Shown four spades and three buckets; tells which set has more (>50%) | 60–68 mo | R & R |
|     One to five houses, one to seven houses (>90%) Which picture has the *most* houses? | 64 mo | McD |
|   2. Identifies set with *less* | 36–72 mo | Wa |
|     Shown four spades and three buckets; tells which set has less (>50%) | 60–68 mo | R & R |
|   3. Compares sets of *same* size | 36–72 mo | Wa |
|     Determines equality of two sets of 10 beads each. The two groups were shown to the subject in plastic boxes or glass bottles. The arrangements of the beads were not predetermined. After each presentation, the child was questioned concerning the equality of the two groups of beads (>50%). | 60–72 mo | Ho |
|     Answers question "Is there a disk for each child?" (four disks, four children) (>75%) | 60–68 mo | R & R |
|     Four frames; marks each of the two frames that look the same (four pictures of ducks) (>50%) | 60 mo | Sch |
|     Four frames; marks the two frames that have the same number (nine circles) (>50%) | 60 mo | Sch |
| IV. Performs ordination tasks | | |
|  A. Places concrete objects in order from shortest to tallest, smallest to largest, etc. | | |
|     Arranges 10 paper dolls in order by size; locates certain dolls by ordinal names (>50%) | 60–72 mo | Ho |
|  B. Orders semiabstract objects | | |
|     Points to left, marks the first duck (>80%) | 60 mo | Sch |
|     Marks the last duck (>50%) | 60 mo | Sch |
|     Identifies "middle" and "last" (>70%) | 60 mo | Bj |
|     Identifies "second" and "fourth" (>50%) | 60 mo | Bj |
|     Identifies first (>50%) | 60–72 mo | Wil |
|     Identifies ordinal concepts *first* and *second* (>50%) | 60–68 mo | R & R |
|  C. Begins ordering sets according to size | | |

V. Identifies numerals

| | | |
|---|---|---|
| A. Matches numerals | 36–72 mo | Wa |
| B. Identifies numerals when named | 36–72 mo | Wa |
| Marks the numeral for 3 (>70%) | 60   mo | Sch |
| Identifies numerals 1–8 (>50%) | 60–68 mo | R & R |
| Marks numeral 4 (>50%) | 60–72 mo | Wil |
| Marks numeral for 6 (>50%) | 60   mo | Sch |
| C. Names numerals | 36–72 mo | Wa |
| Correctly names numerals 1, 2, 3, 4, 5 (>50%) | 60–68 mo | R & R |
| Correctly names numerals 10, 11, 12, 13 (>50%) | 60–68 mo | R & R |
| D. Matches numerals with sets | 36–72 mo | Wa |
| Child matches set of three objects with appropriate numeral by pointing to, placing, or drawing line | No norms | |
| Marks number that shows number of fingers on one hand (four or five) (>50%) | 60   mo | Sch |
| Marks number that shows how many eyes you have (>50%) | 60   mo | Sch |
| E. Seriates numerals | 36–72 mo | Wa |
| Marks the number than comes just before 5 (50%) | 60   mo | Sch |
| F. Provides missing numerals | | |
| Supplies next number in a series, such as; 1, 2, 3,—or 5, 6, 7,—(>50%) | | R & R |
| G. Compares numerals (more, less) | 36–72 mo | Wa |
| H. Writes numerals | 36–72 mo | Wa |
| Writes numerals 1–5, uneven and widely spaced | 60–72 mo | LAP/H |

VI. Uses numbers in math related areas

| | | |
|---|---|---|
| A. Money | | |
| Identifies *money* (in group of pictures: boat, ball, money, umbrella) (>80%) | 60–68 mo | R & r |
| Identifies picture of penny, nickel, dime (>80%) | 60–68 mo | R & R |
| | 60–72 mo | LAP |
| Recognizes *penny,* (80% at 60 mo Bj) | | |
| Marks the frame that shows a dime (>70%) | 60   mo | Sch |
| Identifies $1.00 (Show card with $1.00, $5.00, $10.00) (>50%) | 60–68 mo | R & R |
| Identifies $5.00 ($1.00, $5.00, $10.00) (>50%) | 60–68 mo | R & R |
| Identifies $10.00 ($1.00, $5.00, $10.00) (>50%) | 60–68 mo | R & R |
| Tells which buys less (penny, nickel, dime) (50>50%) | 60–68 mo | R & R |
| Tells which buys most (dime, quarter, half dollar) (>50%) | 60–68 mo | R & R |
| Makes change: "If you have five pennies, how much money will you give me for a piece of gum that costs 1¢?" (>50%) | 60–68 mo | R & R |
| Marks the frame . . . which of four coins will buy the most (three cents and nickel) (>50%) | 60   mo | Sch |
| B. Time | | |
| Relates clock time to daily schedule (i.e., runs to turn on T.V. when sees hands of clock at 5:00) | 60–72 mo | LAP |
| Answers correctly when shown clock and asked: What is this? (80%, 89% at 60 mo—Bj) | 60–68 mo | R & R |
| Answers correctly when shown clock and asked: What does this tell us? (>50%) | 60–68 mo | R & R |
| Four frames with clocks/watches; marks 6:00 | 60   mo | Sch |
| Recognizes time on full hour when referring to clock (>50%) | 60   mo | Bj |
| C. Calendar | | |
| Names calendar (>50%) | 60   mo | Bj |
| Correctly identifies usage of calendar (>50%) | 60–68 mo | R & R |
| Marks something that measures days of month (>50%) | 60   mo | Sch |
| D. Ruler | | |
| Marks something that measures table or how tall you are (>50%) | 60   mo | Sch |
| Answers: What is this used for? >50% | 60–68 mo | R & R |
| Answers: What is this? | 60–68 mo | R & R |
| E. Thermometer | | |
| Answers "Is it getting hotter or colder?" (>50%) | 60–68 mo | R & R |

F.  Geometric shapes

| | | |
|---|---|---|
| Marks two numbers/figures that are the same (>70%) | 60 mo | Sch |
| Marks the two shapes that look alike (>70%) | 60 mo | Sch |
| Recognizes circle (>50%) (91%—Bj) | 60 mo | Wil |
| Marks each circle in the frame (>50%) | 60 mo | Sch |
| Matches shapes correctly when asked to match following shapes to a similar figure drawn on cards or a board with a similar figure cutout. (>80%) | 60–68 mo | R & R |
| Recognizes square (>50%) when shown a picture of square (>70%—Bj) | 60–72 mo | Wil |
| Points to line, as well as sides of triangle (>80%) | 60–68 mo | R & R |
| Points to corner of square (>80%) | 60–68 mo | R & R |
| Places finger inside circle (>80%) | 60–68 mo | R & R |
| Points to longest line (>80%) | 60–68 mo | R & R |
| Tells which parallel lines are closest together, farthest apart (>80%) | 60–68 mo | R & R |

G.  Fractions

| | | |
|---|---|---|
| Recognizes one-half of one item (>50%) | 60 mo | Bj |
| Says number of pieces an object has when it has been cut in half | 68 mo | Slos |
| Recognizes an item divided into thirds (89%) | 60 mo | Bj |
| Responds accurately to one-fourth of an item (>50%) | 60 mo | Bj |

VII. Uses numbers in number stories

| | | |
|---|---|---|
| If–then situations | 60 mo | Sch |

Example: (while demonstrating, "If I have two books and I take one away, then how many will I have left?"

2 − 1 = n   Mark the right frame (81%). Objects pictured.
5 − 2 = n   Mark the frame (70%). Objects pictured.
2 + 1 = n   Mark the frame (50%). Objects pictured.
3 + 3 = n   Mark the frame (50%). Objects pictured.
1 + 1 = n   Make right number of marks (>50%). No objects.
2 − 1 = n   Make right number of marks (>50%). No objects.

| | | |
|---|---|---|
| When asked to respond to a work problem that involved simple addition and subtraction facts by marking a series of similar pictures: | 60 mo | Bj |

Solved problems involving addition combinations (almost 90%)
Solved problems involving subtraction combinations (approximately 75%)

## REINFORCEMENT ACTIVITIES

While examining the many sources cited in the preceding sequences, the authors of the Developmental Pinpoints discovered a number of items which connoted choice, preference, or purpose on the part of the child. These pinpoints did not seem specific to any of the skill areas usually found in developmental sequences. They did, however, seem to suggest a developmental pattern of activity preference which might be used by a teacher of the severely handicapped in planning reinforcement activities.

Through the consideration of the types of activities presented in the Reinforcement Activities listing, the teacher of the severely handicapped child can more easily discover those events which, employed as positive reinforcers, may serve to increase desired behavior on the part of each individual within the classroom. Positive reinforcement involves the use of any event which strengthens or increases the behavior it follows. Those events which serve as positive reinforcers cover a wide range, some occurring naturally in the environment (such as hugs, smiles, or verbal praise), and others, such as food, tokens, or privileges, which are called extrinsic reinforcers. It is important to remember that these positive reinforcers vary from individual to individual: the same events are not reinforcing to all. Although these authors have listed some of the activities found by many to be reinforcing, these specific activities may not be reinforcing to all individuals within a classroom population. It is the teacher's task to discover, through careful observation, which materials, areas, or activities are reinforcing to each child in the classroom.

The task of selecting appropriate, effective positive reinforcers can be a difficult one. It can, however, be simplified by examining a child's choices in terms of the sensory categories through which engagement in an activity is received.

1. Events which are received by the sense of *hearing* belong to the *auditory category*. Music, praise, and even noise may serve as auditory reinforcers. The child at 11 months who squeezes a doll to hear it squeak is responding to reinforcement of an auditory type.

2. The *visual category* includes events such as flashing lights, a star placed on a chart, or a teacher's smile. While a severely handicapped child may not "stand at a window and watch events outside intently" at 15 months, as some sources have found children to do, he may show preference for activities, such as presentation of a flashing light board, similar to a 4-month-old infant's "increased motor activity at sight of a toy."

3. Those reinforcers which appear to the sense of smell belong to the *olfactory category*.

4. The *gustatory category* includes a variety of foods, drinks, or other materials, such as clay, which may appeal to the sense of taste.

5. *Tactual–kinesthetic* reinforcers appeal to the sense of touch and motion of the extremities.

6. The authors of this sequence have added a sixth receptive category—the *proprioceptive*. Proprioceptive reinforcers appeal to the body's sense of inner stimulation. Movement produced by swinging, rocking, being pulled in a wagon, or any number of gross motor activities may provide positive reinforcement of the proprioceptive type.

Of course, not all reinforcer choices represent just one receptive category. Some activities, such as playing with paints or clay, watching T.V., or engaging in "frolic play" (Reinforcement Activities, 5.1 mo.) may appeal to more than one sense.

The following are a few of the high-strength activities which may appeal to children between the ages of 1 month and 6 years. These activities have been arranged according to the age at which they have been noted to occur. The teacher using the list as a pinpointing guideline may wish to rearrange the pinpoints in terms of such reinforcer categories described above. If the pinpoints are arranged within sensory categories, the teacher will notice an interesting pattern. Within each category, a child's initial preferences deal with object use and enjoyment of materials themselves. As the child grows older, high-strength activities develop a social context. This observation may be helpful to a teacher who finds a pupil unresponsive to the usual social reinforcers.

The authors of this sequence hope that the following activities will be useful to teachers planning programs for individuals for whom the task of discovering effective positive reinforcers has often been an extremely difficult one.

### REINFORCEMENT ACTIVITIES

**0.1–6 months**

| | | |
|---|---|---|
| Quiets when picked up | 0.1 mo | Bay |
| Increases motor activity at sight of toy | 4 mo | C/LAP |
| Uses paper in play | 4.8 mo | Bay |
| Likes frolic play | 5.1 mo | Bay |
| Uses string in play | 5.4 mo | Bay |

**6–12 months**

| | | |
|---|---|---|
| Rings bell purposely | 8 mo | LAP |
| Squeezes doll; listens to squeak | 11 mo | LAP/C |
| Likes to be constantly within sight and hearing of adult | 12 mo | Sher |
| Enjoys applause (repeats performances laughed at) | 12 mo | Ges |
| Watches people, cars, animals with prolonged interest | 12 mo | Sher |

**12–18 months**

| | | |
|---|---|---|
| Stands at window and watches events outside intently for several minutes | 15 mo | Sher |

**18–24 months**

| | | |
|---|---|---|
| Enjoys short walks | 18–23 mo | LAP/Ges |

**24–30 months**

| | | |
|---|---|---|
| Enjoys birthday party with just family—food is the party | 24–29 mo | Ges |

**30–36 months**

| | | |
|---|---|---|
| May go through elaborate rituals with own possessions at home | 30–35 mo | Ges |

## CONCLUSION

Although the integration of severely handicapped individuals within the mainstream of community life has been accompanied by general cur- riculum goals, such as development of self-care and self-help skills, social adjustment in the home and neighborhood, and economic usefulness within home or sheltered workshop settings, advocates of the integration process have been slow to establish specific objectives and programs suited to the unique needs of individuals within this difficult population. The teacher of the severely handicapped, when confronted with the task of providing assessment and instruction for children who present multiple physical, behavioral, and learning problems, may well wonder where to begin. It is hoped that the Developmental Pinpoints will provide a starting place.

This pinpoint sequence has been designed to describe normal development within each major skill area. While it is not suggested that the sequence of development for severely handicapped children is the same as that for "normal" children—it may, in fact, differ markedly—the pinpoints do provide a means of initial evaluation and a basis for further programming efforts within the developmental areas. By providing programs to meet objectives in every area, the teacher insures that each child participates in a well-rounded program, regardless of his developmental position within any specific skill category.

It is generally assumed that performance expectations for severely or profoundly handicapped individuals are extremely limited. Programs for the severely handicapped have only recently been developed and have generally been confined to certain areas, such as development of self-help and prevocational skills. Children who perform in the preacademic areas described in the sequence will, of course, no longer be considered severely handicapped. The authors have, however, included these preacademic pinpoints with the hope that the sequences will expand the capabilities and expectations of teachers of the severely handicapped. By discovering a child's behavioral possibilities in any area, the teacher may establish a new goal. Current objectives stress full growth and participation in the community of each severely handicapped individual, within the bounds of his ability. The ultimate goal, however, is that every severely or profoundly handicapped individual have the opportunity, through accurate assessment and careful programming, to discard this label, and to participate in society to the extent of his capabilities as a human being.

## SOURCE KEY

Bay  Bayley N: Bayley Infant Scales of Development. New York, Psychological Corp., 1968

Bj  Bjonerud C: Arithmetic concepts possessed by the preschool child. Arith Teach 7:347–350, 1960

B&N  Brace A, Nelson L: The preschool child's concept of number. Arith Teach 12:126–133, 1965

C  Cattell P: The Measurement of Intelligence of Infants and Young Children. New York, Psychological Corp., 1940

PAR  Doll E: Preschool Attainment Record. Circle Pines, Minn., American Guidance Service, 1966

Vin  Doll E: The Measurement of Social Competence: A Manual for the Vinland Social Maturity Scale. Circle Pines, Minn., American Guidance Service, 1966

Den  Frankenberg W, Dodds J: Denver Developmental Screening Test. Denver, Colo., Ladoca Project and Publishing Foundation, 1966

110                                                    Cohen, Gross, and Haring

Minn  Goodenough F, Maurer K, Van Wagen M: Minnesota Preschool Scale. Circle Pines, Minn.: American Guidance Service, 1940
Ges   Gesell A: The First Five Years of Life: a Guide to the Study of the Preschool Child. New York, Harper, 1940
      Gesell A, Armatruda C: Developmental Diagnosis: Normal and Abnormal Child Development, Clinical Methods and Applications. New York, Hoeber, 1962
Ho    Holmes E: What do pre-first-grade children know about number? Elem Sch J 63:397–403, 1963
H     Hurlock E: Child Growth and Development. St. Louis, McGraw-Hill, Webster Division, 1968
Kep   Kephart N: The Slow Learner in the Classroom. Columbus, Ohio, Merrill, 1971
Ben   Koppitz E: Bender-Gestalt Test for Young Children—Koppitz Method. New York, Grune & Stratton, 1964
Kuhl  Kuhlmann F: A Handbook of Mental Tests: A Further Revision of the Binet-Simon Scale. Baltimore, Md., Warwick and York, 1922
I&A   Manuel H: Inter-American Series—Primary, Preschool Level, Austin, Tex.: Guidance Testing Associates, 1966
R&R   Rea, R, and Reys R: Competencies of entering kindergartners in geometry, number, money, and measurement. Soc Sci Math 71:389–402, 1971
LAP   Sanford A: Learning Accomplishment Profile. Chapel Hill, N.C.: University of North Carolina at Chapel Hill, Chapel Hill Training–Outreach Project.
Sch   Schwartz A: Assessment of mathematical concepts of five-year-old children. Exceptl Edu 37:67–74, 1969
Sher  Sheridan M: The Developmental Progress of Infants and Young Children. London, Her Majesty's Stationery Office, 1968
Slos  Slosson R: Slosson Intelligence Test. New York, Slosson Education, 1964
MPS   Stutsman R: Mental Measurement of Preschool Children, with a Guide for the Administration of the Merrill–Palmer Scale of Mental Tests. Yonkers-on-Hudson, World, 1931
Wa    Wang M: Psychometric studies in the validation of an early learning curriculum. Child Dev 44:54–60, 1973
Wil   Williams A: Mathematical concepts, skills and abilities of kindergarten entrants. Arith Teach, 12:261–268, 1965
PLS   Zimmerman I, Steiner V, Evatt R: Pre-School Language Scale. Columbus, Ohio, Merrill, 1969

M. Ellen Somerton and
Donald G. Myers

# B

# Educational Programming for the Severely and Profoundly Mentally Retarded

The purpose of this chapter is twofold: first, we want to present an overview of an educational program for severely and profoundly retarded individuals; and, secondly, we want to delineate a few areas in the curriculum of particular importance to those researchers who are developing new programs and presently working in this rapidly growing field.

## POPULATION SERVED

The educational program discussed in this book is intended to serve individuals classified as severely mentally retarded. However, when dealing with various definitions concerning the lower levels of retardation, it is very difficult to discern much about the individuals strictly by the label used. While, in general, profound mental retardation has remained as pertaining to I.Q.s below 25 or 30, it is seldom employed. The most common terminology is "severely retarded," but an investigation of the term reveals that it can encompass I.Q.s of as wide a range from 54 to 0, or as small a range from 20 to 0. To complicate the issue even further, many references to severely retarded refer to the lowest level of the classification system, except in the American Association on Mental Deficiency, which applies it basically to I.Q.s from 35 to 20, while the term "profound mental retardation" is reserved for the very bottom category.

We recognize that the intelligence quotient should not be the only criterion used in making a diagnosis of mental retardation, or in evaluating its severity. Ideally, it should serve only to help in making a more accurate judgment of the individual's adaptive behavioral capacity. Also, any classification system tends to lead to oversimplification of problems that are both complex and perplexing. Within each level, there are wide differences of ability potentiality. For these reasons, it is preferable, in educational programming, to downplay etiology and focus on the dimension of adaptive behavior—primarily, the effectiveness with which an individual copes with the natural and social demands of his environment.

In order to better understand the severely and profoundly mentally retarded, the authors offer the following brief list of descriptions that often characterize such individuals:

1. Physical defects are numerous and often severe; i.e., impaired vision, hearing, and mechanisms for motor coordination.

2. May fail to attain an upright and mobile position in space or become ambulatory.

3. May show gross underdevelopment or complete unawareness of the environment.

4. Often display extreme infantile-type behavior.

5. Frequently are unable to interact or communicate with their physical and social environment.

6. Often speech remains undeveloped although sounds are made.

7. Care of bodily functions pose serious problems; i.e., there is absence of feeding and toileting skills.

8. Most often cannot guard themselves against the most common physical dangers.

The great majority of our severely and profoundly retarded population can be found in state institutions or in smaller public and private facilities. Many children do remain at home for as long as the family is able to care for them. However, difficulties in care for the severely and profoundly retarded tend to increase as the child gets older. Parents expect to give a newborn child total care, seeing to his needs 24 hours a day. There is a joy in this helping, caring role, but the joy is often made possible by knowing that the dependent relationship is short-lived. Total care of a 3, 5, 10, or 20-year-old individual places tremendous strain on any family unit, and the mother, in particular.

The need for total care, including feeding, dressing, and toileting, requires an almost constant vigil. However, this is only one demanding dimension. Parents of these individuals often have feelings of guilt, insecurity, and doubt about their ability to care for this person. If there are other children in the family, they must make allowances for the added attention given to the special child. This is not always easy, depending on the age and disposition of the children who are expected to understand this most difficult situation. Some parents, after first worrying when the child appears to be different from a normal child, tend to accept his often existing abnormal postures and difficulties or his inability to move as inevitable. Thus, one often finds a child of 4, 6, or 8 years of age being treated as a young baby. The parents spoil the child by doing everything for him. By assuming that the child is incapable of normal development, parents quite unwittingly aggravate the difficulties.

Society often exerts pressures on parents to place the retarded child in an institution. A mere stare on the street, a guarded conversation by a neighbor, or reluctance to visit in the home brings about a range of emotions which members of the family are not equipped to handle.

The history of the education of the severely and profoundly retarded is not very noteworthy or illustrious and, therefore, will receive limited comment. Most of the educational opportunities for the severely and profoundly retarded were found in residential schools. It was only at the turn of this century that special classes for any retarded in public school systems were initiated, and they have grown steadily since then. However, no specific program provisions were made for severe and profound retardation, and they became specifically excluded from school. At this time, the concept of the ineducable, an unacceptable term, came to be applied to the lower functioning retarded children.

An increasing number of parents and concerned citizens felt the exclusion concept to be unjust. Gradually, from about 1930 on, local parent organizations began to appear and to take a leadership role. About 1950, these groups consolidated into the National Association for Retarded Children. This group, together with a number of interested professional groups, brought the whole problem of the needs of the retarded into clearer focus. As a result of their efforts, on October 7, 1971, the doctrine establishing a zero reject system of free public education and training for the mentally retarded attained the force of law in the state of Pennsylvania. No longer will a Pennsylvania school system postpone, terminate, or in any way deny the mentally retarded the right to a program of free public education and training.

Although much greater public awareness of the lower functioning mentally retarded may now be observed, much remains to be accomplished in providing appropriate educational opportunities and experiences.

### Curriculum Planning: Goals, Objectives, and Principles

In teaching, an educator should constantly ask, "Why am I teaching this?" In teaching the severely and profoundly retarded, the teacher asks, "Why am I teaching this to these children?" Goals and activities are always interchangeable to some extent. Sometimes it is more convenient to think of a goal and to choose activities that will work toward that goal. On the other hand, nearly all activities provide learning opportunities that contribute to more than one goal.

The educational objectives for the severely and profoundly mentally retarded are quite modest and tend to emphasize adjustment in the practical, self-help, social, and communicative aspects of development. They include, primarily, activities which have been demonstrated to be feasible for these individuals, and which relate to a dependent or semi-independent role in society. The fact must be borne in mind that activity modification may be necessary as new information appears. At present, each teacher should feel free to try out a range of experimental activities in the search for a program adapted to their needs and capabilities. In essence, the basic philosophy should be that severely and profoundly mentally retarded are children and students, and that the goal should be to help each realize his maximum potential, just as it is for every child and student.

In working toward an effective program of intended learning devised by the teacher, many aspects must be considered. It is quite unrealistic for a teacher to offer these children experiences merely because such experiences have always been offered, or because they are the procedures the teacher knows. In order to achieve success in teaching severely and profoundly retarded youngsters, the instructor needs sensitivity to the needs of each child, an awareness of the significance of the students' reactions as expressed through body movement, tension signs, and attempts to verbalize. The teacher must be able also to anticipate behavior, and to determine whether the foreseen behavior should be averted, carried through to frustration or success, or be directed to other goals. Each teacher must be aware of the fact that the entire educational program for the severely and profoundly retarded must be directed at developing skills in basic sensory, motor, self-help, and language areas. Such skills seem essential in beginning any type of learning sequence for these students. The program must be highly structured, and present situations and experiences in which the stimuli to which the children are exposed are carefully controlled. Because of the strict curriculum structure, educators must be careful in teaching by the method of imitation. The students being taught will not only learn the correct methods, but also the incorrect ones by the imitative process. The teacher must guard against responding inappropriately to an inaccurate or incorrect task performance. The child's behavior may seem "cute," but such teacher behavior will usually encourage further undesired responding by the student. The teacher must always be aware of her behavior and then of the child's.

## The Use of the Curriculum

In today's educational process, it is quite natural for teachers to participate in sharing efforts in curriculum planning and development. Ultimately, the translation of the curriculum guide into actual experiences for the students is the responsibility of the teacher. In the case of the severely and profoundly retarded, with a vast variety of classroom locations, ranging from institutional, to public school, to home-bound settings, where the classes are few and geographically isolated, the burden of making the curriculum rests heavily on the individual teacher. Also, such teachers will have particular students under their direction for a much longer period of time than is customary in the regular classes; thus the problems of scope and sequence of the program will depend solely on the specific teacher.

While all teachers generally have their own curriculum ideas and plan, the curriculum within this report may offer the educator some new ideas and methods of teaching the severely and profoundly mentally retarded. It is based on action-oriented programming and classroom use. The focus of the curriculum emphasizes experiences needed by individuals at a very low developmental level. A clear, logical sequence of tasks are then presented to the child. The level and sequence of the various learning experiences depend, to a great extent, on the readiness of the child. In most instances, it will be necessary to break down the experiences into very basic competencies and teach these serially. Detailed procedures in the curriculum will order the task to be taught into small, manageable steps. By utilizing such an approach, it is hoped that no behavior, no matter how small or inconsequential it may seem, will be overlooked or disregarded. The teacher must be perceptive even to the child's cooing and babbling; it means something to the child. Likewise, the teacher must learn that any successes of the child will be very, very small, but most important is the process of developing the child's skill areas.

The curriculum developed for use in teaching the severely and profoundly mentally retarded consists of instructional units in five broad developmental areas: (1) sensory, (2) motor, (3) self-help, (4) language, and (5) perceptual cognitive.

Each unit of instruction will be detailed in a step-by-step manner and organized as follows:

1. INSTRUCTIONAL OBJECTIVE

Each objective specifies the competency to be demonstrated or the behavior the instruction is to produce. Each objective is seen as a basis for setting the dimension of the lesson and provides the format for structuring the activities, evaluating the child's performance, and selecting the resources. Objectives must be well stated and well designed. An instructional objective may involve the child being able to successfully chew and swallow chopped food. A situation must then be developed and structured to produce the desired behavior. Later, the teacher can determine whether or not the instructional objective was achieved, for example.

2. READINESS

Student readiness is the absolute minimum behavioral competency needed to start an instructional objective. Establishing readiness levels is desired to encourage the greatest possible program flexibility. For example, if the instructional objective requires the child to successfully chew and swallow chopped food, the readiness would be that no apparent physiologic impairment is present that would prevent such a behavior. The esophagus must be open sufficiently to pass solids.

3. PROCEDURES

The procedures are the tasks available to the child to facilitate mastery of the instructional objective. The procedures are developmental with complex activities broken down into small, specific teaching tasks. For example, one step in the procedures for achieving the chewing and swallowing objective may require the physical manipulation of the jaws.

4. TASK EVALUATION

The evaluation process is essential in determining the successful completion of an instructional objective and in improving an instructional unit. In order to evaluate educational progress, the major target behavior should be day-to-day performance. For example, evaluation would determine to what extent the child was successful in chewing and swallowing chopped food.

5. MATERIALS AND EQUIPMENT

Most educational activities will require teaching or resource materials and equipment. Suggestions and listed items are provided that might assist the teacher in directing the instructional objectives. For example, in chewing and swallowing chopped food, meatloaf, green beans, carrots, and noodles in bite size form are suggested. It must be pointed out that the vast majority of the materials and equipment used in the curriculum are readily available at nominal costs in any neighborhood variety store or supermarket.

### Charting and Behavior Evaluation

Evaluation is an integral part of our program, and all students are assessed on a number of dimensions at various intervals during the program. It has been found that general screening tests or scales using group data are of questionable practical value because of the tremendous variability within the atypical child population. A more valid comparison for any child is probably his own level of functioning. Assessing the students in terms of percent of time attending to task and nontask stimuli, as well as frequency of specific behaviors, has been of assistance in curriculum planning. It has also been informative to video tape samples of student performance to assess behavioral change, as well as teaching techniques.

One of the most difficult tasks for teachers is to list the behavioral charting procedures that will enable teaching personnel to observe and record the presence and level of various types of behavioral competencies demonstrated by the severely and profoundly retarded.

The Competency Checklists are useful diagnostically, prognostically, and particularly for following the instructional program. The checklist permits the teacher to analyze the specific educational needs of each student. A checklist precedes each of the instructional units and is organized according to the complexity of developmental behavior. It provides the user with a curriculum plan, a series of behavioral expectancies and activities to facilitate behavioral change. Through the instructional program, the teacher will have an accurate determination of the student's present level of functioning. This will also provide goals and a reporting system while involved in instruction.

Observing and reporting behavior is an essential part of the curriculum. Therefore, numerous charts were used. A brief description of the various types of charts that may prove valuable in checking and reporting behavior follows.

### Curriculum Chart (Table 1)

This chart identifies general program areas and the competency levels established for a child. In the example provided eight curriculum areas are used for this particular child. The information within this standardized form will vary, depending on the child and teacher needs. A bar graph at the top of the chart is used to depict the child's present level of competency, ranging from zero blocks (no competency), to four blocks (complete competency). Such a visual representation of the child's level of functioning, stated in broad terms, is an aid to the teacher in readily assessing the child's needs and also achievement. This chart is especially helpful if more than one person is involved in the instructional process.

**Table 1.**
Curriculum Chart

NAME: _____ Howie

| | Tactile Discrimination | Visual Discrimination | Gross Motor | Fine Motor | Feeding/ Drinking | Toilet Training | Undressing/ Dressing | Communication Development |
|---|---|---|---|---|---|---|---|---|
| *No blocks* | No response to tactile stimulus | No response to visual objects | No attempt to move independently | No attempt to hold object | Child is completely dependent in feeding and drinking | Not on toilet training program—dependent in toileting needs | Child is totally dependent in undressing and dressing | No attempt to communicate either through gesture or vocalization |
| *1 block* | Responds to tactile stimulation through visual response to observer; vocalizes, moves, frowns | Turns eyes toward light | Turns head in direction of stimuli, while in a prone position | Grasps object placed in his hand and holds it 2 sec | Swallows when stimulated externally | Demonstrates a reaction to stimulation in genital area | Pulls sock off when it is placed at mid-foot position | Vocally (crying) responds when noise is made |

118

| 2 blocks | 2 blocks | 2 blocks | 2 blocks | 2 blocks | 2 blocks | 2 blocks | 2 blocks |
|---|---|---|---|---|---|---|---|
| Brushes or briefly touches objects | Fixes on object momentarily | Lifts head and shoulders while in a prone position | Brings hands to his face and looks at them | Sucks fluids from a nipple | Remains on potty chair or toilet 5 min with complete assistance | Puts sock on when it is placed just over toes | Echoes sound made by others |

| 3 blocks | 3 blocks | 3 blocks | 3 blocks | 3 blocks | 3 blocks | 3 blocks | 3 blocks |
|---|---|---|---|---|---|---|---|
| Manually explores shape, texture, density and temperature of objects | Follows vanishing stimulus momentarily | Reaches for objects while in a prone position | Reaches out in an attempt to grasp object held in front of him | Moves jaws up and down in response to adult's 3 finger control | Responds inconsistently in bowel habits when on potty or toilet | Takes pants off when both feet are in pant legs and pants are down by ankles | Babbles discriminately in response to simuli |

| 4 blocks | 4 blocks | 4 blocks | 4 blocks | 4 blocks | 4 blocks | 4 blocks | 4 blocks |
|---|---|---|---|---|---|---|---|
| Demonstrates ability to discriminate objects unalike in shape, texture, density and temperature | Follows object moving in circular path | Sits with support | Transfers toy from grasp of one hand to grasp of the other | Chews and swallows finely chopped food | Child has sporadic success when placed on potty or toilet for urination | Child releases one arm from armhole of shirt and pulls shirt off | Imitates gestures made by another |

**Table 2.**
Individual Prescriptive Planning Sheet

| Dennis (Student's Name) | 4-7-75 (Date) | Self-Care (Area Involved) | MES (Educator) | Right-to-Ed Center (Educational Facility) |
|---|---|---|---|---|

### INSTRUCTIONAL OBJECTIVE

To have Dennis successfully feed himself, using a hand-over-hand method of feeding, within a 15-min time period, at a 50% accuracy level

### LEARNING MILIEU

Eating area of classroom

Lunchtime

### STEP BY STEP PROCEDURE

1. Sit Dennis at the lunch table, instructor should sit to his right side.

2. Instructor's hand should be over Dennis' right hand, thus enabling him to hold spoon.

3. Instructor's other hand should be supporting his right elbow.

4. With assistance of the instructor, Dennis should scoop a small amount of food from the bowl and place it in his mouth.

5. The instructor should then guide Dennis' arm and hand back to the bowl.

6. Reward Dennis with a light pat on the left shoulder, paired with the words, "Dennis eats nicely," each time he successfully finishes the sequence.

At lunch table with
instructor sitting to
right side of Dennis

No other children at
table with Dennis

## MATERIALS AND EQUIPMENT
Dennis' therapy spoon
Terry cloth bib
Pink bowl
Dennis' chair with feet
    and side support
Mashed food (so it will
    remain on spoon better)

7. Instructor should be certain to hold Dennis' hand and elbow firmly so
   that he senses the support, but not so tightly as to inhibit his movement,
   or discourage initiative.

## Individual Prescriptive Planning Sheet
## (Table 2)

The individual prescriptive planning sheet provides an analysis of the educational program within a selected curriculum area. It is designed to meet the specific needs of the child, rather than those of the class as a whole, and determines what he is taught as well as how he is taught. A prescription may be written on more than one area. In the planning sheet illustrated, self-feeding was the area of immediate concern; thus the step-by-step procedures have been developed.

## Educational Encounter Report

This report is a detailed narrative of the general classroom procedures and results over a specified time period. It serves as a self-check for the teacher, insuring that the objectives of the specific curriculum areas are effective. A summary of the daily instructional sessions will demonstrate strengths and weaknesses in programming. An example follows:

Name: _____Alex_____      Time period: __Week of March 18, 1975__
Concentration Area:   Self-feeding
Submitted by:   _MES_

*General Procedures.*   Alex was worked with at each meal during the day this week. The majority of the food that was given to him was of the type that could be served in a bowl, such as beef stew, chili, etc. The step-by-step method was followed closely. When Alex began to get tired and lax about holding the spoon, he was fed by the instructor to complete his meal.

*General Results.*   Alex certainly seems to have gained skill this week. His grasp is much stronger and he is completing more of the meal before he tires. I have noticed that his motor development is not improving. It is still necessary at times for Alex to be supported while in the sitting position. His head control is very good.

*Specific Notable Events.*   On Wednesday morning, Alex ate his entire bowl of oatmeal without hesitation. This is particularly notable, since prior to this point he has always tired or become disruptive before finishing the meal.

*Recommendations.*   (1) Continued placement on feeding program. (2) Supplemental grasp development exercises. (3) Supplemental time provided for sitting with minimal support.

## Toilet Training Chart (Table 3)

The toileting chart permits a 2-hour check of the child's elimination control. The factor of time is of critical importance. Significant daily remarks should be recorded.

**Table 3.**
Toilet Training Chart

| Toileting Behavior | | | | | | Name:    Alex |
|---|---|---|---|---|---|---|
| Date | | | Time | | | Remarks |
| March | 7 | 9 | 11 | 1 | 3 | 5 | |
| 13 | Wet | Dry | Wet | Dry | Wet | Wet | Had one success; was dry |
|    | X | U | X | X | X | X | when put on toilet |
| 14 | Wet | Wet | Wet | Wet | Wet | Wet | Went entire day without a |
|    | X | X | X | X | X | X | success on the toilet |
| 15 | Dry | Wet | Wet | Wet | Wet | Dry | Made a B.M. in toilet and |
|    | U | X | U | X | X | BM | was able to urinate twice |
| 16 | Wet | Wet | Dry | Wet | Wet | Wet | Had two successes on the |
|    | X | X | U | X | X | BMU | toilet |
| 17 | Wet | Dry | Dry | Wet | Wet | Dry | Was dry more today, and had two successes on the |
|    | X | U | X | X | X | U | toilet |

X—no results; U—urinated; BM—bowel movement; Wet—wet before placed on toilet; Dry—dry before placed on toilet.

## Happenings Chart (Table 4)

This chart is very helpful in any learning environment. The happenings chart provides a teacher with a means of communicating to others the unexpected successes and accomplishments of the children. It adds a new dimension of perceptiveness to the teacher's role making each an alert observer of new and changing behavior.

**Table 4.**
Happenings Chart

| | | |
|---|---|---|
| Denny F. | 1-22-75 | 9:00 a.m.: took spoonful of food himself and returned spoon to the bowl |
| Bobby S. | 1-31-75 | 4:00 p.m.: turned head in direction of loud noise made to his right side |
| Howie S. | 3-17-75 | 8:30 a.m.: rolled from his stomach to his back |
| Mary M. | 4-11-75 | 12:30 p.m.: pulled feet from basin of cold water while being stimulated with warm and cold water |

A happening is a wonderful thing . . . the first time a child does or says something . . . new!

### The Curriculum

To provide a complete and ready-made curriculum guide is not within the scope of this paper. This would violate one of the basic principles of sound curriculum making, which requires teaching staff participation. This report consists of suggested units of instruction in five basic developmental areas: (1) sensory, (2) motor, (3) self-help, (4) language, and (5) perceptual–cognitive (Tables 5–16).

In order to provide the reader with a fundamental understanding of the format followed in developing the curriculum, examples of competency checklists and instructional units will also be presented.

## COMPETENCY CHECKLIST

Name _____     Educational Facility _____
Date _____     Educator _____

Instructional Unit
Sensory Development
Tactile Discrimination

Criterion:     0  No competency (0% correct response)
               1  Moderate competency (25% correct response)
               2  Adequate competency (75% correct response)
               3  Complete competency (100% correct response)

_____     1.  Child responds to tactile stimulus in the environment.
_____     2.  Child responds to tactile stimulation through visual response to observer; i.e., vocalizes, moves body part, frowns, etc.
_____     3.  Child responds to vibrator stimulation by one of above criteria.
_____     4.  Child responds to brushing stimulation by one of above criteria.
_____     5.  Child responds to icing stimulation by one of above criteria.
_____     6.  Child brushes or briefly touches objects.
_____     7.  Child grabs at and attempts to pick up objects.
_____     8.  Child holds objects.
_____     9.  Child explores shape, texture, density and temperature of objects.
_____     10.  Child shows awareness of ability to discriminate objects that are alike in temperature; i.e., hot air, hot water—cold air, cold water.
_____     11.  Child shows awareness of ability to discriminate objects that are alike in texture and shape.
_____     Total
                      Remarks:

## Instructional Objective

To stimulate the body muscles and circulatory processes through the use of various brushing techniques.

## Readiness

No apparent physiologic impairment that would prevent or inhibit response to tactile stimulation.

## Procedure

1. Lay child on soft surface, as carpeted floor or mattress.
2. Remove child's clothing from area or areas of body to be stimulated.
3. Brushes to be used can range in texture from very soft to quite brisk. They can also range in size from the smallest eyeliner brush to a wallpaper brush, with many in between sizes.
4. In the first trial of brushing stimulation, use a soft brush to guard against any irritation of the child's skin. Gradually move to a harder bristle brush in later encounters.
5. Brushing should take the method of long even strokes. Be aware of any excessive skin irritation and cease the exercise if this happens.
6. This stimulation can be done all over the body, but is usually begun on the hands and feet.
7. The face may be stimulated with a small eyeliner brush. At the corners of the mouth, move the brush in shoft swift movements up and down. (Occasionally this is done to execute a rooting and sucking reflex.) The face may also be stimulated in the area of the cheeks, eyelids, and just below the lower eyelashes.

## Task Evaluation

1. Did the child overtly show discontent with the brushing exercise?
2. Did any affected spastic limbs seem to relax in any way with the brushing?
3. Did the child respond verbally to the brushing?
4. Did any of the face stimulation seem to tickle him? Did he move his hand to his face or rub or scratch the itch?

## Materials and Equipment

Variety of brushes (ranging in texture from very soft to hard)
Carpeted floor or mattress

## COMPETENCY CHECKLIST

Name _____     Educational Facility _____

Date _____     Educator _____

Instructional Unit
Sensory Development
Auditory Discrimination

Criterion:                    0  No competency (0% correct response)
                              1  Moderate competency (25% correct response)
                              2  Adequate competency (75% correct response)
                              3  Complete competency (100% correct response)

_____     1. Child searches for sound with eyes.
_____     2. Child turns head toward source of loud sound.
_____     3. Child reacts positively or negatively to loud noise.
_____     4. Child moves body toward loud sound.
_____     5. Child identifies source of loud sound.
_____     6. Child responds to "no."
_____     7. Child changes activity with change of sound.
_____     8. Child listens to echo.
_____     9. Child listens to own voice recorded.
_____    10. Child listens to music.
_____    11. Child listens to stories.
_____    12. Child listens to imitate.
_____    13. Child demonstrates ability to identify animal sounds.
_____    14. Child demonstrates ability to identify mechanical sounds; i.e., cars, trucks, trains,
                           airplanes, etc.
_____    Total
                       Remarks:

### Instructional Objective
To have child turn head toward source of loud sound.

### Readiness
Child is able to move head voluntarily.
Child hears satisfactorily.

### Procedure
1. Lay child on back on comfortable surface.
2. Child should be in such a location that it is easy to approach him from either side, e.g., a mattress or soft rug in the middle of a room.
3. The adult should kneel behind the child and make a loud noise to one side of the child's head. A bell may be used or a decoder or any other piece of equipment that makes a distinct noise that can be operated by the adult.
4. The object should not be too readily observable, making it necessary for the child to turn his head in order to locate the noise.
5. Repeat the noise making several times, going to each side of the head.
6. It is also a good idea to vary the types of sounds, such as hand clapping, music, bells, decoders, and banging on drums.

### Task Evaluation
1. Did the loud sounds disturb the child?
2. Did he turn his head to each side as he was stimulated by the sound?
3. Did he turn to each direction equally well?
4. Did he seem to be turning because he saw the object or because he was seeking the source of the noise?

### Materials and Equipment
Mattress or soft rug for middle of floor
Bells
Decoders or buzzer
Set of small drums
Transistor radio

## COMPETENCY CHECKLIST

Name _____    Educational Facility _____ ___
Date _____    Educator _____

Instructional Unit
Sensory Development
Visual Discrimination

Criterion:
0 No competency (0% correct response)
1 Moderate competency (25% correct response)
2 Adequate competency (75% correct response)
3 Complete competency (100% correct response)

_____    1. Child turns eyes towards light.
_____    2. Child's eyes fix on object momentarily.
_____    3. Child horizontally tracks within 90° arc (not crossing midline).
_____    4. Child horizontally tracks past midline (greater than 90° arc).
_____    5. Child horizontally tracks within 180° arc—eyes and head.
_____    7. Child moves eyes independently of head in 180° arc.
_____    8. Child follows vanishing stimulus with eyes.
_____    9. Child follows object moving in circular path.
_____    10. Child follows moving object held 18 inches from eyes.
_____    11. Child looks for fallen objects by bending over.
_____    12. Child follows moving object along floor 10 feet away.
_____    13. Child follows object dangling on string 10 feet away.
_____    14. Child identifies familiar objects by sight.
_____    15. Child identifies objects as same when position or settings change.
_____    16. Child matches objects, colors, lengths, size, shape.
_____    17. Child sorts objects, size, shape, color.
_____    18. Child makes fine visual discrimination between objects such as colors, sizes, shapes and letters.
_____    19. Child identifies fine differences in pictures.
_____    20. Child identifies missing parts of pictures.
_____    21. Child reports dominant object in visual field.
_____    22. Child identifies whole object and design when viewed in part.
_____    23. Child recalls three objects after 10-sec exposure when less than 1 min has elapsed.
_____    24. Child recalls more than three objects after 10-sec exposure.
_____    25. Child performs tasks using gross eye–hand coordination movement.
_____    26. Child performs task using fine eye–hand coordination movements.
_____    27. Child recognizes differences in sizes by sight.
_____    28. Child recognizes specific shapes by sight.
_____    29. Child matches according to size.
_____    30. Child matches according to shape.
_____    31. Child sorts according to size.
_____    32. Child sorts according to shapes.
_____    33. Child sorts according to color.
_____    34. Child names item in photograph.
_____    35. Child names item in four-color illustration.
_____    36. Child names item in line drawing.
_____    37. Child associates photograph with drawing of an object.
_____    Total
Remarks:

## Instructional Objective
To have child horizontally track past midline.

## Readiness
Voluntarily moves head left to right and right to left.
Adequate sight to follow object within 3 feet.

## Procedure

1. Position child in order that the visual stimuli is optimally visible.
2. Hold a brightly colored object 3 feet from child's face.
3. Stabilize object in one position until child's eyes fixate on it.
4. As soon as child is fixating on object, slowly move object laterally.
5. Instructor should move object from dominant side to nondominant side of child. Thus child moves head from dominant to nondominant side.
6. If child loses sight of object, stop movement and wait until child fixates on it again.
7. Give a physical or verbal prompt if child hesitates in visually fixating on object.

## Task Evaluation

1. Did child keep his eyes fixated on object when instructor began to move it?
2. Did child keep eyes fixated on object past midline?
3. If child took eyes off object, how long did it take for him to refixate on it?

## Materials and Equipment

Brightly colored object that is visually stimulating to child

## COMPETENCY CHECKLIST

Name _____     Educational Facility _____

Date _____     Educator _____

### Instructional Unit
### Motor Development

Criterion:                    0  No competency (0% correct response)
                              1  Moderate competency (25% correct response)
                              2  Adequate competency (75% correct response)
                              3  Complete competency (100% correct response)

_____   1. Relax spasticity (if not applicable—score 2).
_____   2. Correct body alignment.
_____   3. Direct body movement.
_____   4. Increase voluntary movement on the part of the child.
_____   5. Extend child's arms.
_____   6. Open child's hands.
_____   7. Physically direct child to touch objects.
_____   8. Physically direct and assist child in clutching objects.
_____   9. Physically direct and assist child in grasping objects.
_____  10. Physically direct and assist child to pick up and hold objects.
_____  11. Child moves head in direction of stimulation.
_____  12. Child turns head in prone position.
_____  13. Child lifts head in prone position.
_____  14. Child lifts head and shoulders in prone position.
_____  15. Child assumes elbow rest.
_____  16. Child sits with support.
_____  17. Child side sits with assistance.
_____  18. Child side sits unassisted.
_____  19. Child brings self to a sitting position with assistance.
_____  20. Child brings self to a sitting position without assistance.
_____  21. Child rolls supine to prone.
_____  22. Child exhibits ability to move arms and legs in directed movement.
_____  23. Child exhibits ability to move arms and legs in self-directed movement.
_____  24. Child crawls.
_____  25. Child exhibits protective extension of arms forward.
_____  26. Child exhibits equilibrium reactions when prone.
_____  27. Child exhibits equilibrium reactions when supine.
_____  28. Child maintains creeping position with assistance.
_____  29. Child maintains creeping position alone.
_____  30. Child assumes creeping position.
_____  31. Child gets on hands and knees and rocks.

_____ 32. Child exhibits ability to move arms and legs in left-right progression with directed movement.
_____ 33. Child creeps on hands and knees.
_____ 34. Child allows self to be brought to a standing position.
_____ 35. Child brings self to a standing position with assistance.
_____ 36. Child brings self to a standing position unassisted.
_____ 37. Child stands with support.
_____ 38. Child maintains balance in the standing position.
_____ 39. Child cruises sideways with assistance.
_____ 40. Child cruises sideways without assistance.
_____ 41. Child moves legs and arms in left-right progression.
_____ 42. Child walks with assistance.
_____ 43. Child walks without assistance.
_____ Total
Remarks:

## Instructional Objective
To have child lift head when lying on stomach.

## Readiness
Child is able to remain on stomach for an extended period of time.
Child is able to control head movements; lifts head up and down.
Child balances head.

## Procedure
1. Lay child on stomach on a mattress or soft rug. (Mattress or rug should be in center of room so that child is easily accessible to adult.)
2. The adult should also lie on stomach on the floor directly in front of the child. The child and adult should be face to face.
3. Encourage the child to lift his head by first giving him a small taste of pudding or similar food that he likes.
4. When he has tasted the pudding and realizes that it is on the spoon, hold it just above his head, so that it is necessary for him to lift his head to obtain the food.
5. Reward the child with another small taste of pudding when he lifts his head.
6. Gradually increase the amount of time that you require him to hold his head up before rewarding him.

## Task Evaluation
1. Did the child follow the spoonful of pudding after having the first taste?
2. Would he lift his head up to try and get a second taste?
3. Did the child have to strain any to keep his head up?

## Materials and Equipment
Mattress or small rug
Pudding
Spoon, appropriate size for child

## Instructional Objective
To have child bring self to a sitting position and then sit alone.

## Readiness
Directs arm movements.
Directs leg movements.
Can exert a pushing force with one arm and hand.
Can balance head in a sitting position.

## Procedure
1. Lay child on back on carpeted floor or on blanket placed on floor.
2. Direct child to bring arm over his body and place his hand flat on the floor at shoulder height.
3. When his hand is on the floor, direct him to bring his leg up into a bent-knee position and then over to the floor on the side of the body.
4. When the child's knee is touching the floor he should exert force with the hand and arm and begin to push himself up. If necessary, give him some assistance by a small lift at the shoulders.
5. When he is approaching the sitting position, direct him to place his hand and arm on the floor and then push himself up. If necessary, help him keep his hand flat on the floor.

## Task Evaluation
1. Was child able to bring arm and leg all the way over to side of body?
2. Did he keep the hand flat on the floor and push up with it?
3. Was he able to bring his arm up and place it flat on the floor to give himself support?
4. Did he need much help in bringing his upper torso up?

## Materials and Equipment
Carpeted floor or blanket

## Instructional Objective
To have child begin to creep on hands and knees.

## Readiness
Is able to crawl on abdomen.
Can hold hips off floor

## Procedure
1. Place a bed pillow on the floor.
2. Lay the child on his abdomen over the pillow. Place his hands and arms in such a position that he is holding his head, shoulders, and chest up. Place his knees in a kneeling position, raising hips off floor.
3. Attract the child's attention with a mobile or some other object of interest, thus trying to build the length of time he remains in this position.
4. This exercise should be repeated until the child is able to maintain the position with ease and no longer needs the assistance of the pillow.
5. When the child can maintain the position, moving forward can be accomplished by stimulating the child to move toward something of interest such as the pudding.
6. Reward attempts of the child to move forward.

## Materials and Equipment
Carpeted floor.
Bed pillow
Appropriate reinforcer
Mobile

## COMPETENCY CHECKLIST

Name  _____     Educational Facility _____
Date _____     Educator _____

### Instructional Unit
### Fine-Motor Competency

Criterion:

        0  No competency (0% correct response)
        1  Moderate competency (25% correct response)
        2  Adequate competency (75% correct response)
        3  Complete competency (100% correct response)

_____  1. Child will, while lying on back, follow a moving object or a light with his eyes from the center 2 inches to the left and right side of his head.
_____  2. Child will grasp a toy that is placed in his hand and hold it 3 sec.
_____  3. Child will bring his hands to face and look at them.
_____  4. Child will hold toy placed in his grasp for 10 sec.
_____  5. Child will reach out in an attempt to grasp an object held in front of him.
_____  6. Child will move an object held in his hand to his mouth.
_____  7. Child will feel object placed in his hands by moving his fingers and hands around object.
_____  8. Child will fling ball, toy, or paper without direction.
_____  9. Child will transfer toy from grasp of one hand to grasp of the other.
_____ 10. Child will clap his hands together in imitation of an adult.
_____ 11. Child will roll a ball to an adult in imitation.
_____ 12. Child will place three blocks in a cup in imitation of an adult.

_____ 13. Child will place four rings on a peg in any order.
_____ 14. Child will place large peg into hole in pegboard.
_____ 15. Child will build a tower of two blocks by watching an adult perform this task.
_____ 16. Child will build tower of five to six blocks without aid or imitation.
_____ 17. Child will hold a book and grasp several pages and turn them.
_____ 18. Child will throw ball haphazardly without regard to distance or direction.
_____ 19. Child will string at least four beads in two minutes.
_____ 20. Child will imitate a mark (−), (==), (1) made by holding a pencil or crayon in fist.
_____ 21. Child will grasp and place a medium peg in pegboard without aid.
_____ 22. Child will unwrap candy with verbal cues and without physical help.
_____ 23. Child will turn pages of a book, one at a time.
_____ 24. Child will draw an O in imitation of an adult.
_____ 25. Child will draw a V in imitation of an adult.
_____ 26. Child will use blunt scissors to cut paper held by adult.
_____ 27. Child will throw a large ball with direction.
_____ 28. Child will catch a large ball from a distance of 3 feet.
_____ 29. Child will draw a + in imitation of an adult.
_____ 30. Child will be able to copy a square drawn on paper.
_____ 31. Child will build a pyramid of six blocks in imitation of an adult.
_____ 32. Child will copy a diamond ◇ shaped figure made by an adult.
_____ Total
Remarks:

## Instructional Objective
To have child grasp a toy that is placed in his hand and hold it for 3 sec.

## Readiness
Child directs hand movements.
Child has strength in arm and hand.

## Procedure
1. Take a rattle that is dowel shaped or a small toy with the same shape and place it in the child's hand.
2. Fingers of child's hand should mold around toy easily.
3. Instructor should place her hand around child's and help him shake or squeeze the rattle or toy, so that he receives auditory reinforcement for holding object.
4. Instructor should fade her hand over hand assistance to child by relaxing the amount of pressure she uses to give support.
5. She should eventually fade the amount of physical contact she makes with child's hand.

## Task Evaluation
1. Did child object to having dowel-shaped object placed in hand?
2. Did child drop object as soon as instructor faded physical prompt?

## Materials and Equipment
Dowel-shaped rattle or toy

## Instructional Objective
To have child reach out in an attempt to grasp object held in front of him.

## Readiness
Directs arm movements.
Directs hand movements.
Can focus on object held one foot in front of him.

## Procedure
1. Hold a brightly colored object about 12 inches in front of the child. Retain the object in front of the child for at least a minute.
2. If the child does not reach for the object after 1 min gradually lower it down toward his hand.
3. Continue to lower the object until the child moves his hand to grasp the object or until the object touches the child's hand.

4. Instructor should place child's hand around object and then put her hand over his in order that he maintains the grasp.

5. Reduce physical prompt by releasing grasp of child's entire hand and guide by prompting with touch at wrist.

6. Dowel-shaped objects should be used at first as they are easier to grasp.

## Task Evaluation

1. Did child focus on object?
2. Did he swipe at object in order to attain it?
3. Did he maintain the grasp after the instructor reduced the physical prompt?
4. Did he look at object while grasping it?

## Materials and Equipment

Brightly colored dowel-shaped object

## Instructional Objective

To have the child place three blocks in a cup.

## Readiness

Directs hand movements
Directs arm movements
Grasps
Sits with support

## Procedure

1. Sit child in chair appropriate for his size at table also appropriate for his size.
2. Sit opposite him so he has full view of your movements.
3. Place three 1-inch blocks on table along with a wide-mouthed cup.
4. Instructor should then slowly pick up one block with her dominant hand, while holding the cup with her other hand and place the block in the cup.
5. Instructor should do the same for the next two blocks.
6. Instructor should then put the cup and blocks in front of the child and ask him to do the same.
7. If necessary, the instructor should physically prompt the child by guiding his hand. The physical guide should be faded as soon as the child initiates the action independently.

## Task Evaluation

1. Did child focus on the blocks that were on the table?
2. Did he guide his hand directly to them?
3. Was he able to hold the blocks until he delivered them from the table to the cup?
4. Did he try to take the blocks out of the cup after he put them in?

## Materials and Equipment

Three one-inch blocks
Wide-mouthed cup
Table appropriate for child's size
Chair appropriate for child's size

## COMPETENCY CHECKLIST

Name _____     Educational Facility _____

Date _____     Educator _____

### Instructional Unit
### Self-Care Development
### Feeding–Drinking

Criterion:                    0  No competency (0% correct response)
                              1  Moderate competency (25% correct response)
                              2  Adequate competency (75% correct response)
                              3  Complete competency (100% correct response)

_____  1. Child opens mouth when physically stimulated.
_____  2. Child closes mouth when physically stimulated.
_____  3. Child takes fluid from a dropper while in a reclining position.
_____  4. Child retains liquid in mouth without dribbling.
_____  5. Child swallows when stimulated externally.
_____  6. Child swallows independently.
_____  7. Child performs sucking reflex indiscriminately.
_____  8. Child performs sucking reflex with oral stimulation.
_____  9. Child sucks fluids from nipple.
_____ 10. Child reaches in direction of bottle (nipple) with mouth when being fed.
_____ 11. Child moves jaw up and down in response to adult's three finger feeding control.
_____ 12. Child moves jaw up and down independently.
_____ 13. Child moves tongue in lateral movement when stimulated.
_____ 14. Child moves tongue in lateral movement independently.
_____ 15. Child simultaneously moves jaws up and down and moves tongue laterally.
_____ 16. Child opens mouth voluntarily at sight of spoon.
_____ 17. Child opens mouth and voluntarily takes pureed food from spoon with upper lip.
_____ 18. Child opens mouth and coordinates lips to remove food from a spoon.
_____ 19. Child swallows pureed food.
_____ 20. Child accepts finely chopped food in mouth.
_____ 21. Child holds food in mouth without dribbling.
_____ 22. Child simultaneously moves jaws up and down and tongue in lateral movement.
_____ 23. Child chews with lips closed.
_____ 24. Child swallows masticated foods.
_____ 25. Child accepts chopped food into mouth.
_____ 26. Child retains chopped food in mouth.
_____ 27. Child masticates chopped food.
_____ 28. Child swallows masticated food.
_____ 29. Child touches bottle when held by adult.
_____ 30. Child holds bottle when held by adult.
_____ 31. Child grasps bottle independently while sucking.
_____ 32. Child sucks finger food placed in mouth by adult.
_____ 33. Child masticates finger food placed in mouth.
_____ 34. Child swallows finger foods.
_____ 35. Child squeezes and smears pieces of finger food on table.
_____ 36. Child lifts finger food to mouth.
_____ 37. Child places finger food in mouth.
_____ 38. Child retains finger food in mouth.
_____ 39. Child sucks finger food in mouth.
_____ 40. Child masticates finger food.
_____ 41. Child swallows finger food.
_____ 42. Child accepts small pieces of solid food.
_____ 43. Child retains small pieces of solid food.
_____ 44. Child sucks on small pieces of solid food.
_____ 45. Child masticates small pieces of solid food.
_____ 46. Child swallows small pieces of solid food.
_____ 47. Child retains food in mouth.
_____ 48. Child brings solid food to mouth; holds independently.
_____ 49. Child bites off food self-held.
_____ 50. Child accepts liquid from cup when held by adult.
_____ 51. Child retains liquid in mouth without dribbling.
_____ 52. Child swallows liquid.
_____ 53. Child touches partially full cup and accepts liquid from cup held by adult.
_____ 54. Child closes mouth and retains liquid.
_____ 55. Child holds cup partially full independently with two hands and accepts liquid from cup which has been brought to mouth by adult.
_____ 56. Child independently brings partially full cup to mouth and accepts liquid while holding cup.
_____ 57. Child independently brings partially full cup to mouth and drinks liquid holding cup with one hand.
_____ 58. Child independently brings full cup to mouth and accepts liquid.
_____ 59. Child replaces partially filled cup on table with assistance.
_____ 60. Child replaces cup on table independently.
_____ 61. Child independently replaces cup on table without spilling.
_____ 62. Child grasps spoon with aid of adult.
_____ 63. Child balances food on spoon with aid of adult.

| | |
|---|---|
| _____ | 64. Child brings food to mouth with aid of adult. |
| _____ | 65. Child holds spoon and brings food to mouth, guided by adult. |
| _____ | 66. Child lifts food on spoon to mouth independently. |
| _____ | 67. Child inserts spoon in mouth, turning spoon. |
| _____ | 68. Child inserts spoon in mouth keeping bowl straight. |
| _____ | 69. Child places spoon in dish with aid of adult. |
| _____ | 70. Child places spoon in dish, guided by adult. |
| _____ | 71. Child places spoon in dish independently. |
| _____ | 72. Child scoops small amount of food onto spoon with aid from adult. |
| _____ | 73. Child scoops small amount of food onto spoon with guidance of adult. |
| _____ | 74. Child scoops small amount of food onto spoon using bowl as guide edge. |
| _____ | 75. Child independently scoops small amount of food from plate having an edge. |
| _____ | 76. Child scoops small amount of food onto spoon independently, using dominant hand. |
| _____ | 77. Child independently scoops small amount of food from edgeless plate, without pushing food off the plate. |
| _____ | 78. Child brings fork with piece of food on it to mouth. |
| _____ | 79. Child returns empty fork to bowl or plate. |
| _____ | 80. Child pierces food using fork with adult's assistance. |
| _____ | 81. Child pierces food using fork independently. |
| _____ | Total |

Remarks:

## Instructional Objective
To teach child sucking process.

## Readiness
Esophagus opened sufficiently to permit small amounts of liquids and strained foods to pass easily.

## Procedure
1. With dropper, place moderate amount of apple cider vinegar on child's tongue. Check sensitivity of tongue such as the tip. This may also be done with lemon juice. The vinegar or lemon juice should be placed on the front part of the tongue, rather than the back.

2. This procedure should be followed until the child automatically sucks as soon as a drop of any liquid is placed on the tongue.

## Task Evaluation
Does child's tongue go up to roof of his mouth or make any sucking action when lemon juice or vinegar is placed on it?

## Materials and Equipment
Food dropper
Lemon juice
Apple cider vinegar

## Instructional Objective
To have child sufficiently chew and swallow chopped table food while in a sitting position.

## Readiness
Child is able to chew.
Child is able to swallow solids as well as liquids.
Child balances head.
Child maintains a sitting position.

## Procedure
1. Sit child at a table that enables the instructor to sit opposite.

2. Introduce the child to the food he is going to eat.

3. Put some food on the end of a spoon and place close to the child's mouth. Encourage him to take the food from the spoon with his lips.

4. Notice the child's tongue movements. If they are forward and backward rather than to the side, hold his lips together so that he is unable to move his tongue forward. Thus, he will be unable to push the food from his mouth.

5. Do not permit the child to place the tongue out of the mouth when taking the food. Touch his tongue with your finger until he keeps it in. Then introduce the food.

## Task Evaluation
1. Did child take the food with his lips?
2. Did child move his tongue forward, backward, or push the food out?

## Materials and Equipment
Table that enables child and instructor to sit opposite each other
Chopped table food large enough to require chewing but not quite bite size, including meatloaf, peas, green beans, carrots, and noodles

## Instructional Objective
To have child feed himself regular chopped food, using his fingers.

## Readiness
Balances head.
Remains in a sitting position.
Is able to chew.
Swallows sufficiently while in a sitting position.
Has pincer movement developed to point that child can pick up food with three or four fingers.

## Procedure
1. Sit child at table and make comfortable before introducing food.
2. Instructor should sit opposite child and guide movements.
3. Introduce two or three pieces of bite size food.
4. If child does not begin to pick up food, the instructor should place one of the pieces in the child's hand and guide the hand to the mouth.
5. Step four should be repeated if child does not begin to pick at or play with food first.
6. If child does begin to pick at food, wait until he has a piece of food in his hand and then guide the hand to his mouth.

## Task Evaluation
1. Did child sustain interest in feeding himself?
2. Did child learn that the food was to go into his mouth?
3. Was pincer grasp developed to the point where child delivered the food from the table to the mouth without dropping it several times?
4. Did child eat the food or play with it?

## Materials and Equipment
Table which enables instructor to sit opposite child
Bite-size pieces of food, such as french fries or pieces of meatloaf

### COMPETENCY CHECKLIST

Name _____  Educational Facility_____

Date _____  Educator _____

### Instructional Unit
### Self-Care Development
### (Dressing)

Criterion:                          0  No competency (0% correct response)
                                    1  Moderate competency (25% correct response)
                                    2  Adequate competency (75% correct response)
                                    3  Complete competency (100% correct response)

_____  1. Child pulls sock off when it is just over his toes.
_____  2. Child pulls sock off when it is placed at his midfoot.
_____  3. Child pulls sock off when it is positioned at the heel.
_____  4. Child pulls sock off when it is around the ankle.
_____  5. Child removes sock independently.
_____  6. Child pulls sock on from ankles.
_____  7. Child pulls sock on from heel.

_____  8. Child pulls sock on from midfoot.
_____  9. Child pulls sock on from when it has been placed just over his toes.
_____  10. Child puts sock on independently.
_____  11. Child takes pants off when just one foot is in pant leg and the pants are down by ankles.
_____  12. Child takes pants off when both feet are in pant legs and pants are down by ankles.
_____  13. Child takes pants off when they are by his knees.
_____  14. Child takes pants off when they are positioned by hips.
_____  15. Child takes pants off independently.
_____  16. Child pulls pants on when they are on his hips.
_____  17. Child pulls pants up from knees.
_____  18. Child pulls pants up from ankles.
_____  19. Child puts one foot in pant leg and pulls pants up.
_____  20. Child puts pants on independently.
_____  21. Child removes shirt when it is sitting on top of his head.
_____  22. Child removes shirt when it is at eye level on his face.
_____  23. Child removes shirt when it is around his neck.
_____  24. Child releases one arm from the armhole and pulls the shirt up and over his head.
_____  25. Child releases both arms from the armholes and pulls shirt up and over his head.
_____  26. Child removes shirt when it is placed at midstomach.
_____  27. Child removes shirt independently.
_____  28. Child pulls shirt down from midstomach.
_____  29. Child pulls shirt down from under armpits.
_____  30. Child puts one arm in armhole and pulls shirt into position.
_____  31. Child puts both arms in armholes and pulls shirt into position.
_____  32. Child pulls shirt down from eye level, puts both arms in armholes, and pulls shirt into position.
_____  33. Child puts shirt on independently.
_____  34. Child takes shoes off when only tips of toes are in them.
_____  35. Child takes shoe off when heel and back part of foot are released from shoe.
_____  36. Child takes shoe off independently.
_____  37. Child puts shoe on by pushing heel into proper position.
_____  38. Child puts shoe on when heel is completely out of shoe.
_____  39. Child puts shoe on when just tips of toes are in shoe.
_____  40. Child puts shoe on independently.
_____  41. Child takes hat off when it is sitting on the top of his head.
_____  42. Child takes hat off when it is pulled halfway into position.
_____  43. Child takes hat off independently.
_____  44. Child puts hat on when it is placed halfway on head.
_____  45. Child puts hat on when it is sitting on top of his head.
_____  46. Child puts hat on independently.
_____  47. Child removes mitten when thumb is released and mitten is only partially on four fingers.
_____  48. Child removes mitten when it is halfway over thumb and positioned properly over four fingers.
_____  49. Child takes mitten off independently.
_____  50. Child puts mitten on when thumb and four fingers are positioned in it properly and mitten is halfway on.
_____  51. Child puts mitten on when it is only one-fourth of the way on.
_____  52. Child puts mitten on independently.
_____  53. Child can take coat off when hand and arm are released from sleeve and coat is sitting on shoulder.
_____  54. Child takes coat off independently.
_____  55. Child puts coat on by pushing arm and hand through armhole when positioned at armhole and rest of coat is positioned.
_____  56. Child puts coat on by bringing arm around back to armhole of coat, placing arm and hand in armhole and bringing coat into proper position.
_____  57. Child puts coat on when it is held for him at side.
_____  58. Child puts coat on independently.
_____  59. Child opens snaps when hands are positioned properly.
_____  60. Child opens snaps independently.
_____  61. Child closes snaps, when top snap is positioned on bottom, but not fastened.
_____  62. Child closes snaps independently.
_____  63. Child opens zipper when zipper is three-quarters of the way down.
_____  64. Child opens zipper when zipper is halfway down.
_____  65. Child opens zipper independently.
_____  66. Child closes zipper when zipper is three-quarters of the way up.

                67. Child closes zipper when zipper is halfway up.
                68. Child closes zipper when zipper is one-fourth of the way up.
                69. Child closes zipper independently.
                70. Child unbuttons clothing when button is three-quarters of the way through buttonhole.
                71. Child unbuttons clothing when button is halfway through buttonhole.
                72. Child unbuttons clothing independently.
                73. Child buttons clothing when button is three-quarters of the way through the buttonhole.
                74. Child buttons clothing when button is halfway through buttonhole.
                75. Child buttons clothing independently.
                Total
                Remarks:

## Instructional Objective

To have child successfully pull sock off when it is at the ankle position.

## Readiness

Child can grasp.
Child directs arm movements.
Child directs hand movements.
Child directs foot movements.
Child directs leg movements.
Child can compensate for any move to right or left, forward or backward, while in a sitting position.

## Procedure

1. Sit child on chair.
2. Sit on chair.
3. Place sock at ankle position.
4. Give him the command, "(name), take your sock off!"
5. Direct the child to bend at the waist and grasp the top of the sock with both hands. Four fingers should be on the outside and thumb should be on the inside between the foot and sock.
6. Direct him to push the sock down and over the heel and then off the foot.
7. Repeat steps 4, 5, and 6 until child is consistently successful.

## Task Evaluation

1. Did child maintain good balance when bending over to grasp the sock?
2. Did he grasp the sock firmly or did it just keep slipping from his hand?
3. Did he pull the sock off in a smooth motion?
4. Did child exhibit any problem in grasping the sock and pushing it off the foot?
5. How long did it take the child to become consistently successful?

## Materials and Equipment

Chair appropriate to child's size
Chair for instructor that enables him to be at eye level with the child
Sock slightly larger than what the child might normally wear

## Instructional Objective

To have child successfully pull pants up from hip position.

## Readiness

Child can grasp.
Directs arm movements.
Directs hand movements.
Can remain in standing position.

## Procedure

1. Pull slacks to child's hips.
2. Command child to stand up; aid him if necessary.
3. Seat child on chair that brings you to eye level with him.
4. Give him the command, "(name), put your pants on!"
5. Place child's hands on the waist band of the pants by his hips. His four fingers should be on the outside, thumb on the inside.

6. In a hand-over-hand manner, help the child to pull the pants into position.
7. Repeat steps 4, 5, and 6 until the child is consistently successful.

## Task Evaluation
1. Did the child grasp the waist band of the pants firmly or did they keep slipping out of his hands?
2. Did he bring his pants up in a smooth motion or did he pull and tug at them?
3. How long did it take before the child was consistently successful?

## Materials and Equipment
Chair that brings instructor to eye level with child
Chair for child appropriate for his size
A pair of slacks with elastic waist band larger than what the child would normally wear

## Instructional Objective
To have child put both arms in armholes and pull shirt down into place.

## Readiness
Child can grasp.
Directs arm movements.
Directs hand movements.

## Procedure
1. Place child in a sitting position.
2. Give him the command, "(name), put your shirt on!"
3. The shirt should be over the child's head and in position around the child's neck; both arms should be released from the armholes.
4. With the child's hand holding the bottom of the shirt down and out, have him move his hand up and through the armhole.
5. In the same manner, have the child hold the bottom of the shirt down and out while the child moves his other hand and arm up and through the armhole.
6. For steps 4 and 5, the child may need the instructor's hand over hand assistance.
7. When the child puts both arms in the armholes, he should pull the shirt into place.
8. Repeat the process until the child sufficiently goes through the steps himself.

## Task Evaluation
1. Did the child experience difficulty in holding the shirt out with one hand while putting the other through the hole?
2. How much practice did the child need before he could perform the task himself?

## Materials and Equipment
Chair appropriate to child's size
Chair that allows instructor to be at approximately eye level with child
Polo shirt larger than what the child might wear but no so large that it falls into place

## COMPETENCY CHECKLIST

Name _____     Educational Facility_____

Date _____     Educator _____

### Instructional Unit
### Self-Care Development
### (Washing and Bathing)

Criterion:

        0 No competency (0% correct response)
        1 Moderate competency (25% correct response)
        2 Adequate competency (75% correct response)
        3 Complete competency (100% correct response)

_____     1. Child remains in bathtub for an extended period of time.
_____     2. Child plays in bathroom sink by keeping hands under running water.
_____     3. Child attempts to wash self with a washcloth.

_____ 4. Child tries to apply soap to the washcloth.
_____ 5. Child washes all parts of his body except face.
_____ 6. Child dries self with assistance.
_____ 7. Child helps adult wash and dry his face.
_____ 8. Child washes and dries hands and face independently.
_____ Total
Remarks:

### Instructional Objective
To have child attempt to wash body with washcloth while in bathtub or with hands at sink.

### Readiness
Child has good head balance.
Child sits without support.
Child has grasp.
Child stands at sink by himself or with grasp support.

### Procedure
1. Fill bathtub with water to cover child's legs while he is sitting or fill bathroom sink about one-third way full. The water should be lukewarm.
2. Attract child's attention by saying, "(name), let's take a bath!"
3. Assist child into bathtub and command him to sit down. Bath mat is recommended to prevent slipping.
4. Hand child the washcloth and in a hand-over-hand method assist him in washing himself.
5. The communication during this period should be as follows: "(name), wash your arm!" Follow through, "(name), wash your stomach!" Follow through and continue to other parts of the body.
6. Go over the child's entire body by naming the parts before helping him wash.
7. Again, when the child is at the sink, give him the command "(name), wash your hands!"

### Task Evaluation
1. Did child maintain good grasp on washcloth?
2. Did child resist having washcloth cross any body parts?
3. Did he begin to follow commands after naming parts of the body several times?

### Materials and Equipment
Fully equipped bathroom with tub and sink
Washcloth
Bath mat
Lukewarm water

### COMPETENCY CHECKLIST

Name _____ Educational Facility_____
Date _____ Educator _____

Instructional Unit
Self-Care Development
(Nasal Hygiene)

Criterion:
0 No competency (0% correct response)
1 Moderate competency (25% correct response)
2 Adequate competency (75% correct response)
3 Complete competency (100% correct response)

_____ 1. Child does not avoid having his nose cleaned with a tissue.
_____ 2. Child recognizes the need to clean nose and seeks assistance.
_____ 3. Child cleans nose with assistance.
_____ 4. Child tries to clean nose, but is unable to blow nose properly.
_____ 5. Child secures a tissue to clean nose independently.

_____     6. Child cleans nose independently.
_____     Total
                   Remarks:


## Instructional Objective
To have child clean nose with assistance.

## Readiness
Grasps.
Attends to adult.
Imitates adult's actions.
Is not afraid to touch his nose with tissue.

## Procedure
1. Attract child's attention by saying, "(name), let's blow your nose!"
2. Take tissue and hand it to child. In a hand-over-hand method, guide his hand to his nose.
3. When he has the tissue at his nose, give him the command, "(name), blow your nose!"
4. If he does not follow through, make the blowing sound in hope that he will imitate.
5. Reward any effort on his part to blow his nose.
6. When he has finished, command him to throw the tissue away.
7. Make certain that there is a wastebasket nearby and that he disposes of the tissue properly.

## Task Evaluation
1. Did child hold tissue after it was given to him?
2. Did he resist the adult's efforts to guide his hand to his nose?
3. Did he understand what he had to do to make the air come through his nose to remove any mucus in the nose?
4. Did he dispose of the tissue properly?

## Materials and Equipment
Tissue
Wastebasket

### COMPETENCY CHECKLIST

Name _____     Educational Facility_____
Date _____     Educator _____

### Instructional Unit
### Self-Care Development
### (Oral Hygiene)

Criterion:              0  No competency (0% correct response)
                        1  Moderate competency (25% correct response)
                        2  Adequate competency (75% correct response)
                        3  Complete competency (100% correct response)

_____     1. Child is not afraid of toothbrush.
_____     2. Child becomes accustomed to the taste of toothpaste.
_____     3. Child permits adult to brush his teeth.
_____     4. Child brushes own teeth with the assistance of the adult.
_____     5. Child brushes teeth with no assistance.
_____     6. Child puts toothpaste on brush with assistance.
_____     7. Child readies toothbrush and brushes teeth.
_____     Total
                   Remarks:


## Instructional Objective
To have child put toothpaste on toothbrush with assistance and brush his teeth by himself.

## Readiness

Grasps.
Directs arm movements.
Directs hand movements.
Can hold toothbrush steady with hand.
Can exert force in squeezing with hand, thumb and fingers.
Drinks unassisted from cup.

## Procedure

1. Attract child by saying, "(name), let's brush your teeth!"
2. Go to him and accompany him into the bathroom; lead him to the sink.
3. If he is too short to comfortably use the bathroom sink, a small pair of steps should be available for him to stand on.
4. Hand toothbrush to child, expecting him to take it with his hand.
5. Hand him the toothpaste. He should take this with his other hand.
6. In a hand-over-hand manner, assist him in squeezing the toothpaste from the tube. He should do this by grasping the tube with the thumb on one side and the four fingers on the other, then squeeze.
7. You should instruct the child to use the toothpaste sparingly.
8. To put the toothpaste on the brush, have the child bring the toothbrush to the opening of the tube of toothpaste. The opening of the tube should be pointed downward.
9. He should hold the toothbrush steady and move the toothpaste along the bristles to spread on the brush.
10. When the toothbrush is readied, give him the command, "(name), brush your teeth!"
11. When he is finished brushing, encourage him to rinse the toothpaste from his mouth by taking a mouthful of water.

## Task Evaluation

1. Did the child hold the toothbrush steady with one hand, while squeezing the toothpaste with the other?
2. Was the child able to exert enough force with his hand to get some toothpaste out of the tube?
3. Were the child's motions steady enough to hold the toothbrush with one hand and spread the toothpaste with the other?
4. Did he clean and rinse his teeth adequately without the help of the adult?

## Materials and Equipment

Fully equipped bathroom
Child's toothbrush
Toothpaste
Small paper or plastic cup
Water
Small pair of steps

## COMPETENCY CHECKLIST

Name _____     Educational Facility_____
Date _____     Educator _____

### Instructional Unit
### Self-Care Development
### (Toileting)

Criterion:

0 No competency (0% correct response)
1 Moderate competency (25% correct response)
2 Adequate competency (75% correct response)
3 Complete competency (100% correct response)

_____ 1. Child exhibits movement in response to physical stimulus by others.
_____ 2. Child demonstrates a reaction to stimulation in genital area.
_____ 3. Child responds to warm water in genital area.
_____ 4. Child responds to manual stimulation on external and internal thighs.
_____ 5. Child is capable of chewing and swallowing finest chopped food.
_____ 6. Child is capable of chewing and swallowing chopped food.
_____ 7. Child is capable of chewing and swallowing bite-sized food.
_____ 8. Child is using bottle at frequent times for fluid intake.
_____ 9. Child is using bottle to supplement nutritional level and is not dependent upon it as the sole source of sustenance.

_____   10. Child is using bottle or glass for satisfaction of thirst.
_____   11. Child produces a solid stool once or twice a day.
_____   12. Child produces a solid stool once a day.
_____   13. Child produces a solid stool once a day at a regular time.
_____   14. Child urinates at some given times; i.e., after naps, meals, activities.
_____   15. Child is dry from 1 to 2 hours, permitting a toilet training schedule to be implemented.
_____   16. Child demonstrates head balance in sitting position with assistance.
_____   17. Child demonstrates upper torso balance in sitting position with lower extremities held.
_____   18. Child demonstrates head balance in sitting position with no assistance.
_____   19. Child demonstrates upper torso balance in sitting without restraint.
_____   20. Child can maintain a sitting position without assistance for 5 min.
_____   21. Child will remain on potty with direct assistance for 5 min.
_____   22. Child will stay on potty chair with constant supervision for 5 min.
_____   23. Child will stay on potty chair with limited supervision for 5 min.
_____   24. Child will stay on potty chair with *no* supervision for 5 min.
_____   25. Child will remain on toilet for 5 min when held by an adult.
_____   26. Child will remain on toilet for 5 min when prompted by an adult.
_____   27. Child demonstrates the upper extremity strength to balance body weight in moving self to sitting position.
_____   28. Child demonstrates the arm and hand control to hold himself on potty using arms, and on toilet without using arms to maintain balance.
_____   29. Child can use arm control to lift and slide from potty and later from toilet.
_____   30. Child responds inconsistently in bowel habits when on the potty or toilet.
_____   31. Child responds and begins to display some consistent body awareness and resulting muscle control when placed on the potty.
_____   32. Child responds inconsistently in bowel habit to being placed on a toilet at a specified period.
_____   33. Child responds inconsistently to bladder control when placed on or in front of toilet or standing urinal.
_____   34. Child responds and begins to display some consistent body awareness and resulting muscle control when placed on or in front of toilet or standing urinal.
_____   35. Bowel and bladder control regulated to certain times of the day; regular success on the toilet.
_____   36. Gestures toilet needs.
_____   37. Moves to toilet unattended.
_____   38. Child grasps waistband of pants with palmar movement with thumb inside the band.
_____   39. Child pushes outer pants to knee level.
_____   40. Child grasps band of underpants with thumb inside the band, on each side, and pulls up.
_____   41. Child pulls up outer pants in same manner as underpants.
_____   42. Child cares for personal cleanliness in bathroom.
_____   43. Child uses toilet appropriately and independently.
_____   Total
                   Remarks:


## Instructional Objective

Child is dry from 1 to 2 hours, permitting a toilet training schedule to be implemented.

## Readiness

Child is on a regular schedule for meals.
Child eats table food.
Child begins to become regular in voiding after meals, bedtime, naps, and active play periods.
Child should be ready to wear training pants rather than diapers.

## Procedure

1. Take careful notice when child eliminates in pants. This can be done by checking the child every 10 min for a period of at least 5 days and marking the results on a chart. The chart should be similar to the one below.

| 9:40—Dry | 1:20—Dry |
| 9:20—Wet | 1:30—BM & Wet |
| 9:30—Dry | 1:40—Dry |
| 9:10—Dry | 1:50—Dry |

This chart should be readily accessible.

2. When the 5-day period is completed, and it is felt that an accurate accounting of the child's eliminating behavior has been obtained, the chart should be analyzed as to the approximate time of day the child eliminates. Similarities in time of

day for several days should be noted. If the results are not uniform, this may be an indication that, because of the irregularity in eliminating, the child is not yet ready to be put on a toileting schedule.

3. When the chart has been analyzed and specific times of the day are found to be eliminating periods, a schedule for toileting should be made to correspond to the eliminating times. Initially, the child should be placed on the potty every 2 hours for a 10-min period. The following is an example of an appropriate toilet training schedule:

Sun.

| | |
|---|---|
| 7:15 | After awakening |
| 9:15 | After breakfast |
| 11:15 | After play |
| 1:15 | After lunch |
| 3:15 | After nap |
| 5:15 | After dinner |
| 7:15 | After play |
| 9:15 | Before bed |

4. The above schedule allows for the child to be placed on the potty at times when it is most probable that he will eliminate.

## Task Evaluation

1. Was there any similarity in the eliminating periods of the child?
2. Did the child void in his pants any more than once every 1 or 2 hours?
3. Did you notice if the child voided regularly after meals, naps, and vigorous play periods?

## Materials and Equipment

Chart, with attached pen, that shows elimination periods measured for 5 days at intervals of 10 min.
Training pants.

## Instructional Objective

To have child sit on potty chair with assistance.

## Readiness

Is able to remain in a sitting position with the assistance of a potty chair guard.
Is aware that bathroom is different than playroom or bedroom.
Freely accepts bathroom atmosphere.

## Procedure

1. Attract child's attention by stating, "(name), let's go to the potty!"
2. Go to child and accompany him into the bathroom.
3. Direct child to potty and assist him in taking pants down.
4. Guide child into a sitting position on the potty.
5. The above three steps should be accompanied with much verbalization on the part of the adult to reassure the child and to calm his fears or doubts about what is occurring in the bathroom.
6. The chair guard should be positioned properly to reassure the child that he is safe in the potty chair.
7. The 10 min on the potty should be spent supervised by the adult.
8. The 10-min period should not be unpleasant and the child should be kept as interested as possible.

## Task Evaluation

1. Did child accept bathroom and potty without undue fear?
2. Did he remain seated on the potty for the 10-min period, or did he try to squeeze out of the chair?

## Materials and Equipment

Fully equipped bathroom
Potty chair appropriate for child's size with guard for support
Pants with elastic waistband

## Instructional Objective

To have the child relax and achieve results when placed on the potty.

## Readiness

Child's eliminating has been studied and implemented into a toileting schedule.

## Procedure

1. Attract the child's attention by saying, "(name), let's go to the potty!"

2. Go to the child and accompany him to the bathroom.

3. Direct child to the potty and assist him in taking his pants down.

4. Guide child into a sitting position on the potty.

5. Assure the child while on the potty by talking to him and petting him gently.

6. There are various things that can be done to encourage the child to void while on the potty. Some of these are:

    a. Turning on the water faucet in the sink or bathtub, whichever is more visible to the child. The water should run out in a slow stream.

    b. Squirting the child with warm water in the area of the genitals may also aid him in voiding.

    c. Petting the child gently in soft even strokes on the upper thighs or by the genitals may aid in eliminating.

7. Stay close to the child. If he should eliminate, reward him immediately. The reward can be a favorite toy, a piece of sugar-coated cereal, or something else of which the child is fond.

8. Much attention should be given to the fact that the child was successful on the potty.

9. If the child does not eliminate on the potty in the 10-min period, take him off as nonchalantly as possible. Do not praise or scorn.

10. Remember to mark the toilet training chart appropriately in the time slot with either a U for urinate, BM for bowel movement or X for no success.

11. The child may urinate shortly after he has been taken off the potty. This should not be looked at as negative behavior. It is very likely showing that the child's bladder muscles are beginning to respond appropriately to sitting on the potty.

## Task Evaluation

1. Was the child relaxed on the potty, or did he cry and try to squeeze out of the chair?

2. Did the petting or squirting of water in the area of the genitals aid him in eliminating?

3. If the child was successful, did he seem to realize what he did?

4. Did he connect the reward with voiding in the potty?

## Materials and Equipment

Fully equipped bathroom
Potty chair with guard
Squeeze bottle with squirting spout
Toilet training chart
Pants with elastic waistband
Reward appropriate for child

## COMPETENCY CHECKLIST

Name ———————————————————  Educational Facility———————————

Date ———————————————————  Educator ———————————————

### Instructional Unit
### Language Development
### (Language)

Criterion:

0 No competency (0% correct response)
1 Moderate competency (25% correct response)
2 Adequate competency (75% correct response)
3 Complete competency (100% correct response)

——————————  1. Child cries or makes noise indiscriminately, child coos.
——————————  2. Child responds to loud noise.
——————————  3. Child physically moves when noise is made.
——————————  4. Child vocally responds (crying) when noise is made.
——————————  5. Activity of child diminishes when sound is made.
——————————  6. Child reaches or turns toward noise made behind head.
——————————  7. Child moves part of body toward direction of noise.
——————————  8. Child turns head toward direction of noise.
——————————  9. Child looks in general direction of noise.
——————————  10. Child looks in general direction of noise within 5 sec of when noise is made.
——————————  11. Child attends to dominant sound while others are present.
——————————  12. Child locates sources of sound out of sight by turning head in general direction of sound.
——————————  13. Child cries in response to angry vocal tone.
——————————  14. Child stops crying, smiles, and has relaxed cooing movement to friendly vocal tone.

———————— 15. Child locates sources of sound out of sight by turning in general directions of sound.
———————— 16. Child moves tongue in various positions in order to develop muscles for speech.
———————— 17. Child gurgles.
———————— 18. Child grunts or makes other sound through throat.
———————— 19. Child echoes own sound.
———————— 20. Child echoes sound made by others.
———————— 21. Child discriminately makes throat sounds in response to stimuli.
———————— 22. Child indiscriminately babbles.
———————— 23. Child echoes own babbling.
———————— 24. Child echoes babbling when another person babbles.
———————— 25. Child babbles discriminately in response to stimuli.
———————— 26. Child makes gross, nonspecific sounds by movement of lips and mouth.
———————— 27. Child makes specific "m" sound.
———————— 28. Child echoes "m" sound when made by self.
———————— 29. Child echoes "m" sound when made by another person.
———————— 30. Child makes specific "b" sound.
———————— 31. Child echoes "b" sound when made by self.
———————— 32. Child echoes "b" sound when made by another person.
———————— 33. Child makes specific "p" sound.
———————— 34. Child echoes "p" sound when made by self.
———————— 35. Child echoes "p" sound when made by another person.
———————— 36. Child responds indiscriminately.
———————— 37. Child imitates gesture made by another person.
———————— 38. Child responds gesturally to cue gesture.
———————— 39. Child responds gesturally to cue gesture accompanied with sound.
———————— 40. Child responds to simple verbal commands.
———————— 41. Child associates family member with name.
———————— 42. Child says "da-da," "ma-ma" appropriately.
———————— 43. Child recognizes own name when spoken.
———————— 44. Activity stops when he/she hears "no-no."
———————— 45. Child imitates nonspeech sounds.
———————— 46. Child says additional word besides "da-da" and "ma-ma."
———————— 47. Child uses a variety of sounds.
———————— 48. Child imitates simple sounds.
———————— 49. Child combines several vowel sounds.
———————— 50. Child attempts to imitate group of words (sentence) by making several sounds in a row, not necessarily with similar inflection (accurate imitation).
———————— 51. Child waves and claps in response to verbal request.
———————— 52. Child understands simple verbal commands without gestures.
———————— 53. Child tries to imitate gesture and concurrent speech with babbling and appropriate inflection.
———————— 54. Child babbles when gesturing (e.g., babbles while pointing) independently.
———————— 55. Child indicates wants by pointing and vocalizing (with appropriate inflections, not words) e.g., positive inflection, expressions to unfavorable stimuli (removal of food).
———————— 56. Child imitates appropriate number of syllables in simple word.
———————— 57. Child imitates beginning sound of simple word appropriately.
———————— 58. Child imitates simple one-syllable word approximately.
———————— 59. Child imitates simple one-syllable word discernably.
———————— 60. Child imitates sound of object's name when object is shown and its name is said simultaneously (e.g., milk, cup, ball).
———————— 61. Child says appropriate name of object when object is shown to him.
———————— 62. Child imitates touching and says name of body part when person does this.
———————— 63. Child imitates touching of body part when other person simultaneously touches body part and says name.
———————— 64. Child touches appropriate body part when other person says name (person does not touch part).
———————— 65. Child says body part when other person points to it.
———————— 66. Child responds yes or no appropriately when stimulus is presented to him.
———————— Total
Remarks:

# Instructional Objective
To have child imitate sounds.

## Readiness
Attends to adult.
Reacts to noises.
Vocalizes sounds.

## Procedure
1. Seat child on chair.
2. Sit on chair
3. While holding a baby doll or some other familiar object, repeat the word "baby" or other appropriate names several times. While repeating, show the object to the child.
4. Reward the child appropriately for an approximation of the word.
5. When the child makes an attempt at the word, try to build a communication repertoire with him by repeating the sounds that he made and rewarding him if he makes them back.

## Task Evaluation
1. Did the child attend to the adult when speaking to him?
2. Did he seem to associate the word with the object?
3. Did he make any attempt to verbalize in response to the adult?
4. Did he repeat the sound that he initially made after the adult made it?

## Materials and Equipment
Chair, appropriate size for child
Chair for adult that brings him to eye level with the child
Baby doll or any other object of which the child may be able to verbalize the sound

## Instructional Objective
To have child respond to simple verbal commands.

## Readiness
Has adequate vision.
Has adequate hearing.
Directs body movements.
Attends to adult.
Vocalizes voluntarily.

## Procedure
1. The object of this exercise is to build, by imitation, the child's response to gestures and verbalizations. This can be done while working with two or three children. If working with more than one child, make sure that they are congenial and not distracting to each other.
2. Sit with the children and make sure that all children can see you.
3. Begin by requesting that the children attend to you. Reward each child who attends to you. Ignore those who do not attend.
4. When you have each child's attention, begin a "do this game."
5. Start the game with a simple gesture such as a wave and the command, "(name), do this!" Reward each child who imitates the task. Repeat the command and gesture.
6. When each child has successfully imitated the gesture, begin to use other gestures. Repeat until the child is consistently successful.
7. Next, begin to work on verbalizations by starting with simple words such as "ma-ma." Give the command, "(name), say 'ma-ma'!" Repeat until the child is consistently successful.
8. Reward each verbalization made by the child. Add words to increase the child's verbalization.

## Task Evaluation
1. Did the child attend to you?
2. Did the child realize that he was being rewarded for imitating your actions or words?
3. Did the child achieve any imitations or verbalizations on a consistent basis?

## Materials and Equipment
Chair, appropriate size for the child
Chair for adult

## Instructional Objective
To have child move tongue in various positions.

## Readiness

Opens and closes mouth voluntarily.
Directs tongue movements.

## Procedure

1. Seat child on chair using support if necessary.
2. With tongue depressor or index finger, spread a moderate amount of peanut butter or jelly on outer perimeter of the lips.
3. Place a mirror in front of the child.
4. Standing behind the child, demonstrate the tongue movement that you want the child to imitate.
5. He should stretch his tongue out and lick the food off the outside of the lips.
6. If the child does not imitate the motion, stimulate him to bring his tongue out of his mouth by touching it with a tongue depressor or by giving him a small taste of the food.
7. To have the child move his tongue laterally inside his mouth, place peanut butter on either his right or left jaw inside his mouth.
8. In order to get the peanut butter off, he will have to move his tongue.
9. Keep his hands occupied, so that he does not use them to remove the food.
10. Similar exercises should be used to have child move tongue up and down, backward and forward and between the teeth and lips.

## Task Evaluation

1. Did the child become irritated when the jelly or peanut butter was put around or in his mouth?
2. Did he imitate the instructor's movements?
3. Did child initiate any movement of his own to remove the food?

## Materials and Equipment

Chair appropriate size for child
Tongue depressor
Peanut butter
Jelly
Mirror

## COMPETENCY CHECKLIST

Name _____ Educational Facility_____

Date _____ Educator _____

### Instructional Unit
### Perceptual Cognitive Competency

Criterion:

    0 No competency (0% correct response)
    1 Moderate competency (25% correct response)
    2 Adequate competency (75% correct response)
    3 Complete competency (100% correct response)

_____ 1. Child reacts to disappearance of face: "peek-a-boo."
_____ 2. Child anticipates being lifted.
_____ 3. Child's visual regard of objects is present.
_____ 4. Child recognizes a few familiar people.
_____ 5. Child looks for fallen object.
_____ 6. Child consistently tries to reach.
_____ 7. Child responds to "bye-bye."
_____ 8. Child will lift cup to obtain object underneath.
_____ 9. Child recognizes self in mirror.
_____ 10. Child unwraps a cube covered with a piece of tissue or cloth.
_____ 11. Child attempts to imitate scribble on demand.
_____ 12. Child places round blocks in a shapes formboard.
_____ 13. Child uses four to six words in vocabulary.
_____ 14. Child "shows" shoes, clothing, toys, etc., to family and familiar friends.
_____ 15. Child spontaneously scribbles.
_____ 16. Child names any one object; i.e., in response to "what's this?"
_____ 17. Child begins to understand use of familiar objects.

_____  18. Child places round and square blocks in formboard.
_____  19. Child repeats single words heard.
_____  20. Child puts large pegs in a pegboard.
_____  21. Child points to four parts of a doll: eye, hand, nose, etc.
_____  22. Child builds a four-block tower.
_____  23. Child knows concept of "one" as opposed to "many more than one."
_____  24. Child begins to sense ownership: "my."
_____  25. Child understands two prepositions: "with," "to," etc.
_____  26. Child completes three-shape formboard; i.e., circle, square, triangle.
_____  27. Child imitates crayon strokes, both vertical and horizontal.
_____  28. Child names any five objects, i.e. in response to, "what's this?"
_____  29. Child counts two objects.
_____  30. Child points to six parts of a doll: eye, hand, nose, etc.
_____  31. Child repeats a two-digit sequence: 2, 8, etc.
_____  32. Child knows concept of one when asked for one.
_____  33. Child builds an eight- or nine-block tower.
_____  34. Child knows sex or tells name.
_____  35. Child copies a circle from an example—circle does not have to be exact.
_____  Total
                  Remarks:

## Instructional Objective
To have child look for fallen or disappearing object.

## Readiness
Child has ability to see objects at least 3 feet away.
Child directs eye movements.
Child directs head and upper trunk movements.

## Procedure
1. Seat the child on chair appropriate for his size.
2. Instructor should sit in front of and slightly to the side of the child.
3. Take a brightly colored object and hold it above child's line of vision, about 12 inches away.
4. Attract child's attention to the toy by shaking it, and bringing it in and out of his line of vision.
5. When the child focuses on the toy, move it to one side out of his line of vision.
6. If child does not follow the object or loses it while it is moving, hold it in position until he again focuses on it, and then begin moving it.
7. Repeat this exercise several times and keep the direction of movement of the object consistent.

## Task Evaluation
1. Did child focus on object?
2. Did he follow the object when it began to move?
3. Did he just move his eyes or did he move his whole upper trunk in order to look for the object?

## Materials and Equipment
Chair, appropriate size for child
Brightly colored object

## Instructional Objective
To have child lift cup to obtain object underneath.

## Readiness
Child directs arm movements.
Child directs hand movements.
Child grasp developed.
Child has sight adequate to see small objects.

## Procedure
1. Seat child at small table on chair appropriate for his size.
2. Sit opposite the child.
3. Place a piece of cookie under a clear cup and then command the child to get the cookie.

4. If he does not initiate the action, direct him with hand-over-hand assistance.
5. Gradually reduce physical prompts until the child does it by himself.
6. When child has had several successful trials using the see-through cup, use a cup that he cannot see through.

## Task Evaluation
1. Did child initiate activity?
2. Did he focus on cup for a long time before initiating activity?
3. Did he "forget about" cookie when it disappeared under the cup?

## Materials and Equipment
Table and chair, appropriate size for child
Cookie
See-through cup
Opaque cup

## Instructional Objective
To have child recognize self in mirror.

## Readiness
Child sees adequately.
Directs arm movements.
Directs hand movements.

## Procedure
1. Place a full length mirror in front of the child. He should be sitting, if able.
2. Direct child's attention toward the mirror by tapping on it and by a physical prompting, if necessary.
3. When child is focusing on mirror, say "where's (name)?"
4. Take child's arm and direct it to the mirror; pointing to his image, say "there's (name)."
5. Repeat several times until child focuses on self and points.

## Task Evaluation
1. Did the child attend to himself in mirror?
2. Did he attempt to point to his image?
3. Did he make any vocalizations when he saw his image?

## Materials and Equipment
Full length mirror
Chair, appropriate for child's size

## SUGGESTED READINGS AND MATERIALS AND EQUIPMENT

### Program Development

Brady JF, Smilovitz R (eds): APT: A Training Program for Citizens with Severely or Profoundly Retarded Behavior. Spring City, Pa., Pennhurst State School, 1974

Bry P, Nawas MM: Is reinforcement necessary for the development of generalized imitation operant in severely and profoundly retarded children? Am J Ment Defic 76:658–677

Chalfant JC, Silkovitz RG: Systematic Instruction for Retarded Children: The Illinois Program–Experimental Edition. Part 1: Teacher-Parent Guide. Urbana, Illinois University, Institute for Research on Exceptional Children, 1970

Curriculum for Institutionalized Severely and Profoundly Mentally Retarded. Intermediate Unit No. 8, Ebensburg State School and Hospital, Ebensburg, Pa., 1974

Hollis JH, Gorton CE: Training severely and profoundly developmentally retarded children. Ment Retard 5:20–24, 1967

Kleyle HM, Rocereto GM (eds): A Case Study Approach to the Low Functioning Child. Pittsburgh, Duquesne University, 1973

Kleyle HM, Rocereto GM (eds): An Instructional Guide for Parents. Pittsburgh, Duquesne University, 1974

Mager RF: Preparing Instructional Objectives. Belmont, Calif., Fearon, 1962

Mattei AM: Stimulation Procedures for the Extremely Low-functioning Cerebral Palsied and Other Health Impaired Child. Monaca, Pa., Intermediate Unit 27, 1974

Myers DG, Sinco ME, Stalma ES: The Right to Education Child. Springfield, Ill., Thomas, 1973

Shick RL (ed.): Summer trainee workshops in early childhood education for the handicapped. Department of Special Education, School of Teacher Education, Mansfield State College, Curriculum guide for early education of the handicapped, summer sessions, 1973–74

Sontag, E, et al., (ed.): Considerations for serving the severely handicapped in the public schools. Education and Training of the Mentally Retarded, Vol 8, No. 2, 1973

Stephens B, Manfredini D, Malcotti M (eds): Training the Difficult Retardate. Department of Special Education, Temple University, Philadelphia, 1972

Tilton JR, Liska DC, Bourland JD (eds): Guide to Early Developmental Training. Wabash Center for the Mentally Retarded, 1972

Watson LS: Applications of behavior-shaping devices to training severely and profoundly mentally retarded children in an institutional setting. Ment Retard 6:21–23, 1968

Watson LS: Application of operant conditioning techniques to institutionalized severely and profoundly retarded children. Ment Retard Abstr 4:1–18

Western State School and Hospital Education Department: Unit Development Program. Intermediate Unit No. 1: Canonsburg, Pa., 1972

### Motor Development

Auxter D: Motor skill development in the profoundly retarded. American Institute for Mental Studies: Training School Bull 68:5–9, 1971

Bobath B: The very early treatment of cerebral palsy. Develop Med Child Neurol 9:373–390, 1967

Bobath K, Bobath B: The diagnosis of cerebral palsy in infancy. Arch Dis Child 31:159, 1956

Bobath K, Bobath B: Cerebal palsy, in Pearson PH, Williams CE (eds) Physical Therapy Services in the Developmental Disabilities. Springfield, Ill., Thomas, 1972

Bobath B: Abnormal Postural Reflex Activity Caused by Brain Lesions. Germany, Heinemann, 1971

Bucks County Public Schools: Bucks County Intermediate Unit Program for the Severely and Profoundly Handicapped, Intermediate Unit No. 22, Doylestown, Pa.

Cruickshank WM: Cerebral Palsy: Its Individual and Community Problems (rev ed). Syracuse, N.Y., Syracuse Univ Pr, 1966

Finnie NR: Handling the Young Cerebral Palsied Child at Home. New York, Dutton, 1970

Fiorentino M: Normal and Abnormal Development: The Influence of Primitive Reflexes on Motor Development. Springfield, Ill., Thomas, 1972

Gillette HE: Systems of Therapy on Cerebral Palsy. Springfield, Ill., Thomas, 1969

Godfrey G, Thompson M: Movement Pattern Checklist. Columbia, Mo., Kelly, 1966

Keen RA, Sullivan S: Suggestions for Positioning the Severely Involved Child. Pittsburgh, Pennsylvania. Department of Welfare Workshop, July, 1973

Levy J: The Baby Exercise Book, New York, Random House, 1973

McDonald E, Chance B: Cerebral Palsy. Englewood Cliffs, N.J., Prentice-Hall, 1964

Pothier PC: Therapeutic handling of the severely handicapped child, Am J Nursing, 71:321–324, 1971

Smith DK: M-A-P project skill development checklist. Indiana, Pa., Indiana Armstrong Arin Intermediate Unit, 1973

## Self-Care Skill Development

Abramson EE, Wunderlich RA: Dental hygiene training for retardates: An application of behavioral techniques. Ment Retard, 10:3, 3–6, 1972

Azrin NH, Armstrong PM: The "mini-meal"—A method for teaching eating skills to the profoundly retarded. Ment Retard, 11:9–13, 1973

Balthazaar EE: Balthazaar Scales of Adaptive Behavior for the Profoundly and Severely Mentally Retarded. Champaign, Ill., Research, 1971

Bensburg GJ (ed): Teaching the Mentally Retarded: A Handbook for Ward Personnel. Atlanta, Southern Regional Education Board, 1965

Bensburg G, Colwell C, Cassel R: Teaching the profoundly retarded self-help activities by behavior shaping techniques. Am J Ment Defic 69:600–679, 1965

Foxx RM, Azrin NH: Toilet Training the Retarded. Champaign, Ill., Research, 1973

Lebeck M, Elliott C: Toilet training for profoundly retarded with a limited staff. Ment Retard, 8:48–50, 1970

Sullivan S, Keen RA: Feeding Program for Physically Handicapped Children. Pittsburgh Home for Crippled Children. March, 1974

Watson LS: How to use behavior modification with mentally retarded and autistic children: Programs for administrators, teachers, and nurses. Columbus, Ohio, Behavior Modification Technology, 1972

## Sensory-Perception-Cognition

Ball T (ed): A guide for the instruction and training of the profoundly retarded and severely multi-handicapped child. California, Santa Cruz County Board of Education, 1971

Ball TS: Itard, Séquin, and Kephart. Columbia, Ohio, Merrill, 1971
Cibik Edward P (ed): Instructional Modules for a TMR Curriculum. Westmoreland Intermediate Unit No. 7: South Greensburg, Pa.
Edgar, CL: Effects of sensory-motor training on adaptive behavior. Am J Ment Defic 73:713–719, 1969
Ronayne AM, et al: Perceptual—Motor Development Curriculum Guide. Allegheny Intermediate Unit No. 3, Pittsburgh
Sontag E, Burke P, York R: Considerations for serving the severely handicapped in the public schools. Ed Train Ment Retard 8:20–26, 1973
Webb RC: Evaluating the Sensory–Motor Bases of Behavior in the Profoundly Retarded. Washington, D.C., United States Department of Health, Education, and Welfare, Office of Education, 1972

## Communication Development

Anderson RM, Miles M, Mathey PA: Communicative Evaluation Chart from Infancy to Five Years. Cambridge, Mass., Educator Publishing Service, 1964
Baer DM, Guess D: Teaching productive noun suffixes to severely retarded children. Am J Ment Defic 77:498–505, 1973
Bricker WA, Bricker DD: Assessment and modification of verbal imitation with low-functioning retarded children. J Speech Hear Res 15:690–698, 1972
Bricker WA, Bricker DD: Development of receptive vocabulary in severely retarded children. Am J Ment Defic 74:599–607, 1970
Bricker WA, Bricker DD: A program of language training for the severely language handicapped child. Exceptional Children 37:101–111, 1970
Crickmay MC: Speech Therapy and the Bobath Approach to Cerebral Palsy. Springfield, Ill., Thomas, 1966
Hall SM, Talkington LW: A suggested language development program for severely and profoundly retarded. J Spec Educators Ment Retard 6:1970
Pierce RB, Warvi V: Swallow Right. Huntsville, Alabama, Huntsville Rehabilitation Center, 1973

## Materials and Equipment Guides

Bergen A: Selected Equipment for Pediatric Rehabilitation. Blythedale, New York, Blythedale Children's Hospital, 1974
Finnie NR: Handling the Young Cerebral Palsied Child at Home. New York, Dutton, 1968
Nathan C: Please Help Us Help Ourselves. United Cerebral Palsy Center, Indianapolis, Indiana, 1970
Robinault IP (ed): Functional Aids for the Multiply Handicapped. Hagerstown, Md., Harper & Row, 1973
Zinkus C: Feeding skill training in Feeding the Handicapped Child. University of Tennessee, Child Development Center, Memphis, Tenn., 1971

## SUGGESTED RESOURCE MATERIALS AND EQUIPMENT WITH ADDRESSES

Binky Baby Products, Inc.                    Plastic coated spoon
New York, N.Y. 10010                         Trainer cup

| | |
|---|---|
| Childcraft Education Corp.<br>964 Third Avenue<br>New York, N.Y. 10022 | Playtentials |
| Constructive Playthings<br>1040 East 85th Street<br>Kansas City, Mo. 64131 | Unbreakable metal mirror |
| Creative Playthings<br>Princeton, N.J. 08540 | Activator pulling sounds.<br>Infant chimes mobile<br>Rainbow twirler |
| European Folk Craft Shop<br>525 Linden Street<br>Scranton, Pa. 18503 | Big beach ball<br>Prone board |
| General Motors Corp.<br>Any zone office | Love seat |
| Hogg Chair Company<br>Chicago, Ill. | Hogg chair |
| Invalex Company<br>741 West 17th Street<br>Long Beach, Calif. 90813 | Potty chair |
| Oster Corporation<br>Milwaukee, Wis. 53217 | Infrared massager |
| J. T. Posey<br>39 S. Santa Anita Avenue<br>Pasadena, Calif. 91107 | Posey restraint |
| J. A. Preston Corporation<br>71 Fifth Avenue<br>New York, N.Y. 10003 | Large handled therapy spoon<br>Large handled therapy fork<br>Plate guard<br>Relaxation chair<br>Scoot-a-bout<br>Therapy chair |
| Fred Sammons Company<br>Box 32<br>Brookfield, Ill. 60513 | Nipplespoon |
| Sip n' Spin, Inc.<br>Irvington, N.J. 07111 | Drinking cup |

| Skill Development | Fat mat (wedge) |
| Equipment Co. | |
| 1340 North Jefferson | Foam builder mat |
| Anaheim, Calif. 92806 | Odd ball saddle |
| The Kendall Company | Rib type nipple |
| Curity Rib Nipple | |
| Chicago, Ill. | |

Much of the material appearing in this chapter was originally discussed in *The Right-to-Education Child* (1973). It is suggested that the reader refer to this text for a more detailed understanding of educational programming for the severely/profoundly handicapped.

### Bibliography

Finnie, Nancie R. *Handling the Young Cerebral Palsied Child at Home*. New York: E. P. Dutton, 1970.

Hart, Verna. *Beginning with the Handicapped*. Springfield, Illinois: Charles C Thomas, 1974.

Myers, Donald G., Sinco, Michael E. and Stalma, Ellen Somerton. *The Right-to-Education Child*. Springfield, Illinois: Charles C Thomas, 1973.

Deborah D. Smith,
James O. Smith, and
Eugene Edgar

C

# A Prototypic Model For Developing Instructional Materials for the Severely Handicapped[1]

Severely handicapped children frequently have difficulty acquiring basic life skills. Regardless of the difficulty, however, it is important that these children master many varied skills, so that as adults they can lead more independent lives. An individual's ability to function in society is directly related to the number of life skills he possesses. For example, to hold a job successfully, one must be able to arrive at the job on time, perform the work required, prepare or purchase lunch, cooperate with peers, and return home. Success may also depend on the ability to drive a car or read bus schedules, tell time, handle money (deposit pay checks, budget expenditures, and purchase items), and recognize survival words such as "danger," "stop," or "poison." Many skills are necessary to complete this chain.

Normal or gifted youngsters usually do not have to be taught how to put on their coats or tie their shoes; they often learn how to tell time and make change without direct instruction. Those youngsters who do not learn by observing the actions of others, however, need to be systematically taught many of these skills. Since there are numerous life skills children must master, it is vital that educational materials be effective and that time set aside for instruction be used efficiently. Research has investigated a number of antecedent and subsequent events which influence teaching (Smith, 1973). The effects of instructions (Lovitt and Curtiss, 1968; Lovitt and Smith, 1972), feedback (Hillman, 1970; Kirby and Shields, 1972), and reinforcement contingencies (Chadwick and Day, 1971; Smith, Lovitt and Kidder, 1972) have been the topic of much research and have influenced various types of instructional procedures. It follows, however, that if the material presented to the learner is inconsistent or poorly sequenced, learning will be impeded. Unfortunately, at this time, effective curriculum materials for most of the basic educational and life skills needed by the severely handicapped are not commercially available. As a result, classroom teachers are left to select, sequence, and plan lessons to teach self-help and life skills to these children.

## THE PROTOTYPIC MODEL

The prototypic model for developing instructional programs and materials provides the educator with a detailed set of procedures to follow in developing instructional sequences which are nearly errorfree and which teach new skills in a minimum amount of time. The programs resulting from this process are highly structured and pertain to specific skills.

To clarify the procedures outlined in the prototypic model, one instructional program developed through this process was selected as an example for the following description of the model—the Shoe Tie Program (Smith, Smith, and Haring, 1974).

### Prerequisite Knowledge

New skills are developed and mastered by building on those skills already mastered—that is, the prerequisite skills. The educational programmer must come to the task with three mastered entry skills. He must be thoroughly familiar with the skill to be programmed. If he wishes to create an instructional program to teach youngsters how to tie shoes, the instructional programmer must be proficient in the skill of shoe tying.

Besides knowing how to perform the target skill, the programmer should be competent in basic programming techniques such as cueing, fading, and chaining (Skinner, 1968). He must be able to create instructional frames which break the task into steps that are small enough to be mastered, yet still retain the interest of the learner.

In addition to these two general skills, the instructional programmer must be aware of general human learning characteristics. For example, he must be able to build into his sequences enough repetition to allow for overlearning. He should know how to include demonstration sessions to provide modeling, and review sessions to insure that mastered skills are maintained at a proficient level of performance.

### Primary Decisions

When the educational programmer is certain that he possesses the entry behaviors necessary to approach the task of creating educational sequences, he is ready to begin the process of developing a skill-specific instructional sequence. First, the skill to be programmed must be clearly and precisely identified. In our example, shoe tying is that specific skill and the terminal objective of the proposed sequence. In this sequence, only shoe tying is taught; the sequence does not include instruction on putting on or lacing shoes.

The second decision which must be made at this point concerns the intended audience or target population for whom the program is to be written. The instructional programmer will have to recognize specific deficits which may occur in his target population. The Shoe Tie Program was designed for any individual who can pinch, pull against tension, and imitate or model the actions of others.

## Lattice Developed

Once the target skill and population have been precisely defined, a task analysis process begins. The lattice system developed by Woolman (1962) was modified to implement this step of building the prototypic model. As the lattice component of the model seems particularly applicable to the classroom teacher's daily needs, it will be discussed in greater detail here.

The lattice is a graphic display of the analysis of a specific task. Goals and objectives are put into a hierarchy so that educational activities can be planned to help students master various skills systematically.

It is important for teachers of severely handicapped youngsters to carefully specify which behaviors their students need to acquire; for successful learning, goals must be precisely stated. But identifying a task to be mastered is only the first step in developing an educational sequence. Often, subgoals of tasks need to be specified. These subgoals can also be broken down into smaller objectives. By carefully sequencing these objectives, subgoals, and major goals, the educator can plan relevant educational activities that permit the learner to master specific objectives along the way toward his mastery of the target skill.

The lattice system is one way of organizing educational activities and of sequencing skills. The lattice forces the teacher to specify goals and objectives: once a lattice is constructed, the sequence of events leading to the completion of a task is clearly delineated because the integral parts of that task are specified and put into a hierarchy.

The lattice is not an instructional sequence, nor does it outline precise activities to be included in the instructional program. The lattice merely displays the component parts of a skill arranged according to the sequence of behaviors leading to the completion of a specific task. Myron Woolman originated the lattice system to give structure to the ordering of educational activities. He argued that by latticing a task before instruction begins, a teacher could see the relationship and integration of concepts to be taught. Woolman (1962) expressed the intent of his lattice system:

> . . . any body of material to be learned can be organized into a sequence which permits the systematic growth of a pool of relevant responses to the stimulus being learned. . . . as learning progresses, the learner is alternately required to add new information and integrate it into the ever growing pool. This continues until the learning objective is achieved (p. 181).

Since Woolman initially proposed the lattice system, others have adopted his procedures. Budde and Menolascino (1971) showed how the lattice system can be applied to vocational habilitation. Bricker (1972) used a lattice format to display his sequence for language acquisition. Smith and Smith (1974) employed the lattice system to analyze instructional sequences before they developed structured instructional programs to teach self-help and life skills.

Lattices can be very sophisticated or very simple. They can be constructed to show the relationship of one skill to another. They can be three-dimensional to illustrate the difficulty, as well as the sequence of component tasks. However, such complex systems are often confusing. For purposes of organizing educational activities or analyzing instructional skills, complexity is usually not necessary.

For most teachers' purposes, lattices should simply display the analysis of a task. Simplified lattices allow for ease of communication among teachers who use this system for task analysis and for speed of construction. To meet the many educational needs of their students, teachers need to be able to analyze specific skills as quickly as possible. The following section describes the procedures teachers can use to construct lattices to display their analysis of specific skills.

LATTICE CONSTRUCTION.

Since a lattice is a graphic display of a skill analysis, there are specific procedures which must be followed in its construction. Since a sequence of events is involved in constructing a lattice, we will use a lattice to display this sequence (Fig. 1).

In addition to the graphic display, narration is included to explain what the boxes mean and why they were placed on the lattice in their respective positions. Sections of the complete lattice are numbered so the reader can match the narration with appropriate sections of graphic display.

*1. Prerequisite knowledge.* Just as children need to possess specific skills before they can perform complex tasks correctly, so adults must

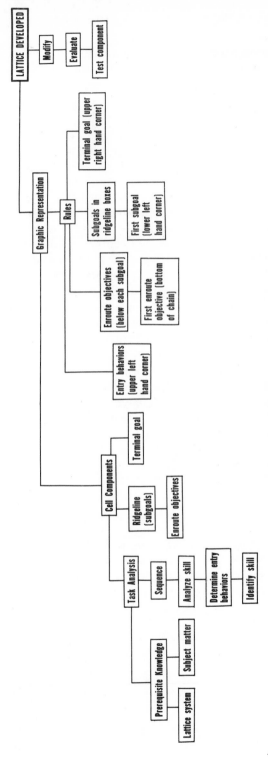

Fig. 1. Procedural lattice for lattice development.

also possess certain skills before they can break down a task for analysis and display that analysis in lattice format (Fig. 2). Before a teacher breaks a skill into component parts and attempts to construct a lattice, he should know what a modified lattice is and how it is used. The sections included in this part of the lattice summarize the knowledge a teacher should possess before attempting to "lattice" a skill.

*1a. Lattice system.* Because the purpose of constructing a lattice is to obtain a sequenced list of the major component parts (objectives and subgoals encountered en route) of the skill to be taught, some rules and conventions are followed in constructing a lattice. After the teacher analyzes the skill and puts the analysis in lattice format, he will refer to the lattice as he develops the instructional sequences designed to help his students attain mastery of the desired behavior. Therefore, the format used should be consistent so that interpretation of the analysis is identical to the sequence originally intended. Moreover, following a prescribed format for lattice construction promotes ease of communication. If other teachers analyze skills in the same manner, lattices can be shared with colleagues so that skill analysis and sequencing need not be done over and over again. Specific details about latticing rules are found under heading 4: Graphic Representation.

*1b. Subject matter.* Prerequisite knowledge of subject matter is more important than knowing the rules and conventions for lattice construction. The teacher should have a thorough knowledge of the subject matter to be analyzed, since it is impossible to break down an academic task or skill if one cannot successfully complete the task oneself. For example, the teacher who needs to teach his students how to tie shoes cannot divide that skill into component parts without knowing how to tie his shoes systematically.

*2. Task analysis.* Once the teacher is familiar with the procedures used to construct a lattice (Fig. 3) and is competent at performing the task to be analyzed, he is ready to begin the task analysis.

*2a. Identify the skill.* The teacher must first determine precisely what specific task he wants to submit to analysis. If a child needs to learn how to tie his shoes, then shoe tying is the specific task to be analyzed—

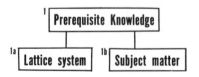

Fig. 2.   Lattice format.

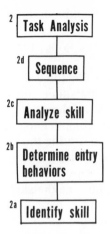

Fig. 3.   Task analysis lattice.

not the more general skill of selecting appropriate shoes for certain occasions, for example. Further, although the learner might also be deficient in putting shoes on his feet, that is a different task and should not be included in the lattice for shoe tying.

*2b. Determine entry behaviors.*   After the task to be analyzed is identified, the teacher should decide what skills he will expect of students beginning the sequence—that is, at what skill level he will begin instruction. For example, if the teacher wishes to teach his students how to tie shoes and plans to lattice that skill, he needs to decide what skills he will and will not teach in his instructional sequence. Fine-motor coordination is an important prerequisite skill. The teacher must decide whether he will expect competence in motor coordination before he teaches shoe tying or whether he will teach that skill simultaneously with shoe tying.

Our experience indicates that more efficient instruction occurs if prerequisite skills are mastered before students begin a specific sequence such as shoe tying. Often, entry behaviors are determined arbitrarily; different teachers expect different entry levels from their students. Nevertheless, some entry levels should be specified.

*2c. Analyze skill.*   Although not a sophisticated or scientific method, one way to analyze a skill is to observe its execution repeatedly. As the teacher performs the task and observes others execute the skill over and over, the major component parts of the skill can be identified, and the sequence in which they are performed becomes obvious. As the teacher repeats the task, he should carefully scrutinize his actions and identify each step. When we analyze a skill, each part of the skill is written on an index card, so that the sequence of these components can be easily ordered and reordered.

*2d. Sequence.* Once identified, the component parts of the skill are sequenced. Frequently, the sequence is dictated by the skill and the end product; for example, in shoe tying, the sequence and the product are constant.

A hierarchy of skills is identified during sequencing. Some parts of the skill are major components; others are subordinate steps which lead to completing the major steps. In shoe tying, completing the half-knot and tying the bow are two major components. These, then, are the subgoals of the final goal for a student mastering the skill of shoe tying. The en route objectives which lead to completing these two subgoals are placed under the subgoals, thereby representing the hierarchy of steps in the task.

All of these steps (identifying the skill, determining the entry behaviors, analyzing the skill, and eventually sequencing the steps used to complete the task) comprise the major elements of the task analysis.

*3. Cell components.* Lattices are comprised of a series of interlocking boxes or cells (Fig. 4). Each of these cells must be placed in position according to the sequence and analysis determined in the preceding step of this process. The terminal behavior, or goal, the subgoals, and the en route objectives have been stated concisely and marked for the graphic representation. The next step in lattice development can now be completed.

*3a(1). En route objectives.* En route objectives are those behaviors which lead to completing the subgoals. If tying the half-knot is a subgoal of the shoe tying sequence, steps such as bringing the shoe laces into a crossed position are the en route objectives. These are placed underneath the subgoals.

*3a(2). Ridgeline.* The lattice ridgeline comprises the subgoals of a task. When the lattice is formed, these subgoals are connected to each step in a stepladder format which leads up to the terminal behavior.

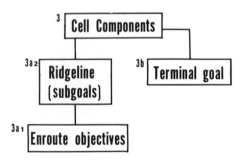

Fig. 4.   Lattices are comprised of a series of interlocking boxes or cells.

*3b. Terminal goal.* There is one terminal behavior or goal for each lattice. Depending on the complexity of the lattice, the terminal goal could be as simple and concrete as "shoes tied" or as complex and conceptual as "time concepts." Regardless of the nature of the skill analyzed, there is only one concisely stated terminal goal for each lattice. All the previously identified steps lead directly to completing the terminal behavior.

*4. Graphic representation* (Fig. 5). For a lattice to be consistently interpreted by many people and to be meaningful to the person who constructed it, certain rules or conventions should be followed. The lattice is a blueprint or master plan depicting the steps and the sequence which lead the learner to mastering a specific task; the graphic display should be clear and easily interpreted.

*4a. Rules* (Fig. 6). Rules for promoting clarity and ease of interpretation follow—those for cell placement are in this section followed by rules for placing the lines connecting cells.

A stepladder format is used for arranging the subgoals' sequence. Cell boxes display this sequence from left to right. The ridgeline is connected by lines which form right angles.

Whenever possible, en route objectives are connected to each subgoal's cell with straight lines (Fig. 7). When it is necessary to show three or more en route objectives not primarily related to each other, these may be placed under the subgoal cell with both straight and bent lines.

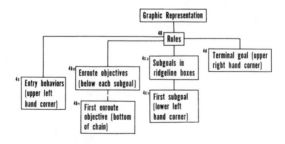

Fig. 5. Rules for a lattice.

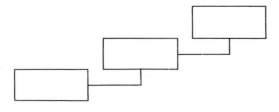

Fig. 6. Stepladder format.

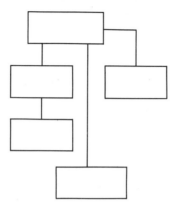

Fig. 7.  En route objectives, connected to each subgoal's
cell with straight lines.


If one en route objective must be completed before another task is
initiated, the cells are put together in a chain. When one task is definitely
prerequisite to the next, the first objective in the chain is put in the bottom
cell. All of the ensuing en route objectives lead up to the subgoal.

Major subgoals may be considered terminal goals of "miniprograms"
within one complete lattice (Fig. 8). In some cases, it is desirable to have
an overall lattice showing how skills relate to each other in order to plan
curricula. This can also be accomplished by using the lattice system. In
the example shown below, two small lattices are put together under one
terminal behavior. This format can easily be adapted for the purpose of
displaying the progression of skills taught in one academic year for particular skill areas such as computational arithmetic or self-help.

*4b (1). Entry behaviors* (Fig. 9).   The behaviors or skills which the
learner must possess before he begins the instructional sequence devel-

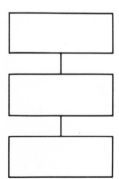

Fig. 8.   Subgoals—terminal goals of "miniprograms."

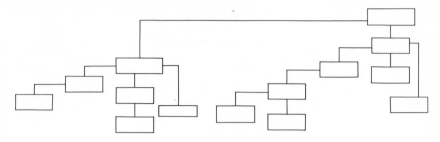

Fig. 9.   Entry behavior lattice.

oped from the lattice are entry behaviors. Entry behaviors do not appear as cell components, but they are listed on the lattice page. A convenient place for them is the upper left-hand corner. They are noted and labeled as entry behaviors, and they are stated concisely.

*4b (2). First en route objective.*   This objective leads the learner to mastering the subgoals which, in turn, lead to his achieving the terminal goal. If the sequence of these objectives is a simple linear progression, the first en route objective is placed at the bottom of the chain. However, if several objectives or a set of objectives are included under one subgoal, the goal which is mastered first is placed to the left of the other en route objectives.

*4c (1). First subgoal.*   The first subgoal in the sequence, the first ridgeline cell, is placed towards the bottom left-hand corner of the page. The en route objectives related to completing that subgoal are positioned underneath this first ridgeline box.

*4c (2). Second Subgoals.*   The remaining subgoals are positioned in stepladder format (from left to right), leading to the terminal behavior. These comprise the ridgeline.

*4d. Terminal goal.*   The terminal goal always appears in the upper right-hand corner. Stated concisely, it is positioned to indicate clearly that it is the end-goal of the sequence.

*5. Lattice developed.*   This is the terminal goal of the task described in this article. Before a lattice is truly completed, however, some final testing and evaluation must be undertaken (Fig. 10).

*5a. Testing.*   The teacher should perform the latticed task once again, following the lattice as it is now constructed. He should scrutinize each component to be certain that the words in each cell adequately describe the behavior. He should recheck the sequence for accuracy.

*5b. Evaluating.*   The teacher should note any evidence he finds that the lattice does not properly display the sequence or the analysis or that wording is misleading.

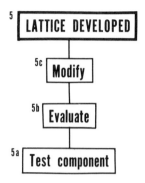

Fig. 10.   Lattice developed.

*5c. Modifying.* If errors in the lattice have been identified, they must be corrected. If entry behaviors were omitted, they must be included. If the ordering of the subgoals was incorrect, it must be adjusted. After these final checks, the task has been analyzed and displayed so that instructional activities can be organized. These activities should aim for enabling the learner to master each en route objective and its subgoals, and eventually, the terminal behavior.

The lattice approach could be helpful to teachers as they plan their curriculum activities for a year, a month, or a week. The system allows teachers to specify which skills they want their students to master; they would also display the analysis of each skill in a simple format so that en route objectives can be identified easily.

The teacher then has an outline from which to plan activities that will help his students acquire needed skills. Further, the outline can identify or pinpoint those skill areas for which effective programs are not currently available, thereby guiding the teacher's own plans for program development. Similarly, for the programmer who implements the prototypic model in its entirety, the lattice serves as a blueprint from which the instructional program is later built (Fig. 11).

### Pretest Package

Once the lattice has been constructed, it plays an integral part in the next stage of the program—developing a pretest. Test items are constructed to sample students' abilities to perform the tasks identified in the lattice. The pretest serves three purposes. (1) It indicates if the learner has already mastered the task and therefore, does not need to enter the instructional sequence. (2) The pretest samples the entry behaviors to determine whether the learner is ready to enter the sequence at Lesson 1. (3)

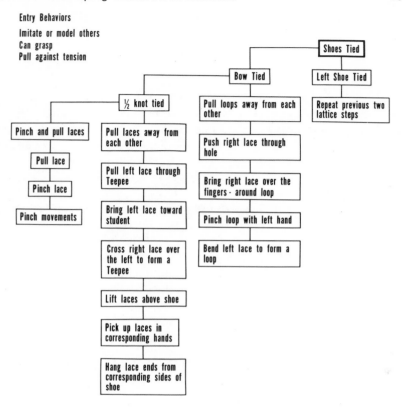

Entry Behaviors
Imitate or model others
Can grasp
Pull against tension

Shoes Tied

Bow Tied | Left Shoe Tied

½ knot tied | Pull loops away from each other | Repeat previous two lattice steps

Pinch and pull laces | Pull laces away from each other | Push right lace through hole

Pull lace | Pull left lace through Teepee | Bring right lace over the fingers - around loop

Pinch lace | Bring left lace toward student | Pinch loop with left hand

Pinch movements | Cross right lace over the left to form a Teepee | Bend left lace to form a loop

Lift laces above shoe

Pick up laces in corresponding hands

Hang lace ends from corresponding sides of shoe

Fig. 11. Lattice for "shoes tied."

The pretest offers information regarding differential placement in the program. For example, if the learner has not mastered the task but can successfully complete some components of the skill, the learner's exact beginning level should be specified. Once the program is fully developed, not all children will begin with the same lesson. Students who initially possess some of the behaviors required to perform a task successfully, but who cannot accurately complete the terminal behavior, can be placed in the sequence according to their initial skill level.

Test items are constructed for each component of the skill; items are included from each part of the ridgeline and from many en route boxes. Materials needed for the pretest are developed, and a data collection system is prepared. For an accurate indication of each learner's skill levels, pretests are individually administered. Because the pretest is a critical part of the entire program package, field testing is required to determine whether the pretest accurately identifies varying skill levels.

## PROGRAM FORMAT

The next program decision relates to format. One option might be a series of worksheets which do not require teacher assistance. In this case, a teacherless program would emerge. Another option might consist of structured lessons administered by teachers or paraprofessionals. This procedure produces either small group or one-to-one programs. The Shoe Tie Program was developed for one-to-one teaching. Since this is an expensive educational procedure, the instructional sequence was designed for administration by untrained as well as trained personnel.

## INITIAL FIELDTEST POPULATION

The first group of learners to receive the instructional sequence is selected through use of the pretest instrument. Those pupils having all of the entry behaviors, but not possessing skills beyond those taught in the first lesson, are selected. Learners possessing advanced skills could enter the sequence; however, those having only the entry behaviors are used for this first field test in order to verify each lesson.

## INITIAL FIELDTEST

*Phase 1.* In this first phase, the program writer writes lessons concurrently with field testing. General criterion levels are established for all of the lessons. In the Shoe Tie Program, the authors decided that no more than 10% error would be accepted for each lesson. Therefore, they rewrote any lesson in which any child failed to meet the criterion of 90% correct responding. A general data collection system was also devised. Data were collected for each frame for each lesson, allowing the programmers to determine when specific frames produced high error rates. When these were identified, the frames were corrected and retested. Rewriting continued until most error was eliminated.

The programmers also developed a format to facilitate lesson writing. Since these instructional programs are highly structured and are intended for administration by personnel with widely varying skills (e.g., parents, volunteers, and classroom aides), a three-column format was developed for ease in administering the lessons. All of the teacher's directions are found in one column. Those actions used to model the desired behaviors are carefully described. Words spoken to the student are printed in capital letters. All of the expected student responses are found in the second column, indicating whether the student is required to answer a question, imitate a behavior, or manipulate supplemental materials. The third column contains suggested remediation activities. In some cases, all possible error cannot be eliminated by rewriting the program. Whenever a problematic instructional frame occurs, an elaboration of the teacher's directions appears in this column. A sample lesson format is included (Table 2).

**Table 1.**
Results of Secondary Field Testing—Shoe Tie Program

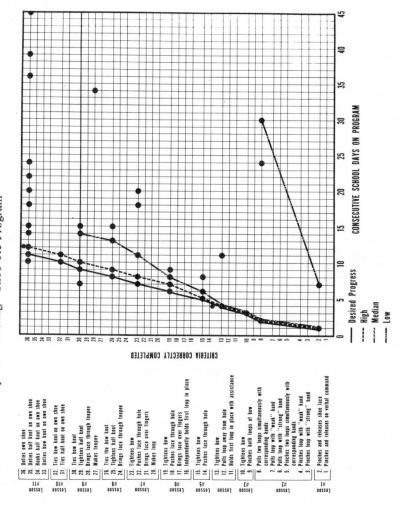

**Table 2.**
Sample Lesson—Shoe Tie Program

| Instructor | Student | Remediation |
|---|---|---|
| Say: THIS IS CALLED A BOW. WHAT IS THIS CALLED? (R-3) | R-3. "Bow" | |
| *Section 2: Student Pulls Bow Tight* Untie the shoe. Tie the laces slowly, stopping at the step where you pull the loops to finish the bow. Say: YOU PINCH THE LOOPS. MAKE SURE YOU PINCH BOTH PARTS AT ONCE. (R-4) | R-4. Pinches loops. | If child hooks loops, say: NO. Then model the pinching movements in the air. Say: PINCH Have students imitate pinching three times correctly in the air. |
| NOW IT'S YOUR TURN TO PULL THE BOW TIGHT. PULL THE LOOPS AWAY FROM EACH OTHER. (R-5) Repeat Section 2 until the student correctly completes the task three consecutive times | R-5. Pulls loops away from each other. Repeats Section 2 three times correctly. | |

The first lesson of the program is written once a convenient lesson format has been designed. Inexpensive teaching aids are developed where necessary. The only teaching aid developed for the Shoe Tie Program was a simple device used to teach pinching and pulling a shoelace. The tasks taught in this lesson aim to bring the student to mastery of the first en route objective of the first component specified in the lattice. Each lesson should bring the learner one step closer to mastering the terminal behavior. Even though more than one lesson may be required to teach one en route behavior, the aim is still to move the learner progressively closer to the target behavior. After the first lesson is written, it is tested on one or two subjects. If error in excess of criterion occurs, the lesson is rewritten and retested. The second lesson is then written and field tested. Once again, if error exceeds the criterion rate, the lesson is rewritten and re-tested. These procedures are repeated until all of the lessons have been written and field tested on a small population of students.

*Phase 2.* When the second phase begins, the entire sequence has been developed, but the whole program has not been tested because of the considerable rewriting that may have occurred in the first phase of initial field testing. Therefore, the whole program is now submitted to field test-ing, administered by one or two of the program writers' colleagues. Feed-back from these administrators enables the programmer to clarify any teacher directions which prove to be ambiguous or incomplete.

Six children at the Experimental Education Unit were selected for this second phase of initial field testing of the Shoe Tie Program. These children possessed only the entry behaviors specified in the pretest and lattice, and they were not differentially placed in the program at advanced levels. The entire sequence was tested to insure that most error had been eliminated in the previous stage. Four of the six students chosen for the second phase were enrolled in the Down's Syndrome Kindergarten. The fifth student was an 8-year-old moderately retarded boy, and the sixth student was an 18-year-old emotionally disturbed young man.

One of the kindergarten students successfully completed the entire Shoe Tie Program in 21 sessions. After 44 sessions, another 5-year-old student completed all but the last lesson. The other two Kindergarten students failed to complete the program due to absenteeism and/or un-cooperative behavior. The 8-year-old completed the entire lesson se-quence in 11 sessions, and the 18-year-old learned to tie his shoes in seven sessions. These field test data indicated that the sequence enabled the children to master the terminal behavior with a minimum amount of error; hence, the program was ready for secondary field testing. If substantial error had occurred during initial field test, the program would have been rewritten and retested, as was the case with several other programs.

SECONDARY FIELD TESTING

Once the instructional program is written, field tested with a limited number of subjects, and rewritten, the sequence is ready for more exten-sive field testing. Multiple packages of the instructional program are pro-duced. The teachers' manuals are edited, typed, duplicated (at least 50 copies), and bound. If supplemental materials, such as teaching aids and student workbooks, are used in the program, they must also be produced in sufficient quantity for the secondary field test population. Teaching aids should be durable and reusable, with the exception of student workbooks.

Additional field testing is required for several reasons. First, it is important for more children to be included in the field test population.

This number need not exceed 50 youngsters, but should be more than the 5 to 10 students who participated in the initial field test stage. Additional students are needed to validate the instructional sequence and to determine whether error pileup occurred because of unclear instructional frames.

Second, wider field testing yields information about teacher-induced error. In the initial stage of field testing, the instructional programmer and those familiar with his procedures have tested the program. Because of the "in-house" nature of initial field testing, elements of the directions may have been omitted or written unclearly. Instructional programmers frequently use jargon familiar only to themselves and their colleagues. This jargon could mislead or confuse the classroom teacher and could result in new student error.

Before an instructional program is ready for full-scale dissemination, those parts of the lesson sequence which caused teacher error should be isolated; this is accomplished by analyzing feedback from teachers using the program. First, data gathered in the secondary field test stage should be analyzed. If numerous errors occurred in sections which were error-free in the initial field testing, it is probable that teachers did not understand the directions. In some cases, error pileup occurs for one teacher and not for another. This kind of inconsistency will appear in children's data, indicating ambiguity in teacher directions.

Often, however, student data fail to indicate ambiguity which does, in fact, exist. For instance, a teacher may not understand the directions in one section, but if he teaches the section appropriately, the student data will not indicate a need for rewriting. For that reason, it is important to collect the second kind of feedback—information from those using the program. Through direct communication, ambiguities can be identified for the instructional programmer. Whenever ambiguity or error occurs, the instructional programmer has an obligation to rewrite affected sections.

For the Shoe Tie Program, 24 special education teachers were contacted and 18 indicated a willingness to use the program with 32 of their students. All of these students had learning problems ranging from severe retardation to moderate developmental lags with considerable behavioral disorders. The students were well past the age when shoe tying is expected to occur and had experienced numerous failures in attempting to learn basic self-help skills. One teacher's comment, "If this child, who has very low academic abilities, can successfully complete this program, I feel almost anyone would be successful," typifies this population. After 45 instructional days, 12 teachers reported data on 25 students. Of those 25 students, 12 successfully completed the program (Table 1).

The range of instructional days needed to meet the final criterion was 10–36, with a median of 19 days. Three additional students (two who did not have laced shoes and one confined to a wheelchair) completed Lesson 9, which required that they be able to tie the model shoe. Thus, 15 of 25 students successfully learned to tie shoes. The remaining 10 students experienced various problems with the program. One student's visual acuity problems impaired his performance, and he was removed from the program until appropriate corrective lenses could be provided. Three other students (the poorest performers) had excessive behavioral problems and could not be controlled by their teachers. One child made no progress after Lesson 4, and several others were frequently absent.

Each frame of the program was analyzed to determine if rewriting was necessary. "Pushes lace through hole," objectives 14 and 18, were the only obvious problem areas in the program (Table 3).

Setting a reasonable criterion of 3 days per lesson, these two objective checks in Lessons 5 and 6 appear to be problematic. By Lesson 7, this same objective (22, "pushes lace through hole") no longer had a high error rate. The final Shoe Tie Program will contain a warning to the teachers that this skill appears to be the most difficult to learn. The teachers will be encouraged to give their students extra practice on this skill and to use tangible reinforcers if they are deemed necessary.

From the follow-up questionnaire sent to all participating teachers, the only suggestion consistent across the majority of teachers dealt with the use of verbal instructions to the students. The revised program will encourage the teachers to alter the verbal directions at their discretion. These alterations will be correlated during the final data analysis period.

FINAL FIELD TESTING

During the last phase of instructional material development, enough program packages are produced to conduct final field testing with another 40–50 students. The procedures used in secondary field testing are repeated in order to validate the entire program, including all of the revisions. Each field testing stage has had a slightly more sophisticated purpose. The initial stage tested the first draft of the program, with emphasis on student error. The secondary field test stage specifically monitored both student and teacher error. After these steps have been completed, the instructional program is ready for dissemination. Final field testing insures that revisions made after the secondary field test stage actually reduced student and teacher error.

INSTRUCTIONAL PROGRAM DEVELOPED

To summarize, the specific skill taught by the instructional sequence was carefully selected and analyzed in such a way that each step in acquiring the skill was precisely identified and sequenced. The lessons were written so students could master each step, and the emerging program

**Table 3.**
**Number of Instructional Days per Student per Criterion Test**

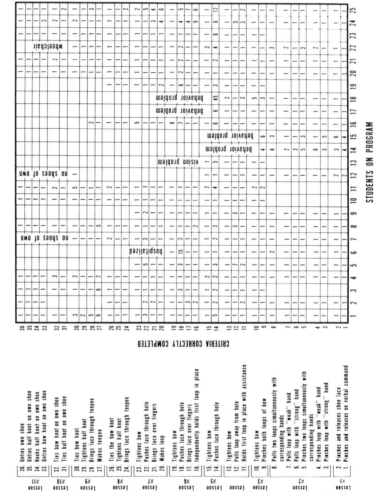

was field tested at least three times. There are various ways to disseminate these programs, including federally sponsored clearing-houses and commercial publishers. The instructional programmer needs to determine the most appropriate vehicle to disseminate the fully developed instructional program—one that has been through all the stages noted above.

## CONCLUSIONS

The prototypic model for developing instructional materials, as described in this chapter, is one systematic approach that provides hard data on the effectiveness of any given instructional material before it is placed on the open market. A recent commentary by a publisher of instructional materials (Bleil, 1975) notes that professionals (consumers) must demand quality materials before the publishers (producers) will be compelled to maintain high standards. If this attitude of "buyer beware" prevails at the marketplace, only the consumers can effect a change; they must purchase only proven materials!

Bleil (1975) also comments on the need for both child and teacher data statements. Basically, this means that educational materials must report not only on children's skill acquisition, but also on teachers' ability to use the material effectively and efficiently. The prototypic model produces data on both student and teacher performance. Initial, secondary, and final field testing provide specific child performance data. Secondary and final field test data yield information on teachers' ability to use the materials appropriately.

Latham (1974) questioned the willingness of teachers in the field to evaluate instructional materials. He speculates that teachers are too busy to take the time to respond to material evaluation questionnaires, and they are uninterested in the results of such surveys. Our experience has been completely the opposite. Without the use of incentives (money or even retention of instructional materials), 24 of 34 teachers contacted (73%) agreed to use the Shoe Tie program with their students. Of these 24 teachers, 12 (50%) returned the completed data after 45 possible instructional days (9 calendar weeks). All of these teachers completed a specific teacher questionnaire, and all indicated that more instructional programs should be field tested in this manner. When contacted, the remaining 12 teachers indicated they were still using the Shoe Tie Program with their students or that their students had moved away. All 24 teachers indicated

*The Prototypic Model for Developing Instructional Materials for the Severely Handicapped was developed under a grant from the National Institute of Education, Grant OEG-0-70-3916(607), Project 572247. The authors would like to thank Jennifer Maser for her help in the preparation of this manuscript.

they were interested in using this program in the future and would take part in field testing other programs, if appropriate for their students. Perhaps teachers are too busy and are uninterested in evaluating poorly constructed or inappropriate materials, but our data indicates that teachers are willing and even excited to be included in the validation process of well-constructed and appropriate instructional materials.

The development of effective instructional materials for handicapped children requires considerable time, effort, and money. Shortcuts in program development result in shortchanging handicapped students. As professionals responsible for the education of handicapped children, we must demand quality products. To do less is to abandon our responsibilities.

**REFERENCES**

Bliel G: Evaluating educational materials. J Learn Disabil, 8:19–26, 1975

Bricker WA: A systematic approach to language training. *In* Schiefelbusch RL (ed): Language of the Mentally Retarded. Baltimore, University Park Pr, 1972

Budde JF, Menolascino FJ: Systems technology and retardation: Application to vocational habilitation. Ment Retard 9:11–16, 1971

Chadwick BA, Day RC: Systematic reinforcement: Academic performance of underachieving students. J Appl Behav Anal 4:311–319, 1971

Hillman BW: The effect of knowledge of results and token reinforcement on the arithmetic achievement of elementary school children. Arith Teach 17:676–682, 1970

Kirby FD, Shields F: Modification of arithmetic response rate and attending behavior in a seventh-grade student. J Appl Behav Anal 5:79–84, 1972

Latham G: Measuring teacher responses to instructional materials. Educat Tech 14:11–15, 1974

Lovitt TC, Curtiss KA: Effects of manipulating an antecedent event on mathematics response rate. J Appl Behav Anal 1:329–333, 1968

Lovitt TC, Smith JO: Effects of instructions on an individual's verbal behavior. Except Child 38:685–693, 1972

Skinner BF: The Technology of Teaching. New York, Meredith, 1968

Smith DD, Lovitt TC, Kidder JD: Using reinforcement contingencies and teaching aids to alter subtraction performance of children with learning disabilities. *In* Semb G (ed.): Behavior Analysis and Education—1972. Lawrence, Kansas, Univ Kansas Pr, 1972

Smith DD, Smith JO: Research and application of a prototypic model for instructional material development. *In* Haring NG (ed.): A Program Project for the Investigation and Application of Procedures of Analysis and Modification of Behavior of Handicapped Children: Annual Report. National Institute of Education Grant OEG–0–70–3916 (607), 1974

Smith DD, Smith JO, Haring NG: The Shoe Tie Program. Experimental Edition, Experimental Education Unit, Child Development and Mental Retardation Center, University of Washington, Seattle, Washington, 1974

Woolman M: The concept of the program lattice. Washington D.C. Institute of Educational Research, Unpublished manuscript, 1962

# III

# Assessment and Performance Measurement

Wayne Sailor
and R. Don Horner

# A

# Educational Assessment Strategies for the Severely Handicapped

Assessment is the first step toward education of the severely handicapped. As a process, it enables the educator to know the student's skills, abilities, and existing behavior patterns. It provides a system for becoming familiar with the student early and in a way which is functional for the student's education. As a useful tool, assessment tells the educator where to begin with a severely handicapped child. Used skillfully, the assessment will specify educational goals for the class and instructional objectives for the individual student.

There are many varied kinds of standardized and published assessment systems applicable to the field of special education. These vary from precise behavioral scales and checklists, through specialized ability tests (e.g., reading readiness), to specific skill and ability assessment tools such as those used by speech therapists for language assessment, occupational therapists, etc. The focus of this chapter is on "global" educational assessment tools which are applicable to the severely handicapped student. The five scales and two checklists reviewed and discussed in this chapter are global in the sense that they tap different areas of the student's behavioral repertoire which will be subjected to learning or to the educational experience. Some of the assessment tools reviewed were developed from a different philosophical position on education than that which applies to severely handicapped children today. These tools were to be used by parents or "care personnel," frequently found staffing wards of large state institutions. The purpose of the assessment was to find out how "retarded" a new arrival to the ward really was, rather than to determine where and how to begin the student's educational process.

The severely handicapped student poses some unique problems for traditional educational assessment. The term "severely handicapped" has come to include one or more of the following parameters; physical disabilities so severe or complex that they restrict ambulation or locomotion via typical transportation modes; behavior characteristics which are injurious to self or others; gross hyperactivity; impulsiveness; frequently uncontrolled bowel and/or bladder functions; epilepsy; grossly inadequate communicative skills; and mixed or multiple sensorimotor disabilities. These parameters embrace severely and profoundly functionally retarded individuals, who may or may not be characterized by orthopedic, perceptual, and/or emotional handicaps. Given the nature and extent of these handicapping conditions, the definition of education necessarily becomes broad-based and flexible. It must include, for example, in addition to academic skills, basic learning functions associated with survival and coping. Curriculum must take the form of training programs for remediation of behavioral deficits; medicoprosthetic deficits; self-help, motor, social, and communicative skill deficits. The process of getting started with a class of severely handicapped children must be translated into identifying skill deficit areas and designing or implementing existing programs to alleviate those deficits.

It is hoped that in presenting, in some detail, descriptions of a number of applicable assessment devices, we will provide the educator with the information necessary to select an assessment tool which best meets his or her needs in getting started with a class of severely handicapped students.

### Vineland Social Maturity Scale

The Vineland Scale, developed by Dr. Edgar A. Doll at the Vineland Training School at Vineland, N.J. (Doll, 1947), is one of the oldest and one of the most extensively used assessment scales. The items on the scale are brief two-to-five word phrases backed up with one-to-three-sentence elaborations in the manual of directions. The items are grouped into 17 age ranges, and sample behaviors from six domains: self-help, self-direction, locomotion, occupation, communication, and social relations. The self-help domain is divided into three subdomains of self-help—general, self-help eating, and self-help dressing. The scale is said to provide "a definite outline of detailed performances in respect to which children show a progressive capacity for looking after themselves and for participating in those activities which lead toward ultimate independence as adults." (Doll, 1947, p. 1).

The initial standardization data was collected on "normal" individuals, 10 males and 10 females from each year of chronological age from birth to 30 for a total of 620 subjects. The final items for the scale were arranged statistically with average age norms provided for each item, a technique which is said to have resulted in "a precise order of progressive difficulty."

The recommended uses for the scale include measurement of growth or change, individual differences, variation in development, improvement following training, and reviewing developmental histories. The scale has 117 items. The number of items in each of the 17 age categories ranges from 17 in the birth to 1 year and 1 to 2-year age categories, to three in the 9–10 and 11–12-year age categories. The number of items in each domain which sample behaviors from birth to 30 years ranges from 10 in locomotion to 39 in the combined self-help subdomains.

The score for each item is necessarily subjectively determined. A recorder interviews an informant who is required to judge and then describe how much, to what extent, and in what ways the individual usually or habitually behaves. The recorder has to make a number of judgments in order to determine a score. To score an item "plus," the judgments required are: (1) does the behavior as described by the informant conform to the one-to-three-sentence description in the manual; (2) if so, is the behavior usually or habitually performed; (3) if so, is performance dependent upon undue urging or artificial incentive; or (4) is performance dependent upon occasional assistance under special circumstances. To score an item "plus F," the judgments required are: (1) does the behavior as described by the informant fail to conform to the one-to-three-sentence description in the manual; (2) if so, is this due to special restraint or lack of opportunity; and (3) if so, did the behavior formerly conform to the description when restraints were absent or opportunity was present. To score an item "plus 0," the following judgments are required: (1) is this a behavior the individual has not performed in the past and does not perform now; (2) if so, is this due to special restraint or lack of opportunity; (3) if so, would the individual usually or habitually perform the behavior or quickly learn to do so if restraints were removed or opportunities were provided; and (4) is absence of performance due to physical or mental disability (if so, the item cannot be scored "plus 0"). To score an item "plus and minus," the recorder has to judge: (1) if the behavior is occasionally performed but not ordinarily performed with full success; and (2) if so, is the performance more than cursory or fitful. To score an item "minus," the recorder has to judge: (1) if performance has not yet been successful; or (2) if successful, has it been only (a) rarely successful, or (b) successful when under extreme pressure, or (c) successful when under unusual incentive.

Different credit or point value ranging from 0 to 0.5 to 1 is given to different scores, and the total credit is converted to an overall social age ranging from 0.06 years of social age for one point to 30 plus years of social age for 110 or more points. If an individual's social age matches or exceeds his chronological age, his social maturity is considered average or above. The extent to which social age is below the chronological age is the extent the individual is considered socially immature.

### Cain–Levine Social Competency Scale

The Social Competency Scale (Cain, Levine, and Elzey, 1963) was developed during the course of a federally sponsored research project at San Francisco State College. The authors acknowledged the work of Dr. Edgar A. Doll as their initial starting point. The items on the scale are brief one-to-four-word phrases followed by four or five sentences 3 to 16 words long describing four or five levels of increasingly independent performance. The items are placed under five categories: personal care, mealtime skills, general tasks and responsibility, interpersonal skills, and communication. These are recombined in the scoring into four domains: self-help, initiative, social skills, and communication. The authors define social competency as "the development of learned skills which ultimately permits the child to achieve self-sufficiency and socially contributory behaviors" which "is measured along a dependence–independence continuum." This continuum is reflected in the sentences describing increasingly independent performance in four ways: (1) increase in manipulative ability; (2) moving from other-directed to self-initiated behavior; (3) moving from self-oriented to other-oriented behavior; and (4) through increased ability to be understood (Cain, Levine, and Elzey, 1963, p. 2).

The final standardization of the scale was based on ratings of "mentally retarded" individuals, 414 males and 302 females, enrolled in public, private, and parent-operated schools or residents of state institutions in California. They ranged in chronological age from 5 to 14 years. The scores of each of the four domains and total score were statistically converted to percentile ranks for five different age groups of mentally retarded individuals, which permits the determination of an individual's relative standing in relation to other mentally retarded individuals in each of the four domains and in overall social competency. The items themselves were not arranged in any particular sequence within a category, but the four or five sentences under each item were sequenced along a continuum of increasing independence by means of rank-order agreement among judges.

The scale has 44 items with which to sample the behaviors of children ranging in age from 5 to 14 years. The number of items in each domain is 10 (initiative, social skills, and communication) and 14 (self-help).

The score for each item is determined subjectively, but the authors have attempted to reduce the number of judgments that have to be made in comparison to the number required by the Vineland Scale. An interview format is recommended. Informants are asked to describe the behavior of the individual. The rater must judge which sentence under the item best conforms to the verbal responses of the informant. A score of 1 on the item reflects the most dependent level, and a score of 4 or 5 on the item reflects the most independent level, with the scores of 2 and 3 reflecting the transition from dependence to independence. This takes the place of the "plus and minus" scoring used in the Vineland Scale. The "+F" and "+0" scoring categories used in the Vineland Scale are not used in this scale, with the rationale that determination of what behaviors are actually performed and at what level of independence is more relevant information than an informant's conjecture, inference, or interpretation of what might happen under hypothetical conditions. Even though this probably reduces some of the judgments required of a rater, there are still difficult judgments such as does the behavior occur: (1) occasionally, frequently, or nearly always, and (2) rarely, sometimes, or usually.

## AAMD Adaptive Behavior Scale

The American Association on Mental Deficiency Adaptive Behavior Scale (Nihira, Foster, Shellhaas, & Leland, 1974) is perhaps the most widely and intensively used assessment procedure at this time. It was developed at the Parsons State Hospital and Training Center in Kansas under the sponsorship of the American Association on Mental Deficiency with a grant from the National Institute of Mental Health.

The items on the scale are primarily brief, one-to-four word title phrases that are sometimes followed by four to seven phrases describing decreasingly independent behavioral performance, and, at other times, are followed by phrases describing 4–12 behaviors which are examples of members of the class of behavior identified by the title of the item. The scale items are divided into two broad categories. Part One contains developmental items and Part Two contains maladaptive items. The items in Part One are grouped under 10 domains: independent functioning, physical development, economic activity, language development, numbers and time, domestic activity, vocational activity, self-direction, responsibility, and socialization. The independent functioning domain is divided into the eight subdomains of eating, toilet use, cleanliness, appearance, care of clothing, dressing and undressing, travel, and general independent functioning. Physical development is divided into the two subdomains of sensory and motor development. Economic activity is divided into the two subdomains of money handling and budgeting, and shopping skills. Language development is divided into expression, comprehension, and social language development; domestic activity into cleaning, kitchen duties, and other domestic activities; and self-direction into initiative, perseverance, and leisure time. The items in Part Two are grouped under 14 subdomains: violent and destructive behavior, antisocial behavior, rebellious behavior, untrustworthy behavior, withdrawal, stereotyped behavior and odd mannerisms, inappropriate interpersonal manners, unacceptable vocal habits, unacceptable or eccentric habits, self-abusive behavior, hyperactive tendencies, sexually aberrant behavior, psychological disturbances, and use of medications.

The authors state that the term adaptive behavior "primarily refers to the effectiveness of an individual in coping with the natural and social demands of his or her environment" (Nihira, Foster, Shellhaas and Leland, 1974, p. 5).

The standardization data is based on mildly, moderately, severely, and profoundly mentally retarded male and female persons in residential institutions. They ranged in chronological age from 3 through 69. The scores on each of the 10 domains of Part One and 14 domains of Part Two were statistically converted to percentile ranks for 11 different age groups. This allows the determination of an individual's relative standing in relation to institutionalized mentally retarded individuals on each of the 24 domains. The items in Part One are arranged in presumed developmental sequence.

The recommended uses for the scale include: identification of areas of deficiency, comparison of an individual's ratings over time, comparison of ratings on the same individual in different situations, comparison of ratings by different raters, providing information exchange, development of new training programs and research, and providing descriptions of groups of individuals.

The authors also suggest the following administrative uses: program planning and design, resource allocation, administrative control, and program evaluation.

The Scale has 66 items in Part One and 44 items in Part Two to sample behaviors from 3 up to 70 years. The number of items in each domain ranges from 2 to 21 in Part One and 1 to 7 in Part Two.

The score for each item is determined subjectively, but the authors in the 1974 revision have improved the wording of the items and increased the emphasis on observable behavior in an effort to reduce the possible bias and ambiguity. Three methods are recommended for obtaining the information upon which to base the score for each item. One is called first person assessment. In this case, a person who knows how to use the scale is also familiar with the person being rated and scores all the items in the scale. The second method, called third party assessment, is for several individuals who may possess relevant information, but who are not familiar with the use of the scale. Each is asked for information about each of the items on the scale. The third method is called the interview method. In this case, an individual familiar with the person being rated is asked a series of questions designed to elicit verbal responses which describe the behavior of the individual being rated. The rater must judge which description or (on some items) descriptions under the item best conforms to the verbal responses of the informant.

There are three types of items in the scale, each with its own scoring procedures. Each requires that the rater judge which of the descriptions best conforms to the description provided by the informant (or best conforms to the behavior of the individual being rated if the rater and informant are the same person). One scoring procedure requires that the rater select and circle the number of the description which represents the level of independent performance of the individual and enter this number as a score. A second scoring procedure requires that the rater place a check beside each description judged to conform to the behavior of the individual being rated. The descriptions checked are summed and entered as the item score or, in the case of descriptions of negative behaviors, subtracted from the total number of descriptions and entered as the item score. The third scoring procedure requires that the rater judge not only whether a description conforms to the behavior of the individual but whether it occurs occasionally or frequently. Each description scored as occurring occasionally receives 1 point and each scored as occurring frequently receives 2 points. The total number of points is entered as the score for the item. The item scores within each domain are summed and a profile of all the domains is plotted. This profile shows not only relative standing on each domain in relation to an institutional population, but it also shows which domains are lower than others.

The authors suggest possible ways to interpret the profile. For example, if the individual ranks high on Part Two (maladaptive behaviors), consideration should be given to reducing the individual's maladaptive behavior to see what happens to the adaptive behaviors in Part One. It is also suggested that an individual with domain scores at or near the top of the percentile ranks probably performs well enough in these domains that a trainer can concentrate on the remaining domains. Of the remaining domains, the authors suggest that programs be developed for the higher ones, as their experience has shown that this results in improvements in the lower domains. An exception to this is if lower scores are the result of restrictive policies or opportunities which can be changed. It is also suggested that the domains themselves follow a developmental sequence, with behaviors in the domain of physical development being acquired first, and those of economic activity last. If both these domains are low, programs for physical development should take priority. As program goals are met, the scale should be given again to provide a basis for determining the next remedial program. The suggestions for interpreting the second part of the scale center mainly around the impact the maladaptive behavior is having on the individual and his environment, and the age of the individual in relation to the behavior. The behavior of setting fires may have a higher priority for reduction than the behavior of spitting on others; and the behavior of throwing self on floor, screaming, and yelling may take less priority for reduction in a 3-year-old than it would in a 30-year-old.

### Balthazar Scales of Adaptive Behavior

The Balthazar Scales (Balthazar, 1971 a, b, c, d; 1973), designed for use with the severely and profoundly retarded, were developed at the Central Wisconsin Colony and Training School in Madison, Wis., at about the same time Nihira, Foster, Shellhaas, and Leland were developing the AAMD Adaptive Behavior Scale.

The Balthazar Scales are divided into two sections. Section I contains the scales of functional independence which are said to provide "a comprehensive study of adaptive, functionally independent behaviors of ambulant severely or profoundly retarded or younger moderately retarded individuals" (Balthazar, 1971a, p. v). Section II contains the scales of social adaptation which are said "to yield objective measures of coping behaviors" (Balthazar, 1973, p. 3).

Section I is divided into: (1) eating scales designed to measure specific eating skills observed during the course of one or more meals. The skills are grouped into five major classes with up to 13 items each: dependent feeding, finger foods, spoon usage, fork usage, and drinking. A supplementary eating checklist includes self-service, use of assistive devices, type of food, position in which fed, rate of eating, advanced utensil usage, and supervision. (2) Dressing and undressing scales which involve a rater observing or taking the rated individual through a series of steps to put on and take off shoes; tighten, tie, and untie laces; put on and take off socks; put on and take off briefs; put on and take off an undershirt; put on and take off a shirt or blouse; put on and take off pants or skirt; and put on and take off a dress. (3) A toileting questionnaire with information obtained in interviews and divided into questions about daytime bladder and bowel control; and general information about nighttime bladder and bowel control.

Section II is divided into eight categories, which are further subdivided as follows: (1) unadaptive self-directed behaviors, including failure to respond; stereotypy (stereopathy); posturing, including objects; nondirected, repetitious verbalization; inappropriate self-directed behavior; and disorderly, nonsocial behavior; (2) unadaptive interpersonal behaviors, including inappropriate contact with others; aggression; and withdrawal; (3) adaptive self-directed behaviors, including generalized, exploratory, and recreational activity; (4) adaptive interpersonal behaviors, including fundamental social behaviors—noncommunication; fundamental social behaviors—social vocalization and gestures; and appropriate response to negative peer contact; (5) verbal communication, including nonfunctional, repetitious, or inarticulate verbalization; and verbalization; (6) play activities, including object relations; playful contact, and play activities; (7) response to instructions, including response to firmly given instructions; and cooperative contact; (8) a checklist consisting of personal care, assisted or unassisted, and other behaviors. All of the items on each of the scales are brief phrases backed up by one or more sentence elaborations in the rater's handbooks.

The population studied in developing Section I included 451 and, in Section II, 288 ambulant individuals 5–57 years of age who resided at the Central Wisconsin Colony and Training School between 1964 and 1969. Standardization data were derived from 122 individuals for the eating scales, 200 for the dressing–undressing scales, and 129 for the toileting scales.

The recommended uses for the scale include: (1) providing precise objectives for the design and development of behavioral programs; (2) providing a standardized method for measurement, evaluation, and feedback of results of behavioral programs; (3) grouping of subjects for classification purposes; (4) evaluation of manpower staffing patterns and inservice training programs; and (5) research.

Primary emphasis is given to information which is obtained by direct observation. The observations are made on various items which measure very small differences in behavior. Each rated individual is observed while engaged in "typical" activities, and in "familiar" situations. The rater must judge which aspects of an individual's behavior are representative of typical behavior and must eliminate from the observations any behaviors judged to be: (1) influenced by chance; (2) reflecting inadequate training of others; and including (3) interview information of doubtful reliability. A rater is supposed to discontinue rating an individual (1) not in the visual range of the rater; (2) engaged in therapy or training; (3) in bed or sick; (4) being held or restrained; and (5) when handling and/or supervision is improper or inappropriate.

The procedures for administering the eating scales by the rater include: (1) neither initiating nor responding to the behavior of the individual being rated; (2) ignoring any attempt by the individual being rated to interact with the rater; (3) remaining in an appropriate position for observing without affecting the behavior of the individual being rated; (4)

not influencing the rated individual's interactions with others; and (5) avoiding looking directly at the individual being rated.

The procedures for scoring the eating scales include: (1) scoring all items individually on a 0–10 point scale; (2) scoring all items on the proportion of each 10 occurrences, a "0" if the behavior does not occur and "10" if it occurs at each opportunity or attempt. One occurrence in each 10 is scored "1," 2 scored "2," 5 scored "5," etc; (3) never scoring an item higher than the one from which it is indented; for example, if "holds finger foods" receives a score of "5," then the score of the indented item "hand to mouth movement" cannot exceed "5." The supplementary eating checklist is scored by placing a checkmark by those that apply, leaving blank those that do not apply, and printing N.O. (no opportunity) if opportunities to perform the behavior are not provided.

The procedures for administering the dressing–undressing scales include: (1) providing the opportunity for the individual being rated to perform all of the dressing and undressing independently; (2) if independent performance does not occur, providing opportunities to perform at each step, putting on or taking off clothing as outlined in the manual; (3) providing appropriate verbal or material reinforcers for successful independent performance of the entire behavior, but only delivering verbal reinforcers upon successful completion of a step; (4) allowing 10 sec for the individual being rated to begin his performance and, if performance does not occur, providing additional cues, a demonstration, and a 1-min wait for performance before performing the step for the individual.

The procedure for scoring the dressing–undressing scale is to score each item on a 0–6-point basis. Six points are given for "independent performance"; 5 points for "independent, imperfect performance"; 4 points for "supervised performance"; 3 points for "assisted, partially"; 2 points for "assisted, primarily"; 1 point for "cooperative performance"; and 0 points for "no participation." More detailed criteria for point scoring are provided in the rater's handbook.

The toileting scale is administered in an interview format. The person being interviewed is asked a series of questions and is asked to estimate, on the basis of an average of 10 times that the individual eliminates, the number of times the behavior referred to in the question occurs. The estimated number becomes the score for the one item. Two interviews are required if a different person attends the rated individual at night.

The scales in Section II employ direct observations of individuals while engaged in "typical" activities in "familiar" situations. The measurement system in Section II is frequency counts per unit of time. The score for each item is based on six 10-min observation sessions per individual. The observations should extend over a period of at least 3 days in a given rating week. Scoring is done by occurrence (a tally made each time the behavior occurs) or by 1-minute intervals (a tally made in each minute containing at least one instance of the behavior). Several behaviors occurring together are each tallied beside the appropriate item on the tally sheet. These tallies are then transcribed to the scoring summary sheet, and the cumulative frequency, mean, or median becomes the score for the item.

A profile on each of the scales in Section I can be plotted, using either raw scores or percentile scores. Performance tables which show percentile ranks for various raw scores are provided in the supervisor's handbook. The author emphasized that they are guidelines, but they can be used cautiously as standardized tables if the means and standardizations of the rated population are comparable to those presented in the tables. It is further pointed out that the development of percentile tables for the specific population under study is the preferable procedure for serious attempts to use the scale empirically. In profiling or graphing the observations in Section II, the performance areas (categories, scales, or items) are marked off on the horizontal base of the graph. The scores (cumulative frequency, means, or medians, etc.) are marked off on the vertical axis. Line graphs, histograms, bar graphs, etc., represent the actual scores in each area. The type of presentation and the areas selected for presentation depend on the use to be made of the information. The mean cumulative frequencies of the standardization group for each scale of Section II are presented in the handbook for Section II. The author cautions the test administrator not to consider the means as norms, but as descriptions of the behaviors observed at a given time in a specific population; serious users of the scale are encouraged to develop means for their populations.

Once the scores in Section I are profiled, the high and low scores can be studied and certain skills can be selected for improvement. In Section II, the profile provides for identification of low points in coping. Programs can be developed to improve skills or to increase the frequency of "desirable" behaviors and thus to reduce the frequency of "undesirable" behaviors. In addition, programs can be developed to reinforce and extend desirable behavior already present.

Repeated administration of the scales can determine the progress that has been made, which programs are strong and which are weak, provide a basis for the selection of new targets and a criterion for moving individuals into new training environments.

### Camelot Behavioral Checklist

The Camelot Behavioral Checklist (Foster, 1974) was developed by the second author of the AAMD Adaptive Behavior Scale. It has three distinctive features; (1) a large number of items (399) which sample behaviors over a wide range of ability; (2) all of the items can be directly stated as instructional objectives; and (3) the items are arranged in an empirically derived increasing order of difficulty (defined in terms of the percent of the original sample that needed training on the behavior).

The items on the scale are brief two-to-seven-word behavioral descriptions. The scale has 10 domains which are divided into 40 subdomains as follows: (1) self-help, including eating behaviors, dressing and undressing, toilet use, cares for own health, knowledge of self, bathing, hair care, and grooming; (2) physical development, including balance, walking, posture, body movements, hand movements, and sensory development; (3) home duties, including house cleaning, clothing care, cooking, yard care, car maintenance, and operation of appliances; (4) vocational development, including work-related skills and job skills; (5) economic behavior, including shopping, money handling, and use of credit; (6) independent travel, including transportation and travel skills; (7) numerical skills, including arithmetic skills and time; (8) communication skills, including receptive language, expressive language, reading, writing, and use of the telephone; (9) social behaviors, including spectator activities, participation, and interaction with others; (10) responsibility, including social responsibility, response to emergencies, and security.

The Camelot was designed "to identify specific training objectives for an individual" and then to provide "a summary or classification score which is directly based on these objectives" (Foster, 1974, pp. 2–3). It can be administered in three different ways: (1) one person completing each of the items from memory; (2) two or more persons completing different items from memory; or (3) one or more persons completing the items by directly observing the behavior of the individual being rated. The author recommends the use of one of the first two methods as a basis for preliminary selection of targets, then use of direct observation of the behaviors selected for training during the pretest or baseline.

The checklist is scored by judging whether the individual "Can Do" each of the 399 behavioral descriptions or whether he "Needs Training." " 'Can Do' refers to those behaviors the client can now do and further training is not required. 'Needs Training' means the individual cannot presently perform the behavior or performs it in less than normal manner, and further training should be planned" (Foster, 1974, p. 5). There are some exceptions to the scoring, such as when items refer specifically to males and females and when physical limitations preclude further training. The general rule for scoring all such items is: if the item cannot be considered a target for further training, score it "Can Do" to indicate it should not be selected as a target behavior. If an individual has had no opportunity to perform the behavior, the rater is instructed to either guess or actually test the individual to determine if he can do it. If doubt arises, it is recommended that the item be scored "Needs Training," rather than have the individual miss being provided any needed training because the behavior was scored "Can Do."

The items on the scale scored "Can Do" are transferred to the Camelot Behavioral Checklist Profile which consists of 40 columns of numbers, one column for each subdomain. The numbers in each column correspond to the numbers of the items. Each item scored "Can Do" is circled. Each item scored "Needs Training" is left uncircled. The numbers in each column representing the items are in a descending order of difficulty. The level of difficulty is based on the percentage of individuals in the original sample of 624 mentally retarded individuals who needed training on that item. Therefore, the selection of "targets" for training should start with the lowest uncircled item number in any subdomain and proceed upward. When all gaps have been filled, targets can then be selected which will expand an individual's behavioral repertoire beyond the highest item circled on the item profile. The selection of subdomains from which to choose targets probably should be based on the percent of the original sample that needed training on the behavior. For example, behavioral descriptions 1, 2 and 3 on the subdomain "eating behavior" are all lower percentages (and presumably less difficult behaviors) than item 1 on the subdomain dressing and undressing; therefore, if items 1, 2, and 3 of the eating behavior subdomain need training, they should be trained before item 1 of the dressing and undressing subdomain.

The number of "Can Do" items in each domain is totaled and entered in the appropriate box on the item profile sheet. The totals for each domain and the total for all domains are transferred to the Camelot Behavioral Checklist Score Profile which consists of 11 columns, one column for each domain and one column for the checklist total. The score profile provides a quick overall representation of the number of behaviors within each domain already acquired and the number not yet acquired by the individual. It also shows the individual's relationship to the original group in terms of the percentage of that group who had also acquired that level of behavior within each of the domains and for the total score.

If the data plotted on the score profile are the mean scores of a group, then it is possible to determine where that group stands in relation to the scores of the original group. If the scores of both an individual and the mean of the group are plotted, it is possible to determine where the individual stands in relation to the group.

Once the target or terminal behaviors have been determined, a Skill Acquisition Program Bibliography (Tucker, 1974) is used to identify any programs that have already been developed for those behaviors. The references list programs by title and author (or project) that are known to exist and where they can be obtained. Each program included in the references was evaluated and assigned one to four "stars" on the following criteria: One star—"Plausible task analysis and teaching strategy (defined as meeting the subjective quality standards of Camelot Behavioral Systems)." Two stars—"Plausible task analysis and teaching strategy and field tested in one location with 40 or fewer students." Three stars—"Plausible task analysis and teaching strategy and field tested in two or more locations with more than 40 students." Four stars—"Plausible task analysis and teaching strategy, field tested in two or more locations with more than 40 students, and is commercially available." (Tucker, 1974, p. 1). Programs were "not available" (which means they either did not exist or could not be found) for 176 or approximately 45% of the 399 behavioral descriptions.

### Portage Project Checklist

The Portage Project Checklist (Shearer et al., 1970) is a checklist of behaviors which, according to the authors, usually appear in normal children between birth and 5 years. The checklist is one part of the Portage Guide to Early Education; the second part is a card file containing a behavioral description and suggested activities and materials for each item on the checklist. These materials are recommended for use (1) with normal or handicapped children; (2) in the home, classroom or institution; (3) in a one-to-one or group situation; and (4) with professionals, paraprofessionals, or parents. The checklist was developed by pooling items from several inventories, scales, charts, and records. The card file was developed from experience with children in establishing the behaviors on the checklist.

Both the checklist and card file are color coded and divided into five categories: (1) cognitive, (2) self-help, (3) motor, (4) language, and (5) socialization. The items within each category are listed as nearly as possible in the order and age level at which they are thought to appear in normal development. As the child is assessed, a checkmark is placed in the "entry behavior" column beside each behavior which the child is now exhibiting or has previously exhibited. Those nonchecked behaviors following the checked behaviors are potential "target" behaviors. The potential target behaviors from each of the five categories can be organized into a curriculum sequence for that particular child. As each behavior is selected as a target and is learned by the child, the date on which the behavior is considered to be learned is written beside the behavior in the "date achieved" column. The card file provides suggested activities for each behavior.

## TARC Assessment System[2]

The TARC System (Sailor and Mix, 1975), called TARC because it was developed at the Topeka (Kansas) Association for Retarded Citizens Community Day Services Center, represents an example of a short-form behavioral assessment tool which is geared directly to the formulation of instructional objectives and subsequent curriculum selection. The system is predicated on the fact that there currently exists a wide spectrum of applied technology immediately available to meet educational goals of a severely handicapped population, but which, for various reasons, has been inadequately disseminated. Commensurate with the current surging trend in the field of special education to provide functional educational experiences for this heretofore neglected population, and to establish classes in regular school district schools for the severely handicapped, a means of getting this curriculum technology out to teachers and para-professional personnel is urgently needed. The TARC System is designed to provide a means for meeting this need in special education by relating curriculum selection directly to assessment and the derivation of instructional objectives.

The system is short-form, as opposed to comprehensive, and is primarily intended to help personnel charged with the education of the severely handicapped to get started in the classroom, day-care center, institution, etc. It seeks to go beyond providing a simple, categorical statement of a child's current strengths and weaknesses relative to education, and seeks instead to provide an immediate basis for curriculum planning and selection. In meeting this need, the system functions as a mechanism for the dissemination of curriculum technology which otherwise is, in many cases, located only after extensive and time-consuming searches of a wide variety of resources.

Traditionally, the formulation of educational goals, the writing of instructional objectives, the process of curriculum planning and design, the writing of lesson plans, grading of papers (on-line measurement), etc., has been the exclusive domain of competent, well-trained and experienced teachers in the field. These teachers have relied extensively on the large body of literature encountered in their training and in regular perusals of educational journals and in daily contacts with their peers in the school system. The teacher of the severely handicapped child currently enjoys none of these advantages. The chances are great that this teacher will have been trained for the education of a qualitatively different population such as Educable Mentally Retarded, Trainable Mentally Retarded, Learning Disabled, Emotionally Disturbed, etc. Training programs for the preparation of personnel for the severely handicapped are only just beginning (Sontag, Burke, and York, 1973). The chances are equally great that this person will operate, at least initially, in a relative vacuum. At any one school, for example, there will probably be only one classroom for the severely handicapped. Today, one is surprised to encounter even one such class in a given school district. Some states as yet have no classes for the severely handicapped. The teacher will, in addition to these problems, find relatively little in current educational journals to assist in curriculum planning. Many existing educational programs were developed during the past decade on various federally funded research projects and practically ceased to exist when the project expired.

The TARC System, in short, provides a procedure for getting started with a severely handicapped class, a procedure for personnel caught in the time-training lag prevalent in the field of special education with this population. In the manner to be described in the rest of this chapter, it affords a relatively quick behavioral assessment of the child's capabilities and disabilities; formulates, with the aid of a computer program, instructional objectives for the child's initial educational programming; and, finally, selects from existing, available curriculum technology those educational programs which were specifically designed to meet the instructional objectives, and describes these curricula in sufficient detail to enable the teacher to make reasonable decisions on selection and purchase. The TARC System utilizes a four-stage procedure to arrive at curriculum selection which consists of (1) assessment, (2) profiling, (3) derivation of instructional objectives, and (4) curriculum selection. The teachers' creative ability will be challenged extensively at the point of implementation of the purchased curriculum modules, some of which are poorly designed and written, some of which do not work, and many of which are largely unsupported by field test research efforts. Curriculum selection for severely handicapped students is, as yet, a relatively undeveloped territory, and will most likely remain so for the next several years. On the more optimistic side, however, many of the materials discussed elsewhere in this book are representative of successful educational technology when skillfully applied to the severely handicapped student.

STAGE ONE: ASSESSMENT.

The TARC Assessment Inventory is the keystone component of the system. It was developed to provide a short-form educational assessment of the current level of skill development of severely and profoundly retarded or otherwise multihandicapped children on a variety of skill domains. It can be utilized to provide an immediate index of the current level of functioning of a child in a given educational setting. When scores are averaged across children in the setting, it can be used to provide an index of the current level of educational functioning of a group or class. Assessing a child with the TARC Inventory requires a rater to make a series of scaler judgments (e.g., choose one of five or six scaled items which best describes the child on a particular skill) and categorical judgments (e.g., choose any number of a series of items which best describes the child's current performance) based upon careful observation of the child in a group or class setting. The rater must be at least minimally familiar with the child (or class) and should have observed his or her behavior for at least 2 weeks prior to making the assessment. The rater is encouraged to put the child through various "skill-tapping" activities, dictated by the inventory, to determine if various behaviors are or are not present in the child's repertoire.

Utilized in this fashion, the TARC Inventory may be used to:

1. Provide a means of communicating with parents, agency personnel, and others over various educationally related performances relevant for a severely handicapped population of children.

2. Demonstrate accountability for educational or rehabilitative efforts by (potentially) showing changes across a wide variety of skill areas, with repeated measures at 6 months or greater intervals. For example, a class utilizing a particular language development program may supply field test data for the program's effectiveness by demonstrating averaged significant elevations, over time, on the communication skill domain of the inventory. These data would provide a form of concurrent validity if strongly associated (correlated) with on-line, day-to-day performance data from the language program being tested.

3. Provide an educational assessment upon which to base the formulation of educational goals for a group or class. Utilizing averaged scores for the group, the rater may determine, for example, that the class average is low on fine-motor skills relative to other performances. This information might translate into a decision to devote a particular portion of the class time to block teaching of activities comprising the fine motor development skills.

4. Provide an educational assessment on which to base the formulation of precise instructional objectives for individual children.

The TARC Inventory is not intended to provide a comprehensive, global assessment of the type available through the Balthazar Scales or the Adaptive Behavior Scales. It is rather intended to selectively tap a few representative skill areas within each of four domains: self-help, motor, communication, and social skills. The inventory was standardized on a population of 283 severely handicapped children in institutions and day centers. It has been rather extensively tested and revised, and has been shown to be a reliable instrument over time and across independent observers. The manual which accompanies the inventory (Sailor and Mix, 1975) presents statistical data on the standardization of the instrument. Research which is presently under way at Kansas Neurological Institute and through the services of the Arkansas Department of Social and Rehabilitation Services, Division of Developmental Disabilities, is tending to show, by way of short-term validity, that the instrument is particularly discriminative at lower ranges of intellectual and behavioral functioning. It becomes less sensitive to performance changes at the moderate levels of functioning and tends to be insensitive to performance differences among and within mildly or borderline retarded children.

The overall structure of the inventory is as follows. Within the self-help skill area, the inventory provides data on the child's level of functioning for toileting (a composite of performance on urinary and bowel functions); washing; eating (a composite of utensil use, neatness, drinking, and behavior at mealtime); and clothing (a composite of dressing and undressing abilities).

Within the motor skill area, the inventory produces scores for small muscle (a composite of fine-motor skills); large muscle (a composite of physical education, play, and related gross-motor skills); and pre-academic skills (a composite of specific behaviors requiring motor coordination and perceptual–motor skills judged to be of direct relevance for classroom curriculum).

The communication skill area supplies performance data on expression (production) and reception (comprehension) as parallel communicative abilities. It also provides a preacademic communication skill score which is a composite of specific classroom-related communicative behaviors.

Within the social skill area, the TARC Inventory provides data on behavior as it pertains to responsiveness-to-directions on the part of an adult, to functioning in a group, and to functioning on a one-to-one basis. It also taps interaction with peers and adults as well as cooperation, parallel play, and emotional stability or control. Data are provided on preacademic social skills, which are a composite of specific classroom-related social behaviors.

The inventory is accompanied by a manual of operation (one for each package of 10 assessment forms ordered); a biographical data sheet, for recording supplementary information which might modify interpretations of outcome scores (e.g., severe auditory or visual impairment, severe orthopedic handicap, etc.); a profile sheet, for producing a graphic representation of the child's functioning within his various skill areas as they compare to the standardization sample; and a score sheet, which is detachable for mailing in order to activate the computer options discussed below.

STAGE TWO: PROFILING.

Scores on an assessment summary score sheet are meaningful only within some specifiable context which enables the rater to translate them into prescriptive educational programming efforts. The TARC Assessment System includes, with the inventory, a blank profile sheet which enables the rater to transfer scores to a graphic descriptive system which lends them some degree of statistical meaningfulness. The profile sheet is constructed in such a way that the child's scores on the various domains and subdomains sampled can be examined in terms of a comparison with the averaged scores of the standardization sample. By connecting the child's scores with a felt-tipped pen after plotting them on the profile sheet, the rater constructs a graph of the child's overall performance which may be interpreted two ways. First, the scores which fall below the midpoint of the profile sheet indicate that the child scored below the average of the standardization sample of 283 on those particular items. In formulating instructional objectives, the TARC System employs the logic that the child should first receive educational instruction and training on those areas in which he is most deficient relative to his peers. The second interpretation that can be made from the profile sheet is an analysis of the child's relative strengths and weaknesses from the standpoint of his own overall level of functioning. A given child may have a profile where no single score falls below the midpoint on the scale. The child is, thus, relatively ahead of the standardization sample in all areas. The lowest point on the graph, however, might fall on the eating subdomain of the self-help skill section. This would indicate that, relative to the child's overall level of functioning, his eating skills reflect the most impairment; therefore, an educational program to develop eating skills would constitute an initial instructional objective. The term "instructional objective," as it is employed in the context of the TARC System, refers to behaviors to be engaged in on the part of the teacher, rather than terminal performances on the part of the student.

Figure 1 presents a sample profile sheet from the TARC System. Data are presented on the profile from one of the children in the standardization sample, to illustrate how the profile may be used.

The profile sheet is designed so that scores can be transferred from the score sheet to an appropriate spot on the profile sheet under each of the subdomains assessed (e.g., toileting); under the total score for each assessed domain (e.g., self-help); and for the total inventory score (last column on the profile sheet). The distribution of numbers on each column of the profile sheet represents the spread, for each of the columns, of the average scores for the standardization sample, transformed statistically into standard scores with a mean of 50 and an SD of 20. Thus, if the averaged scores for the entire standardization sample were plotted on the sample profile sheet, the resulting graph would be a straight line at the standard score 50 location (for the left and for the right margins). The sample data presented in Fig. 1 show how far one child deviated from the average and by how much in statistical terms. This particular child, who was 11 years old at the time the profile was made, is considerably below the average of the standardization sample on his total scale score (25). This child has been assessed on other measures and found to be profoundly retarded (I.Q. below 25). The TARC Profile data show him to be particularly deficient in both communication and social skill areas. He reveals essentially no skills in language, and he does not wash himself. Relative to the standardization sample, the child shows some strength only in toilet regulation and eating. Relative to his own overall performance, the child is particularly lacking receptive communication skills, and washing as a specific self-help skill. The low receptive language score might suggest severe hearing impairment, but this finding was not confirmed in audiological screening.

The rater using the TARC System has an option, at this point, of utilizing the system's two additional stages, or stopping with profiling. The inventory contains a blank profile sheet of the type illustrated in Fig. 1. The rater can produce the graphic profile and, in conjunction with a careful study of the raw assessment data, arrive at a series of instructional objectives for the child and seek curricula to meet the specified objectives. The second option is to return the score sheet to the author to activate the computer options in deriving instructional objectives and listing available curricula.

Under the computer-programmed option, the rater receives first a printout of the profile, plotted by the computer and identical to the one included in the inventory, with the graph points connected in the manner illustrated in Fig. 1. On the next three pages of the printout, the computer program generates a series of three tables identifying specific behaviors which the child was and was not able to perform, as identified within the raw data of the inventory. These tables simply recall for comparative display the items on the preacademic scales from the motor, communication, and social skill domains. Table 1 lists the motor skills for the child depicted in Fig. 1. The numbers in parentheses (not included in the computer printout) are shown here to illustrate the logic of the computer program in formulating instructional objectives, a logic very similar to that of the Camelot Scale, but quite dissimilar, for example, to that of the Adaptive Behavior Scale. The numbers represent the percentages of children, within the standardization sample, who were capable at the time of their assessment of performing each specified behavior. For example, this child has "grasps with thumb and fingers" as an item on the "can do" side. This behavior was in the skill repertoire of 86% of the children in the standardization sample. On the "can't do" side, this child shows, for example, "catches ball." This behavior was present in 53% of the standardization sample.

Table 1

| Can Do Items—Preacademic Motor Skills | Can't Do Items—Preacademic Motor Skills |
|---|---|
| (83) Uses crayons with help | (52) Uses scissors with help |
| (76) Uses puzzles with help | (63) Uses paints with help |
| (71) Uses pencil with help | (71) Uses books with help |
| (93) Walks | (56) Uses dolls with help |
| (82) Runs | (63) Uses toy trucks with help |
| (41) Uses slippery-slide | (41) Hops on one foot |
| (79) Crawls | (63) Jumps, both feet |
| (85) Rolls over | (26) Skips |
| (85) Bends | (68) Climbs |
| (87) Throws ball | (72) Swings |
| (86) Grasps with thumb and fingers | (47) Rides tricycle |
| (85) Imitates some large muscle movements—jumping, clapping, etc. | (53) Catches ball |
| | (31) Splashes in pool safely |
| (11) Ties shoes | (56) Puts on coat alone |
| (38) Buttons own clothing | (65) Strings large beads |
| (48) Zips and unzips own clothing | (48) Folds paper |
| (28) Combs own hair | (26) Traces around objects |
| (67) Imitates small muscle movements | (84) Opens door (by turning doorknob) |
| (59) Completes three-piece form board | (30) Puts on mittens |
| | (85) Transfers objects from one hand to the other |
| (76) Normal or near-normal gait | |
| (37) Matches basic colors | (78) Stacks blocks |
| (24) Colors or marks within lines | (68) Stops and returns a rolled ball |
| (93) Does not drool | (36) Sorts objects by color, size and/or shape |
| (88) Pulls self upright from lying to sitting position | |
| (92) Stands up alone without support | |
| (89) Holds head up normally when walking | |
| (93) Releases object held in hand | |

For at least some of these behaviors (e.g., buttoning, shoe tying), there are existing, available, structured curricula for the severely handicapped. The educator need not "reinvent the wheel" in cases where instructional objectives can be met with existing curricula. The chief advantage of the computer program in the TARC System is in the facility of matching existing curricula to logically derived instructional objectives.

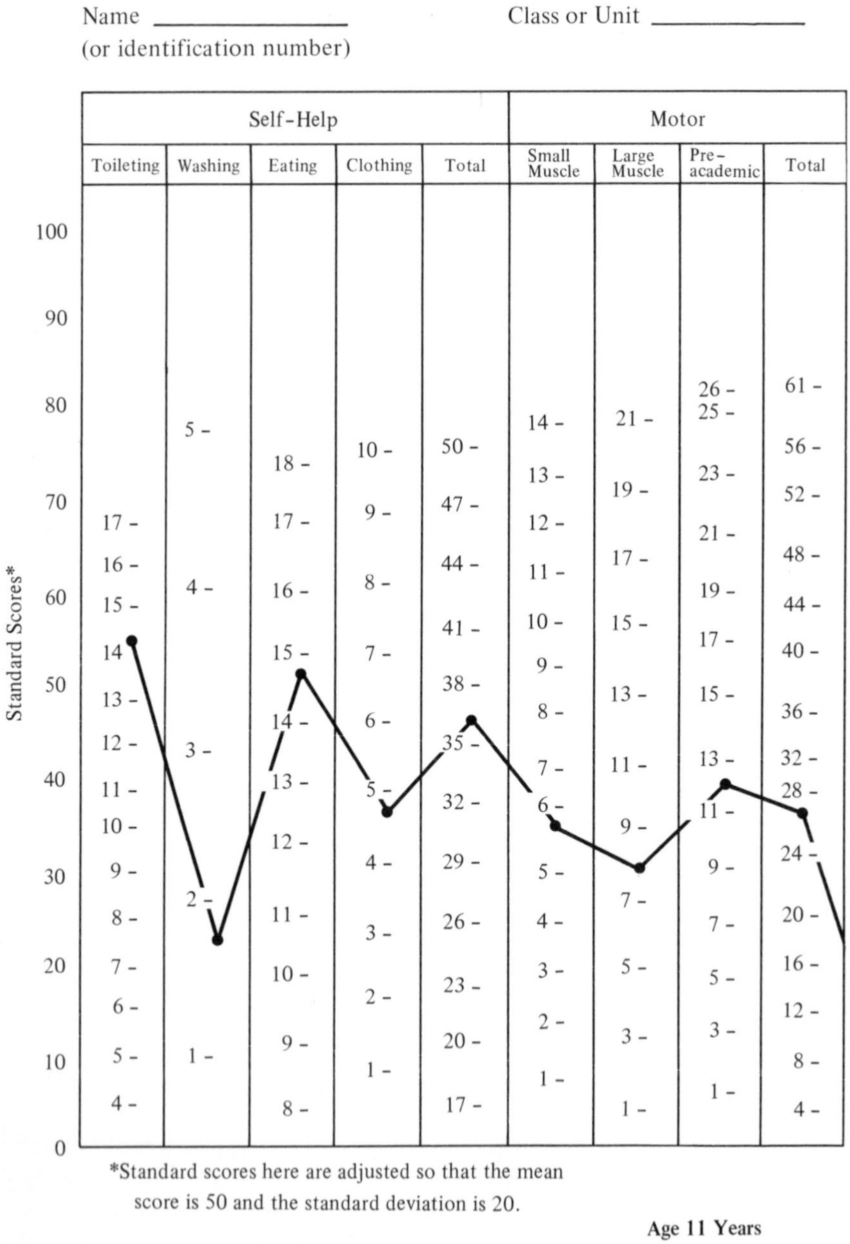

Name _____     Class or Unit _____

(or identification number)

*Standard scores here are adjusted so that the mean
score is 50 and the standard deviation is 20.

**Age 11 Years**

Fig. 1. An example profile sheet from the TARC Assessment System with

Rated by ______________ Date ______________

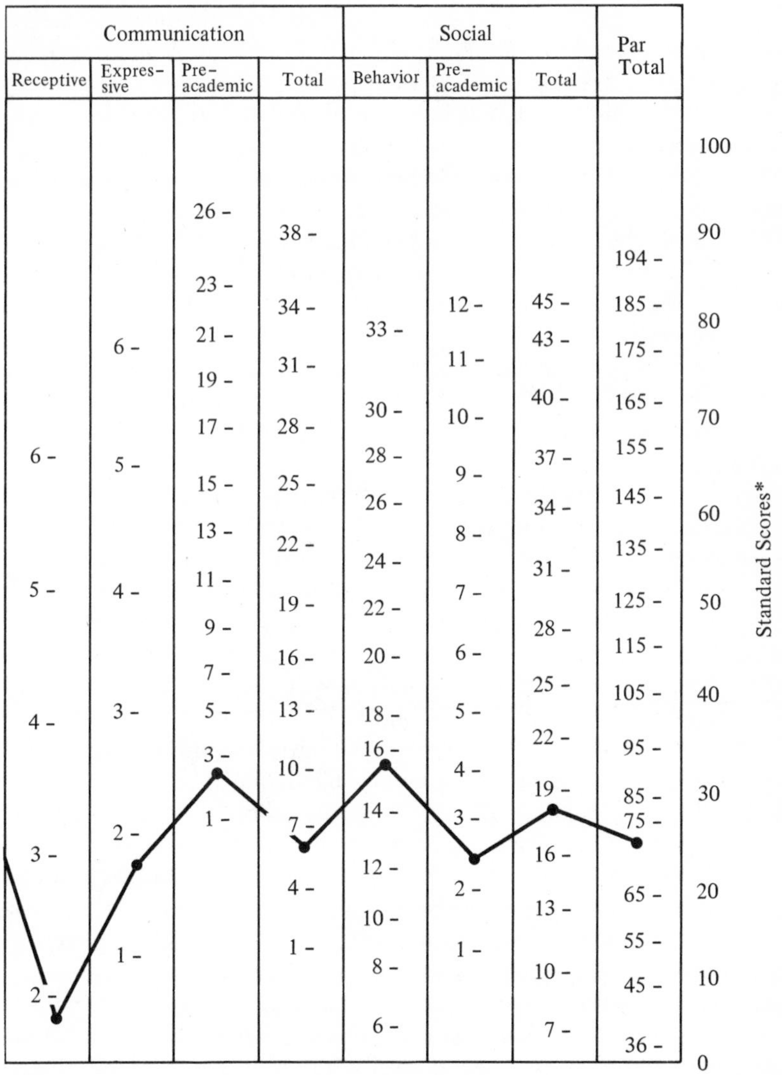
Communication
Social
Par Total
Receptive
Expres-sive
Pre-academic
Total
Behavior
Pre-academic
Total
6 - 5 - 4 - 3 - 2 -
6 - 5 - 4 - 3 - 2 - 1 -
26 - 23 - 21 - 19 - 17 - 15 - 13 - 11 - 9 - 7 - 5 - 3 - 1 -
38 - 34 - 31 - 28 - 25 - 22 - 19 - 16 - 13 - 10 - 7 - 4 - 1 -
33 - 30 - 28 - 26 - 24 - 22 - 20 - 18 - 16 - 14 - 12 - 10 - 8 - 6 -
12 - 11 - 10 - 9 - 8 - 7 - 6 - 5 - 4 - 3 - 2 - 1 -
45 - 43 - 40 - 37 - 34 - 31 - 28 - 25 - 22 - 19 - 16 - 13 - 10 - 7 -
194 - 185 - 175 - 165 - 155 - 145 - 135 - 125 - 115 - 105 - 95 - 85 - 75 - 65 - 55 - 45 - 36 -
100
90
80
70
60
50
40
30
20
10
0
Standard Scores*

graphed data from one child presented as an example.

STAGE THREE: FORMULATING
INSTRUCTIONAL OBJECTIVES.

The computer program is arranged so that it formulates instructional objectives from the standpoint of the following logical premises: (1) a severely handicapped child should be trained first and most intensively in those educational skills in which he is most deficient relative to his own overall level of functioning; (2) the specific behavioral components of those skills should be trained in an order which corresponds to the frequency of those behaviors in a "normative" sample, in this case, the TARC standardization sample. Thus, if a child is showing the least development in the gross-motor skill area, relative to the rest of his overall performance, then motor skill development will dictate the first instructional objective. If "grasps with thumb and fingers" is scored as not present in the child's motor repertoire and is the deficit behavior in this skill area which the highest percentage of the standardization sample was capable of performing, then this specific skill will be stated within the first instructional objective. The computer program follows this sequence through six instructional objectives, ranked in their logical order of importance, with up to six specific behavioral components within each objective (also ranked). Of course, a different set of logical premises could be established toward the same end. For example, some skill areas could be weighted more heavily than others, regardless of their position in the percentage rankings of the standardization sample, as in the Adaptive Behavior Scale. The logic of the TARC System was selected primarily, as was the Camelot Scale, on the basis of the availability of existing educational technology which corresponds, albeit roughly, to the percentage rankings of the standardization sample.

The computer program, in formulating instructional objectives, begins by scanning the data on the biographical data sheet of the inventory. Factors such as "nonambulatory," "severe vision loss," etc., modify the interpretations of data from the inventory. Second, the program scans the profile to determine the rank order of the six lowest, relative points on the scale. The third step in the program calls for a scan of all the assessment data within these six skill areas, some of which appear on the printed tables (e.g., Table 1) and some of which do not (those items not contained in the preacademic skill categories). The program next compares the assessment data against the percentage data from the standardization sample norms, and it selects the rank order of the objectives and their specific behavioral components. The program will then direct the computer to print out the list of six instructional objectives, with up to six specific behavioral components each, ranked on the basis of severity of deficit. If the computer is asked to average scores for a group or class, it will bypass its tabling option and print a list of more general educational goals based upon the class profile.

Table 2 presents an example of the actual computer printout of the first four of the six instructional objectives formulated for the child whose profile was presented in Fig. 1 and whose motor skills, preacademic scale scores, were presented in Table 1. The reader cannot trace the logic of the

**Table 2.**
Instructional Objectives

---

The following instructional objectives for this student are presented in ranked order as to their judged importance for the student's educational goals. Thus, the first instructional objective is intended to train a skill which this student needs most, relative to his own performance, and to the average performance of the standardization sample. The second objective is judged the second most important, etc. It is suggested that, following educational programming leading to fulfillment of 50% or more of the stated objectives, the student be reassessed with the TARC System, and new instructional objectives formulated. The author would be particularly grateful for and interested in feedback from users as to their successes, failures, problems encountered, etc., in the use of the TARC System. Write to the author, Dr. Wayne Sailor, at Kansas Neurological Institute, 3107 West 21 Street, Topeka, Kansas, 66604.

Instructional Objective No. 1
Initiate reinforcement program to respond to name with eye contact from different face to face positions (assume hearing intact unless proven deaf or hearing impaired). If successful, initiate beginning stages of receptive speech skills program.

Instructional Objective No. 2
Initiate face and hand washing program.

Instructional Objective No. 3
Initiate expressive language program at the level of vocal imitation. The program should include the following specific skill—imitate simple sounds (achieve imitative stimulus control with several vowel and vowel–consonant sounds).

Instructional Objective No. 4
Initiate the development of preacademic social skills (to include the following special skills):
Respond with and initiate social gestures (e.g., wave bye-bye).
Appropriate mouth–object contact (learns not to place inedible substances in mouth).
Signal help when needed.
Learn to play appropriately for level of functioning (e.g., recreation skill program).

computer program in deriving these objectives without a detailed examination of the child's total TARC Assessment data but the general logic is
apparent. The first instructional objective is based upon the low profile
point for receptive communication skills (See Fig. 1). The objective specifies an attention-training program prerequisite to beginning a receptive
language curriculum. The second objective corresponds to the next lowest point, washing skills, and so on.

The computer program, at this point, has accomplished no more than
the teacher might have done by carefully examining the TARC Assessment data and making decisions as to where to begin the educational
process with the child. The computer program has the slight advantage of
knowing something about the relative frequency of the various behaviors
in a "normative" sample of severely handicapped children. The process
of curriculum selection, the final stage of the TARC System, may best be
provided by the computer option for those educators who are not immediately familiar with existing, available educational technology for the
severely handicapped. The instruction to "initiate face and hand washing
program" is of little help if the teacher has no idea how to approach the
problem. Fortunately, face and hand washing curricula exist and are readily available for implementation with severely handicapped children. The
final stage of the TARC System is designed to put the educator in touch
with the curricula most likely to succeed in fulfilling the instructional
objectives derived from the computer program.

STAGE FOUR: CURRICULUM SELECTION.

The Personnel Preparation Program for Education of the Severely
Handicapped at Kansas Neurological Institute has compiled a comprehensive bibliography of educational technology for the severely handicapped (Sailor, Guess, and Lavis, 1975). This bibliography forms the
basis for the computer-programmed library retrieval system which is a
component of the TARC System. Each of the entries in the bibliography
consists of an existing, available, "canned" program to meet a particular
instructional objective or educational program need. The computer library system includes a reference for the program under its domain and
subdomain (e.g., self-help; toileting), together with its cost, where it can
be purchased, how much, if any, training is required to administer it,
where such training may be obtained, whether it is backed up with research data, to what population parameters it is restricted, etc. Each
program referenced in the system contains, in addition, a descriptive
abstract.

The library retrieval system can be utilized either of two ways. The
first is by a "key-word" classification system which allows the user to
retrieve educational curricula according to designated entries. For exam-

ple, entering the request "self-help; toileting" will cause the computer to print all known references to existing toilet-training programs, together with the descriptive information and abstracts. A small manual of key-word "descriptors" accompanies the system for using this option.

The second option, and the one of most relevance to this chapter, is activation of the library system by the TARC System computer program. The TARC Assessment System, having derived instructional objectives in stage three, automatically activates the library retrieval system to print out a list of available curricula, with descriptive information and abstracts, to meet each component of each instructional objective. The printout appears in a ranked order for each objective component, with those programs ranked first, second, etc., which, in the authors' judgment, are most likely to succeed in training the designated skill. The judgment process of ranking curricula was based upon consideration of all known information about the various educational programs, including information supplied by program authors, published research reports, reports from field test users, etc. The library system is continually updated so that rankings are subject to change based upon receipt of new information, new field test data, etc. Many of the programs listed are being field tested at Kansas Neurological Institute and Project MESH (Model Education for the Severely Handicapped) at Parsons State Hospital and Training Center, Parsons, Kansas.

In the case of instructional objectives for which no known curricula have been developed, the computer simply prints the statement "No curriculum available." In this case, the user is in the same situation as everyone else and must develop his or her own curriculum. The chapters, in this book, on developmental sequence and curricula should prove particularly helpful in this effort.

## CONCLUSION

A number of approaches to the educational assessment of the severely handicapped have been reviewed and discussed. Some guidelines have been presented to facilitate decisions about which assessment tools are appropriate for various populations and assessment needs.

Several issues of importance to educators emerge from an examination of the five scales and two checklists above. The first is that most of the items in most of the assessment tools are too general to provide specific target behaviors. The conditions under which a behavior occurs and a criterion by which to score a behavior as present or absent in an individual's repertoire are frequently missing.

A behavioral definition should specify the conditions under which the behavior is to be performed, the action to be performed, the object of that action and a criterion for successful performance. One or more of these four components is usually missing. For example, the item "balances head," lacks condition and criterion. The conditions could add "when in a sitting position" and the criterion "for at least 10 sec."

The action in many of the scale items is usually present, but it is often too ambiguous to be useful in a behavioral definition. Such actions as "goes," "uses," "gets," "cares," "does," and "makes" should be expanded into a phrase to reduce ambiguity. Such actions as grasps, reaches, sits, drinks, stands, chews, unwraps, buttons, cuts, etc., may, on the other hand, communicate the behavior to be observed without further elaboration. Such verbs as "enjoys," "trusts," and "inspires" are not directly observable, and items using such words would require total revision if translated into behavioral definitions.

Several issues arise with reference to scoring criteria. First, most of the scales and checklists use a "present" or "absent" scoring dichotomy. A strict interpretation of "present" could result in this category being scored for any behavior that has occurred one or more times in the individual's lifetime. Scoring a behavior as present or absent forces the rater to dichotomize a range that may go from once in the individual's life to hundreds a day. The rater, with several scales, has to judge from an interview with a person supposedly familiar with the individual's behavior if this behavior conforms to or exceeds an unknown norm and can be scored "present," or whether the behavior deviates below the unknown norm to the point that it should be scored "absent."

Given that items on some of the scales rely on the verbal report of others, do not specify conditions or criteria, have ambiguous action, and have a "present–absent" scoring system, the extent to which those scales accurately represent the individual's behavior can be questioned. The use of the scales as a rapid assessment procedure, as opposed to direct objective measurement of specific behaviors, would be lost if the scale consisted of a comprehensive set of specific, objective, behavioral items. The time required to set up or expose the individual to all the conditions, measure all the responses, and repeat this across a number of individuals, a number of different times, could result in several raters' time taken up entirely with assessment procedures, if scores are required on all items.

In conclusion, an educational assessment provides a useful function as a subjective, shorthand procedure for a quick look at several classes of behavior in order to make a preliminary determination of what instructional objectives might be defined for a given individual. One or more objectives should be selected, translated into behavioral definitions, and accurately measured. A program should be identified or developed for each behavior found to be deficient. When implemented, this program should result in the behavior's reaching and maintaining the criterion specified in the behavioral definition. The assessment should be repeated as a first step to selecting new instructional objectives and to detect any deficiencies appearing in previously established behaviors.

[1]This material was prepared with support from USOE, Bureau of Education for the Handicapped, Division of Personnel Preparation; Grant OEG-0-74-2766 to Doug Guess, Wayne Sailor, and Leonard Lavis of Kansas Neurological Institute.
[2]The TARC System was developed with support from funds made available from USOE to the Kansas State Department of Education, Title 1, P.L. 89-313, Grant 72269; USOE/ BEH OEG-0-74-2766; and USOE/BEH OEG-0-74-7991. All proceeds go to the Topeka Association for Retarded Citizens, Benefit Fund.

## REFERENCES

Balthazar EE: Balthazar Scales of Adaptive Behavior, Part One: Handbook for the Professional Supervisor. Champaign, Ill., Research Press, 1971a
Balthazar EE: Balthazar Scales of Adaptive Behavior, Part Two: Handbook for the Rater Technician. Champaign, Ill., Research Press, 1971b
Balthazar EE: Balthazar Scales of Adaptive Behavior, Part Three: The Scales of Functional Independence. Champaign, Ill., Research Press, 1971c
Balthazar EE: Balthazar Scales of Adaptive Behavior, Part Four: Workshop and Training Manual. Champaign, Ill., Research Press, 1971d
Balthazar EE: Balthazar Scales of Adaptive Behavior II. Scales of Social Adaptation. Palo Alto, Consulting Psychologists Press, 1973
Cain LF, Levine S, Elzey FF: Manual for the Cain–Levine Social Competency Scale. Palo Alto, Consulting Psychologists Press, 1963
Doll EA: Vineland Social Maturity Scale—Manual of Directions. Minneapolis, American Guidance Service, 1947
Foster RW: Camelot Behavioral Checklist Manual. Parsons, Kansas, Camelot Behavioral Systems, 1974
Nihira K, Foster R, Shellhaas M, et al: AAMD Adaptive Behavior Scale Manual. Washington, D.C., American Association on Mental Deficiency, 1974
Sailor W, Guess D, Lavis LW: Educational technology for the severely handicapped: A comprehensive bibliography. Unpublished syllabus, Kansas Neurological Institute: Personnel Preparation Program for Education of the Severely Handicapped, 1975
Sailor WS, Mix BJ: The TARC Assessment System (User's Manual). Lawrence, Kansas, H & H Enterprises, 1975
Shearer D, Billingsley J, Frohman A, et al: The Portage Guide to Early Education: Instructions and Checklist (Experimental ed). Portage, Wisconsin, Cooperative Educational Service Agency No. 12, 1970
Sontag E, Burke P, York R: Considerations for serving the severely handicapped in the public schools. Educ Train Ment Retarded 8:20–26, 1973
Tucker DJ: Skill Acquisition Program Bibliography. Parsons, Kansas: Camelot Behavioral Systems, 1974

Dale Gentry and
Norris G. Haring

# B

# Essentials of Performance Measurement

Historically, the public education system in the United States has provided educational services only to "educable" children and youth; that is, those who were considered intellectually capable of benefiting from the educational process provided by the schools. This rationale resulted in the denial of services to a large number of individuals with severely handicapping conditions, such as severe or profound intellectual retardation, extreme emotional disorders such as autism and schizophrenia, extreme motor impairments, multiple sensory handicaps, sensory handicaps in combination with other handicaps, or other combinations of handicapping conditions which combine to result in severe learning and functioning impairment. More recently, however, social, judicial, and legislative actions have affirmed the right of severely and profoundly handicapped persons to utilize the same public educational system that has served less impaired and normal persons.

In response to these mandates, public school educators have hastened to provide school programs for the severely handicapped, who are attending public school programs in increasing numbers. Because their rates of learning under typical conditions are very low, however, they require much more precise arrangements of their learning environments to make observable and substantive progress toward more independent levels of functioning. In fact, it is fair to assert, based on past experience, that without precise and systematic arrangements of their learning environments, these individuals will make no appreciable behavioral or educational progress over a period of time.

The phrase "precise and systematic arrangement of the learning environment" has a definite meaning to us. It includes the careful assessment of the individual in each area of development; the clear formulation of learning objectives; the orderly sequencing of each step in the curriculum through which the pupil is to progress; the exact specification and implementation of instructional events; the precise determination and use of feedback, correction, and reinforcement techniques; and the appropriate use of formative and summative classroom evaluation procedures. The omission of any one of these components from the teaching process decreases the probability that severely handicapped pupils will make orderly progress toward their learning objectives. This chapter considers one of these components, the use of formative and summative measurement procedures in the teaching process.

## FORMATIVE AND SUMMATIVE EVALUATION

The distinction between formative and summative evaluation should be noted. Formative evaluation is the collection and use of data to make relatively immediate determinations about whether or not the intervention process must be altered to maintain or improve a pupil's performance. Summative evaluation is the collection of data to describe or summarize a pupil's progress over a longer interval of time. There can be overlap between the two types of evaluation. Summative data can be used to make longer-term program modifications, and formative data can sometimes be used to describe progress over time.

For severely handicapped individuals, learning tasks must be refined into very small units, and even then, progress may be extremely slow. It is essential for the educator to utilize precise and frequent classroom measurement to determine whether a severely handicapped pupil is making progress, whether or not the rate of his progress is adequate, or whether he has mastered one learning task and is ready to advance to another. Additionally, exact measurement of a pupil's performance is invaluable in assessing the relative influence of different components of the instructional process.

Since the essential purpose of formative measurement is to make instructional decisions for the individual, it would be pointless to collect formative data unless they actually led to decisions which help the pupil. Data collection is justifiable when it leads to the modification of instructional programming that facilitates the individual's progress. However, data which are collected but not used to benefit the child are a costly waste of resources. Ordinarily, the successful use of data for decision making requires the teacher to formulate "decision rules" or guidelines which help the teacher to use the collected data easily and efficiently to determine necessary program changes for individual children.

## STANDARD DATA PROCEDURES

In recent years there has been much interest in, and discussion about, standard data procedures among special educators. From this discussion, it is apparent that there are some general conclusions on which most persons would agree: (1) significant progress in any field of endeavor is at least partly dependent upon the use of standard measurement procedures; (2) such procedures would provide a basis for comparing data from different settings and sources; (3) standard data procedures and formats would lead to quicker and clearer communication among professionals; (4) research would benefit from the use of common data procedures; and (5) teachers and children would ultimately benefit from usable standard procedures.

There are some additional reasons for developing standard data procedures, although not all of these reasons would lead to the same conclusions or formats: (1) some types of data are more appropriate than other types of data for certain behaviors. Duration data, for example, are more appropriate for some behaviors, while frequency data are more appropriate for others; (2) some types of data are more sensitive than other types of data; (3) some data are more easily collected and recorded than other data. Practitioners usually prefer the more easily usable procedures; (4) some types of data displays contain more information than other types of displays. Generally, the "standard behavior chart" (Behavior Research Company, P.O. Box 3351, Kansas City, Kansas, 66103) includes more information than do other displays; (5) some types of displays are either more difficult to use or are more foreign to users than other types of displays.

We generally advocate the use of frequency measures, displayed on a standard behavior chart, and the use of "decision rules" with such a display. However, we also recognize that there are other factors which may compel the use of alternate data procedures. In the subsequent discussion, we will attempt to take those factors into account.

## REQUIREMENTS FOR FORMATIVE
## CLASSROOM MEASUREMENT

There are a number of requirements which formative classroom measurement procedures should fulfill in order to be useful to the teacher and the child. These are discussed below.

1. The measures should be taken directly on the task or objective being taught. Ratings scales, in contrast to direct measures, are dependent on the rater's ability to discriminate change. Measures which are taken on related or broader tasks are not apt to provide immediate information about the pupil's learning on the task being taught. Standardized tests usually are not good tools for direct classroom measurement, since they often measure a broad variety of learnings with relatively few items.

2. The measure taken should provide information about the intended or critical outcome of the learning task or phase. For example, if one is trying to teach a youngster to wear his glasses or hearing aid, then duration of time spent wearing the device is a more appropriate measure of performance than a frequency count of the number of times the child puts on the device. On the other hand, a frequency measure might well be the most appropriate indication of proficiency on a motor task, such as sorting objects.

3. The measurement scale and the behavior unit should be sensitive enough to readily reflect change in the learning task or behavior being measured. Generally, the larger the number of potential units in a scale, the more sensitive the scale will be to change. A binary scale such as a "yes-no" scale, or a 5-point scale such as "A-B-C-D-E" usually requires large amounts of change in behavior before a corresponding change shows on the scale. A percent scale with a range from 0 to 100 is often quite sensitive to behavioral change, providing there is a reasonably large number of opportunities for the child to respond. However, a percent scale limits behavior change at either end; as behavior change approaches 0 to 100 percent, it can change no further. Open-ended scales, such as listing behavior counts or duration, tend to resolve this problem at the upper limit. Frequency measures (behavior counts divided by time) resolve the problem at both the upper and lower limits of the scale. Generally, a frequency scale provides the most sensitive reflection of change in behavior.

The behavior itself should also be defined in small enough units to reflect small increments of change. For example, the specification of a behavior unit as "tying a shoe" would result in a behavior unit that would not reflect change readily with children who have severe motor impairment. By refining shoe tying into a series of small steps, such as "grasps end of shoelace with thumb and forefinger," it is possible to select behavior units which will reflect change readily as a result of instruction.

4. Measures should be taken frequently. Usually, behavior measures should be taken daily. Frequent or daily measures are important for several reasons. (1) Repeated measures are necessary to assure that the obtained results reflect the actual performance of the individual. A typical performance will show up clearly in a series of data points. (2) Several

data points are necessary to determine change or progress across time. If no progress is being made within a few sessions, the teacher will want to make a change, so that ineffective procedures are not continued with the learner. Only if data are taken frequently can this determination be made within a relatively short span of time. (3) Frequent measures will allow a teacher to sort out the relative effectiveness of different intervention procedures. This is especially important in determining what procedures are most effective for a given individual.

5. Measurement results should be reliable. Different observers should obtain the same results when observing the same behavior, or the same observer should obtain the same results across time (assuming the behavior has not changed). Reliability is often a function of the clarity with which the behavior is defined and also of the behavior-recording techniques. Generally, behaviors which are defined in terms of movement cycles (Kunzelman, 1970) will lend themselves to reliable observation. Simple and immediate data recording procedures will also greatly aid reliability.

6. Measurement procedures should be practical. The teacher or other manager should be able to keep data on a pupil's performance while implementing the instructional or management process. Procedures which require external observers or sophisticated apparatuses have generally not been practical in the classroom. Two main factors help make classroom measurement practical: the procedures for counting and/or timing behavior should be simple and easy to use; and, the teacher or other manager should be proficient at using the data procedures.

7. Data procedures should be efficient and economical. The major factor to consider here is the amount of information provided in return for the cost to obtain the data. For example, suppose the teacher can collect as much useful information about a pupil's performance by taking a 2-minute sample at the end of an instructional period as by recording the child's behavior for an entire 30-minute period. The briefer sample would be more "cost-efficient" and should probably be used instead of the more costly measurement. There are, however, some behaviors and conditions which require more lengthy or costly measurement, such as observing behavior change over time in order to monitor the effects of a medication or monitoring behaviors which require an outside observer.

## TYPES OF DATA

There are several types of direct data which may be collected on behavior; each has a different use and relative advantages and disadvantages. Generally, the different types of data include those which are binary, item, count, percent, frequency, duration latency, trial, and time-ruled. Intensity is not described here because of its limited practicality in most classroom situations.

### Binary Data

"Binary" data are, perhaps, the simplest form of data, but all other more sophisticated types of data incorporate "binary" decision making in some way. Binary information is information which can be assigned to one (either) of two categories. For example, a teacher might want to know if John does have his lunch ticket or if he does not—it is an "either–or" occurrence. Such information, then, is binary. Instances of binary classification include such categories as yes–no, correct–error, and off–on.

In collecting binary data, the first step is to define the behavior of concern and the time period during which the behavior is to be monitored. The teacher might be concerned if Timothy hit other children on the bus ride to school. The bus driver could report to the teacher each morning, "Yes, Tim hit another child," or "No, he did not." Because the behavior is clearly defined, and the time period in which it is to be monitored is clearly specified, it is a very simple matter for the bus driver to report the binary (yes–no) occurrence of the behavior. (A more sensitive measure of hitting behavior will be cited later.)

Binary data can be used for a variety of behaviors where the relevant characteristics are the behavior's occurrence or nonoccurrence, its completion or incompletion, or its correctness or incorrectness. Taking medicine, completing a task, hanging up a garment, or bringing lunch money are examples of behavior which might be monitored using binary data.

The greatest advantage of binary data is their simplicity and ease of use. The greatest limitation of binary data, as described above, is their insensitivity to behavior change. Changes in performance are often slow to be reflected in binary data. It is important to note, however, that the sensitivity of binary data is greatly increased when behaviors are refined into smaller and more frequent components and behavior counts are taken, or when some other dimension of the behavior is measured. It will become obvious in subsequent discussions how this occurs.

### Item Data

A second type of measurement is the collection of "item" data. This is mainly a refinement of binary data described above. Item data are binary data collected on the separate components or items of a task or on a sequence of activities. Item data are collected by refining a task or activity into its component steps and noting a pupil's correct or erroneous performance on each step. (Refinement of a task into its component parts is referred to as "task analysis.") For example, handwashing might be divided into many steps, beginning with standing in front of the sink, moving the right hand to the cold water faucet handle, grasping the faucet handle, and continuing on through the sequence. The teacher or other manager records whether or not the pupil correctly completes each step of the sequence.

Item data are readily collected on tasks or activities that are of a "task sequence" nature, or where correct or error on specific items may be clues to instruction (analysis of specific errors is referred to as "error analysis"). An example of the latter might be on counting skills, where a child always errs on the same numbers in the counting sequence.

The advantages of item data are that they provide specific information about which components of a task a pupil is having difficulty with, and hence they provide the teacher with cues about which items may need more instruction. Item data are much more responsive to small changes in performance than more global binary data.

The main limitation of item data is that they do not provide information about proficiency. In addition, they do not provide an overall perspective of an individual's progress, as do some types of data discussed subsequently. However, item data have had much appeal to educators working with severely handicapped persons.

## Behavior Counts

Behavior counts are a third type of data, wherein a behavior is recorded each time it occurs. Usually, behavior counts are obtained by defining a behavior, as noted previously, and by counting its occurrence for a fixed interval of time each day or session. Returning to the example of Tim's hitting on the bus, instead of simply noting the occurrence or nonoccurrence of hitting, the bus driver would count the number of times Tim hit another child. Behavior counts are most appropriate where behaviors have the opportunity for reoccurrence within a specified period of time. Taking medication during the school day would not be an appropriate behavior on which to obtain a count if that behavior had only one opportunity for occurrence each day. However, the number of bites taken at lunch, the number of steps correctly completed on a task sequence, or the number of times a child initiates a communicative interaction, are all appropriate behaviors on which to obtain "count" data.

The main advantage of count data over previous types of data is that it more sensitively reflects overall improvement than either "binary" or "item" data, and may be visually displayed more readily on a behavior chart. Behavior "counts" require no transformation when plotting them on a behavior chart. It is important to note that when "count" data are collected, the time period should be held constant, so that data are comparable from day to day. In a few cases, the number of opportunities to respond may be held constant, but under such conditions one might choose to use percent data.

### Percent Data

Percent data are the number of times a behavior occurs out of the total number of opportunities for the behavior to occur, or the number of "correct" occurrences of the behavior. Percent data are obtained by presenting a number of opportunities for the behavior to occur, counting the number of "correct" occurrences, and dividing that count by the total opportunities. ("Correct" behavior count ÷ number of opportunities = percent of the behavior).

Percent data are often collected on academic or preacademic behaviors, or on other tasks where the individual can make "correct" or "error" responses to items. Teachers have long scored math pages and spelling lists with percent scores.

An alternative use of percent data has been with "time-ruled" measurement of events. An observer watches a pupil for a specified interval of time, for example 10 seconds. At the end of each time interval, the observer records the occurrence or nonoccurrence of a specified behavior. This information is a form of repeated "binary" measures. However, the total number of intervals is divided into the number of intervals during which the behavior occurred to derive a percent of intervals during which the behavior occurred. This type of data is often collected on behaviors which are difficult to translate to movement cycles, such as "playing in proximity (e.g., within 3 feet) to another child."

The main advantage of percent data is that they convert to a common scale. Variations in data which occur because of different numbers of opportunities to respond are "equalized" by using a percent scale. Percent data do reflect accuracy of performance well. They are also more familiar to many people, so that they understand percent data readily. Like count data, percent data also summarize overall progress and are easily plotted on a visual chart, although they require a transformation to do so.

The disadvantages of percent data are the limits at the upper and lower end of the percent scale. Percent data do not well reflect proficiency of performance, nor amount of time over which a behavior was measured.

## Frequency

Frequency (or rate) data are the number of behaviors which occur within a standard unit of time. They are obtained by counting the number of times a behavior occurs within a given time period and dividing the number of behaviors which occurred by the number of time units (e.g., the number of minutes) during which the behavior was counted (behavior count ÷ minutes observed = frequency).

Frequency measures are appropriate for many of the same behaviors for which "count" and "percent" data are appropriate. This includes social behaviors such as initiating a communication, asking a question, talking out in class, hitting another child, and interacting with peers. It also includes educational tasks, such as saying vowel sounds, reading survival words, placing pegs in a board, or placing puzzle pieces.

The advantages of frequency measures are that they usually provide the greatest sensitivity of all scales to behavior change. In addition, they convert measures to a common scale so that data from different days and sources are comparable. When both correct and error data are charted on a standard behavior chart, they allow the teacher to note accuracy, speed, endurance, change across time, and to predict the pupil's performance in the future. Also, "data decision" procedures are readily usable with frequency data plotted on a standard behavior chart.

There are also disadvantages to frequency data. Many people are unfamiliar with the standard behavior chart on which frequency data are plotted, and they often experience difficulty in using it. Also, when a behavior is paced or controlled by the presentation of the teacher or the type of material, changes which appear on the chart may reflect change other than in the learner. In this case, it may be a matter of the measure being "too sensitive." Some persons have had reservations about the use of frequency measures and the standard behavior chart because they have felt that the procedures were too complex.

## Latency

Latency is the amount of time it takes an individual to begin to respond after the teacher has provided a cue to start. Data are obtained most easily by using a stopwatch and timing the interval from the cue to the beginning of the response. Latency measures have been most useful on such behaviors as compliance with directions and initiating tasks upon receiving instructions.

## Duration

Duration is the length of time that a pupil continues to respond once he has begun a behavior or task. Duration is obtained by noting the start and stop times for a task. Duration has two main uses. (1) Behaviors which should be continued for a time, such as wearing glasses, are appropriately measured by collecting duration data. (2) Duration may be an important dimension when trying to build endurance, such as on a vocational or prevocational task.

Both latency and duration have limited use as classroom measures. They are appropriate only for a limited number of behaviors, and usually they should be used in conjunction with other measures. For example, endurance on a vocational task should also be accompanied by some measure of productivity, such as number of units completed during the work session.

## Trials to Criterion

Finally, the number of trials it takes a pupil to reach criterion performance may be an appropriate measure for some behaviors. Trials to criterion data are obtained by setting a desired performance level, such as three correct responses in succession, and recording the number of opportunities (or trials) a child has for responding before he reaches the criterion of three successive correct responses. Trials to criterion data are usually collected when the teacher is teaching a very primitive response to a pupil. For example, if the teacher is working on a grasping response, she may record the number of times she must assist a child in grasping an object before that child is able to grasp the object independently.

The advantage of trials to criterion data are that they are easy data to collect on behaviors which require much prompting and assistance. In addition, trials to criterion provide data which are comparable to much historic research. The major limitations of trials to criterion are lack of sensitivity and lack of provision of formative information.

## STEPS IN PLANNING AND IMPLEMENTING
## DATA COLLECTION

The collection of data can be simplified if the teacher follows a series of steps when planning the data collection process. The following steps, although not in a necessary sequence, will provide the teacher with one model to use in selecting and implementing data procedures. The reader will note that some of these steps appear to represent instructional planning in general. However, they are attended to only to the extent necessary for their consideration in data collection.

## Specifying the Behavior

The first step in collecting data is the precise specification of behavior. In most cases, it will be possible to specify behavior as "movement cycles," or as repeatable and observable behaviors. Even in those cases where movement is not the important dimension of behavior, it will be useful to begin with complete movement cycles, since all types of measurement depend on the observation of at least one part of the movement cycle.

Examples of movement cycles which teachers have selected for modification with severely handicapped individuals are listed below to exemplify the way in which movement cycles can be stated. The list purposely includes both refined and larger unit movement cycles. Obviously, the behaviors actually selected for modification with an individual pupil would be based on comprehensive curriculum and systematic assessment of the pupil's performance in relation to the curriculum.

Some examples of movement cycles which might be selected for acceleration include: fixing eyes on object, tracking object with eyes, grasping object with thumb and forefinger, pointing to named object, following one-step direction, placing (sorting) objects into two bins, placing shapes in a form board, counting pennies to 10, collating pages, reading survival words orally, washing hands, writing name, assembling bicycle brake, placing object "in" or "on" box upon command.

Examples of movement cycles which have been selected for deceleration include: head banging, taking food from another person's plate, flicking fingers in front of eyes, throwing objects, soiling pants, removing shoes.

## Determining Critical Outcomes

A second step in the data collection process is the determination of the critical or expected outcomes for desired behaviors. There are several critical dimensions of behavior that relate to the evaluation strategy. These include accuracy, discrimination, fluency, endurance, latency, and duration.

ACCURACY

It should be noted that response accuracy is inevitably part of the desired outcome of any selected behavior. There are almost no conditions in which society will accept a high proportion of inaccurate responses. Therefore, accuracy is one expected outcome common to all behavior targets. The expected outcome for many behaviors will also include a number of other criteria.

ACCURACY ON CUE.

For some tasks, cue discrimination coupled with response accuracy is the critical dimension of behavior. These tasks are usually those for which only one response or one chain of responses is required to an initial cue. Responding to one's name is an example. When a teacher calls a child's name, the expected response is usually for the child to look at the teacher, listen, and perhaps verbally indicate that he/she has heard the cue by saying "yes." With such a behavior, discrimination of the cue (calling the child's name), coupled with the "correct" response chain, is a most important dimension of the behavior. Similarly, such behaviors as following a direction, turning on a light when entering a darkened room, and responding to greeting are all behaviors where response accuracy to a single cue are especially important.

Response accuracy to cues is also important in some behavior chains. Consider, for example, the act of washing one's hands or assembling a brake part. An initial cue is provided by either the manager or the environment. The individual completes the first step of the sequence, which serves as a cue for the appropriate step to follow. Only if the individual accurately discriminates each cue in the sequence and emits the appropriate response will the behavioral chain be completed correctly.

Cue discrimination and response accuracy is also important for most application and generalization phases of learning. In many acquisition tasks, a pupil is taught to respond in the presence of a single or limited number of distracting cues. However, in many application and most generalization situations there are many irrelevant or confounding cues. In such situations it becomes especially important for the pupil to discriminate and respond correctly to an appropriate cue. An example would be where a child has learned to count change in a classroom situation for a familiar teacher. When the child is called on to count change for a small purchase in a grocery store, there are many unrelated cues and people. The child must discriminate the relevant cue, that of the clerk quoting the price of the item, and respond correctly by counting out the change.

PROFICIENCY

With many tasks, response fluency is an important behavior dimension, in addition to correct cue discrimination and response accuracy. There are at least three important reasons for this. (1) Proficiency is often necessary on some basic performance tasks for successful completion of more complex tasks. For example, proficiency at grasping and releasing objects is necessary for successful completion of many sorting, assembly, and collating tasks. Or proficiency on basic math facts is necessary for needed proficiency on higher level math skills. (2) Proficiency is more likely to lead to successful application, generalization, and maintenance.

(3) External criteria sometimes require specified "rates" of performance. Production rates, for example, are often dictated by an industrial employer or sheltered workshop.

ENDURANCE

With some tasks, endurance is an important behavior dimension in addition to accuracy and fluency. Usually this is true on work tasks. Not only does the correct production rate have to meet a certain standard, an employee must be able to sustain the performance rate for a long period of time.

LATENCY

In some cases, response latency is important. Usually, this is true for tasks that require a cue. Following the cue, it is desirable for the pupil to emit the correct response within a reasonable time interval. Compliance with directions usually means the individual must emit the correct response within a given time period.

DURATION

The development of specified response durations for a single movement cycle is occasionally important. Examples of this would include sitting, holding up one's head, standing, and wearing glasses or hearing aids.

## Specifying Objectives

A third step in selecting and implementing data collection and evaluation procedures is specifying the desired objective. This usually follows readily once the desired behavior and the critical behavioral outcomes have been specified. An objective for the task of washing one's hands might be stated as follows: "Before beginning meal preparation, the child will complete all steps within the handwashing sequence within 3 minutes." With this simple statement, a number of response requirements have been imposed: (1) responding to the cue of entering the kitchen and starting to prepare a meal; (2) accurately completing each step in the handwashing sequence; and (3) proficiently performing the task. By recognizing the response requirements he is imposing, the teacher is aided in selecting appropriate measurement procedures.

## Selection of Teaching Strategies

A fourth step in implementing data collection and measurement procedures is consideration of the teaching strategy and tactics selected.

There are several different teaching strategies which have implications for implementation of evaluation procedures to be used. Some representative strategies and their implications for measurement are discussed below. It should be noted that all strategies are not necessarily mutually exclusive.

One strategy is that of analyzing a task into component steps and teaching the task as a behavior chain. Tasks such as handwashing, bicycle brake assembly, sandwich making, zippering, and parts assembly have been taught using this approach. When teaching tasks as a chain of behaviors, teachers have characteristically provided a large amount of prompting, modeling, and physical assistance in the initial stages of learning, and have gradually withdrawn or faded these events as the pupil acquires the task, until the pupil is able to complete the entire sequence without assistance.

One way in which teachers have collected data with this teaching strategy has been to devise a data collection sheet listing each step in the sequence, with columns at the right to indicate child performance. An example of this data collection form is shown in Figure 1.

**Washing Hands**

Pupil's Name _____ Manager's Name _____

| Behavioral Progression | Date | | | | | | | | |
|---|---|---|---|---|---|---|---|---|---|
| 1. Get towel from cupboard, if not out | | | | | | | | | |
| 2. Get soap from drawer, if not out | | | | | | | | | |
| 3. Roll up sleeves, if needed | | | | | | | | | |
| 4. Turn on water | | | | | | | | | |
| 5. Test temperature, not cold | | | | | | | | | |
| 6. Adjust water temperature | | | | | | | | | |
| 7. Pick up soap from soap dish | | | | | | | | | |
| 8. Hold soap under running water | | | | | | | | | |
| 9. Remove soap from water | | | | | | | | | |
| 10. Rub soap between hands until lather forms | | | | | | | | | |
| 11. Replace soap in soap dish | | | | | | | | | |
| 12. Rub lather over front of hands | | | | | | | | | |
| 13. Rub lather over back of hands | | | | | | | | | |
| 14. Rub lather between fingers | | | | | | | | | |
| 15. Rinse hands under running water until all soap is removed | | | | | | | | | |
| 16. Turn off water | | | | | | | | | |
| 17. Remove towel from rack | | | | | | | | | |
| 18. Dry hands by rubbing on towel | | | | | | | | | |
| 19. Return towel to rack | | | | | | | | | |

+ - Pupil completes step correctly without assistance
v - Pupil completes step correctly with verbal instruction
d - Pupil completes step correctly with demonstration
p - Pupil completes step correctly with physical assistance
o - Pupil does not complete step correctly

Fig. 1.   A data collection form, with columns at the right to indicate child performance.

Different types of data can be collected using the task-chaining approach, and the resulting data can be summarized or used in a variety of ways. One type of data would simply indicate correct or error performance for each step of the task. The teacher can then observe on successive days those steps in which the pupil is making improvement. A second type of data would indicate whether the pupil performed a step correctly or required a prompt, demonstration, or physical assistance. Generally, this would enable the teacher to observe smaller increments of progress.

The collected data could be used or summarized in a variety of ways. (1) The teacher might use the data in an "item" fashion. That is, she would inspect the pupil's performance on each step of the task sequence on subsequent days, and, if the pupil showed little or no progress on given steps, she would provide extra instruction on those steps. (2) The teacher might summarize the behavior counts and chart those counts. For example, if correct and error scores were recorded, the teacher would count and chart those. (3) The teacher might convert the counts to percent correct scores and chart those. (4) The teacher might time the performance on that task, transform the data to frequency scores (correct and error response per minute), and chart those scores. An example of displaying both the percent and frequency scores on the same data are shown below in Figure 2.

A second teaching strategy is to analyze a learning task into component parts or task categories and to teach each component part to some criterion ("proficiency") before advancing the pupil to a subsequent step of the task. Such a strategy is often associated with repeated drill and practice procedures. Counting skills, math computation, reading survival words, sorting, puzzle completion, and matching tasks are examples of tasks with which this strategy has been used. Usually, data collected on these tasks consists of correct and error counts which are taken from a brief "timing," transformed to frequency scores, and charted for display. An example of such data is shown in Figure 3. Actually, the data in Figure 3 were obtained when the teacher provided the pupil with instruction specifically on the "hand rubbing" step of the handwashing sequence, because the pupil was not improving on that step. Frequency scores are especially useful with this strategy because proficiency is best indicated by frequency scores.

It is possible to collect and use other types of data using this strategy of repeated practice on one step of a task before advancing to another step. Some teachers have converted the data to percent correct scores and charted those. This does yield accuracy information, but it does not provide information about fluency or proficiency.

Another measurement approach is to collect correct and error data on each trial. When a child has completed several consecutive correct trials, he is advanced to the next step in the task sequence. This procedure is very easily used, even though it does not provide as much information about child performance as the other data approaches. An example of such data is provided in Figure 4.

A third teaching and management strategy might be referred to as a free-responding and reinforcement strategy. With this strategy, the teacher looks for the occurrence of a behavior over a time period and provides reinforcement of that behavior as it occurs. This type of strategy

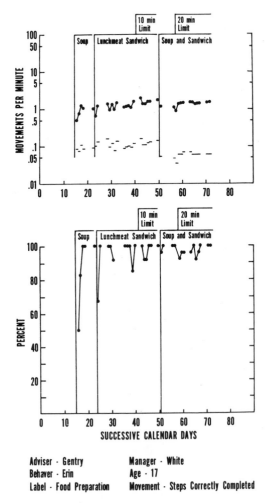

Fig. 2.    An example of displaying both the percent and frequency scores on the same data.

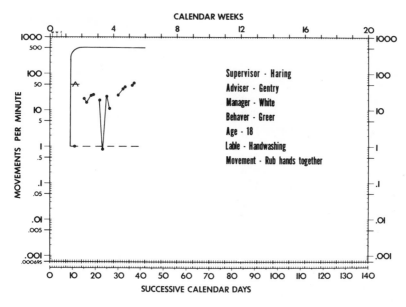

Fig. 3. Data, collected on various tasks, consisting of correct error counts which are taken from a brief "timing," transformed to frequency scores, and charted for display.

has been used with the development of some communication and social skills such as emitting vocalizations, initiating "communicative interactions" with other children, and using gestures or words to solicit teacher assistance.

It should be noted that many classroom deceleration targets also fit this "free-responding" paradigm. Head banging, hitting other children, self-stimulatory behaviors, etc., are generally behaviors that can be emitted at any time. Although the consequences provided for these behaviors are not the same, the measurement strategy would be.

Such behaviors are usually best measured by keeping behavior counts over given time periods, transforming the data to frequency counts, and charting for display and decision making. An example of such data is shown in Figure 5. An autistic child's manager recorded the child's frequency of several different interaction behaviors during a play session where children were allowed to blow bubbles. The number of times the child initiated verbal interactions with a peer is shown in Figure 5. Such behavior data also have been charted as behavior counts.

There is a fourth type of teaching strategy which assumes some importance. This can be termed a "limited-response" strategy. With this approach, a pupil is provided a limited number of opportunities to re-

Pupil's Name   Fred          Manager's Name   Hanawalt

Behavior              Fold and tape box flaps

| Day | Date | Correct Trials | Time | Comment |
|-----|------|----------------|------|---------|
| M | 31/3/75 | 13 | 10" | With assistance |
| T | 1/4/75 | | | |
| W | 2/4/75 | 12 | " | " |
| Th | 3/4/75 | 6 | " | " |
| F | 4/4/75 | 10 | " | " |
| M | 7/4/75 | 4 | " | " |
| T | 8/4/75 | | | |
| W | 9/4/75 | 12 | " | " |
| Th | 10/4/75 | 10 | " | " |
| F | 11/4/75 | 12 | " | " |
| M | 14/4/75 | 12 | " | " |
| T | 15/4/75 | 12 | " | " |
| W | 16/4/75 | 16 | " | " |
| Th | 17/4/75 | 12 | " | " |
| F | 18/4/75 | 16 | " | " |
| M | 21/4/75 | 18 | " | " |
| T | 22/4/75 | 14 | " | Without assistance |
| W | 23/4/75 | 12 | " | " |
| Th | 24/4/75 | 28 | " | " |
| F | 25/4/75 | 32 | " | " |
| M | 28/4/75 | | | |
| T | 29/4/75 | 24 | " | " |
| W | 30/4/75 | 32 | " | " |
| Th | 1/5/75 | 28 | " | " |
| F | 2/5/75 | 34 | " | " |

Fig. 4.   An example of data of a measurement approach collecting correct and error data.

spond. Usually, the number of opportunities depends on the number of times the teacher or environment presents a cue for responding. Teaching a pupil to respond to his name, visually track an object, or hang up his coat are examples of behaviors that often utilize this teaching approach. Using this approach, an appropriate way to measure behaviors is to record behavior counts and the number of opportunities a child was provided for responding. The data then can be converted to a percent of correct or appropriate responses and charted for visual display.

## Selecting the Type of Data to Be Collected

A fifth step in establishing the data collection process is to actually determine the type of data to be collected and used. This determination requires the teacher to review both the previous factors and some additional considerations.

1. The behavior to be measured should already have been specified in terms of movement cycles.

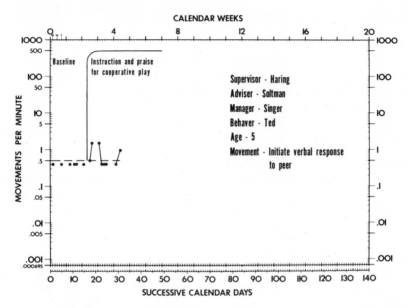

Fig. 5.   An example of data transformed to frequency counts, charted for display and decision making (see text).

2. The critical outcome should have been determined. If accuracy, proficiency, endurance, latency, or duration are especially important, these will have an important bearing on the type of data to be collected.

3. The performance objective should have been established. If performance objectives include specific statements of accuracy or proficiency, then data collected on performance en route to those objectives should include the same type of data as that specified in those performance objectives.

4. The teaching strategy should have been specified and will place some constraints on the data collection process. Different instructional strategies impose some constraints on counting, timing, and/or recording procedures. Once collected, data can be transformed, with some limitations, to desired data types; they then can be summarized, charted, and used for decision making.

5. The resources a teacher has will affect the type of data selected and used. The teacher who has few children, much professional assistance, and efficient data collection devices will probably collect more elaborate data than the teacher with many pupils, little assistance, and no timing or counting devices. The amount of previous training and experience that a teacher has had in collecting and using data is also an important factor.

### Formulating Data Collection
### and Use Procedures

Following the determination of the specific type of data to be collected and used, the sixth step in establishing the evaluation process is the selection of specific procedures for collecting and using data. These steps are discussed below.

WHEN TO COLLECT DATA

The teacher must determine when and for how long to collect data. Several factors affect this decision. If the behaviors occur infrequently, as with many social behaviors, then it is desirable to collect data for a longer session, such as a half-hour to a full day. Usually, it is desirable to have at least 10 occurrences of a behavior during an observation period.

Another situation which would require a longer observation period is one in which endurance of performance across time is desired. For example, if an individual needs to maintain productivity for an hour, then the observation time should extend for an hour. The data collection process might also extend over an entire teaching period if the teacher is interested in recording the pupil's performance on each step of a task or problem in a teaching sequence.

Brief measurement times may also be used for some tasks. The teacher may have a half-hour instructional period, but take a "probe" or timing of a pupil's performance lasting only 1 or 2 minutes. This procedure is appropriate when the "critical effect" information desired about a pupil's performance can be obtained in a brief sample of his behavior. For example, a teacher may be teaching counting skills to a pupil for a 10-min period. But the teacher can determine progress toward acquisition and proficiency by evaluating counting performance during a 1-minute timing. The same rationale may hold for a large number of behaviors. The actual time sample will be determined by the behavior being measured.

Actually, brief samples or probes of a pupil's behavior often provide a better indication of progress than data collected over a longer period of time, since it is often easier to carefully control measurement conditions for a brief timing than for an entire instructional period. In fact, much of a pupil's performance during instruction is affected by cues, prompts, assistance, and reinforcement, and these factors vary and change from day to day. However, during a brief measurement period, these factors can be held constant from day to day, so that change in the data reflects actual change or progress in the pupil's performance, not change in the environment.

Some teachers prefer to take probes at the beginning of the instructional period, reasoning that they are interested in measures that reflect "retention" from the previous day's instruction. Other teachers prefer to administer probes at the end of the instructional period, because they want to assess immediate increments of performance.

## Counting, Timing, and Recording Procedures

After deciding when and for how long they wish to take data, the teacher must select counting, timing, and recording procedures. These procedures need not be sophisticated or costly. In fact, the simpler and less complex the procedure and equipment, the more usable and practical are the procedures in the classrooms.

Counting procedures vary somewhat with the behavior. For low frequency behaviors, such as social behaviors, the teacher may use a small pad or a piece of tape on which to make tally marks for each occurrence of a behavior. Some teachers have used wrist counters, such as golfers wear, to count low frequency behaviors. For more frequent behaviors, such as usually occur with instructional tasks, there are several options. In some cases, the end product can be counted after the child is finished. For example, after a child has completed a matching task, puzzle, or written assignment, the teacher can often count the numbers of items completed correctly and erroneously. For "process" data, where there is not a product to count at the end of the measurement period, the teacher can use a form with appropriate places to make tally marks for each occurrence of a behavior. Or a single bank "gate tally counter" is available at many hardware stores for 5 to 10 dollars. A more durable and usable counting tool is a double bank Veeder-Root counter, but its purchase price is higher than the "gate" counter.

Timing procedures also vary from the use of simple and inexpensive procedures to the use of relatively costly stopwatches. Many measurement procedures require the use of timing procedures in order to obtain performance frequencies or rates. Timing procedures vary from the use of available or inexpensive clocks and watches to the use of more costly timing devices. Perhaps the most common classroom timing procedures involve the use of wall clocks, wrist watches, or digital clocks. A teacher starts a pupil on a "timing," watches the clock, and asks the pupil to "stop" at the end of a time interval.

Watches and clocks are useful for brief timings of from 1 to several minutes, and where length of the timing is fixed. For longer fixed timings, the use of kitchen timers and laboratory timers, such as the ones used in darkrooms, are useful. The audible signal produced by timers at the end of the timing period makes it less likely for a teacher or pupil to forget to stop the measurement sample at the appropriate time. For more precise timing, many teachers use a stopwatch. Generally, a stopwatch with a full 60-second sweep on the face is easier to read and use for classroom timings than one with a 30-second sweep.

For the orderly collection and use of data, it is important to plan for the recording of data once they are collected. Most teachers adapt or create a data recording form that allows them to record the information that is relevant to them. An example of a recording form which allows the teacher to record correct and error counts and performance time is shown in Figure 6.

Teachers sometimes use their desk calendars or grade books to record direct performance data. Whatever the procedure, it is important that data be kept in such a way that they are not inadvertently lost between their collection and use.

The teacher must formulate decision criteria that will enable her to use the collected data. Since the purpose of collecting formative data is to provide information to the teacher to make intervention decisions about pupils, the teacher must formulate "data decision rules" which facilitate such decisions. When data are collected without such rules in mind, the use of the data is almost always inefficient and/or inappropriate.

## DATA DECISION RULES

Data decision rules potentially include three areas: (1) rules for placement of pupils in curriculum; (2) rules for evaluating progress of

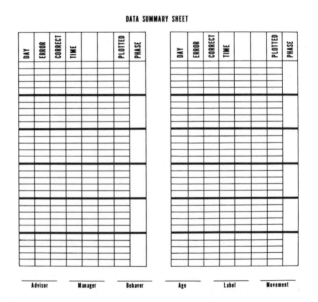

Fig. 6.    A recording form which allows the teacher to record correct and error counts and performance time.

pupils toward objectives; and (3) rules for advancing pupils to new tasks or new steps in a task. Placement rules relate to assessment and will not be discussed here. Rules for determining when to advance pupils to new tasks or steps in tasks and for evaluating their progress on learning tasks enroute to objectives, are the rules which teachers can use in their daily evaluation of pupil progress.

### Rules for Determining When to Advance Children to New Tasks

Appropriate rules for advancing pupils to new steps or tasks have two major benefits. (1) They help the teacher to avoid moving pupils from one task to another before they have had an opportunity to master the first task. (2) They help the teacher to avoid keeping pupils on one learning task for an extended time after it has been learned, thus retarding their advancement to new learning tasks.

Rules for advancing pupils to new steps or tasks generally require two steps: (1) determining what performance criteria represent acquisition, mastery, or proficiency; and (2) determining how many times, or for how long, a pupil must achieve the criterion of performance before he advances in the curriculum. Determining criterion performance may coincide with establishing performance objectives. Rules for advancing to new steps or tasks generally do not require charting for visual display. For "item" or "binary" data, a rule may relate to a number of successive correct trials or sessions. For example, one might specify that when a pupil performs each step of a task correctly for three consecutive trials, he will be advanced to the next step of a learning sequence.

For count, percent, or frequency criteria, it is necessary to specify both the performance criterion necessary for mastery (e.g., 100 percent correct or 40 correct responses per minute) and the number of times that the criterion must be reached (e.g., two trials in succession) before advancing to the next task. These data do not necessarily require a visual display, but they usually do require some simple calculation to convert the data to the desired terms. For example, to determine what percent of correct responses 13 is of 20 total problems, it is necessary to divide 13 by 20 to arrive at the percent correct, which is 65 percent. To determine frequency, it is necessary to divide the number of correct responses by the amount of time to arrive at the number of correct responses per time unit. By comparing the derived figures with the performance criterion specified for a task, it is a relatively easy matter to determine if the pupil has achieved the criterion. Such determinations may also be made from a visual display or chart by noting the desired performance criterion on the chart and noting when the plotted data reach the criterion.

## Rules for Evaluating Children's Progress
## Toward a Learning Objective

There are two beneficial results of using decision-making rules for evaluating pupil progress in reaching objectives. (1) They help teachers avoid persisting with teaching procedures that are not resulting in pupil performance gains. (2) They help teachers avoid making changes in teaching procedures when the procedures are resulting in pupil gains.

Usually these decision rules have two important components: (1) the rate of progress pupils must make on successive days, sessions, or trials; and (2) how long pupils must fall below this rate of progress before a teacher will alter an intervention.

In considering the rate of progress which pupils should make, it is reasonable to assert that children should perform better than "no progress." Teachers have sometimes selected small increments of progress, such as achieving 5–10 percent gains per week on a given learning task. Other persons have indicated that a 25 or 30 percent gain each week is an acceptable rate of growth. It is important to note that the rate of growth pupils make is partly dependent on the size of the learning task the teacher has presented the pupil. Pupils characteristically show greater rates of progress on tasks refined into small units of instruction than on tasks consisting of large units.

A less sophisticated criterion, but perhaps easier to use, is the selection of a minimal progress rate that surpasses "no change" in the pupil's performance. The selection of this criterion may not be as absurd as it first seems. Suppose the teacher requires a pupil's average performance on succeeding weeks to exceed his performance on the previous week. The teacher is, in effect, saying that the child must make more than "zero" progress.

After the teacher has selected the rate of progress which is desirable, it is then important to determine the number of days which a pupil must fall below that rate of progress before the teacher will make an instructional or management intervention. One might select a number of consecutive days below the criterion rate of progress, such as the 3 days advocated by White and Liberty (1975). As an alternative, one might select a criterion such as 3 out of 4 days, or 4 out of 5 days below the selected rate of progress as being the criterion for making an intervention.

Progress criteria can be used with or without a visual display. If used without a visual display, the teacher is required to formulate a table or other listing of the performance criterion for each day the pupil performs. The pupil then must equal or exceed the listed value of a given day. If he falls below the listed values for the specified number of days, the teacher then makes an intervention.

A second way to use the progress criteria is to mark a "minimal progress line" on a chart. As the teacher plots the pupil's performance each day, it is readily apparent whether or not the pupil has achieved his desired rate of progress. It is also readily apparent when the pupil's performance falls below the line of minimal progress for the specified number of days.

## Visual Display

The next step in establishing measurement procedures is the selection of visual display or charting procedures, or even whether the teacher will elect to use a chart.

As indicated previously, the teacher may collect data and apply data decision rules that enable the use of data without requiring a visual display. The main advantage of this system may be economy of teacher time, while the main disadvantage could be the loss of information about a pupil's rate of progress and characteristics of performance change. It is probably easier for a teacher to see and compare pupils' performance changes when displayed on a chart.

Most charts indicate successive time (days, sessions, or trials) across the horizontal axis (abscissa), and the score (count, percent, or frequency) on the vertical axis (ordinate). The lines on the arithmetic charts familiar to most persons are equally spaced on both vertical and horizontal scales. Arithmetic charts are easily constructed by teachers or are available from graphics and paper supply stores. Semilogarithmic charts have equally spaced lines on the horizontal axis, and proportionally spaced lines on the vertical axis and are available from fewer outlets. The relative merits of the semilog or "standard behavior chart" have been discussed elsewhere. The "standard behavior chart" is especially suited to use for decision making using a line of minimal progress, as described by Liberty (1972) and White and Liberty (1975).

Presented in Figure 7 is an example of the use of data collection in decision making concerning when to implement certain phases of a self-help task.

Figure 7 represents a student's progress across two successive phases of a handwashing task. The chart is a display of a frequency measure of a certain behavior: hand rubbing motions per minute. The object or criterion for each phase was approximately 50 rubs/minute—rubs being the back and forth movement of the student's hands. After the hand rubbing behavior was learned to criterion, phase 1 was implemented. During this phase, a washcloth was introduced between the student's hands. As the data reveals, rubbing motions dropped from about 50 rubs/min to none. However, over the succeeding days of phase 1,

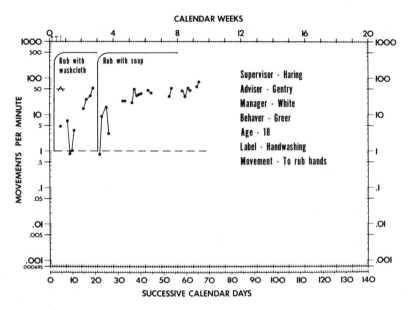

Fig. 7.   A student's progress across two successive phases of a handwashing task (see text).

frequency of rubbing again returned to criterion (50 rubs/minute). Once criterion was reached on phase 1, phase 2 was implemented by introducing a bar of soap between the hands. Again, rubbing motions dropped from 50 to zero/minute—and again, they returned to criterion over the succeeding days of phase 2.

This type of data display aids the teacher in making decisions concerning whether or when to implement phase changes in a program or even whether to continue with a particular strategy. By setting a criterion for phase change ahead of time—in this case, 50 rubs per minute—the teacher can easily see when a new intervention is necessary, and how quickly a child learns each aspect or phase of the total skill being taught.

Befor leaving the discussion of formative data, it is important to note that selection of the amount and type of data to be collected and the specific procedures to be used may depend, to a large extent, on the resources and goals of the program serving severely handicapped individuals. In a setting where instructional and curricular development, personnel training, and/or research are components of the program, and where resources are available, it may be imperative to collect large amounts of relatively sophisticated data which are comparable across individuals, classrooms, instructional programs, and instructional situations. However, in a program where the sole emphasis is service to pupils or where resources are limited, then less extensive and sophisticated data may be sufficient or desirable.

This chapter has attempted to provide a rationale for and description of essential components of a formative measurement system. Only slight emphasis has been placed on an analysis of the relative merits and disadvantages of different kinds of data. The reader is referred to White and Liberty (1975) for an extensive and thorough discussion of these issues.

## SUMMATIVE DATA

The purpose of summative data for severely handicapped individuals is to provide summary and descriptive information about children's performance through time. Usually the summative data are related to standardized tests, which may be either "norm referenced" or "criterion referenced." However, there are few standardized tests or measures which are appropriate for a variety of severe handicaps and which measure performance in a variety of areas. Some measures which have been used widely for infants and young children such as the Bayley Scales of Infant Development, the Denver Developmental Screening Test, the Portage Project Checklist, and the Sequenced Inventory of Communication Development, have been used to describe handicapped individual's progress in different performance areas. Recently, scales have been developed or refined which are intended for use especially with handicapped individuals. These include such measures as the AAMD Adaptive Behavior Scales, The Gunzberg, The Camelot Behavior Checklist, The Calyer-Azusa Scales, and the TARC Assessment Scale. The Experimental Education Unit of the University of Washington is currently developing the Uniform Performance Assessment Scale, which is intended to provide summative evaluation of performance of individuals with a variety of handicapping conditions and over a broad age range in several performance areas. An increasing interest by teachers, administrators, and funding sources is resulting in considerable effort to develop summative measurement tools for the severely handicapped.

An alternate type of summative information is the description of individual's "rate of change" of performance across time. The "rate of change" or "celeration" statements derived from frequency measures plotted on semilogarithmic charts provide a technological base for collecting and using this type of summative data.

## SUMMARY

In the eduation of severely handicapped individuals, there are both specific and general needs. Specifically, educators must arrange effective instructional programs for individual pupils, using feedback about the pupil's performance to assure that the pupil is making adequate progress and to determine those instructional procedures which are most effective with the individual. Generally, educators must determine those interventions which have the highest probability of success with pupils and the measurement procedures which provide the most information for the least expenditure of teacher time and energy. Both of these efforts require the further development and validation of a technological base of information in curriculum, instructional strategies, learning hierarchies, and reinforcement procedures with severely and profoundly handicapped individuals. The success of these efforts depends on the use of a sound measurement base which itself can be applied with individual pupils.

**REFERENCES**

Kunzelmann HP (ed.): Precision Teaching: An Initial Training Sequence. Seattle, Wash. Special Child Publications, 1970
Liberty KA: Data decision rules. Working Paper No. 20. Eugene, Oregon: Regional Resource Center for Handicapped Children, College of Education, Department of Special Education, University of Oregon, August, 1972
White OR, Liberty KA: Behavioral assessment and precise educational measurement. *In* Schiefelbusch R, Haring NG (eds): *Teaching Exceptional Children*. New York, McGraw-Hill, 1975

# IV

# Intervention Strategies

Alice H. Hayden, Gael D. McGinnes,
and Valentine Dmitriev

A

# Early and Continuous Intervention Strategies for Severely Handicapped Infants and Very Young Children

It is sobering to realize that if we had been writing this chapter only 10 years ago, it would have been a chapter devoted almost entirely to residential care strategies. Today, we have raised our sights remarkably; no longer content to see even the severely handicapped individual relegated to a life of custodial care, we are determined to fulfill a dream that few dared to dream some short years back. In earlier years, institutionalization was the norm because there were limited expectations and, hence, few strategies for helping severely handicapped individuals achieve self-determination. Thus institutionalization and custodial care were the general solutions, and seemingly the best solutions society had to offer. Now, we have the strategies to intervene successfully to promote self-dependence. Now, we are committed to the ideal of "normalization"—that is, to providing the "least restrictive alternative" in care, and to providing each person, regardless of his or her handicap, with the skills to function as independently as possible in a setting as near to the normal community setting as possible. A large order? Yes, and one which requires that intervention begin early, and continue for as long as the individual needs help.

## PREVENTION: THE EARLIEST INTERVENTION

It may seem illogical to begin talking about prevention of handicapping conditions when the topic we set out to discuss was intervention; after all, "intervention" presupposes that a handicap already exists and that something needs to be done about it. But it is impossible to discuss the topic of intervention without feeling impelled to raise the important, related issue of preventing severely handicapping conditions initially and of preventing more severe degrees of handicap or "secondary" handicaps after an initial insult is apparent. Moreover, there are several reasons why the issue of prevention is important to the interventionist. To begin with, prevention may concern "second-stage" prevention of the subtle handicaps which often go undetected in a child with severe involvement; occasionally these subtler manifestations are masked because the initial presenting handicap is so dramatic that attention is naturally drawn away from the less salient behaviors. Occasionally, too, the subtler handicapping conditions actually were secondary to the initial development insult, and therefore, may not have existed at the time of the child's first complete diagnostic workup. For all these reasons, it is necessary to be concerned with ongoing prevention through screening, periodic evaluation with appropriate standard assessment instruments as a backup monitor to the daily observation of a child's progress, and remediation of potentially handicapping conditions before they develop into full-blown disorders.

The more usual sense of prevention does not concern prevention of secondary handicaps, however, but rather refers to prevention of a handicap in the first place. Here the interventionist, whose primary goal is remedial instruction of a child with an already existing handicap, is nevertheless in need of information about prevention. It is a topic which cannot be considered tangential to his/her primary area of responsibility—remediation. Two topics are particularly relevant to prevention of handicapping conditions: education for parenting and genetic counseling.

## Education for Parenting

It is by now a truism that we educate our citizens for almost every role but those most important to family life—marriage and parenthood. There are some efforts to provide junior high school, high school, and college students with important bits of information about biologic parenthood and about developmentally facilitating or obstructing "social" elements in marriage and family life. However, instruction in the aspects of parenting necessary to insure reduction in incidence of handicapping conditions and to promote optimum development in children can only be termed understressed in most school curricula. In order to prevent severe and profound handicaps in their offspring, prospective parents need to be aware that multiple factors have been identified as having substantial influence on the outcome of a pregnancy or a parenting experience.

Among the topics which should be covered in education for parenting courses are the following. This list is not to be considered complete, but is rather merely exemplary; it is meant to stimulate further thought, particularly since, in the nature of our rapidly changing society, any list of this sort will be outdated within a few months to a year.

1. MATERNAL NUTRITION

The adequacy of the mother's diet, particularly during pregnancy, but actually during her entire lifetime, has important influence on the health of her children. Information about the basic seven food groups and about increased protein, calcium, vitamin, and general caloric requirements during pregnancy should be provided by her physician to every prospective mother—but this information should actually be made known in an informational way as early in her lifetime as she is able to understand it. Elementary school children may have little actual control over the diets they are fed; however, they can begin to learn about nutrition and can convey brochures, pamphlets, and other information to their parents.

Training for parenthood can begin in the primary and elementary grades, by teaching all children the basics of good nutrition, as well as the basic principles of child care. In doing this we can reach the parents, especially mothers, at a time when it can have a direct effect on the health of the existing family, as well as any additional children who may be born in the future. Adults who learn about and practice good nutrition from childhood are more likely to continue doing so prior to and during the crucial years of parenting. They are also more likely to be in better physical health themselves and are, therefore, more likely to produce healthy children. Almost any means to improve early nutrition should be undertaken, using whatever community resources are available.

2. EFFECTS OF DRUG INGESTION/DRUG ABUSE

In 1961, information began to emerge about the devastating damage a drug called Thalidomide could have on a developing fetus when taken by the mother during pregnancy (*Life,* August 10, 1962). Prior to that date physicians frequently prescribed drugs for their pregnant patients to quell "morning sickness," to aid in sleeping, and so on. In the past decade or so, an expanding list of such drugs has been implicated in the causation of developmental disabilities, with the result that even some drugs formerly prescribed to prevent the loss of a pregnancy due to miscarriage (such as "DES"–diethylstilbestrol or its equivalents) have been shown to cause long-delayed cancers of the reproductive tract in young women whose pregnant mothers took the drug.

Physicians are now reluctant to prescribe even so seemingly "harmless" a drug as aspirin to a pregnant or potentially pregnant patient; dentists, alarmed at the developmental anomalies caused by x-rays administered to pregnant patients, now routinely use a lead apron when x-raying their female patients of child-bearing age, whether the patients have declared themselves to be expecting a child or not. The toxic effects of alcohol, ingested by alcoholic pregnant mothers, on their offspring has been demonstrated by researchers at our own Child Development and Mental Retardation Center (Smith and Jones, 1973), giving impetus to earlier information efforts cautioning the expectant mother to reduce or eliminate alcohol intake in pregnancy. Conservative obstetricians now ask patients to eliminate tobacco and to reduce caffeine (coffee) intake as well. These trends are significant; they point to the importance of educating even very young people about the extremely harmful effects that may occur when an expectant mother takes drugs.

The topic, of course, has particular relevance because of the increase, in recent years, of deliberate "recreational" abuse of drugs such as amphetamines or barbiturates; teenagers, who make up the larger percentage of drug abusers, also tend to abuse drugs such as LSD-25, which has, in some studies (Hsu, Strauss, and Hirschorn, 1970) been implicated as a cause of chromosomal damage—a prominent cause, in turn, of severe developmental deficits in offspring. Educating the preteen or teenage youngster might prevent some such instances of severely or profoundly handicapping conditions.

Educating preteens and teenagers about the dangers of drug abuse is an effort which, like education in nutrition, should begin in the earlier grades. Younger children and preteens are more likely to accept teachers and other adults as authority figures and are less likely to be swayed by undesirable influences and pressures of peer groups, as is often the case with high-school age youths. If all children get the same basic information about nutrition and drugs over a period of years, a much larger segment of the population will be reaching adulthood and parenthood with the knowledge of these facts firmly established.

## 3. EFFECTS OF AGE-RELATED FACTORS

The fact that mothers under age 20 or over age 40 have a much higher risk of producing developmentally damaged children than do mothers in the optimum childbearing years (ideally, from ages 24–28) is not sufficiently known. Women who wish to plan pregnancies in order to maximize their chances of giving birth to healthy babies ought to be informed about age-related aspects of reproduction well in advance of the time they actually become pregnant. Even where a woman of advanced years—the highest risk group for producing children with Down's syndrome, for example—wishes to become pregnant, the knowledge that she belongs to a group at risk may lead her to take advantage of procedures now available to diagnose the presence of Down's syndrome and other anomalies while the child is still in the womb, and the pregnancy can be legally terminated. (These procedures are described below; see Genetic Counseling.) If the woman has no knowledge that she is at risk, she may neglect such important steps to insure the best pregnancy outcome.

## 4. EFFECTS OF DISEASE

With the widespread rubella epidemic in the United States during 1964–1965, many mothers who had contracted the disease during the first trimester of pregnancy subsequently gave birth to infants who were deaf/blind, or who showed substantial visual or hearing impairment, or both. It has been shown that parental venereal disease can damage an unborn child, and that viral diseases have damaging effects on a developing embryo or fetus, even though the organism is not directly in contact with the disease-producing agent, but is still in the womb. This information has produced intensified efforts to isolate the factors which cause such anomalies, to develop vaccines (now available, for instance, to prevent rubella) or other preventive measures (such as public health education campaigns to convey information about the dangers of venereal diseases and the available treatments for them). These efforts have done a great deal to insure the safety of a developing child and, significantly, to educate the public so that vaccines and preventive measures will be used. Much more needs to be done in this area, but recent advances have done something to reduce a prominent cause of severely/multiply handicapping insults.

## 5. EFFECTS OF CHILD ABUSE/NEGLECT

As education for parenting becomes more sophisticated, it must begin to deal with the troublesome issues related to parents' own treatment of their children. Since 1961, when the term "the battered child syndrome" was coined (Journal of the American Medical Association, Kempe et al., 1962), there has been increasing awareness of the appallingly high incidence of cases of child abuse and neglect, including failure to provide nutritionally adequate diets, shelter, or care in times of illness. The National Center for Child Abuse and Neglect has recently documented (*Time,* March 17, 1975) that an increase even above that noted in the past decade has begun to be reported. Center spokesmen speculated that there is a relationship between reported abuse and nutritional or physical neglect of children and the difficulties presently experienced by many families in finding employment and in providing adequately for their children. Apparently, then, education is very timely right now—education which stresses the long-term and truly devastating effects on a young child's neurologic integrity when he/she is subjected to harsh physical abuse. Even "spanking," as some parents call it, has harmful physical effects—not to mention the harmful psychological sequelae when a helpless child is verbally and physically abused by an angry, unpredictable adult. Educational efforts should also stress that parents who believe their behavior is harmful to their children can find help from a number of social and health agencies in their communities— and that seeking such help carries with it no stigma, whereas conviction following prosecution on a charge of child abuse certainly harms both parent and child.

6. IMPORTANCE OF EARLY AND CONTINUING
   PRENATAL CARE

We have the dramatic evidence of a precipitous fall in our infant mortality and maternal mortality rates in America during the last 75 years as testimony to the fact that not only can adequate prenatal care insure better survival for both infant and mother, but most prospective mothers know this and take advantage of the care that is available. However, our mortality rates are still higher than those of England, Japan, and some of the Scandinavian countries; further, many of the mothers at greatest risk for producing handicapped children—the poor, the young or older mother, the uneducated—are the very ones who make least, and latest, use of predelivery medical care. Many of the factors we have just mentioned as having the most detrimental effects on the developing baby could be prevented if the child's mother had good prenatal care, beginning at the time she planned her pregnancy, or at least when it is newly established. This topic will be discussed further below, in connection with the issue of genetic counseling—one of the important services that are presently available to parents who seek advice prior to conceiving a child. This service can make a great difference to decreasing the number of severely and profoundly handicapping conditions in children.

7. ACCIDENT PREVENTION

No discussion of the prevention of handicapping conditions would be complete without some reference to the importance of accident prevention for both the pregnant woman and for the newborn child. The pregnant woman must realize that an injury to herself may also affect her unborn child. Many falls and other injuries may be avoided through careful planning and attention to safety precautions. Accident statistics point to the many mishaps that occur in the home; yet a careful room-by-room survey will pinpoint many potential hazards that could be rather easily corrected. Such attention could greatly reduce falls, burns, scaldings, and would generally benefit all the members of the household.

The pregnant woman often feels awkward, and is not as agile as she is normally when she is not carrying a child. Her movements during pregnancy may need to be more considered and deliberate. She may find hand rails and other supporting or guiding mechanisms helpful; she may find it beneficial to make some changes in footwear, just as she has found or will find it necessary to make modifications in her clothing.

Planning for the child's arrival should also include attention to child safety. There are frequent articles in popular magazines and books on crib and clothing selection; other articles discuss safety and other criteria that should be taken into account in toy selection.

As the child begins to move about and to explore his or her environment, the parents must take additional precautions to make certain that the child does not fall or get into things that could be detrimental to health, or possibly even cause death. The average household does indeed contain a number of dangerous or poisonous items which, if ingested or spilled on parts of the body, can be damaging or fatal to a child. Of particular concern should be all cleaning materials, such as detergents, ammonia, bleaches, and other poisonous or inflammatory items. These should always be kept beyond the reach of a child. The family medicine cabinet, also, usually contains a large number of items which can be harmful.

However, accident prevention must not be limited to the home environment. Car accidents resulting in brain damage or other handicapping conditions are an ever-present hazard. For this reason, we cannot stress too emphatically the importance of using car seats and seat belts for children. Every parent or adult transporting children by automobile or bus must make vehicle safety a firm and unbreakable rule.

Precautions need to be exercised most rigorously as the child grows and explores areas he can reach or climb up to explore. As the child becomes verbal, he should be taught safety measures and expected to observe them. The child may then be counted on to take progressive responsibility for safety. For the family of a severely handicapped child, both of these stages may be reached more slowly. Mobility may come later to the handicapped youngster; so, inevitably, will the ability to appreciate accident potentials in substances or situations, and to guard against them. And, even though parents may have done everything they can think of to avoid or prevent accidents, they will find a knowledge of first aid useful. Few of us will go through life without being subject to some accidents. The effects of many accidents or injuries can be diminished greatly by the application of appropriate and immediate first aid.

## 8. IMPORTANCE OF EARLY STIMULATION

Probably the most frequently neglected topic in education for parenting through the years has been the importance of stimulating activity for the child from the earliest weeks and months of life. Parents do not usually think of the child as being educated in the early weeks, but it is nevertheless true that many of the developing child's most significant instructional experiences take place long before school begins. Indeed, much of the emphasis on early childhood education in recent years has come about precisely because of the mounting evidence that, particularly in the case of a handicapped child, educational intervention that awaits school age is initiated too late to have optimum impact. Because this theme is so familiar to those early intervention specialists who have been trained to appreciate the value of early childhood education, they tend to be unaware of how many parents have been told that a young infant spends up to 20 hours in 24 asleep, and the remaining time largely in eating or crying to "exercise his lungs." Parents do indeed require instruction about the importance of early education, for many reasons, such as the following.

The infant not only is capable of performing complex visual and auditory discriminations within the first few days after birth (Smart and Smart, 1973), but must do so in order to develop normally. Function develops in a dynamic fashion from the interactions of environmental stimuli with the evolving structures of the senses and the central nervous system. Without either an intact sensory system or continuing stimulation from the environment, the organism does not develop normally. Dramatic evidence of the devastating developmental effects of stimulus deprivation was produced a few years ago, when a group of psychological researchers separated monkeys at birth into three experimental classes: members of the first class were deprived of sight at birth by being anesthetized and having their eyelids sutured shut; the second group were given normal rearing experiences until 2 months of age, when they were given eyelid-suturing treatment identical to that of the first group; a final experimental cohort did not receive the temporary "blinding" treatment until near adulthood. The results of these differential deprivation schedules were extremely significant. The monkeys who were "blinded" from birth had the sutures removed at 2 months of age, at about the time when the second cohort began the deprivation treatment. But though the second group underwent a longer period of stimulus impoverishment, the first group suffered the most devastating effects. The first group of monkeys never developed normal sight at all; the second group, "blinded" for 3 to 4 months beginning at 10 weeks of age, did show later impairment of visual patterning and visually related functions, but they were not nearly so impaired as the first group, who were functionally blind for life. The third group, not "blinded" temporarily until near adulthood, showed almost no permanent visual impairment.

Such experiments suggest that deprivations during the developmental period have the most serious consequences for later functioning. On the other hand, studies have shown also that stimulation supplied during this early period can be extremely beneficial; particularly to a child in a population "at risk" for developmental disabilities. A population that was studied to examine the effects of early stimulation was born to mothers in Philadelphia General Hospital in 1971; the babies were all premature, and all were born to mothers in the lowest socioeconomic stratum (a high-risk group for producing babies with developmental deficits). But these babies were given a program of intensive sensory stimulation from birth, even while still in the hospital nursery's isolettes. The sheets of their isolettes were colored and patterned to provide visual stimulation, colored mobiles were hung so that the children could see them, and auditory stimuli such as music or the simulated sound of a mother's heartbeat were provided for several hours during the day. The babies were also frequently held and cuddled, talked and sung to by the nurses, and by their mothers during feeding. The mothers were instructed in the importance of early education while they were still in the hospital; when they returned home with their babies, they were visited by social workers who brought stimulating toys for the babies, helped the mothers to locate necessary social and health services, and assisted in finding employment for the mothers if asked to do so. The program combined assistance, training, and support of several kinds to the mothers, with stimulation and frequent positive adult contact for the children. It produced dramatic results: whereas fully one-third to one-half of the premature, "at risk" children could have been expected to show significant developmental delay at 1 year of age, all of them were functioning at or above normal levels at that testing.

Rick Heber of the University of Wisconsin has recently completed a 5-year study of a group of children in the Milwaukee area who were similarly "at risk" when born to mothers whose own intelligence was in the mildly to moderately retarded range. These children, too, showed the effects of appropriate early stimulation; most are functioning above normal levels now, when they have been prepared to enter first grade, and some have recorded I.Q. scores as high as 130 (Heber et al., 1972).

It must be acknowledged that expectations will usually have to be adjusted downward for the child who is born with an already present handicap of a severe to profound degree. But, as will be elaborated in the concluding section of this chapter, the evidence suggests that whatever errors we have made in setting expectations for the severely disabled children so far have been in the direction of expecting too little. The severely involved child may not be brought to function at I.Q. 130 after intensive early and continuous intervention. But he or she will certainly be able to attain an incomparably higher level than otherwise—if given stimulating activity from the first hours after birth.

## Genetic Counseling

Counseling has two main things to offer. It can, first of all, provide prospective parents with an estimate of the probability, based on what is known about genetic or hereditary factors, that they will produce healthy offspring. Such information can be of great value to couples who know, for example, that inherited disorders have appeared in their families. Such couples might wish to alter plans for a pregnancy, should the probability of handicap in the child be above 25 percent; many parents would find the financial and personal demands made upon them by the presence of a handicapped child in their families too great.

Secondly, genetic counseling can refer parents who wish to undergo direct diagnostic procedures to disclose the existence of a developmental anomaly in an established pregnancy. Normally, referrals would be made to a specialist who would use fetal monitoring devices; developmental histories of the mother's previous pregnancies, if any; a history of the mother's own health; and various bits of evidence (using urine and blood samples, for example) of adequate or troubled progress in the present instance to guide him in making a prognosis about the outcome of the pregnancy.

If there is substantial reason to fear a negative outcome of the pregnancy, or if the mother-to-be is in a high-risk age group for producing offspring with developmental deficits, there may be a recommendation to perform further tests, such as amniocentesis. This procedure is ordinarily done under local anesthesia by a gynecologist specially trained to carry it out with minimal risk to the fetus or the mother; it involves inserting a hollow needle through the mother's abdominal wall, and finally into the uterine cavity. The needle is then used to extract a small amount of the uterus' amniotic fluid in which the baby floats while in the womb. This amniotic fluid contains cells from both the mother and the infant, which can be studied for chromosomal damage. If there is no damage evident in any of the cells studied, there is a high probability that the infant will exhibit neither Down's syndrome (the disorder for which this diagnostic procedure was first developed), nor several other handicapping conditions which can also be detected by amniocentesis.

The body of knowledge concerning heredity of genetic abnormalities is increasing at a fast rate; there are new discoveries almost weekly, and such knowledge will lead to greater and greater accuracy in predicting whether the answer to a mother's age-old question, "Will my baby be normal?" is probably yes, or probably no. It is possible now to isolate many of the correlates between parental or other variables and the presence of developmental disabilities in the offspring. One day, this will in turn lead to information about causal relationships, and even to genetic manipulation to prevent handicaps.

If the cells studied show that a damaged infant is developing, the procedure has, at the very least, provided the prospective parents with important information on which to base their plans. The couple may feel that the stress which rearing a handicapped child would place on their family will be too great, and they may elect to terminate the pregnancy for that or for other, related reasons. Yet the desire for a child is so great in some couples that many we have talked with would choose to continue a pregnancy, even knowing that a child born to them would have severe handicaps. The procedure just discussed may be desirable for these parents, too, however; since the financial and personal sacrifices required of parents of a handicapped child are so much greater than those demanded of parents whose children need only average care, a half year or more to prepare for these sacrifices may be crucial to maintaining the family's equilibrium.

No matter what other topics we address in preparing parents who may one day face the reality of bringing up a handicapped child, we should emphasize most a note of hope. It is, indeed, the parents who can make the most far-reaching changes possible in their child's performance. This is true of even the severely or profoundly handicapped child. The joys of watching a complex organism develop increasingly complex skills, find increasing joy in other people and the events of life, and developing increasing ability to return his or her parents' affection—all these rewards are waiting for the parents of a handicapped child, too.


## EARLY AND CONTINUOUS INTERVENTION WITH PARENTS AND CHILDREN

One day, advances in medical and physicochemical sciences, generally, may make it possible to detect and treat biologically the disorders which produce the more severe handicaps. More than the mild to moderate handicaps which often result from environmental factors, the severe handicap tends to be the result of biologically based insult to the organism during the developmental period. Today, however, there is almost no severely handicapping disorder which can be treated totally through the traditionally administered types of medical intervention.

Traditionally, management of developmental disability cases has fallen to physicians, even though the majority of disabilities are not medical in nature. Of the 6 million Americans classed as mentally retarded, an estimated 10 to 25 percent have medical problems. The great majority mainly need special education and occupational training. [Howard, 1974–1975, p. 19.]

The educator therefore becomes involved in work with the severely and profoundly handicapped early, if the best practices are followed, and continues to have an important role in the child's treatment throughout at least the late adolescent period, and perhaps longer, if the individual requires work rehabilitation programs.

At Children's Hospital in Boston, Massachusetts, *a vocational rehabilitation program is underway with children 3 years old and above*. Started by William E. Kiernan, the program is aimed at helping the parents develop realistic long range occupational expectations for their offspring and to inculcate in the youngsters habits which will have vocational utility later on. Training of retarded children with handicaps usually stops with getting them to feed, dress themselves, go to the toilet, and handle other daily needs along with whatever education they can absorb. But ways have been developed for giving very young children experience in assuming responsibility for various chores to prepare them for adult work later on. The idea is to build on a work component in the child's training as soon as he can grasp it and to teach parents to think of their children as growing into useful adulthood. [Howard, 1974–1975, p. 20.]

The educator must, then, take the long view in preparing programs for a child at any given stage or age level. No single program or intervention is likely to hold all the answers, but must instead be visualized as another step in an integrated progress toward a set of life skills.

As will be the case repeatedly throughout the child's development, the first step is to assess the child's development at the moment, particularly in relation to the known normal developmental status of the child's age peers. This allows the educator to have factual information on which to base a program; rather than simply initiating treatment at an arbitrarily defined point, the instructor will teach only those skills the child does not already possess in his repertoire, and will not try to teach skills that are too far advanced for the child to grasp with his present level of functioning.

The need for better and better tools for assessment and testing tools can hardly be overemphasized. The controversy which has grown up in recent years over I.Q. testing and other standard assessment devices arises in large part out of the fallibility of such instruments.

The key to success with the severely to profoundly handicapped child in the early years is immediate and intensive intervention. Exercises to promote early physical mobility and muscle control are essential prerequisites to later development. For example, the ability to "track" a moving object with the eyes is a visual skill which most babies develop in a seemingly effortless way within the first 3 months after birth. The very handicapped child, however, must be systematically trained to do this and many other simple physical acts; if the child fails to develop these skills, the implications are profoundly serious. The lack of some very early developing skills, such as ability to focus visually or to track a moving object with the eyes, presages later inability to receive and process important stimuli on which a significant fraction of learning depends, and/or the inappropriate application, interpretation, and use of the results.

## The Handicapped Infant

Once a handicapped child is born, prevention of secondary handicaps and of more extreme degrees of primary handicaps is essentially a matter of instituting screening, identification, and fine-focus assessment procedures as a preliminary to remediation/intervention. Screening efforts should begin with administration of Apgar scales and other measures of neonatal status in the delivery room, should go on to monitor such newly validated diagnostic signs as sleep patterns (Barnard, 1974), active responses according to developmental age-expectations (presence or absence of classic neonatal reflexes such as the Babinski or Moro motor response patterns in newborns), and feeding abilities. Today, much is known about the significance of an infant's ability to maintain intervals of quiet sleep and states of quiet alertness, as well as to cry lustily in response to food deprivation, cold, etc. (Smart and Smart, 1973). Doubtlessly, new knowledge will soon be added which will make it even more important for an intensive infant-monitoring program to be a routine procedure in hospitals, at least for premature infants (known to be a high-risk group for developmental handicaps) or those in whom a handicap is identifiable at birth. Ideally, this will be done for all babies. Ideally, too, the child who presents an identifiable handicap at birth—and most severe to profound handicaps can indeed be identified at birth or within a few weeks to months after birth—should begin early motor development exercises as soon as his/her caregiver is able to handle him/her freely, even in the incubator or isolette. In the newborn nursery, as mentioned earlier in this chapter, programs of visual, tactile, auditory, kinesthetic, and social stimulation for developmentally delayed infants, particularly the premature baby (Scarr–Salapatek and Williams, 1972; Wright, 1971; Barnard, 1975), can do much to remediate developmental lags.

## The Parents of a Handicapped Child

Immediate support is absolutely required for parents during the classic period of "mourning" which parents undergo following the birth of a child with severe handicaps (Fraiberg et al., 1969); parents need help in expressing feelings; in developing realistic expectations for the child—neither underestimating nor overestimating the infant's potential; aid in locating high quality health care, and information about community programs for handicapped children and their families. Parents may also require referrals to social welfare agencies if finances are a problem.

Parents will generally feel more comfortable if they believe that there is something positive they can do to help their own child. Many are still trying to adjust to the fact that they have a handicapped child; some feel overwhelmed and woefully inadequate to cope with the many problems a handicapped child may present. Parent response generates child response and, conversely, child response generates parent response. The Early Intervention Specialist can give the parent something positive to do, and can help to rebuild what may be damaged confidence or feelings of inadequacy. Parents need understanding support and knowledge that assistance is available to answer questions and to demonstrate how the parent can work with the child. It is important to establish a parent–professional partnership whose aim is to maximize the handicapped child's learning opportunities from the earliest weeks of life.

Truly well-developed programs of intervention with the severely handicapped infant are almost nonexistent outside the University-Affiliated Facilities (UAF's) in the United States (Howard, 1974–1975, p. 20). However, these facilities are presently training 52,000 professionals in 14 disciplines, and these trained personnel are "feeding" into countless programs around the country: these "Johnny Appleseed" or ripple-effect efforts will soon be felt.

The cadre of highly trained professionals to emerge from these UAF centers in the next few years will fill a great need. Until recent years, parents of a handicapped child were never taught to adopt the orientation that their child's adjustment will depend primarily on educational strategies. Doctors were the first lines of appeal sought out by parents when they began to search for help in dealing with the need for services and training. But, as William Howard (1974–1975) indicates, although medical care of high quality is a necessary condition for the severely/profoundly handicapped child, it is not a sufficient one to produce a "whole child" care program:

> By the nature of their work and training, UAF officials say, doctors may not be well equipped to deal with nonmedical cases. Most doctors work alone or with other doctors and nurses. As a result, they may be only vaguely aware, for example, of what a psychologist specializing in emotionally disturbed children could do. . . . Many doctors are not conversant with the new techniques of the speech therapist or the reading laboratory specialist in assisting the dyslexic child. And very few know what a social worker does, or that 15

*percent of the nation's welfare caseload involves retarded persons
. . . .* Training at the UAF centers takes place in a clinical setting.
There are approximately 20,000 client-patients, allowing trainees to
cope directly with the handicapped. . . . The interdisciplinary approach is expected to yield new techniques in aiding the handicapped
and some are already being tried. [pp. 19–20.]
UAF promises to have a long-range impact on the financing and
administration of programs for the handicapped. Presently, some
200,000 persons, or 4 percent of the mentally retarded, are institutionalized. Hopefully, UAFs will substantially reduce the high
cost of patient maintenance . . . provide an important portion of the
specialized manpower to screen patients in institutions and determine
which patients can be released for training and treatment in the community.

Nevertheless, parents may need to seek information and specific
training, with a view to becoming their child's primary interventionist for
the first weeks and months of life. This will be true even if the parents
elect to make the often tragic decision to place the child in an institution,
since it is only rarely that placement will be obtainable during the first
year of the child's life (Barnard, 1975, in press).

INTERVENTION WITH A YOUNG CHILD

Once a handicapped infant is born, and his/her parents have spent the
earliest weeks and months in training of motor skills, simple discrimination skills, and related early learning acquisitions, the next strategy will be
to enroll the child in a preschool or day care program which will continue
the excellent developmental work begun by the parents under the direction of an early intervention specialist. The educator's role at this point
becomes such a critically important one, with so many aspects to be
considered that we wish to discuss it at length in the following section.


## THE EDUCATOR'S ROLE, TRAINING, AND RESULTING
## COMPETENCIES


### ROLE: The Educator as Very Early
### Intervention Specialist

Most writers in discussing the educator's role, make an assumption
which is in sharp conflict with our deepest convictions about the ideal
nature of early childhood education—namely, that the educator does not
enter the picture during the earliest weeks and months of a child's life, but
rather begins to see the child first in brief periods of 2 hours or so each

day, and then only in a preschool program setting. Ideally, as we have indicated in a general statement above (The Handicapped Infant), the early intervention specialist would be in frequent contact with the severely handicapped child and his or her family from the earliest days; in particular, the educator should be designing programs for the parents to carry out during the first weeks and months of the child's life. The specialist would then monitor the parent's training of the child on a daily basis until good teaching skills were established, and periodically thereafter. In a case where a parent works and cannot be with the child more than a few hours a day, the day care worker or other caregiver must be the focus of concern for the early intervention specialist who designs the severely handicapped child's program for the parent and the primary caregiver. The educator assumes increasing responsibility for the child's developmental progress after he/she is enrolled in a school or preschool program.

## The Educator's Goals and General Strategies in Work with the Severely/Profoundly Handicapped

"But what is early intervention?" This question is asked with great frequency by parents who bring a child to a doctor or to a center for child health and development and who are puzzled when instructed to plan for an intensive intervention effort during their child's early years. It is well for the early intervention specialist to have a full and vividly illustrative explanation at hand, since only by engaging the parents' sympathy, cooperation, and active involvement with the program will it succeed. This is best accomplished by educating the parents about the goal and the general strategies of an early intervention program.

The goal of intervention is to provide the experiences which will allow a child to develop skills that approximate or even reach those which a normal child develops. Strategies are discussed below.

EMPLOYING MORE INTENSE AND FREQUENT
STIMULI

To accomplish this task with a severely handicapped child requires that the stimuli employed in input to the organism be more intense and often more frequent than would be the case for a child with average ability. Impaired sensory functioning may require that letters used to teach simple words be larger or perhaps colored red to attract attention (Doman, 1964) in work with the severely handicapped, and repetitions may have to be more numerous if a severely involved child is to learn a word or concept.

RECOGNIZING AND REINFORCING
APPROXIMATIONS TO A CORRECT RESPONSE

A teacher must be able to recognize rather remote, weak approximations of a target response and to reinforce the approximation so that it begins to occur more frequently. Once a remote approximation is established, the instructor can begin to shape and selectively reinforce only closer approximations to the target behavior. Soon the behavior begins to assume very nearly the identical characteristics aimed at, and the instructor can focus on more advanced behaviors in the hierarchy of skills.

HAND-SHAPING RESPONSES WHEN NECESSARY

Strategies such as modeling the desired response or direct verbal instructions (very good instructional techniques with average ability or mildly handicapped pupils) may be less useful with the profoundly handicapped than the strategy of hand-shaping the approximation to the correct response. If a teacher desires to teach head control or to eliminate a child's drooling, initial strategies that use physical holding of the child's head or hand positioning of muscles in the face can do much more to establish the required mastery than will simple "showing" or "telling" the child what is required.

TEACHING "TOOL SKILLS" ESSENTIAL FOR MORE
ADVANCED LEARNING

A teacher may have to teach the foundation skill of imitation, which other children seem to acquire almost spontaneously. Since this skill is one of the essential "tool skills" upon which much of the developing child's learning depends, it must be developed early. If it does not appear spontaneously in the child's repertoire of behaviors, it must be taught by this just-mentioned process of physically shaping an imitative response, such as patting the child's hands together in a game of pat-a-cake; then reinforcing the patting with verbal praise ("Good! You can pat-a-cake!") and perhaps a bite of some food the child enjoys as soon as the child is performing the response, however imperfectly or involuntarily; then selectively reinforcing only better or more nearly self-initiated pats until the response is a good imitation.

The next step in programming would be to model other responses for imitation until the child had generalized this imitating skill, showing an ability to imitate a modeled response rather easily, simply from observing its characteristics visually, tactually, or aurally, rather than requiring a hand-shaping procedure by the teacher.

As is obvious, the acquisition of a basic skill such as imitation or making simple discriminations (big, little; hard, soft) will allow the child to employ these thinking aids to acquire many other basic skills and concepts.

## TEACHING BASIC PERSONAL/SOCIAL BEHAVIOR SKILLS

One of the problems of adjustment for the handicapped child which has received little attention to date is that presented by the child's hygiene, personal or social behavior, and physical appearance. Those who have worked with the handicapped have often been aware that the child's acceptance by others was made more difficult or less complete by virtue of the fact that the child looked either cosmetically unattractive or simply "different" to those around him. Indeed, one of the earliest court cases testing the handicapped child's right to placement in a public school classroom rested on the assertion that the child's drooling, difficult-to-understand speech, and unusual appearance "created a nauseating and depressing effect on the other pupils and the teacher":

(From the records of the Supreme Court of Wisconsin, of April 29, 1919 . . . ) "(R__T__) 13 years of age on March 27, 1918, a resident of the city of Antigo for 11 years, has been a crippled and defective child since his birth, being afflicted with a form of paralysis which affects his whole physical and nervous make-up. He has not the normal use and control of his voice, hands, feet and body. By reason of said paralysis, his vocal cords are afflicted. He is slow and hesitant in speech, and has a peculiar high, rasping and disturbing tone of voice, accompanied with uncontrollable facial contortions, making it difficult for him to make himself understood. He also has an uncontrollable flow of saliva, which drools from his mouth onto his clothing and books, causing him to present an unclean appearance. He has a nervous and excitable nature . . . his condition and ailment produce a depressing and nauseating effect upon the teachers and school children." [Zedler, p. 49, 1974.]

The early intervention specialist can help parents to develop many skills that will be beneficial not only to the parent but to the severely and profoundly handicapped child as well. Some of these skills will help to increase the responsiveness, alertness, appearance, and hence, the acceptance of the child. Pronounced changes in the appearance of some severely/profoundly handicapped children can frequently be effected through helping the child to attain head control or muscle control, as discussed in the section of this chapter dealing with modeling and shaping. Naturally, the appearance of the child is greatly enhanced through teaching the child patterns of cleanliness, grooming, and social behaviors that are acceptable, for example, at the dining table—whether the child is at home or in another setting.

It takes time to help the child develop these skills, using whatever intact resources he or she may have. Simply setting interim goals in a program to teach socially acceptable eating skills to a severely mentally retarded child, as one of our staff did last year, can take great skill in slicing a task into small, easily mastered steps. (Billingsley, 1974). Most of us are unaware, on day-to-day basis, what the small steps in a simple task such as buttoning actually are, far less which ones can most profitably be learned first, depending only on skills the child has already mastered and leading logically into those he is now ready to acquire. Keen observation of a model performing a task, and sometimes stop-motion videotapes, may be necessary to tease out many of the more subtle components of an action that is complex. But, as most parents and teachers will attest, it takes time for the normal child to learn such skills, too.

Parents can most effectively be shaped with tact and positive suggestions about ways to work toward making their child's physical appearance, dress, and grooming as attractive as possible. Teaching the child strategies for controlling gait, positioning of the limbs and features are only partly the parent's province, however; the teacher or intervention specialist must assume a large responsibility in this area. If possible, a physical therapist can help to design exercises for the child to perform. The Mimosa cottage program successfully taught severely handicapped girls skills related to dressing, hygiene, and grooming (Lent, 1968).

That children themselves ultimately value suggestions of this sort can readily be seen in the following passage from a young man's account of his gratitude to his mother in teaching him "deportment" skills which would help him to overcome the effects of his blindness:

> The reason blind children often retreat into their private, frightening or (as tragic), comfortable world is that the schools fail in their first task, which is to show them life as it truly is. (A blind child at school age) . . . is already anesthetized to the real world. Unless he has a mother like mine, he looks like a slob because nobody taught him how to label his clothes . . . that a light-blue jacket, a white shirt, and grey pants go well together. He has already begun to shake his head back and forth as if he were watching a Ping-Pong game. He is already picking at his eyes and his movements are becoming spastic. No wonder when he becomes an adult he is ready to run back to the security of a blind institution. But who's responsible? . . . You want to help a blind child? Then start by teaching him the common courtesies: how, for instance, to turn his face toward the person who is addressing him, how to mix with sighted children, not as a freak, not

as someone to be pitied, but as a person, an individual with feelings and hopes, little hells and talents, too. [Sullivan and Gill, 1975, pp. 170–172.]

## TEACHING THE USE OF "HUMAN RESOURCES"

All of us rely on the help that other human beings can give us to help get us the information or other assistance we need in daily living. But there is obviously a wide range of individual variation in skill when it comes to eliciting help.

For the handicapped, calling on others for aid in situations where the individual himself is simply unable to perform a task or requires assistance with a novel set of circumstances before he or she is able to perform is an absolutely essential ability. Yet it is not often systematically taught.

A small child signals his or her need for help with a generalized, undifferentiated cry for help; older children often get the assistance they need by yelling simply, "Mama!!" Mama then appears, interprets the need, supplies what seems to be lacking, and, if she is a good interpreter, no further wails are emitted. But by the time a severely handicapped child must deal with the community, he or she needs to be able to say, "I have trouble understanding. Can you tell me slowly/louder/again, please?"

The educator can benefit a child by taking time to explain that a problem must be stated clearly, help must be asked for specifically, but with courtesy, and that an individual must be made to feel that his contribution of help or information is useful and appreciated.

These skills are best taught through role-playing practice sessions dramatizing actual encounters the child is likely to have. Since the common school or day care settings offer many opportunities for such interactions naturally, the teacher should have little difficulty teaching skills such as courteous terms of address in asking for more juice or requesting help in building a block tower. Once these skills are established reliably in one area, the teacher can ask the child to exhibit them in other areas. Simply withholding requested help or saying "When you ask me to help you, I will open the puzzle box," can exploit natural learning potentials in everyday situations.

### TEACHING THE USE OF CUES

As will be mentioned later in this chapter, there is a great need to undertake research that will elucidate this vital but poorly understood aspect of work with the severely handicapped. At present, teachers can be aware that a child with impaired vision can be taught to use sound cues or residual vision as an aid to promote better functioning. Lip-reading is an example of using partial cues to help "fill in" the missing sounds where

## The Educator as Trainer of Parents and Other Interventionists

Training of parents, who are partners in the educational process, as well as of the paraprofessionals who are absolutely necessary assistants in work with the severely to profoundly handicapped, is a major responsibility for the educator. We must commend the efforts of "Closer Look" as a national effort to attempt to respond to parents' search for assistance. We can use this resource to get some insights into the problems presented and the need for services and assistance. We need such "listening posts" and the encouragement of parents to share their problems, frustrations, and expressions of needs such as those expressed in the May 1975 issue (The Parent–Professional Partnership) of *Exceptional Children*. There will be a continuing need for teachers to "train" members of other professional disciplines to recognize both the possibilities and limitations of education for the severely handicapped. There will be the need to interface with these people in many ways that involve training, if only to make it possible to share data, to cooperatively plan programs, and to teach some of the instructional skills which these professionals may need, but often lack.

## The Educator as Researcher

Research is an area of concern to a relatively small percentage of the professional population, but it is a large area of responsibility in the sense that there is an almost total lack of appropriate applied educational research to delineate materials and curricula for teaching the severely to profoundly handicapped. Questions which need attention are legion. For instance: what skills are truly critical "life skills"—that is, basic to achieving some degree of independent living as an adult? Toileting and the self-dressing and hygiene skills on which toileting partially depends are obviously needed; but what other dressing skills are really critical, and what could be either dispensed with or taught using alternate methods or alternate materials? For example, can a child with a severe motor problem be taught to use Velcro* fasteners instead of buttons, snaps instead of hooks and laces?

Velcro fasteners have been used in tourniquets and special corsets by health service professionals for years, but special educators have not applied these devices to an *instructional*-prosthetic use. Frequently, an instructor spends many hours and great instructional expertise in trying to

*Velcro fasteners use two strips or round "spots" of material; one side is faced with fuzzy fabric which adheres readily to the plastic "hooks" on the opposing strip's side. They would make clothes fastening easy for any motor-handicapped person, since the fastening can be done by a simple place-and-press motion.

teach a task that could be rendered unnecessary by making a simple modification in the environment. The substitution of Velcro fasteners for difficult buttons, snaps, hooks and eyes is just one example; another might be substitution of a digital watch for a more difficult-to-use conventional one with hour and minute hand.

Our question is, "Can the educational task in part involve isolating those already available or easily designed 'prosthetic' devices in the environment which will make mastery of basic skills easier or less time consuming?" Or, "How can other disciplines and education interface to bring about better learning?" And so on. These questions need systematic, applied investigations by researchers immediately. Often, the technology for teaching the severely handicapped is available now, but is merely unidentified for that purpose.

Few people concerned with the severely and profoundly handicapped and their families would deny the need for concentrated study and research directed to some basic problems in providing service and training, in efforts to prevent handicapping conditions, and in other areas discussed earlier in this chapter. At a recent Workshop on the Severely Handicapped sponsored by the Bureau of Education for the Handicapped held at Educational Testing Service in Princeton, N.J., researchers and "consumers of research" arrived at some agreements and made recommendations about research priorities in the area of the severely/profoundly handicapped. The participants recovnized the imperative requirement to develop and evaluate early invervention strategies to help professionals, paraprofessionals, and parents work effectively with severely and profoundly handicapped infants and young children.

Not the least of research priorities is the need to develop "systems" or networks for feedback from "consumers," whether the consumers are the severely or profoundly handicapped themselves, the parents or caregivers, professionals, or paraprofessionals. Indeed, very little attention has been given to the possibility of using feedback from the severely/profoundly handicapped themselves. Yet there are, in addition to data on their performances and responses to different stimuli, intervention strategies and the like, other types of feedback that should prove most useful to those working with them and eventually to the "consumers" themselves.

Only a few people have considered the information that might be gained, for example, through biofeedback data and through different modes of communication with the severely and profoundly handicapped to determine what cues they use or could possibly use in coping with their environment. Nearly all handicapped individuals consciously or unconsciously use cues and various types of feedback to help them make decisions and cope with certain types of stimuli. For the most part, they have to discover these helpful cues themselves, although some are taught routinely in good programs for the deaf and the blind, for example. But the handicapped individual could help educators and other handicapped individuals as well, through sharing in the discoveries of particularly useful cues. A recent and delightfully readable book, *If You Could See What I Hear* (Sullivan and Gill, 1975) provides such feedback from a young man who was blinded at birth. We have hardly begun to teach most handicapped individuals to utilize cues—partly because we ourselves have not identified those that could be used with different populations, more particularly with the severely and profoundly handicapped.

There is need too for gathering and analyzing feedback from consumer groups—parents, caregivers, paraprofessionals, and professionals—about their observations, new discoveries, successes, and frustrations in working with the severely/profoundly handicapped. Systematic observation and recording of information can provide a basis for objective examination of some of our efforts. We need such information for decision making, program planning, evaluation of strategies, evaluation of competencies, and performance. We need to learn to ask why, what, who, how, and when. In short, we need to "think" about everything we do in working with the severely/profoundly handicapped, and routinely ask ourselves the question, "Is there a better way?" Out of our observations, out of examination of the literature which can be greatly aided by ERIC and other information sources, and from "sharing" concerns and strategies with others, we can identify "researchable problems," and work to delineate an appropriate research design.

## The Educator as Evaluation Facilitator

How do we evaluate our efforts in the prevention of handicapping conditions; in providing services to improve the quality of life for the severely/profoundly handicapped and their families; in providing essential community services; in creating "public awareness" about the need to prevent handicapping conditions through "reeducation" and change in many of our attitudes, priorities, and practices; putting "our best collective minds" to work to identify and serve handicapped children and their families in those crucial early days, months, and years of the handicapped child's life?

Some of these questions lend themselves to evaluation more readily than others. In some instances, however, we do not even have a good baseline at the present time. For example, how can we measure our efforts to reduce child abuse and neglect, when in many areas we do not even have accurate information as to the extent of the problem? Only now is there a general public awakening with regard to its scope and nature, despite its devastating effects on children. Presently, too, every state is making an attempt to determine the nature and extent of available services for handicapped children within its state boundaries. There are efforts to coordinate services, but few states have delivery systems that will meet the needs of the different populations in both urban and rural areas.

### The Educator as Disseminator

Feedback and dissemination are important to those who seek to serve the severely and profoundly handicapped and to train personnel to work with this population. Time is too precious, funds are too short, and deployment of personnel resources to conduct research are too important to scatter or dissipate or even to duplicate efforts; there must be careful coordination and planning. In short, we need to determine research priorities, to consider who or what teams can best undertake what research, and to coordinate our efforts in the accumulation and dissemination of information effectively and efficiently to benefit the population to be served. Evaluation of our efforts in providing service and training, as well as of programs, research, feedback, and dissemination mechanisms requires careful scrutiny by all those who share common goals and objectives as they work with the severely handicapped. Exchange and constructive criticism of our efforts can be attained through the network of centers, projects, and programs and through associations, agencies, and consumers working together to improve the quality of life and the quality of service for the severely and profoundly handicapped.

### TRAINING: COMPETENCY-BASED, INTERDISCIPLINARY PREPARATION FOR WORK WITH THE SEVERELY HANDICAPPED INFANT/YOUNG CHILD

There are a number of efforts directed toward improving training programs in different disciplines, in "regular" education, in special education, in early childhood/special education, in paraprofessional preparation, in parent education (of those who are already parents), and education for parenting (for prospective parents who may be children themselves when taught the foundation skills). Many of these evaluation efforts are "competency-based." But what specific competencies are needed by educators who work with the severely or profoundly handicapped and their families?

In meetings and workshops, members of the American Association for the Education of the Severely/Profoundly Handicapped have underscored the need for determining basic competencies needed by educators in this field. In some areas there are agreements; in other areas, there are differences of opinion. Agreement regarding the basic competencies needed will probably be derived only through careful further study by trainers and trainees working together closely in settings serving the severely and profoundly handicapped.

After the basic competencies have been agreed upon, there still remains the question of formatively evaluating the trainee's attainment of the basic competencies and, therefore, of the activities selected to lead him or her to mastery of competencies. There is obviously a need to move quickly to specify basic competencies required, to develop programs to help personnel acquire these competencies, and to allow trainers to evaluate attainment of these competencies by the trainees. Fortunately, we are not without some background and experience to draw upon, but we would be less than naive if we did not recognize that educators have had, for the most part, limited experience in working with severely/profoundly handicapped infants and young children and their families. For too long, these children have been relegated to institutions and there has been little "market" for the well-trained early intervention specialist to work with this population. In the case of work with infants, educators even now have only limited access, considering the popular view that a child is its mother's responsibility until the traditional school-entrance age of 5 or 6 years.

### Basic Elements in Training for Work with the Severely/Profoundly Handicapped

In order to effectively prepare early intervention specialist personnel working with severely/profoundly handicapped children, there are several basic components that must be addressed:

1. Thorough knowledge of normal child development is essential. Regardless of how handicapped a child may be, the goal of the early intervention specialist should be to help that child move as closely as possible to developmental norms in gross- and fine-motor skills, communication, and social, cognitive, and self-help skills. Basic to the attainment of some of these skills is the early development of discrimination skills, utilizing whatever senses the child may have intact or whatever residual vision or alternate sensory avenues that can function to benefit the child's learning. The educator must use what he or she knows about normal development in assessing, in programming, and in working with parents and others who have contact and impact on the child's care and education.

2. In addition to a thorough knowledge of normal child development, the early intervention specialist must also have a good knowledge of

deviant development. The body of knowledge in this area is increasing rapidly, as is also our knowledge of how to work more effectively and efficiently with the severely and profoundly handicapped. Developmental disabilities and other forms of deviant development present a challenge too long studied from a distance, rather than at close range and, importantly, over time. The development of competencies in working with this population must involve supervised practicum that provides opportunities to work directly with these children and their parents and other caretakers.

3. Interdisciplinary training. The early intervention specialist must learn to work effectively and closely with personnel from a number of disciplines, as well as with parents and paraprofessionals. Each individual in the team must learn what types of integration of expertise and knowledge can be beneficial for the child and his or her family and what expertise is available locally to benefit the child. Effective interaction among personnel from different disciplines is best accomplished through providing part of their training in conjoint courses and in supervised practicum settings serving severely/profoundly handicapped children and their families. The actual application of the inter- and multidisciplinary approaches must be carefully planned and programmed. No single discipline can possibly cope with all the problems presented by severely/profoundly handicapped people and their families.

4. The specialist working with the severely handicapped needs training in behavior modification principles, such as the use of positive reinforcement of successive approximations to a desired response. This was discussed earlier in the section on general strategies that the educator may use. The latter also needs training in the application of those principles with the specific population of the severely/profoundly handicapped.

5. Training must emphasize complete mastery of the systematic observation and assessment techniques mentioned earlier as the first steps, and the most frequently repeated steps in intervention with the handicapped. Systematic observation and assessment are the bases for all programming decisions; these skills, therefore, are indispensable to effective intervention.

6. Supervised practical experience in work with parents, including acquisition of interviewing and effective listening skills which are all too often thought of as the exclusive province of the social worker or counselor. While we would not suggest that an educator's function is to provide therapy or counseling, a thorough mastery of some of the recently developed techniques employed by such specialists can serve the educator well, both in interactions with parents and other adult staff and with the children themselves.

## STRATEGIES WITHIN THE COMMUNITY AND SOCIETY

Any discussion concerning effective intervention strategies with se-verely handicapped infants and young children would be incomplete without some mention of those strategies operating on a large scale. By this, we mean strategies addressed to long-term and comprehensive care issues that necessarily involve the participation of many more people than the handicapped child and his immediate caregivers.

The most obvious reason for needing such strategies is that there is no "cure" for most severely handicapping conditions, no magical pills or treatments that will reverse the course of the handicap and enable the afflicted person to live completely independently. In the absence of mira-cle cures and treatments, we must rely merely on human ingenuity and hard work to improve the quality of life for handicapped persons and their families. Medical and social science have indeed produced many near-miracles in improving the physical health and life expectancies of afflicted persons; many more of them survive into relatively healthy adulthood than just a few short years ago. But precisely because more severely handicapped persons survive, there is all the more need for addressing ourselves to the long-term comprehensive care and educational needs of this population. Stein and Susser (1971) have noted that one of the means for reducing the prevalence of mental retardation and other handicapping conditions is achieved by "limiting the functional disability and social handicap in impaired persons, and cultivating the maximum intellectual and social potential for those affected." That is obviously a long-term effort, requiring the skills and expertise of many different professional and citizen groups, and public and private agencies.

Moreover, strategies involving wide-scale participation are not only required, they are entirely appropriate. There is hardly a family in this country without some personal interest in the care of a severely handi-capped person, whether a relative, neighbor, or friend. The quality of life for severely handicapped persons concerns us all. But even if that were not the case, there would still be other reasons for caring. The social and economic costs of providing long-term care for severely handicapped per-sons are very high indeed, and there are practical economic as well as altruistic reasons for finding strategies to improve that care. Not the least of these reasons is related to discussions earlier in this chapter concerning the interdependence of remediation and prevention. One of the long-range results of increased attention to remediation should be prevention, and a reduction not only in the prevalence, but also in the incidence, of severely handicapping conditions. Further, since "15 percent of the nation's wel-fare caseload involves retarded people, there is an obvious need for voca-

tional training specific to this population to help them function as independently as possible." [Howard, 1974–1975, p. 19.]

Where should these strategies begin? After all, "improving the quality of life for severely handicapped persons" is a very large and very
broad task, one that could cover the range from providing better health
care for one individual to providing vocational training and appropriate
home environments for all afflicted persons. Perhaps one way to sort out
the issues is to bear in mind two national goals whose achievement dates
are drawing near. First, we have a national Bureau of Education for the
Handicapped commitment to provide appropriate educational programs
for all handicapped children by 1980. Second, we are committed to reducing by half the incidence and prevalence of mental retardation in this
country by the end of the century. Although there is no question that
increased funds would make these goals far easier to achieve, the present
state of the economy and some uncertainty about national priorities for
allocating existing funds force us to consider other avenues for reaching
these goals. Certainly, one of our highest priorities at this time is the need
to coordinate efforts and to seek more efficient, effective, and creative
deployment of existing resources.

Coordinating efforts should produce several beneficial short-range
results that will have more impact on the long-range effort than may at
first be apparent. There are, first, the obvious benefits to be found in
reducing duplication of efforts so that if one group really is reinventing the
wheel, at least we do not need to have five other groups doing so; they can
divert their energies to less explored areas of need. Second, bringing
together people with varying skills in a concerted effort virtually guaran-
tees a broadening of outlooks and increases the probability of addressing
unmet needs. While it may be true that some problems are best not left to
committees to solve, the problems we face in providing appropriate service to severely handicapped persons are of such scope that their solution
demands more than individual genius or expertise.

However, the most critical benefit to be derived from coordinated
efforts is that a community, whether a city, state, or region, can maintain
a truly accurate assessment of existing needs that must be addressed and
can deploy resources to meet those needs. Through concerted effort, it
should be possible to develop both cross-sectional and long-range pictures
showing where the community stands in relation to its delivery of service
to citizens. The cross-sectional survey should indicate the nature and
scope of present unmet needs; the long-range picture should yield information about changing trends and the planning that will be necessary to
reverse or maintain those trends, as the need may be. One example of the
kind of information that lends itself to concerted action is the following. In
Washington State, education-for-all legislation has been interpreted to

cover children from school-entering age to 21; school districts throughout the state, however, determine the entering age for children in their bailiwicks. In some districts, handicapped children are eligible for public education and services at age 3; in other districts that eligibility begins at age 5. Yet educators and others throughout the state recognize that by the time a child reaches age 3 or 5, it may be almost too late for him to reap maximum benefits from intervention that should instead have begun at the time of his birth. Therefore, one of the ongoing efforts among many professional and citizen groups in our state is to work towards reinterpretation of our legislation and, in the meantime, to develop programs and deploy resources more effectively so that very young handicapped children can be provided the services they need, beginning with identification, screening, and assessment of this population and continuing with appropriate intervention for the child and his or her family.

The following are suggestions for activities and outcomes related to strategies that involve coordinated efforts toward improving the quality of life for severely handicapped persons.

The first section deals with the need to disseminate information generally. This need has been emphatically underscored in recent months by the establishment of the Developmental Disabilities Technical Assistance System (DDTAS) National Public Awareness Task Force (see Ruder and Finn, Inc. in references). The mission of this task force and its recommendations have been set out in a publication issued in Spring, 1975, whose epigraph (from the Report of the Committee on Labor and Public Welfare on S. 3378, the Developmentally Disabled Assistance and Bill of Rights Act, September 24, 1974) reads as follows:

> The Committee feel that there is a lack of public awareness of the persisting life problems of the developmentally disabled individual. This problem is of sufficient national significance to warrant a project of public understanding which would alert the American public to the plight of these individuals . . . and the potential for a more humane life. [p. 1]

The need for understanding of the plight of the handicapped is only one of the communication gaps that urgently require filling. Some of the others are presented in sections which follow.

### Information: Dissemination for Greater Accessibility

At the very least, any community should gather and disseminate as widely as possible information about available resources. In communities where appropriate services do exist, the family of a severely handicapped child is faced with a frightening maze of public and private services to grope through before they find the services they need. This problem is compounded for families who are new to communities, who must generally waste a great deal of time and effort merely finding landmarks in the new setting. The directory should specify how persons living in communities in which there are only minimal services can avail themselves of other communities' programs. Eligibility requirements should be spelled out. There should be a copy of this directory in the office of every pediatrician, in every clinic, and in every social service agency throughout the community. The directory should be organized for maximum ease in locating appropriate services and should be written in nontechnical language. It should also have a format which will permit updating easily.

Another kind of information gap that needs to be filled—one that can only be filled through coordinated efforts—relates to the vital information that needs to be disseminated about the known causes of some handicapping conditions and the means for reducing the incidence and prevalence of these handicaps. It is simply insufficient to write in academic journals or books about the relationship between maternal age and the incidence of Down's syndrome, for example. Unless that relationship is understood by every woman over 40, there is little that can be done to reduce the incidence of this anomaly. Further, although amniocentesis and therapeutic abortions are available to women who recognize that they may be at risk for bearing Down's syndrome children, these are no means "routine" procedures, either physically or psychologically, and should not be considered routine alternatives or substitutes for the more effective preventive tactic of providing information. That is only one example. Others involve creating greater public awareness of other preventive measures, mentioned earlier, which are all too rarely publicized. For instance, these include the need for proper prenatal care of the mother and developing embryo; the importance of nutrition in a child's development; preparation for parenthood that emphasizes the role of nurturing parenting in the child's early and continuing development and learning; and, finally, the critical importance of safety considerations to prevent many accidents that can cause irreversible damage to young children. This kind of public dissemination of information demands a coordinated approach precisely because of its importance and scope. A message delivered during a TV spot announcement may be forgotten as soon as it is over; but that message will more likely be recognized, remembered, and acted on if it appears frequently in other contexts as well. Messages delivered through television and pamphlets will have even greater effectiveness if service personnel repeat them with conviction. If a child's teacher, for example, conveys the same message that a parent has already seen in a booklet, that message will have even more impact. So, too, pediatricians, psychologists, educators, architects, neighbors, parents, friends, and anyone whose work or care impinges on the quality of life of severely handicapped persons, should be receiving and giving messages that can affect that care and that can do much to prevent further occurrences of the handicapping conditions whose victims require specialized care. The power of parent involvement, the formation of parent-to-parent groups, and the impact of parent groups on state legislatures, as well as on federal legislation and appropriations cannot be underestimated.

## Information: Matching Services and Needs

Still another reason for a coordinated approach to the care of severely handicapped persons and to disseminating information needs, services available, and preventive measures, is that it may be possible to develop innovative programs offering new or unusually creative service delivery systems, often using untapped resources. For instance, anyone familiar with the Foster Grandparent Program operating in many communities knows that these programs offer at least twofold benefits. Children who need specialized care and "extra" attention receive these from persons who have "something special" to give, but whose opportunities for giving are restricted by their age or retirement from work. There is ample evidence in the literature to show that these special attentions can alter the course of handicapped children's development, including their intellectual development (Skeels and Dye, 1939). We are also beginning to reckon with the needs and development of the "givers." Their own growth as human beings should never be allowed to atrophy merely because they have reached an arbitrarily set age; they, too, benefit from the exchange. Parent-to-parent programs, mentioned earlier, offer exceptionally beneficial exchanges and opportunities for creating a ripple effect. The message or training given by one parent to another will often reach a far wider audience than the initial receiver.

Using parents, elderly or retired persons, and other paraprofessionals for various forms of service delivery will be a continuing tactic in strategies designed to improve the quality of life for severely handicapped persons. Yet, all of these would benefit from some attempt to coordinate the services—for instance, a matching plan that strives for optimum deployment of resources; coordinated training so that those "giving" the care can do so with assurance and those receiving can receive the best possible services. The same considerations obtain, of course, in deploying professional services as well.

## Coordination: Better Service, Training, and Research

It is almost axiomatic that service directed towards meeting known needs, research investigating unexplored areas, and training for necessary competencies will result in vastly improved service, research, and training. But there is no way to effect such improvements without the accurate needs assessment mentioned earlier, and there can be no accurate needs assessment without input from many different sources. Furthermore, any efforts to improve these activities at a fundamental level involve the same kind of concerted activity. In the realms of legislation or policy making, for example, informed citizens working in concert have more chance of effecting change than do single persons or special interest groups. Similarly, anyone who has ever attempted to raise funds for research, service, or training programs knows that the probability of receiving those funds is increased if the program has wide impact or implications for replication; if the work is related to, or coordinated with, the work of others, and if needs addressed arise from a true service delivery gap.

One of the means for keeping ongoing and accurate records of needs in a community in order to track service delivery and pinpoint areas of concern is to keep a registry of persons needing service. Although registries of any sort are fraught with possiblities for infringing on the rights to privacy of persons listed, there are existing means for protecting these rights; moreover, one can argue that denial of services through incomplete or inaccurate records may prove to be a more serious infringement of rights than is any potential invasion of privacy arising from the listing. For example, a recent program in Oregon was designed to track service delivery and to match services with needs; the program merits attention. Although it is restricted to educational services, it has many components that can be replicated in other service areas as well. The Oregon Student Progress Record assembles and computerizes information on all trainable mentally retarded children in the state and uses these data to plan state services responsive to identified needs, as well as university courses for those preparing for careers in special education. Very stringent controls are imposed on dissemination and use of these performance data. We are using a similar program at the Experimental Education Unit; information yielded by the Uniform Performance Assessment System will be used for program design or changes; for placement decisions; for filling gaps in the curriculum; for identifying research needs; and, finally, for giving teachers and administrators an accurate picture of what is actually happening at the Unit. The system, to a very large extent, places accountability for children's progress exactly where it belongs—not on the children, but on those developing and implementing their instructional programs (Haring, 1975). A state-wide or region-wide registry of all severely handicapped persons, who are registered at the moment that their service needs are identified, would give to those responsible for coordinating and delivering service the information they require for intelligent planning to meet these needs.

## CONCLUSION

We conclude this chapter by recapitulating a theme stated at the outset—that we have come a long way in recent years, raising our sights and expectations of, and for, the severely handicapped. No longer does society deny the rights of this population to an education; no longer does society consider that many of these individuals have little or no potential. Our "great expectations" are not for the severely handicapped alone, but for society, parents, professionals, paraprofessionals, or other caregivers working with or in behalf of the severely/profoundly handicapped, utilizing what is presently known about human development, human behavior, and modern technology.

Those who seek to make changes in the quality of life for the severely and profoundly handicapped are not idle dreamers. They know that the road that lies ahead is rough and sometimes almost unmapped. They build their expectations on the best that has been done in the past, on the concerted efforts and advances of the present, and on a plan for the future. As the National Association of State Directors of Special Education has pointed out in "Special Education Futures" (Schipper and Kenowitz, 1975), "Clearly the onus is now on society and its institutions, especially educational institutions, to take into account, plan for, and include the handicapped in all possible social milieus to fulfill the promise of a bright future for the nation's exceptional children and youth." We cannot and need not be fatalistic about the future: we can help shape it through planning for it—through setting goals, objectives, and timetables. We have seen how far we have come as a direct result of the goal set by the Bureau of Education for the Handicapped to provide services and educational programs for all handicapped children by 1980. We may fall short of some of our goals, but surely we will never attain them at all unless we set, accept, and work toward goals that seem beyond us now. In the search for and attainment of "a better way," we must have a philosophy that is fair and fit to live by; an attitude that is fit to live with; values that help to create an environment for all that's fit to live in; and a plan for the future that's fit to live for.

## REFERENCES

Abortion: with the future dim, should the unborn die? Interview ed. by D. Niven with S. Finkbine. il *LIFE, 53*:32–33. August 10, 1962

Barnard KE: State of the art: Nursing high risk infants. in Tjossem T (ed): *Intervention Strategies for Risk Infants and Young Children*. Baltimore, University Park Press, 1974 (in press)

Billingsley F: Eating program for the severely mentally retarded. Working Paper No. 26, Experimental Education Unit, Child Development and Mental Retardation Center, University of Washington, Seattle, 1974

Christensen S: The effects of self-marking on an inappropriate classroom behavior. Working Paper No. 45, Experimental Education Unit, Child Development and Mental Retardation Center, University of Washington, Seattle, 1975

Doman G: *You Can Teach Your Baby to Read*. New York, Random House, 1964

Feldman M, Byalick R and Rosedale M. Parents and Professionals: A Partnership in Special Education. Exceptional Children 41:550–554, May 1975

Fraiberg S, Smith M, Adelson MA: An educational program for blind infants. J Spec Ed 3:121–139, 1969

Hard times for kids, too. *TIME*, March 17, 1975, p. 88

Haring NG: Applied behavior principles in teaching handicapped children, in Proceedings of the Conference on the Moral and Ethical Implications of Behavior Modification. University of Wisconsin, School of Education, Madison, March 20–21, 1975

Heber R, Garber H, Harrington S, et al: *Rehabilitation of Families at Risk for Mental Retardation*. Rehabilitation and Training Center in Mental Retardation. Madison, University of Wisconsin, 1972

Howard W: Interdisciplinary management of developmental disabilities. Soc Rehabil Rec 2: 1974–75, 18–21

Hsu, LY, Strauss L, Hirschorn K: Chromosome abnormality in offspring of the LSD-user: D trisomy with D/D translocation. JAMA 211:987–990, 1970

Kempe CH, Silverman FN, Steele BF, et al: The battered child syndrome. JAMA 181:17–24, July, 1962

Kirk SA, Lord FE (eds): Exceptional Children: Educational Resources and Perspectives. Boston, Houghton Mifflin, 1974

Lent JR: Mimosa Cottage: Experiment in hope. Psychology Today, 2: 51–58, June 1968

Ruder & Finn, Inc., in cooperation with the DDTAS National Awareness Task Force. Recommendations and guidelines for a national public awareness effort for developmental disabilities. Chapel Hill, N.C., DDTAS, the Frank Porter Graham Child Development Center, University of North Carolina, Spring 1975

Scarr-Salapatek S, Williams ML: A stimulation program for low birth weight infants. Am J Public Health, 62:662–667, 1972

Schipper VW, Kenowitz LA: Special education futures: A forecast of events affecting the education of exceptional children: 1975–2000 in Journal of Exceptional Children, 1975, in press

Skeels HM, Dye HB: A study of the effects of differential stimulation on mentally retarded children. Proc Am Assoc Ment Defic 44:114–136, 1939

Smart MS, Smart RC (eds.): Infants. Development and Relationships. New York, Macmillan, 1973

Smith DW, Jones K: Fetal alcohol syndrome. Presented at the Charles R. Strother Lecture, Child Development and Mental Retardation Center, University of Washington, Seattle, Dec. 1973

Stein ZA, Susser MW: Changes over time in the incidence and prevalence of mental retardation, in Hellmuth J (ed.), The Exceptional Infant, Vol. 2, New York, Brunner/Mazel, 1971

Sullivan T & Gill D. *If You Could See What I Hear*. New York: Harper & Row, 1975

Wright L: The theoretical and research base for a program of early stimulation care and training of premature infants in Hellmuth J (ed.): The Exceptional Infant, Vol. 2, New York, Brunner/Mazel, 1971, pp 276–304

Zedler EY: Public opinion and public education for the exceptional child. Court decisions 1873–1950 in Kirk S and Lord F (eds.): Exceptional Children: Educational Resources and Perspectives. Boston, Houghton Mifflin, 1974, pp 43–54

Diane Bricker, William Bricker
Richard Iacino, and Laura Dennison

**B**

# Intervention Strategies for the Severely and Profoundly Handicapped Child

Although for years a small group of people have believed it was possible to educate even the most severely handicapped child, only recently have major efforts been undertaken to provide an objective base for demonstrating the efficacy of educating this population (Lovaas, 1968; Lent, LeBlanc, and Spradlin, 1970; Bricker and Bricker, 1972b; Guess, Sailor, and Baer, 1974). These demonstrations, in conjunction with recent legislative and judicial actions, have produced a mandate for school systems to provide public education for all school-age children, regardless of degree or type of handicap (Sontag, Burke, and York, 1973). Unfortunately, this mandate alone has not yet produced widespread action or change, since few teachers have been trained to work effectively with the lower-functioning child, and curriculum materials are limited and inappropriate. In fact, the movement toward unrestricted public education opens a new professional field in which certification requirements, professional skills, and curriculum materials will have to be developed if we are to serve this population adequately. We believe solutions to the educational problems posed by these children are possible, given the opportunity to employ early intervention and parent involvement strategies, using carefully prescribed programs of instruction. Our experience during the past several years (Bricker, 1967; Bricker and Bricker, 1970, 1971, 1972, 1972a, 1973, 1974) has indicated that instruction for profoundly handicapped children can and must be extended beyond the usual expectations of behavior management and training in self-help skills into the areas of cognitive and linguistic development if the children, their parents, and the community are to benefit fully from the training efforts.

The finding that most children, as well as their families, benefit from educational intervention is beginning to counter some of the pessimism previously generated by professionals frustrated in their attempts to educate significantly handicapped children; much of this frustration can be traced directly to ineffectual intervention strategies.

For example, in 1968 Lloyd Dunn articulated the difficulties confronting special educators and indicated that, for the most part, they had failed to provide adequate education for those children who were referred for special services. Not only did Dunn suggest that special education services were inadequate, but that they might even be doing irreparable harm to some children. The social, legal, and legislative forces operating since the early 70s have compounded the issues, rather than eased the problems for the special educator. This state of affairs has stimulated one notable special educator to suggest that "special education for exceptional children faces challenges to its very existence" (Cruickshank, 1972, p. 5).

We must take this challenge as an exciting opportunity to build a more functional, effective system for all children needing special educational services. The many mandatory education laws which are being enacted in the majority of the states may well be one vital mechanism for meeting this challange and rejuvenating special education. We believe that information accumulated across the years, along with new data being generated by careful classroom research, can be synthesized into relatively efficient and effective educational programs for those children who, in the past, were considered educationally hopeless. Perhaps we can be more intelligently optimistic about the futures of many profoundly impaired children if we substitute new concepts for old ones which have little utility. We should talk about ameliorating deficiencies rather than "curing" severe handicaps. Similarly, our language must now reflect a concern for building socially acceptable behavioral repertoires, not with making children "normal." Using this type of approach, we should be able to build a reasonable set of developmental prospects for each child, no matter now handicapped.

Resources previously not available for low-functioning children are being demanded, and legal precedents for the acquisition of these services have been established (Gilhool, 1972). Resources in this sense refer not only to the direct input of money, but also to the more appropriate use of existing teachers, facilities, and materials for those severely handicapped children who have not been previously served by the public schools. This inclusion of significantly impaired children within the public education domain and the movement to bring mildly and moderately handicapped children back into regular education classes will probably necessitate shifts in all areas of public school education (Filler et al., 1975). These moves toward noncategorical education should promote far different educational configurations than currently exist (Reynolds and Balow, 1972). That is, children will be grouped on the basis of behavioral repertoires, rather than categorical classification. Diagnostic testing as it is currently defined will be increasingly replaced with educationally relevant systems (Hunt, 1972; Neisworth, 1969). An additional dividend of these shifts will be that developments in those instructional routines which benefit the severely and profoundly handicapped may help make explicit the instructional requirements of the education of all children. This effect has been demonstrated in the area of language instruction. Research on language development and instruction with the low-functioning child has produced a body of literature that is relevant to all children (Schiefelbusch, 1972; Schiefelbusch and Lloyd, 1974). A reasonable conclusion to draw is that expanded public school programs for severely and profoundly handicapped children are not only desirable for the targeted children and their families, but that efforts in this direction will also benefit all children in terms of improved educational programs.

In their discussion of the problems and priorities related to the education of severely and profoundly impaired children, Sontag, Burke, and York (1973) suggested that concern should be focused on six major areas when considering program implementation at the functional level. These are as follows:

1. The development of relevant and efficient preservice and inservice teacher training programs.

2. The development of highly specialized doctoral level teacher training, research, and instructional design personnel.

3. The development and dissemination of a more efficient instructional technology, instructional content (scope and sequence), and instructional materials.

4. The development of parent training programs which will enable the parents to prepare their severely handicapped child for school and to work intensively with teachers toward optimal student development.

5. The development of relevant vocational skill training programs.

6. The development of life-encompassing service plans, so that after 15 or 18 years in a public school program, the student can avoid spending the remainder of his life in dehumanizing residential institutions (Sontag, Burke, and York, 1973, pp. 25–26).

Surely, one of the more significant problems is the training of personnel to serve this population. Davis (1972) has succinctly stated the simple but pervasive problem of teacher training for the severely and profoundly handicapped child: " . . . the educator has failed to make the necessary adjustment because he has not received the proper preparation and is not equipped to deal effectively with the severely and profoundly retarded" (pp. 217–218). The roots of this training deficiency can be traced to various causes. For instance, the majority of severely handicapped children are placed in institutions; teachers in public schools have never had to cope with this population (Kugel and Wolfensberger, 1969), nor have they been taught the skills to cope with the variety and severity of problems that these children present. Consequently, the first objective of educational systems, when working with this population, should be to structure a practical as well as didactic training program that will equip the teacher to provide relevant methods and materials for educating severely and profoundly handicapped children.

A second allied objective is the provision of parent training programs. Special education has a long history of seemingly disavowing parents as effective teachers of their own children. Clearly, this is an exclusion policy that we cannot afford with the profoundly handicapped child. The education of these children must extend beyond the classroom and into the home if they are to realize their potential.

It would seem apparent that a teacher well trained in educational techniques can increase her effectiveness when her instructional materials are relevant to the developmental level of the child. Unfortunately, few materials are currently available, either of appropriate content or sequencing for training low-functioning children. Although some educational materials are purported to be useful for the profoundly handicapped child, these are often inappropriate for the child still operating within the early sensorimotor period, where the predominate repertoire consists of primitive preverbal sensorimotor acts and simple reflexive forms of behavior. Clearly, we need a method for designing and validating curriculum approaches and materials for this population of children.

These opening statements should indicate our belief that the field of special education must undergo some major changes. Consequently, in this chapter we would like to offer some variations on educational systems which may be of benefit to the profoundly handicapped child. The remainder of this chapter will focus on discussing two intervention strategies that, we believe, will lead to effective educational programming with the profoundly handicapped. One strategy focuses on the elimination of inappropriate behavior and is thus a corrective or problem-oriented approach; the second strategy focuses on the development or construction of appropriate behavioral repertoires.

**INTERVENTION APPROACHES**

The first of the two previously identified intervention strategies for use in structuring an educational intervention program for severely and profoundly retarded children is a corrective approach. This strategy focuses primarily on the deceleration of socially maladaptive or inappropriate behavior and the substitution of more desirable targets. Most programs that concentrate on the profoundly handicapped child have, by necessity, employed a corrective approach. Traditionally, the profoundly retarded child is offered no opportunity for educational intervention until after age 5; and by that time, his repertoire is often replete with a variety of unacceptable and difficult to extinguish responses. Observation of this target population in most institutional settings makes the accuracy of this statement agonizingly apparent.

The second intervention strategy, which we call a constructive approach, focuses on arranging antecedent events to assist children in the development of new, more adaptive skills. A constructive approach has rarely been used with the profoundly retarded child, because until recently educational programs for these children simply did not exist. Once a diagnosis of severe or profound retardation was made, parents were generally counseled to take the child home until the child was admitted to an institutional setting. Because no educational facilities existed for young children, the parent was left with little professional support to provide any environmental stimulation until the child was admitted to a residential facility.

While the corrective approach is often necessary to produce important and essential changes in behavior, we believe that the basic solution to the problem lies in placing all children with significant development problems into a constructive intervention system at the moment of detection. We adopted the constructive approach almost exclusively in an early intervention program we initiated in 1970 at Peabody College (Bricker and Bricker, in press). Now, at the Mailman Center for Child Development, University of Miami, we are serving a broader range of handicapped children which has necessitated the incorporation of both corrective and constructive strategies in our intervention programs.

### Corrective Strategy

We are currently using a corrective approach in an experimental program which was begun in the fall of 1974 for the profoundly retarded school-age child. This program is a joint effort between the Florida State Department of Education, the Dade County Public Schools, and the Mailman Center for Child Development. The 24 children included in this program are typically unresponsive to unstructured environmental stimulation and have repertoires that abound with inappropriate responses. The majority of these children have a history of convulsive disorders and are on drug therapy. Also, many of these children have extensive physical and metabolic problems which contribute to the complexity of intervention. To effectively deal with the multitude of problems and precautions necessary with this group of children, we have developed a corrective strategy termed the Problem Oriented Educational Record (POER). After the major behavioral problems have been resolved with a child, this corrective strategy is integrated into a constructive educational program.

The POER is still in the pilot stage of development, and it will undoubtedly undergo change as the approach is employed and information is gathered concerning its usefulness. A schematic of the POER system is presented in Fig. 1. The system is predicated on a format that places demographic and programmatic variables on a 5- × 8-inch card. Each child admitted into the program has his own set of POER cards that are filled out in conjunction with the parents after the teaching personnel have had ample time to observe the child. We have found it useful to video tape several individual sessions of the teacher–child interaction. These tapes are then used to analyze the child's response patterns to various training materials and settings. After the initial observation period, followed by an analysis of the child's performance taken from the video tape, the POER cards are completed. The information placed on these cards should guide and direct the individual training routines for each child in the program. The various cards used in this system are described below.

### 1-G. COVER CARD

This is the first card in each child's file and contains information on the family such as address and telephone number, the age of the child, the primary physician or medical treatment facility used by the family, and other information that would be useful in an emergency. The card also contains information concerning immunization and whether evaluations have been completed by psychology, nursing, speech and hearing, medicine, and education. In addition, the current educational placement is recorded. This card is thus a summary of the information available on the child. To complete this card, a teacher must research the psychometric and other diagnostic information available on the child, as well as acquire relevant details concerning the nature of the family and the child's home environment.

### 2-G. PRECAUTIONARY CARD

This is the second card in each child's file. On it will be recorded all items of information pertaining to the health and safety of the child. For example, if the child is diabetic, has seizures, or particular allergies or sensitivities, such information is recorded along with a statement of the precautions to be taken. Any person who is planning to intervene with the child in any capacity is obligated to read this card (or cards) before the initial contact with the child. In this way, a student or staff member has a

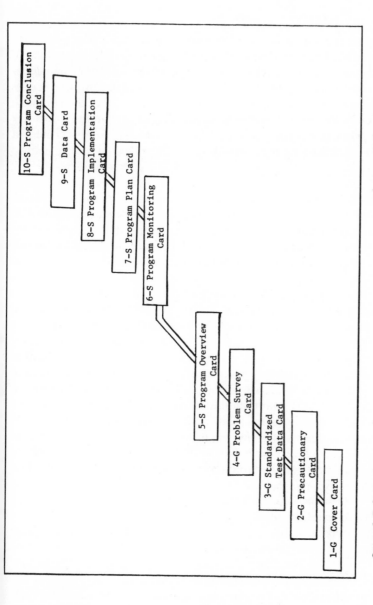

Fig. 1.   Schematic of cards contained in the POER and the sequence of use.

systematic basis for obtaining the necessary information for the protection of the child (e.g., this child is allergic to orange juice) as well as for themselves (e.g., this child bites).

### 3-G. STANDARDIZED TEST DATA CARD

This card is kept in an envelope which indicates those who have access to this information. The card contains a summary of the results of standardized tests given by psychology, speech and hearing, or education. While the scores are reported on these cards, the use of these scores is predicated on prior reading of the full reports contained in the complete chart, which helps insure proper interpretation of this information. By having the entire test history of the child, the user is able to see the test variability as well as long-term trends.

### 4-G. PROBLEM SURVEY CARD

This card contains a listing of problems targeted for possible educational intervention. The problems are coded along three basic dimensions. The first coding indicates whether the targeted form of behavior will require educational techniques designed to decelerate the behavior, accelerate the behavior, or maintain the behavior at a desired rate. The second coding indicates the degree of urgency or importance given to the noted problem. Thus, a form of behavior such as biting other children is coded as a deceleration target having a high priority for intervention. If the child is walking but has not learned to run, running would probably be listed as a low priority acceleration target. Complete lack of speech in the repertoire of a 6-year-old child would surely be listed as a high priority item to be accelerated. High priority items are given immediate program attention, while low priority items are scheduled for intervention at a later date in the program. A third coding notation used on this card indicates the current status of each problem. This code designation specifies whether the problem is targeted as an ongoing problem, whether it has been concluded as a program (e.g., the behavior no longer requires intervention), or provides the date when the program is scheduled to begin. The Problem Survey Card allows the teacher, student, or other relevant personnel to consider a wide range of observational and test data in determining the range of possible intervention targets, their classification, and priority ranking. This ranking should lead to a systematic, sequential organization of the individualized intervention plan.

### 5-G. PROGRAM OVERVIEW CARD

Once an intervention program has been devised and initiated in a given target area (e.g., teeth grinding, biting, verbal imitation, receptive vocabulary, object permanence), then a brief description of the program, date of program, location of the program plan, and the date of program termination is recorded on this card. This card provides an efficient method for checking the number and types of programs which are currently operational for each child. In addition, this card provides summary data of the programs through which the child has moved. The Program Overview Card contains a cross-reference code to other programs which are interrelated. For example, biting is programmed as a deceleration target, but is correlated with programs which are designed to accelerate the development of socially appropriate skills as competing responses to biting.

These first five cards are designed to provide an efficient, accurate summary of the child's demographic data, deficit areas, and information necessary to his health and safety. The remaining cards that complete the POER are organized into sections according to the specific acceleration, deceleration, or maintenance programs. Each program is tracked through the use of a sequence of cards that describe the procedures to be followed, the data derived from the implementation of those procedures, and the final summary of the data which resulted in program termination. The basic cards used in the program format are described below.

6-S. PROGRAM MONITORING CARD

This card is placed first in a specific program section because it provides a data monitoring system which can be used to indicate whether the program should continue as planned. Data from each program are collected at specific time intervals, and the results are evaluated in terms of rate of response or probability of response. For example, a program for receptive language training specifies that a probe is to be given once each week. The dates for these probes are then marked on the appropriate Program Monitoring Card as "Date due." When the probe is given, the teacher marks the score obtained on the Program Monitoring Card and then signs and dates the card, indicating that the probe has been given as scheduled. Each child's cards should be scanned frequently in order to see that no probe has been omitted.

7-S. PROGRAM PLAN CARD

This card (or cards for a program of a long duration) summarizes the program plan using the basic problem-oriented method. This method requires a synthesis of information in four specific areas: subjective information, objective information, assessments, and plans of intervention. Teeth grinding, which would probably be designated as a high priority deceleration target for a child, will be used to illustrate this method of program planning. The first area of subjective information calls for the teacher to note the personnel who have observed this behavior and under what general conditions it tended to occur. This should lead to a more formal baseline situation in which both location and rate of teeth grinding are recorded by a designated person under specified conditions. These baseline data provide the objective information for program planning. The assessment area would include a discussion and evaluation of the objective and subjective observations by relevant participants. The final area is the development of a plan of intervention based on a series of questions that are generated by the target behavior. For example, does the child grind his teeth when involved in an interesting activity? Does the teeth grinding occur in the presence of people? What response seems incompatible with teeth grinding for this child? The answer to such questions will be generated from the intervention. Thus, each relevant question is noted, and the cards describing the intervention plan, and the card for recording the data are clipped to the question card. Several such questions can usually be studied simultaneously in the course of the intervention plan. Thus, the Program Plan Card provides an overview of the subjective and objective information concerning a specific problem, the assessment of that problem, the proposed intervention in the form of questions, and the subsequent answers in the form of data.

## 8-S. PROGRAM IMPLEMENTATION CARD

This card contains a more specific description of the intervention plan in terms of materials used and antecedent arrangements, the response form being assessed, the procedures for evaluation, and the consequent events that are used to strengthen or weaken the particular target responses. If the program involves a form of intervention that is controversial in the field (e.g., calling for brief periods of food deprivation), then the plan is explained fully to the parents and their signatures are required on the bottom of the program format card. In addition, each plan is reviewed by a relevant professional who also indicates approval of the plan by signing the format card. This system has been implemented to prevent teachers or other professionals from using questionable programs without a thorough professional review or without the informed consent of the parents. Once approved, the program is implemented according to the plan, along with the schedule of data collection procedures that assess the effectiveness of the plan. The data are plotted on data cards (described below) which are attached to the program format card.

## 9-S. DATA CARD

The data cards are individually designed in order to best represent the data collection procedures selected for a particular target. For deceleration targets such as biting, teeth grinding, hitting, self-injurious behavior, the data are usually plotted on a daily basis, using response per minute.

For acceleration targets such as verbal imitation, receptive vocabulary, expressive vocabulary, and other complex behaviors, the data cards are generally arranged to record the number of correct responses in relation to the number of opportunities, which provides a probability of rate of occurrence. These latter measures may only need to be taken on a weekly basis.

10-S. PROGRAM CONCLUSION CARD

The final card for every program is the conclusion card, which briefly summarizes assessment, plan, and results of each implemented program. Any conclusions or recommendations derived from the program are noted on this card. The information from the conclusion cards is used to formulate program evaluations. The information on the data cards is summarized and appended to the conclusion card. This data analysis is used to support the program summary and conclusion sections.

As mentioned earlier, the POER is in its pilot stage of development and has been used with only a few profoundly retarded children. The teaching personnel have indicated that they are finding the system to be useful in targeting responses, generating intervention programs, and monitoring these approaches across time.

## Constructive Strategy

The constructive approach to intervention described in this chapter is an extension of the early intervention system we have been evolving during the past 4 years (Bricker and Bricker, 1971, 1972a, 1973, 1974). Data and experience generated from this early intervention project for developmentally delayed children have led us to establish six major objectives:

1. To demonstrate that service and research components can be successfully blended into a single project.

2. To demonstrate that early intervention with young developmentally delayed children is not only desirable, but also necessary and feasible.

3. To demonstrate that thoughtful integration of children with a variety of developmental disabilities can result in an effective program for all the children.

4. To demonstrate that assessment can be more useful for structuring intervention programs when linked directly to training procedures.

5. To demonstrate that parents or care-givers can and should be included as integral parts of an intervention program.

6. To train various levels of professionals to provide effective educational intervention services to a wide range of low-functioning young children.

Although the present writers have moved to the University of Miami, Mailman Center for Child Development to develop a major intervention program for handicapped children, these original goals seem equally appropriate and worthy of serving as the guidelines for this new program. We believe the meeting of these six objectives necessitates a program composed of four major components: classroom demonstration programs, parent involvement, research activities, and training of teachers and allied professionals.

The demonstration component is composed of infant, toddler, and preschool classrooms, as well as special public school units. Each unit is staffed with a minimum of two teachers and a teacher assistant. Their basic responsibilities are to develop and implement an individualized educational program for each child enrolled in their class. The research conducted in these units focuses on classroom training procedures and content, particularly in the areas of language and cognitive development. The chronological age of the children in these classroom units range from 2 months to 12 years. Approximately one-fourth of the children are developmentally normal, while the remaining three-fourths have varying handicapping conditions which result in mild to profound impairments.

Parent involvement in the program occurs within both the research and service units. The research unit is designed to generate data that will be used to develop effective training programs for parents and/or caregivers of developmentally delayed children. Often, the problems studied have been generated by the difficulties encountered by the program personnel involved in service delivery. The service unit is divided into three basic intervention areas for parents: the presentation of information which exposes the parents to strategies for seeking community and state resources available to handicapped children and their families; the development of effective teaching strategies; and the provision of special counseling services for particularly involved problems or difficult family situations. Intervention is implemented through the use of individual sessions and small or large group meetings with a specially trained cadre of full-time parent advisors. The parent program personnel includes parent advisors who do the individual and small-group training, a liaison worker who handles social service needs, advanced clinical and social work students who provide special counseling, and a coordinator who supervises these varying activities.

The research activities have focused on the investigation of the various parameters of linguistic and cognitive development. The information derived from these investigations has then been used to develop effective training programs for handicapped children. A second important research activity has been to explore techniques for training parents to become more effective teachers. Communication between service, research, and training components is of particular importance in order to ask and answer the complex questions that have direct relevance to education of the parents and children. When a specific training procedure breaks down, the research component is consulted concerning existing options. The problem can be studied under more carefully controlled conditions, modifications can be made within the present setting, or the procedure can be tried with a different population. The research component makes these judgments in cooperation with the classroom and parent components.

The final component which we feel is necessary, not only for reaching our goals but also for providing excellence in programs for severely and profoundly handicapped children, is personnel preparation. A program of intervention for a parent or child can only be as effective as the interventionist. Not even the most adequately programmed curricular materials can completely offset a poorly trained teacher. In the constructive approach to intervention, well-trained personnel are clearly the critical variable in maximizing the child's developmental progress.

Our intervention system for educational programming is based on an approach to complex human behavior recommended by J. McV. Hunt more than a decade ago (1961). Hunt's approach was in turn predicated, at least in part, on over 50 years of research and thought on human behavior by Piaget and his colleagues (Piaget and Inhelder, 1969; Piaget, 1970). The structure of this intervention approach, which we have called constructive interaction adaptation, is derived from two major sources. Cognitive formulations about development is the first major source. These formulations describe the form and organizational patterns of the structures, schemes, or operants which developed from an infant's reflexive behavior. The behavioral approaches to human development which emphasize the mechanism for changing behavior and altering patterns of behavioral control exhibited by antecedent stimulus events is the second source. This integration of what appear initially to be divergent notions has precedents (Lynch and Bricker, 1972; Catania, 1973). With few exceptions, infants are born equipped with basic physiologic reflexes, such as sucking and grasping. The constructive interaction adaptation position suggests that the exercise of these reflexes forms the basis of all subsequent development. The sensorimotor stages as defined by Piaget and Inhelder (1969), which occur approximately from birth to 2 years (developmentally), are a continuing elaboration of these basic reflexes which result from environmental interaction. Even undifferentiated random movements exhibited by a young baby or profoundly retarded older child have an effect on his environment, which in turn changes the probability for alterations of the rates, the intensities, or the topographies of those behaviors. If, for example, a crying baby were picked up and comforted, the probability of fussing and crying might increase. Following the initial sensorimotor stage of primary circular reactions, in which an infant's behavior is being controlled primarily by consequent events, a form of antecedent discrimination becomes observable. During the secondary circular reaction stage, the infant apparently begins to discriminate objects on an object–action dimension. For example, some things are better for sucking, some better for shaking, and some better for grasping. As these action–object relationships increase in number, they also increase in complexity and become coordinated. That is, some objects are simultaneously or sequentially trackable, graspable, and shakable. Piaget has called this stage the coordination of secondary schemes, which generally occurs between the 8th and 12th month of development. It is during this stage that the child begins to provide overt evidence of a practical and intentional understanding of his physical and social environment.

With Piaget providing the theoretical underpinning, our task becomes one of translating this developmental approach into an operational curriculum that is appropriate for either infants or profoundly retarded children. We believe the first step in generating an operational curriculum is to construct a map of the milestones that occur during a specific developmental period. This form of mapping for the sensorimotor period has been done previously by W. Bricker and G. Chatelanant and is contained in Fig. 2. This map or lattice represents not only a conceptual framework for development within the sensorimotor period, but it also provides the key content areas for training. Increasingly complex forms of behavior, which are constructed as a function of more and more sophisticated environmental interactions, are represented by the vertical dimension of the lattice. It should be emphasized that constructive interaction adaptation has no requirement for maturation or normative type of conceptual explanations. Consistencies among children in development can be viewed as a function of approximately equivalent experiences occurring and being assimilated at a similar rate by children. For example, although an adult might perceive seemingly numerous and detailed qualitative differences for a baby in an economically advantaged home, the salient stimuli differences of those environments may not be apparent from a baby's point of view. A flapping torn window curtain may be just as effective for visual fixation and tracking as the most expensive crib mobile. An old stuffed sock is just as graspable, suckable, and shakable as the most sophisticated piece of the doll-maker's art.

Starting at the bottom of Fig. 2 with the exercising of the reflexes, and continuing upward on any vertical path provides a theoretical hierarchy of the way in which a baby might adapt to his environment. The right–left dimension reflects developmental sequencing with schemes located the same distance from the baseline coming into existence approximately simultaneously. The uppermost boxes in the figure can be viewed as the terminal states of the sensorimotor period. These states include the pre-verbal cognitive prerequisites for semantic, phonological, and syntactic language processes; and for understanding space, time, physical causality, seriation, and number; and a primitive classification of environmental events, including social relationships.

Armed with this type of lattice structure, which implies developmental order and relationship between the various action schemes, programming for children becomes a matter of creatively engineering environmental interactions which have, at least, face validity as an exercise of that action scheme.

An example of how this lattice structure can be used to provide a direct intervention routine can be seen by following the object constancy sequence which appears in the far left-hand vertical column of Fig. 2. Assuming that a child has the necessary prerequisite skills, one method for training object constancy is to use an object such as a noise-making toy, to elicit an attention response from the child. The toy is held in front of the infant's eyes until the child is judged to make direct visual contact with the object, at which point the toy is activated to produce its sound (a probable reinforcement). This is repeated a few times until the child looks at the toy which is being slowly moved a few centimeters in a horizontal arc. If the infant tracks the object, the noisemaker is again activated, and if not, the toy remains in the new position until the child makes visual contact, and then the noise is produced.

Generalization of this type of tracking skill should be tested and trained across a wide variety of objects, trainers, and settings. The inference that a child does, in fact, have a visual tracking scheme can be made with much more confidence if he will demonstrate such a skill at home with his parents and his favorite toys, as well as in the classroom with the teacher. Similarly, many types of generalized object tracking, such as horizontal, vertical, circular, proximal, and distal, all provide targets for daily training activities.

The interrelationship of the vertical columns of the lattice represented by the horizontal arrows deserves emphasis since the coordination of various simple action schemes becomes important early in sensorimotor development. After the fourth month of development, it would be unrealistic, and in fact cause for worry, to find that a child does not reach for the object he is tracking. Coordination of schemes such as a hand–eye or grasp–suck can and should be emphasized in the training sequences via overlapping training routines. The teacher could, for example, move the tracked object toward the child until it is easily within his reach. His hands can be physically guided to the object and held in the bimanual grasp position as the object is moved (by the adult during the early phases) to the child's mouth, where he can explore the object orally

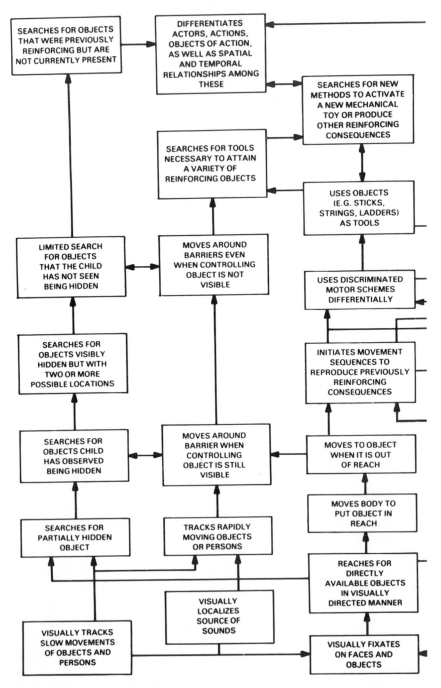

Fig. 2.   A representation of the theoretical framework for sensorimotor

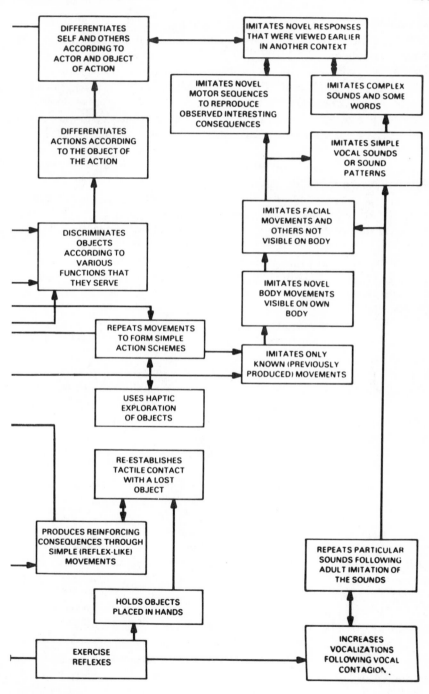

training activities.

for a few moments. As the cycle is repeated several times (the number of repetitions will be determined by the child's rate of improvement), the use of physical guidance can be gradually faded until the child is reaching, grasping, and then moving the object to his mouth without assistance. As a cautionary measure, prior to or during the training sessions, the teacher must attend to various parameters of the task, such as object preferences, since the selection of a nondesired object can mask the extent and limitations of the child's repertoire by reducing his motivational state (Filler, 1973). Again, the parent or trainer must endeavor to shape the target behavior in a variety of functional settings, as well as with a variety of objects which are usually present in the child's environment. Thus, the training goal can be either the child's production of a novel form of behavior or the consolidation of a response that may already be in the child's repertoire but which is used inconsistently or only with a restricted range of objects.

As the infant or profoundly retarded child gains certain skills, it becomes increasingly possible to program exercises which target more complex skills; each succeeding exercise is constructed on the previously demonstrated simpler action scheme. For example, once a child can reliably track a wide variety of objects in different settings, the teacher can end the tracking sequence by partially hiding the object being visually tracked under a screen. Since the child had also previously demonstrated the ability to reach out and grasp objects, it becomes a logical step for him to retrieve the object of interest which is now partially hidden. Note how in each succeeding lattice step on the progressive path, training becomes more complex and interrelated, requiring a subtle elaboration of existing skills. Again, this is the basis of the notion of constructive functional behavior based on successful adaptation (assimilation and accommodation) in environmental interactions.

This training system can be viewed as a process in which the teacher (or researcher) asks the child a sequence of nonverbal questions through presentation of the materials. For example, in the area of object constancy, such questions (which would approximate lattice steps) might include: (1) Can the child fixate on a wide range of objects in a variety of settings with various types of interested participants (parents, teachers, baby sitters, the family pet)? (2) If he does fixate, can he track those interesting objects in various directions (vertically, horizontally, circularly)? (3) Does the child ever reach out and grasp at objects being tracked? (4) Will he reach out for objects when they are partially hidden, or completely hidden either while he watches or when he has not watched the object hidden? (5) Will the child look for a hidden object where it was last seen or where he last found it? Reliable answers to such questions not only help locate a child's skill level in the sensorimotor domain but also provide an immediate answer to the teacher's question, "What do I train?" Every child is located somewhere in the developmental hierarchy, and the next step in that sequence is the logical curriculum target for training. Such examples of sensorimotor activities are only isolated illustrations from one of the many different curricular domains in which developmentally delayed children could benefit from intervention. A well-rounded educational curriculum would include training routines in upright mobility and other gross-motor activities, fine-motor skills, development of basic self-help skills (such as drinking, self-feeding, dressing, and toileting), and the prerequisite skills for language. The constructive interaction adaptation position has been used to develop lattices and subsequent training routines in all of these areas. A continuing research goal is the refinement and validation of both the components and sequences of these hierarchical behavioral topographies.

The full implementation of the constructive interaction adaptation position specifies not only the content and development of the curricula as described above, but also defines the role of the teacher. The important Piagetian principle of "moderate novelty," or just tolerable disequilibrium, is critical in the adaptation process. Adaptation occurs as a function of the assimilation of new environmental inputs which, in turn, permits or requires accommodation of these inputs to existing schemes or structures. The effectiveness of this interactive adaptation appears to depend, to some degree, on an optimal amount of discrepancy between the novel environmental information to be assimilated and the current scheme to be accommodated. If the degree of discrepancy is too great, adaptation does not occur, possibly due to a paucity of external/internal cues pointing to a common linkage between the new circumstances and the existing scheme (Hunt, 1961). Similarly, if the degree of discrepancy is too small, the child's interest is not maintained. The interaction which serves as the vehicle for providing new environmental input is reduced or ceases, and the adaptation process in relation to this environmental situation is terminated (Robinson, 1972).

The problem of match or just manageable disequilibrium seems important in determining an effective teacher training model. Katz (1969; 1970) postulated three models of early childhood teachers: the maternal type, who focuses on creating a warm supportive comfortable environment; the therapeutic type, who emphasizes clinical analytical processes; and the instructional type, whose main concern centers on the transmission of specific content. Spodek (1972) added a fourth type, the facilitator, whose concern is environmental engineering toward significant learning experiences. Constructive interaction adaptation would seem to require that the teacher be a facilitator if a child's developmental progress is to be maximized.

Major competencies required of an effective teacher of infants or the profoundly retarded would include familiarity with relevant skill domains, knowledge of component behavior and sequences in any educationally targeted skill domain, a discriminating understanding of operant technology, and modes of engineering daily events into educationally relevant interactions. The effective teacher would have a clear conception of the component behavior which comprises the field in any given domain. In the sensorimotor area, for instance, the teacher would have to know that inferences about the general structure of object constancy could be made by observing the child demonstrating such behaviors as retrieving partially hidden objects, searching for hidden objects, or tracking. Equally important to this knowledge of the basic behavioral building blocks is an understanding of the hierarchical appearance of such behaviors. A teacher must know that object tracking is probably prerequisite to searching for objects partially hidden which, in turn, is necessary before a child can be expected to retrieve objects he has not seen hidden. The effective teacher must be intimately familiar with such behavioral topographies and practically experienced at seeing their various manifestations in the child's ongoing activities. This would enable the teacher to make the necessary continuous assessment about a child's current level of sophistication in relation to any given scheme or structure. With this knowledge, the teacher could then proceed directly into some type of creative intervention. If these basic skills can be demonstrated, then the teacher ought to be well on the way to successful management of the match on a continuing basis.

Just as knowledge of developmental components and sequences are vital to continuous effective assessment, knowledge of operant technology is basic to creative intervention. The notion of consequation is important within the constructive interaction adaptation framework because it provides the motivation for the maintenance of the child–environment interaction which must be present for adaptation to occur. The effective teacher of difficult children will constantly work toward creating situations which are functionally reinforcing for the child, rather than relying on social or appetitive reinforcers. After exercising basic reflexes, the functional consequences of those reflexive behaviors then increase the rate and complexity of a child's interaction with his environment.

The notion of antecedent arrangement is probably one of the most important of the operant technological skills required by a teacher working within the constructive interaction adaptation position. Another way of looking at environmental engineering is as the process of setting up situations in which moderate amounts of novelty or an adequate discrepancy exists between new information and existing schemes. It is absolutely crucial for an interventionist to remember that adaptation occurs as a function of meaningful interaction with the environment. The most stimulating environment that could possibly be developed would not be a learning environment for a child if he is not able to discern the relationship of new inputs to his existing schemes. The teacher in this situation must be carefully and constantly managing the match, must be limiting the choices, arranging the cues, chaining the stimuli, providing the prompts—all of which have as their goal the child's developmental progress.

Obviously, we believe the constructive interaction adaptation position and its subsequent effects on curricula and teacher roles have particular relevance to intervention with delayed children. The constructive interaction adaptation position suggests that development follows a relatively consistent order, with each new behavior elaborating on the previous one. If organisms do, in fact, develop their behavioral repertoire in similar sequential order independent of rate, then the types of activities contained in our various lattices should be appropriate for any child.

## SUMMARY

We have attempted to discuss two educational intervention strategies for the profoundly handicapped child, as well as to provide a rationale for the necessity of educational intervention. Such a rationale may be somewhat unnecessary, given the current status of BEH funding priorities and the strong case made in the courts to provide educational services for all children. If one accepts the premise that all children, no matter how handicapped, deserve the right to educational services, the next step is to begin to develop the necessary resources for providing these services. Clearly, providing facilities and teaching personnel falls to the domain of public education; however, the development of the actual programmatic content and the application of that content falls to the leaders and innovators in the fields of education, psychology, medicine, and other allied professions.

Those of us associated with the movement to provide educational services to profoundly handicapped people are deeply involved in the development, validation, and subsequent dissemination of information on training procedures and curriculum content, as well as in building an overriding position that will help direct future educational systems. In this chapter we have attempted to describe two of the more useful strategies that have been developed within the context of our intervention program within the Mailman Center. Direct application or replication of any training strategies or curricula without careful adaptation to the developmental level of the target group, physical setting, and behavioral objectives decreases the probability that those strategies will be maximally effective. This, of course, holds true for the material presented here. We do hope that we have presented information that may suggest alternatives, stimulate debates, generate discussion, or even disagreement, which then may lead to further advancement for the profoundly handicapped child.

**REFERENCES**

Bricker DD (ed.): Cumberland House studies in behavior modification. Interim reports on the re-education of emotionally disturbed children. The Department of Mental Health, The State of Tennessee, Nashville, 1(4): 1967

Bricker DD, Bricker WA: Toddler research and intervention project report: Year I. IMRID Behavioral Science Monograph No. 20. Institute on Mental Retardation and Intellectual Development, George Peabody College, Nashville, Tenn., 1971

Bricker DD, Bricker WA: Toddler research and intervention project report: Year II. IMRID Behavioral Science Monograph No. 21. Institute on Mental Retardation and Intellectual Development. George Peabody College, Nashville, Tenn., 1972a

Bricker DD, Bricker WA: Infant, toddler and preschool research and intervention project report: Year III. IMRID Behavioral Science Monograph No. 23. Institute on Mental Retardation and Intellectual Development, George Peabody College, Nashville, Tenn., 1973

Bricker WA, Bricker DD: A program of language training for the severely language handicapped child. Except Child 37:101–111, 1970

Bricker WA, Bricker DD: The use of programmed language training as a means for differential diagnosis and educational remediation among severely retarded children. Final Report, George Peabody College, Contract No. OEG2-7-070218-1629, U.S. Office of Education, 1972b

Bricker WA, Bricker DD: Assessment and modification of verbal imitation with low-functioning children. J Speech Hear Res 15:690–698, 1972c

Bricker WA, Bricker DD: An early language training strategy, in Schiefelbusch R, Lloyd L (eds): Language perspectives: Acquisition, retardation, and intervention. Baltimore, University Park Press, 1974

Bricker WA, Bricker DD: The infant, toddler and preschool research and intervention project. in Tjossem T (ed), Intervention strategies with risk infants and young children. Baltimore, University Park Press, (in press)

Catania AC: The psychologies of structure, function, and development. Am Psychol, 28:434–443, 1973

Cruickshank WM: Special education, the community and constitutional issues, in Walker DL, Howard DP (eds): Special education: Instrument of change in education in the 70's. Charlottesville, Univ of Virginia Pr, 1972

Davis WE: Responsibilities of the educator in programming for the severely and profoundly retarded. Train Sch Bull, 68:217–220, 1972

Dunn LM: Special education for the mildly retarded—Is much of it justified? Except Child 35:5–22, 1968

Filler J: Sensorimotor assessment performance as a function of task materials, in Bricker D, Bricker W (eds): Infant, toddler and preschool research and intervention project III, IMRID Behavioral Science Monograph No. 23. Institute on Mental Retardation and Intellectual Development, George Peabody College, Nashville, Tenn., 1973

Filler J, Robinson CC, Smith RA; et al: Evaluation and programming in mental retardation. in Hobbs N (ed): Issues in the classification of exceptional children. San Francisco, Jossey-Bass, 1975

Gilhool TK: Why "due process" for parents of special educational children in Pennsylvania? Paper presented at the 50th Annual Convention of the Council for Exceptional Children, Washington, D.C., March 1972

Guess D, Sailor W, Baer D: To teach language to retarded children, in Schiefelbusch R and Lloyd L (eds), Language Perspectives: Acquisition, Retardation, and Intervention, Baltimore, University Park Press, 1974

Hunt JMcV: Intelligence and Experience. New York, Ronald, 1961

Hunt JMcV: Psychological assessment in education and social class. Paper presented at Conference on the Legal and Educational Consequences for the Intelligence Testing Movement: Handicapped Children and Minority Group Children. University of Missouri, Columbia, 1972

Katz LG: Children and teachers in two types of Head Start classes. Young Child 24:342–349, 1969

Katz LG: Teaching in Preschools: Roles and Goals. Children 17:43–48, 1970

Kugel RB, Wolfensberger W (eds): Changing Patterns in Residential Services for the Mentally Retarded. Washington, D.C., U.S. Government Printing Office, 1969

Lent JR, LeBlanc J, Spradlin JE: Designing a rehabilitative culture for moderately retarded adolescent girls, in Ulrich RE, Stachnik T, Mabry J (eds): The Control of Human Behavior. Vol. II. Glenview, Ill., Scott Foresman, 1970

Lovaas OI: A program for the establishment of speech in psychotic children, in Sloane H, MacAulay B (eds): Operant Procedures in Remedial Speech and Language Training. Boston, Houghton-Mifflin, 1968

Lynch J, Bricker WA: Linguistic theory and operant procedures: Toward an integrated approach to language training for the mentally retarded. Ment Retard 10:12–17, 1972

Neisworth JT: The educational irrelevance of intelligence, in Smith RM (ed): Teacher Diagnosis of Educational Difficulties. Columbus, Ohio, Merrill, 1969

Piaget J: Piaget's theory. In Mussen PH (ed): Carmichael's Manual of Child Psychology. Vol. I. New York, Wiley 1970

Piaget J, Inhelder B: The Psychology of the Child. New York, Basic Books, 1969

Reynolds MC, Balow B: Categories and variables in special education. Except Child 38:357–366, 1972

Robinson CC: Analysis of stage four and five object permanence concept as a discriminated operant. Unpublished doctoral dissertation, George Peabody College, Nashville, Tenn., 1972

Schiefelbusch RL: (ed): Language of the Mentally Retarded. Baltimore, University Park Press, 1972

Schiefelbusch RL, Lloyd LL (eds): Language Perspectives: Acquisition, Retardation, and Intervention. Baltimore, University Park Press, 1974

Sontag E, Burke PJ, York R: Considerations for the severely handicapped in public schools. Educ Train Ment Retard 8:20–26, 1973

Spodek B: Staff requirements in early childhood education, in Gordon I (ed): Early Childhood Education: The Seventy-First Yearbook of the National Society for the Study of Education. Chicago, Univ of Chicago Pr, 1972

Doug Guess, Wayne Sailor,
William J. Keogh, and Donald M. Baer[1]

# C

# Language Development Programs for Severely Handicapped Children

The severity of language and communication problems among severely handicapped children cannot be overemphasized as a major area of concern. Almost by definition, the severely handicapped are afflicted with a profound delay in speech development and a grossly inadequate ability to understand others. Usually, these behavioral deficiencies have far-reaching effects on the quality of life, and indeed, on the very existence of the severely handicapped person. Without expressive language skills, severely handicapped persons cannot adequately indicate basic human needs and feelings. They can neither express to others the joys and satisfactions of childhood experiences, nor organize their world symbolically in a way that new learning can be assimilated into an existing frame of reference. Too frequently, tantrums, head banging, and other types of self-destructive and socially inappropriate behavior constitute an alarmingly large proportion of a speech-deficient child's behavior.

A decade ago, it would have been easier to dismiss the problem completely, rationalizing that the communication problems of the severely handicapped are inherently and unalterably resistant to intervention—that no amount of effort and time would produce significant and beneficial results for this population. However, within recent years, there have been many published reports demonstrating successful intervention in numerous specific areas of language development among children and adults, despite diagnostic labels such as autistic, schizophrenic, profoundly retarded, brain damaged, etc. The relative success of these specific, yet highly complex, skill-development programs suggests the possibility of construction of more comprehensive speech and language training programs for the severely handicapped. Today, more and more comprehensive speech and language programs are being applied. While most of these programs share many common features, they also contain many distinct and unique characteristics.

The authors intend, with this chapter, to provide the reader with an abbreviated sketch of several existing language training programs which are in various stages of becoming comprehensive curricula for linguistic intervention. Program development within many of the research and development centers is interdependent to a large degree. Frequently, data from the laboratory in Wisconsin will be reflected in new directions for curriculum development at the Kansas laboratory, and so forth. The ultimate production of efficient and reliable language training curricula for the severely handicapped will be dependent upon progress within these various sites, each of which contributes its unique slant on the problems of assessment, acquisition, generalization, etc.

Miller and Yoder (1972a, 1972b, 1974) have developed a language training program structured primarily upon the psycholinguistic data currently available on language development in normal children. Some of the minimal requirements for a child's entry into the program are: (1) an absence of physical impairment to speech mechanisms, (2) an ability to approximate single words, either imitatively or spontaneously, and (3) the cognitive awareness of one or more relational or substantive functions. The program is not intended for nonimitative children, and it is assumed that a generalized imitative skill is present before training begins. Special emphasis has been placed on semantic structures as the basis for instruction, rather than on syntactic structures. First utterances such as "no," "more," etc., (which are communicative within specific contexts) are reinforced and expanded into three-term relations such as *agent + action + object*. Contingencies of reinforcement are applied only when an appropriate form is expressed in context. Thus, the basis for reinforcement rests on the judgment of the semantic function of an utterance by an observer.

Stremel and Waryas (1974) have also structured their language intervention program on psycholinguistic theory. The training sequence has been designed to closely follow the order in which language structures emerge in normal development. Special emphasis has been placed on expansion of the child's utterances, the use of imitation only when it is paired with relevant environmental stimuli, and, in particular, on the role of the semantic component of language. Operant conditioning principles are used to teach the contents of the following three major areas of instruction: (1) early training; (2) early-intermediate training; and (3) late-intermediate training. The first part stresses the comprehension and production of basic grammatical structures such as *noun + verb + preposi-*

*tion + noun*. Part 2 expands the grammatical structures and teaches the use of pronouns, negation, and questions, as well as many other basic language concepts; and Part 3, although still being formulated by the authors, will include procedures to teach plurality, and past and future tense verbs.

Bricker and Bricker (1974, 1970) have described language training procedures which comprise one component of the comprehensive Infant, Toddler, and Pre-School Research and Intervention Project. In developing their language training procedures, the Brickers have considered the contributions from linguistics, psycholinguistics, and operant speech and language research. In addition to language development, the project focuses on several other major areas, including social development and motor and cognitive processes. Retarded children, their nonretarded brothers and sisters, as well as the childrens' parents participate in group and individual instruction. Children can enter the program shortly after birth and remain as long as 6 years. The nondelayed children attend the same classroom sessions as their retarded brothers and sisters, thus providing models for the retarded children, as well as data on the normal acquisition of cognitive and language processes. Concurrently with the child's classes, parents receive counseling and instruction in teaching self-help skills, language training, toileting, etc., which help to integrate classroom and home procedures. Emphasis on early detection of possible handicaps, combined with adequate stimulation, provide a setting which is likely to enhance the effectiveness of the Brickers' language training procedures.

The language training sequence provides procedures for operant auditory assessment, to teach receptive vocabulary, to teach verbal imitation of sounds and words, to teach object and event naming, and finally, to establish the production and comprehension of syntactic structures.

Kent (1974) has recently published the *Language Acquisition Program for the Severely Retarded*. This training manual evolved after 8 years of work by the author and her colleagues, synthesizing clinical experiences, research, and reinforcement theory. Although many of the training sequences can be conducted with two children during a single session, the author emphasizes the importance of one-to-one instruction. The manual's three sections include preverbal, verbal-receptive, and verbal-expressive. The preverbal section teaches attending skills and motor imitation. The verbal-receptive session teaches object and body-part identification and strengthens the child's ability to follow instructions by expanding phrases associated with actions, color, size, etc. Both the preverbal and verbal-receptive sections set the stage for verbal-expressive training. In the last section, emphasis shifts to verbal imitation, expressive identification of body parts, room parts and other objects, and the child's speech repertoire is expanded to include appropriate use of prepositional relationships, verb–noun combinations, colors, numbers, etc. One additional feature of Kent's program is its adaptation to a nonoral approach for use with hearing-impaired and deaf children.

Tawney and Hipsher (1972) have designed a programmed instruction package to teach functional language skills to speech-deficient children. Children who emit no vocal or motor responses are considered acceptable candidates for training, as are children who possess varying degrees of language competence, but who are considered speech deficient. The program has been written so that teachers who are relatively inexperienced in the area of speech and language instruction can effectively carry out the specified procedures. Operant conditioning techniques provide the foundation for the programmed sequences, and each step in a sequence specifies the "target" behavior to be mastered, the prerequisites necessary to enter that step, and a pretest–post test procedure to examine whether the child can pass through the step, or whether he/she has mastered the step after training. Although each step can be carried out in a one-to-one training format, special emphasis has been placed on small-group instruction. The general sequence of instruction as outlined by the authors is as follows: (1) shape attending behavior in tutorial sessions; (2) shape other skills, such as the touch response, which are prerequisite to further instruction; (3) teach concepts at the motor level through a discrimination learning procedure; (4) establish speech sounds; (5) shape sounds into one-word responses; (6) teach "touch" in conjunction with the vocal responses; (7) fade touch instructions, and teach concepts at the verbal level; (8) expand one-word utterances to two and three words; (9) combine noun and verb phrases; and (10) reinforce spontaneous utterances both in and out of training settings.

Other speech and language training programs, which should be of interest to the reader include Gray and Ryan (1973), Drash and Leibowitz (1973), and Hartung and Hartung (1973).

## BACKGROUND OF THE GUESS, SAILOR, AND BAER LANGUAGE DEVELOPMENT PROGRAM FOR SEVERELY HANDICAPPED PERSONS

During the late 1960s and early 1970s, numerous experiments were conducted at Kansas Neurological Institute and the University of Kansas that were relevant to the training and acquisition of language skills such as imitation, morphological grammar, syntax, and the relationship between productive speech and receptive language (cf. Guess and Baer, 1973, for a partial review of these studies). These experiments demonstrated that speech and language acquisition could be studied and analyzed in the same manner as other areas of human behavior, that severely handicapped children could be taught a variety of rule-governed speech skills, and that the techniques used in training could be effective for a diverse array of the linguistic deficits of the severely handicapped population. These investigations provided the optimism needed to develop a larger, more comprehensive intervention program for nonverbal or seriously speech-deficient individuals.

The task of designing a language development program which can progressively and demonstrably move a child from no speech to modest conversational skill was undertaken with several prominent considerations: (1) the program must emphasize the functionality of speech and language—that is, it must rapidly bring children into contact with the potential of speech as an effective mode of controlling the environment; (2) the structure of the training sequence must emphasize the teaching of skills which allow children to expand their own language repertoire; (3) the sequence of instruction must allow flexibility in reordering the content areas to be trained, in accordance with ongoing data analysis.

The structure of the program currently under development has been detailed elsewhere (Guess, Sailor, and Baer, 1974; Guess and Baer, 1973). It includes an initial assessment and evaluation, a comparison of imitation procedures, and the teaching of functional speech and language skills. This chapter will concentrate on a newly revised training sequence for teaching functional speech and language skills and, for illustration, on one subsection of that sequence.

The training program is an interlocking sequence of individual training steps, to be implemented for children (and adults) who have acquired verbal imitation skills. The total sequence is subdivided into 10 major content areas. Two of the areas, *Persons and Things* and *Action with Persons and Things,* are learned by all students. However, after training in these two areas, the program branches into a two-track system, as shown in Table 1.

The first track is labeled Preacademic. It is designed for severely handicapped children who, by virtue of their age, demonstrated ability, living environment, and future educational opportunities, could benefit from an academically oriented program which prepares them for classroom experiences. Included in the Preacademic track are linguistic content areas appropriate to *Possession, Color, Size, Relation* and *Morphological Grammar* (plurals, suffixes, tenses, inflections).

The second track, Community Living, is designed for those severely handicapped individuals who need specific, direct training in the language skills facilitating life in their home, or in a community sheltered workshop, half-way house, nursing home, or any other setting where basic

**Table 1.**
Schematic Presentation of the Training Sequence Categorized in
Content Areas in Their Two-Track Order of Training

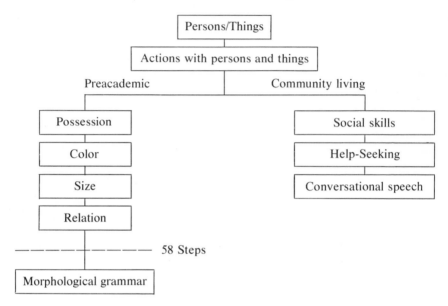

social and survival communication skills assume a major importance in enhancing the eventual move of these individuals to a less protective situation.

The sequence of training steps within each content area is further organized, according to five dimensions: the Reference, Control, Self-extended Control, Integration, and Receptive functions of speech and language.

Reference assumes that the fundamental function of language is to symbolize. This requires the existence of a convenient language event which can be responded to, and responded with, in much the same manner as one would respond to or with some real and important event. When the convenient events are words, an immense gain in control of the social world is achieved for the word-user, for then word-users may exchange words with each other to manage their mutual interactions, and the exchange of words is much more convenient, and can be much more efficient, than the direct teaching of others to help in dealing with the world. In this program, "reference" is used in a variety of contexts, ranging from the relatively simple labeling of objects, the description of actions, the identification of ownership (my/your), the attribution of color, and the identification of relational properties (size, position). However, the lesson is only implicit, in teaching these reference skills, that labels are powerful.

The second dimension, Control, makes that power more explicit by teaching request forms of language as a productive skill, such as in the form, "I want [thing], or [action]"; "I want [action-with-thing]"; and "I want you to [action-with-thing]." At the receptive level, Control is used to acknowledge others questions about the child's wishes, as in saying "yes" or "no" to "You want [thing]?" or "You want [action]?"; "You want [action-with-thing]?"; and, later, "You want me to [action-with-thing]?" Further explicitness about the controlling function of language is added in both the productive and receptive mode through the inclusion of possessive, descriptive, and relational properties which further identify the object or action appropriate to the request. Thus, training within the Reference and Control dimensions is meant to show children that, to the extent that they know referents, they can manage their environment. However, after this has happened, the children are bound to find that they cannot control their environment sufficiently, simply because they do not know the necessary labels for the things, actions, and actions-with-things that they wish. Thus, it is important in maximizing childrens' use of language to control their environment, that they learn how to remedy their lack of labels. This requires teaching them to request further information in the case of specified ignorances. Thus, a Self-extended Control dimension is added to the program. It is designed to teach the children to request further, specific training inputs, based on their discrimination of what they do not know from what they already know.

Self-extended Control is developed by teaching the children to ask questions, such as "What (is) that?" in response to unknown things, "What (are) you doing?" in response to unknown actions, "Whose (label)?" in response to identifying ownership of objects, "What color?" when confronted with novel color stimuli, "What size?" to inquire about the largeness or smallness of objects, and "Where [object] or [person]?" to identify or establish location. Obviously, it is important that the childrens' newly acquired techniques of Self-extended Control (with which they request further instruction about what they do not yet know) be used in a functional manner—i.e., are not only used to invite instruction, but are followed by memory and later use of the instruction given in answer to these requests.

The program contains contingencies designed to make sure that such memory and use actually occur. It is additionally important that language skills taught in Reference, Control, and Self-extended Control are put together in such a manner that previously taught skills are integrated with currently taught skills to maximize appropriate interaction with the environment. Thus, the fourth dimension, Integration, calls for training steps that teach the children to discriminate when to seek appropriate information via question-asking, and when to respond with appropriate referents when the information already exists in their repertoires. A second function of Integration is "dialogue" which, conceptually, provides a teaching framework requiring the children to chain together all or some of the previously learned skills, so that they can carry on a simple but appropriate conversation centered around a functional activity or theme. The dialogue ranges from a relatively simple two-response chain at the end of the Persons and Things category, to 15-response chains in several of the more advanced categories.

Reception is the final dimension on the program structure. Corresponding to specific attainments in productive speech, concepts are also taught at the receptive level, to make complete the childrens' ability to speak and listen. The previously described four dimensions have already indicated the interrelationship between production and reception in the training sequence. Thus, for example, a Reference skill taught at the productive level would have a corresponding Reference concept taught at the receptive level. The training of productive skills first in the program, followed by receptive training (if necessary) of the same skill is not intended to minimize the importance of receptive training, but to emphasize the productive nature of the program which, by design, has the purpose of bringing the children rapidly into the speaking community, (as contrasted to the mute but instruction-following community).

It is usual to assume that receptive training should precede productive training in a language curriculum. It seems logical that a child should "understand" a thing and/or an action with a thing before he can express that relationship. This assumption, of course, is predicated on the equation of "understanding" with receptive speech, an equation frequently exemplified in psycholinguistic literature. This may constitute a quasi-problem of semantics among language researchers, for recent data tend, rather impressively, to demonstrate that productive and receptive repertoires may be trained independently, and that there is little enhancement of either repertoire as a function of which is trained first, even when the content is identical. Guess and Baer (1973) have recently presented research bearing on this training issue. Perhaps the two repertoires (receptive and productive) are indeed independent, with neither order-of-training requirements nor invariable cross-repertoire generalization characteristics; or, perhaps, the central issue is simply that receptive speech skills are far from an infallible measure of the hypothetical "comprehension" which seems so logically to be a prerequisite of productive speech. Pragmatically, at present, two considerations explain the priority for productive speech in this training program: (1) in general, in this program and in other related studies, productive forms have been trained reliably, without a preceding receptive training of the same target skill; and (2) too much emphasis on receptive speech (especially if it is more easily achieved than the comparable productive skill) seems aimed at training an instruction-follower rather than a speaker.

One additional point of importance to the training sequence is the fact that response units are increased both in length and syntactic complexity as the children progress through the steps. Furthermore, the entire sequence is interlocking, so that new skills are introduced as much as possible within the context of previously learned skills. Thus, the children are not abruptly exposed to concepts for which adequate prior training has not already taken place. Also, children are not introduced to later categories and step sequences without having demonstrated that they already possess the skills programmed at earlier levels.

## STRUCTURE OF THE TRAINING STEPS

At present, 58 individual training steps have been designed and written for the categories of *Persons and Things, Action with Persons and Things, Possession, Color, Size and Relations*. The steps are assembled in the form of an experimental training manual.[2] Each step in the manual follows a similar outline which includes the training goal, stimulus materials needed, instructions to the trainer, and a section on programming for generalization.

### Training Goal:

This section describes the specific skills or concepts to be trained in the step, with a brief statement as to how the step is integrated with a previous one.

### Stimulus Materials Needed:

The materials and props needed for the procedures are frequently left to the discretion of the trainer, who, with his knowledge of the student and his/her environment, can select the best items. For the most part, however, the training materials include items which are common, readily available, and functional. The use of objects, rather than pictures, as stimulus items is preferred in order to increase the authenticity of the training environment. The initial steps in the program typically include the following items:

(Food) cookie, Coke/pop, apple, candy, gum, juice, crackers, peanuts, milk

(Toys) ball, car, top, doll, puzzle, block, drum, gun, ring

(Clothing) pants, dress, shoe, shirt, sock, coat, cap, pajamas, mittens, hat, watch

(Body parts) nose, tummy, eye, ear, mouth, foot, chest, arm, leg, knee

(Miscellaneous) chair, table, T.V., spoon, pan, cup, soap, toothpaste, towel, comb, brush, paper, pencil

## Instructions:

Each step includes written instructions to the trainer, describing the order in which items and trials are to be presented, what the trainer says to the student, and the expected response from the student. The trainer's instructions to the student are always printed in capital letters (e.g., WHAT IS THAT?). The response from the student is enclosed with quotation marks (e.g., "ball"). When appropriate, the instructions also explain how training items are to be arranged for the session, and the position or location of the student in the room.

For each trial in a session, the trainer provides the student with a stimulus, which could be a question, a command, and/or the presentation of an object or action. The student, in turn, can give a correct response, a partially correct response, a wrong response, or no response at all. The trainer must react in accordance with the response given. When correct responses are given by the student, they are usually reinforced and praised by the trainer. The trainer is given responsibility to select the types and amounts of reinforcers designated for correct responses by the student. A considerable effort has been made, however, to construct many steps so that a correct response is intrinsically reinforcing for the student, especially in the higher level steps in the training sequence.

Obviously, the student will not respond correctly on every trial. Indeed, some students may require lengthy periods of training before correct responses or even partially correct responses are emitted. The trainer, must, therefore, be prepared to deal with partially correct responses, incorrect responses, or no responses. The various steps in the manual use either one of two basic procedures when the student does not respond correctly. These are the trainer correction procedure and the second trainer modeling procedure.

The trainer correction procedure (presented in detail in the training manual) describes how the trainer should utilize prompts, put-throughs, and shaping techniques to correct errors made by the student in response to specific training trials. The trainer correction procedure allows for flexibility in reacting to individual and often idiosyncratic responses made by the student, yet the procedure provides a systematic framework which allows the trainer to be consistent and thorough when correcting response errors.

There are certain skills and concepts for which a second trainer can best serve as a "model" for the correct response following an error or no response by the student. These situations occur when the concept to be taught involves a reversed discrimination, depending upon the person who originated the response. The concept of "I–you" is a good example. The first person singular pronoun, "I," is used by a speaker, whereas the second person singular pronoun, "you," generally refers to the person or persons spoken to. In teaching the "I–you" discrimination, as well as similar concepts (e.g., "my–your"), a second trainer is helpful, since this person (whether another adult or student who has mastered the concept) can provide the correctly modeled answer by assuming the same speaker-listener role as the student. Accordingly, a second trainer modeling procedure is used in those steps in the program where a reversed discrimination is taught. (Again, the training manual fully describes the second trainer modeling procedure).

Recent experiments with application of group-training techniques with this program have utilized children as second trainers. Thus, child A, for example, who has passed Step 16 and is receiving training on one of the later steps in the sequence, serves as a model for correct responding on Step 16 for child B, who has yet to acquire this training element. Early data on this aspect of the program suggest that peer modeling may present training advantages apart from the sheer economics of employing two adults to one child.

### Programming for Generalization:

Many of the steps in the manual have an additional subsection which describes instructions for extending a newly learned skill or concept to the student's natural environment. Ordinarily, the generalization training procedures are to be administered by the student's parents, parent surrogates, teacher, or other significant persons who have daily contact with the child. The purpose of the generalization procedures is to increase the use of a newly taught skill with persons different from the language trainer, and in environments different from the student's training area. Additionally, the generalization training procedures assist in keeping others aware of the student's progress across time. Thus, by including the child's caretakers as integral parts of the language-training environment, parents, child care personnel, etc., become familiar with the skills available to the student as he/she advances through the program, so that such skills can be properly attended to (and reinforced) when they occur spontaneously.

### Scoring Form and Summary Sheets

Each step includes scoring forms (data sheets) specifically designed for the training sequence in that step. The scoring sheets include space for the student's name, the name of the trainer, the date, and session number. Wherever possible, the scoring sheets provide cues for the trainer in administering the procedure for a particular step. Each scoring sheet includes a summary table for tabulating percent correct responses for each session.

Summary sheets are also provided for each step to record progress across sessions. Additional space on the summary sheets is used to indicate the date on which training was started for that step, the date in which criterion performance was reached, plus the total number of sessions needed to achieve criterion performance.

### An Illustration:

Table 2 illustrates how the training program is organized across the five dimensions. This section will describe the step-sequence for the initial (and relatively simple) *Persons and Things* category.

The student enters Step 1, after having demonstrated an ability to imitate common objects and body parts. The trainer selects 16 items for training, based upon how well the student can articulate the labels, and on the appropriateness of the items for the student's age and living environment. As indicated previously in the discussion of reference, the goal of Step 1 is to teach the student that words are symbolic for common, useful environmental events. The purpose of Step 1 is to teach the student to accurately and reliably label 16 objects. For purposes of example, the complete training instruction for Step 1 is reproduced in Table 3.

The student continues in Step 1 until he/she can label the objects accurately to the specified criterion of mastery. The student is then tested to determine if he/she can point accurately to the same objects that were trained as productive labels in Step 1. If so, the student advances to Step 3 in the sequence; if not, the student is placed in Step 2. This step teaches the students to identify the objects receptively, via a pointing response. Initially, two objects are selected and trained as a pair until criterion performance is reached. A second pair of objects is then trained to a similar level of mastery. At this point, both pairs (four objects) are trained together randomly until the student can reliably identify (point to) each object presented. A skill-test is administered following criterion performance on the four-item block. The skill-test includes all 16 items, presented in random pairs. Successful performance in the skill-test (80% accuracy) enables the student to exit from the step without further training. If the student fails to pass the skill test, a new pair of items is trained to criter-

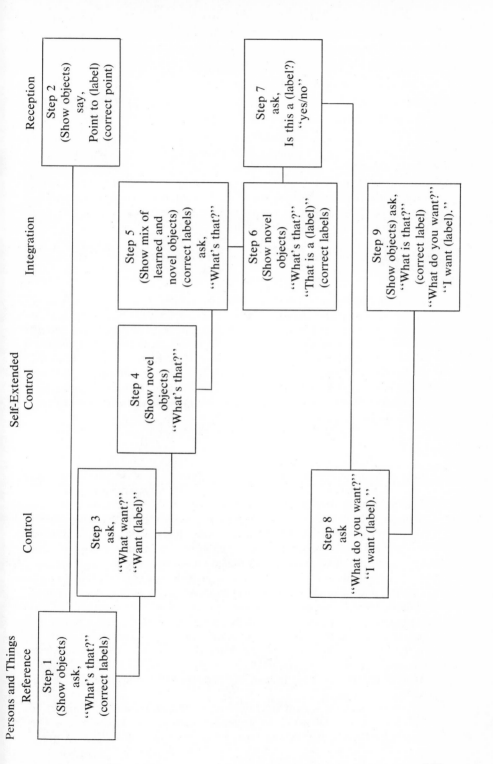

Persons and Things
Reference

Self-Extended
Control

Control

Integration

Reception

**Step 1**
(Show objects)
ask,
"What's that?"
(correct labels)

**Step 2**
(Show objects)
say,
Point to (label)
(correct point)

**Step 3**
ask,
"What want?"
"Want (label)"

**Step 4**
(Show novel
objects)
"What's that?"

**Step 5**
(Show mix of
learned and
novel objects)
(correct labels)
ask,
"What's that?"

**Step 6**
(Show novel
objects)
"What's that?"
"That is a (label)"
(correct labels)

**Step 7**
ask,
Is this a (label?)
"yes/no"

**Step 8**
ask
"What do you want?"
"I want (label)."

**Step 9**
(Show objects) ask,
"What is that?"
(correct label)
"What do you want?"
"I want (label)."

**Table 3.**
Specimen Training Step From Training Manual

---

STEP 1

*Training Goal*: To teach correct labeling (naming) of 16 objects.

*Stimulus Materials*: Sixteen objects or body parts, the labels of which the student can imitate. (Refer to Introduction of Manual for suggested training items). The most important element in making these choices is the selection of objects that are useful to the student.

*Instructions*: Use *Trainer Correction Procedure* as described in Introduction of Manual.

This step includes a skill test which is administered just before training and at various points during training. The student exits from step 1 when criterion performance is achieved on the skill test (80% or more correct responses, or 12 correct responses in a row). To administer the test, present, one at a time, all 16 objects to be trained. Hold each item in front of the student or point to it (if a body part, your body part is pointed to), and then ask, "WHAT'S THAT?" Each object is eventually presented twice, resulting in a total of 32 trials. The *Trainer Correction Procedure* is also used in giving the skill test.

To train the labels of the 16 objects, the following instructions are provided.

Initially, select two objects (1 and 2) and (if they are not body parts) place them in front of the student. Next, pick up or point to an object and ask, "WHAT'S THAT?" (In the case of a body part, always point to your body part, not the student's). For correct responses, the student must say the appropriate label (e.g., "ball"). During the session's trials, the objects in the pair are presented in random order, but for an equal number of trials. Training is continued until criterion performance (80% or more correct responses, or 12 correct responses in a row) is reached on the two objects.

The procedure is then repeated for a second pair of objects (3 and 4) which is trained in the same manner to criterion. Following completion of training on the second pair of objects, next present all four objects (1, 2, 3 and 4) in random order; they are similarly trained to criterion. At this point, the skill test is given (including the four trained objects plus the 12 objects yet to be trained). If the student fails to reach criterion performance on the skill test, proceed to train, separately, the next two pairs of objects (5 and 6; 7 and 8). All four objects are then trained together, as before, and the skill test is administered again.

The procedure is continued until all 16 objects have been trained; the skill test is given following the training of each two pairs of objects. The outline for the training sequence may be abbreviated as follows:

Train to criterion,
  items:
    1 and 2 (e.g., ball and cup)
    3 and 4
    1, 2, 3, and 4
    Administer skill test (if criterion is reached, proceed to Step 2)
    5 and 6
    7 and 8
    5, 6, 7, and 8
    Administer skill test (if criterion is reached, proceed to Step 2)
    9 and 10
    11 and 12
    9, 10, 11 and 12
    Administer skill test (if criterion is reached, proceed to Step 2)
    13 and 14
    15 and 16
    13, 14, 15, and 16
    Administer skill test (if criterion is reached, proceed to Step 2)

*Programming for generalization*: Upon completion of the step, a list of trained objects should be given to the student's parents, parent surrogates, teacher(s), etc. Every few days these individuals should present the same objects to the student and ask, "What's that?" New (nontrained) objects and body parts should be added gradually to the list, if the student maintains an acceptable level of performance (above 80%) in labeling the already learned objects. A record of the student's performance should, of course, be kept for review.

---

Note: If the student fails to reach criterion on the final skill test, you have the option of discontinuing training on this step, and moving the student on to step 2; or continuing to train randomly chosen sets of four objects to criterion, while also continuing to administer the skill test until the student reaches criterion. This decision depends on whatever reasons you may have for concluding that failure to reach criterion will not prevent progress in step 2.

ion, then still another new pair of items. These two pairs are then trained together in random fashion until criterion performance is achieved. The skill test is readministered as before, including all 16 items. The student can again exit from the step if criterion performance is now achieved. If the student again fails the skill test, a fifth or sixth pair of items is trained to criterion, then trained together randomly. The procedure continues with items trained in pairs, then in blocks of four, with the skill test administered following criterion performance on each new block of four objects. Training continues until the skill test is eventually passed or until the student has been trained on all 16 items.

The experimental question, discussed earlier, of whether students should be trained receptively first (Step 2) before the object labels are trained productively (Step 1), comprises one part of the overall experimental analysis. Some students are routinely placed in Step 2 prior to training on Step 1, and vice versa. These results will eventually provide additional data on the interdependence or functional independence of productive and receptive skills.

Step 3 introduces the first Control dimension of the program. Specifically, students are taught to request items, using the two-word response, "Want object-label." The trainer introduces each item by asking "WHAT WANT?" To succeed on this step, the trainer must select items that the student does indeed want, and items that the student can already label with accuracy. This step has been relatively easy to train, in terms of teaching the semantic content of the utterance. Extensive anecdotal reports indicate that the response generalizes very well to the student's natural environment and that the response does, indeed, serve as an important skill which enables the student to at least partly control his/her environment.

Step 4 introduces the first example of the Self-extended Control dimension of the program sequence. It is based on the premise that students will not know the labels of all, or even most, of the objects in their environment, and that a useful skill would indeed be to teach the students to ask for the labels of objects which are unknown to them. Specifically, Step 4 teaches the student to simply ask, "What's that?" when presented with objects for which the labels are unknown. In contrast to previous steps, the student must now respond to the object alone, without a verbal question or command from the trainer (i.e., the students must ask "What's that?" when the novel objects are shown to them). The initial phase of the step includes procedures for identifying novel objects to assure that the student does not, indeed, know the object label. A second phase in the step includes imitation training to improve articulation of the required utterance. The third phase establishes the response, ("What's that?") to novel objects using the trainer correction procedure. The response called for in Step 4 has been relatively easy to teach, and observations have indicated that the students do use the skill during their normal interactions outside of the training sessions. An initial difficulty was posed by poorly articulated responses from many of the students. A later revision of the step introduced imitation/articulation training of the utterance prior to establishing the functionality of the response with novel objects.

For many students, the ability to discriminate when to ask, "What's that?" and when to label previously learned objects is not readily apparent. Step 5 is introduced as one form of Integration, by teaching the differentiated usage of naming known objects and asking the question, "What's that?" when presented with novel objects. The procedure involves the random presentation of both known-label objects and novel objects (those for which the student has not already acquired productive labels). In this procedure, the trainer labels the object following the question, "What's that?" by the student. Some students will remember these labels, and thus start to spontaneously label these previously novel objects correctly, immediately after the trainer presents the objects. This, of course, is the desired process, indicating success for the intent of the training procedure. Upon reaching criterion performance on the step, the students who are able to shift from asking "What's that?" to the appropriate labeling of the objects are advanced to Step 7. Many students, however, continue to ask "What's that?" to repeated presentations of novel objects, indicating that they are not remembering the labels, or that they have not learned to use question-asking behavior in the functional manner desired in the step. These students are then placed in Step 6, which is another step in the Integration dimension.

Both previously learned and new novel objects are again presented randomly in Step 6 training sessions. The specified goal of Step 6 is to teach the student to remember the labels for novel objects provided by the trainer in response to the student's question, "What's that?", and to shift to a response which consists of the appropriate object label. In this procedure, the student must correctly label known objects and ask "What's that?" when presented with novel objects. As in Step 6, the trainer provides the correct label for the novel objects (e.g., THAT IS A _____."). Now, however, the trainer asks the student to also provide the correct label for the novel object (e.g., TELL ME WHAT IT IS). The desired outcome is for the student to spontaneously label the object when first presented, rather than ask the question "What's that?" At this point, the object is now considered learned, and a new novel object is added to the training list. Final criterion for Step 6 is achieved when the student successfully remembers and produces the correct labels for three novel objects within 10 presentations of each object.

Step 7 introduces the use of "yes" and "no" as an index of the student's ability to identify object labels receptively. Teaching the student to use yes/no in response to questions is necessary for subsequent steps in the training sequence, many of which cannot be implemented with just a pointing response. The response thus becomes a productive index of receptive acquisition. The yes/no training in Step 7 essentially follows a match-to-sample paradigm. The trainer holds up an object and asks the student, IS THIS (LABEL)? If that spoken label matches the response to the previously trained (and faded out) response to the question, then the correct answer is "yes"; if the label does not match, the answer is "no." This particular skill has been most difficult to train. Numerous revisions in the training step have been made, following a succession of failures.

The latest revision is a shortened version of a 16-phase training sequence which has been successful in teaching the desired skill (Ramberg, Guess, and Sailor, 1975).

Step 8 is identical to Step 3, except that now the student is trained to use the first person pronoun "I" when requesting objects (i.e., "I want (object-label)"). Again, careful selection of items which are salient to the student is considered essential. Step 8 increases the verbal response to a three-word unit, and this fact alone does predict difficulty for a few students.

Step 9 concludes training in the *Persons and Things* category. This step exemplifies a second type of integration, in that two previously learned responses are chained together to form a very brief dialogue. The trainer displays an assortment of objects which are reinforcing for the student. On a random basis, the trainer asks the student to label selected objects (e.g., WHAT IS THAT?). Following the appropriate labeling response by the student, the trainer confirms the correct answer (i.e., YES, THAT IS A (LABEL), and then further asks, WHAT DO YOU WANT? Students must then make the appropriate request (i.e., "I want (object)); whereupon they are given the item. The procedure continues until the objects have been both identified and requested by the students.

Following completion of the *Persons and Things* category, the students will have been taught to label expressively and identify receptively a large number of objects, to ask questions to obtain names of objects they cannot already identify, to use "yes" and "no" when confirming or denying the identification of objects, to request objects using a three-word sentence containing the pronoun "I," and to chain two verbal responses together. These are modest yet quite significant achievements for the typical student who enters the program. Significantly, the skills and concepts trained in the *Persons and Things* category provide a solid foundation for subsequent training in the sequence which increases in complexity of content, length of the response units, and the number of specific units which are chained together to form appropriate conversational skills.

## SOME PRELIMINARY RESULTS

The program is currently being conducted with approximately 400 severely handicapped children and adults residing in day care centers and institutional settings in the states of Kansas, Arkansas, and Nebraska. Currently, many of the participants in the program are in one of four verbal-imitation training procedures, yet the number of students who have advanced into the functional speech and language component has steadily increased to the point at which some preliminary analyses can be made.

Figure 1 presents data (up to July 1974) reflecting the mean number of trials required to reach criterion for each step, across the nine steps contained in the *Persons and Things* category.[3] Means for each step are based upon the following numbers of subjects: Step 1, 53; Step 2, 34; Step 3, 34; Step 4, 29; Step 5, 23; Step 6, 21; Step 7, 20; Step 8, 17; and Step 9, 16. The figure shows a general decrease in the number of trials required to reach criterion, across the steps. Other data (not presented) indicate that this trend is even more pronounced for those subjects who have completed the 20-step sequence in the *Action with Persons and Things* category. These initial results show that, as the students progress through the training sequence, they acquire new language skills more rapidly, even though the complexity of these skills is ostensibly increasing. (A small

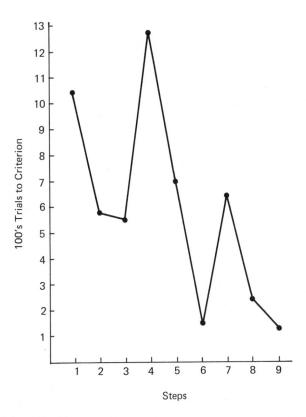

Fig. 1.   Trials to criterion (in blocks of 100) for each of nine steps in the *Persons and Things* category.

number of students have now advanced through most of the steps of the preacademic track.)

Figure 1 also confirms that Step 4 is relatively difficult. This is probably due to an earlier version of the instructions for the step which contained a prose error that allowed some trainers to extend training sessions much longer than the required criterion level.

Eventually, a sufficient number of students will have advanced through the entire sequence to allow some careful analyses of the program with respect to: (1) a comparison of the five dimensions for their relative ease of acquisition; (2) the identification and subsequent revision or resequencing of apparently difficult steps; and (3) a comparison of the subjects' progress with respect to their age, etiology, measured intelligence, and other conceivably important variables. Thus, in the final analysis, the sequence of the program will be based upon data from the subject population, rather than upon some predetermined model of how severely handicapped people logically should, but do not necessarily, acquire communication skills.

The Guess, Sailor, and Baer program continues in a state of development (even after approximately 3 years of development and experimentation). It is not the authors' expectation to produce now, or in the immediate future, a fully completed sequence of instruction for remediating the speech and language deficiencies of severely handicapped children. It is hoped, however, that the program *in its present state* will help to serve at least some of the severely handicapped children and adults. It is further hoped that the program will serve as a catalyst in generating the types of research and conceptualizations required to understand more completely the nature of speech and language deficits among the severely handicapped.

**REFERENCES**

Bricker W, Bricker D: A program of language training for the severely language handicapped child. Except Child 37:101–111, 1970

Bricker W, Bricker D: An early language training strategy, in Schiefelbusch R, Lloyd L (eds): Language Perspectives: Acquisition, Retardation and Intervention. Baltimore, University Park Press, 1974

Drash PW, Leibowitz JM: Operant conditioning of speech and language in the non-verbal retarded child—Recent advances. Pediat Clin North Am 20:233–243, 1973

Gray B, Ryan B: A Language Program for the Nonlanguage Child. Champaign, Ill., Research Press, 1973

Guess D, Sailor W, Baer DM: To teach language to retarded children, in Schiefelbusch R, Lloyd L (eds): Language Perspectives: Acquisition, Retardation and Intervention. Baltimore, University Park Press, 1974

Guess D, Baer DM: Some experimental analyses of linguistic development in institutionalized retarded children, in Lahey B (ed): The Modification of Language Behavior. Springfield, Ill., Thomas, 1973

Hartung SM, Hartung JR: Establishing verbal imitation skills and functional speech in autistic children, in Lahey B (ed): The Modification of Language Behavior. Springfield, Ill., Thomas, 1973

Kent L: Language Acquisition Program for the Severely Retarded. Champaign, Ill., Research Press, 1974

Miller J, Yoder D: On developing the content for a language teaching program. Ment Retard 2:9–11, April 1972a

Miller J, Yoder D: A syntax teaching program, in McLean JE, Yoder DE, Schiefelbusch RL (eds): Language Intervention with the Retarded: Developing Strategies. Baltimore, University Park Press, 1972b

Miller J, Yoder D: An ontogenetic language teaching strategy for retarded children, in Schiefelbusch R, Lloyd L (eds): Language Perspectives: Acquisition, Retardation and Intervention. Baltimore, University Park Press, 1974

Ramberg J, Guess D, Sailor W: Training Generalized Functional Acquisition of "Yes" and "No" in Three Retarded Children, AAESPH Review, 1975, 1:3

Sailor W, Guess D, Baer DM: Functional language for verbally deficient children: An experimental program. Ment Retard 11:27–35, 1973

Stremel K, Waryas C: A behavioral-psycholinguistic approach to language training. Am Speech Hearing Monog 18:96–124, 1974

Tawney J, Hipsher L: Systematic Instruction for Retarded Children: The Illinois Program (Part II). Systematic Language Instruction. State of Illinois, Office of the Superintendent of Public Instruction, 1972

[1]The authors are grateful to the following individuals who have, and are, actively participating in the development of the training program described in this chapter: Hugh Sage, Beatrice (Nebraska) State Home and Training School; Sue Porter, Arkansas Developmental Disabilities Services; and Leonard Lavis, Kansas Neurological Institute. The preparation of this chapter was supported in part from USOE/BEH Grant OEG-0-74-2766 to Doug Guess, Wayne Sailor, and Leonard Lavis at the Kansas Neurological Institute, and in part from USOE/BEH Contract OEG-0-74-9184 to Doug Guess and Wayne Sailor at Kansas Neurological Institute.

[2]The training manual is currently being revised and edited for dissemination to persons working with nonverbal and speech deficient children. Part I of the program is now available from H & H Enterprises, Inc., Box 3342, Lawrence, Kansas 66044.

[3]These results are based upon a prior sequence of steps which does not have a direct 1:1 correspondence with the revised sequence presented in the previous section. There is little reason to doubt, however, that the same general trend will not persist (and probably be even more pronounced) for the new step-sequence.

Example
Scoring Sheet for Step 1

Name__John Brown_____ Date__4-19-75_____ Session #___11__

Trainer__Sue Jones_____

This scoring sheet can be used for either the one-pair or two-pair presentations described in Step 1 training instructions. For training pairs of items, assign numbers (1) and (3) to the first object (for a total of 32 trials); assign numbers (2) and (4) to the second object in the pair (for the remaining 32 trials). When training all four objects, assign each to a single number (16 trials each).

List objects trained:

(1) __cup__     (2) __ball__     (3) __shoe__     (4) __spoon__

| (1) | + | (4) | + | (1) | + | (3) | + |
|-----|---|-----|---|-----|---|-----|---|
| (3) | + | (2) | + | (4) | + | (2) | + |
| (2) | + | (3) | + | (2) | − | (4) | + |
| (4) | + | (1) | − | (2) | + | (1) | + |
| (1) | − | (4) | + | (3) | + | (3) | + |
| (1) | + | (4) | + | (4) | + | (2) | + |
| (2) | − | (1) | + | (3) | + | (3) | + |
| (3) | + | (2) | + | (1) | + | (1) | NR |
| (4) | + | (3) | − | (3) | + | (4) | + |
| (2) | − | (4) | + | (2) | + | (2) | + |
| (1) | + | (2) | + | (4) | + | (4) | + |
| (4) | + | (1) | + | (1) | − | (1) | + |
| (3) | + | (1) | + | (2) | + | (2) | + |
| (2) | + | (3) | + | (1) | + | (3) | − |
| (4) | − | (2) | + | (3) | NR | (1) | + |
| (3) | − | (3) | + | (4) | + | (4) | + |

Score trials as correct (+); incorrect (−); or no response (NR).

Summary for session (%)

|  | + | − | NR |
|---|---|---|---|
| Two objects | − | − | − |
| or |  |  |  |
| Four objects | 81 | 16 | 3 |

Example
Skill Test Scoring Sheet for Step 1

Name__John Brown_____ Date __2-25-75_____ Session #__1__
Trainer __Sue Jones_____

In blanks 1–16, list the 16 objects (and body parts) that are used in Step 1; then list them again (not in the same order) in blanks 17–32.

| | Object | Score | | | Object | Score |
|---|---|---|---|---|---|---|
| 1. | cup | NR | | 17. | shirt | − |
| 2. | ball | + | | 18. | table | − |
| 3. | chair | NR | | 19. | shoe | − |
| 4. | nose | − | | 20. | pants | NR |
| 5. | hat | − | | 21. | ear | − |
| 6. | spoon | − | | 22. | hat | + |
| 7. | ear | NR | | 23. | chair | − |
| 8. | milk | − | | 24. | cup | − |
| 9. | pants | − | | 25. | eye | − |
| 10. | cookie | + | | 26. | T.V. | − |
| 11. | shoe | NR | | 27. | car | NR |
| 12. | car | − | | 28. | cookie | + |
| 13. | table | − | | 29. | milk | − |
| 14. | T.V. | NR | | 30. | spoon | + |
| 15. | shirt | NR | | 31. | nose | − |
| 16. | eye | − | | 32. | ball | + |

Score trials as correct (+); incorrect (−); or no response (NR).

Summary for skill test (%)

| + | − | NR |
|---|---|---|
| 19 | 56 | 25 |

Example
Summary Sheet for Step 1

Name  John Brown                    Trainer  Sue Jones

    Date training started:  2-26-75

    Date training ended: _____

    Total sessions to criterion: _____

| Objects | Percent Correct Responses Across Sessions* | | | | | | | | | | | | | | | | | | |
|---|---|---|---|---|---|---|---|---|---|---|---|---|---|---|---|---|---|---|---|
| | 1 | 2 | 3 | 4 | 5 | 6 | 7 | 8 | 9 | 10 | 11 | 12 | 13 | 14 | 15 | 16 | 17 | 18 | 19 |
| 1 (ball) and 2 (cup) | 39 | 57 | 56 | 79 | 91 | | | | | | | | | | | | | | |
| 3 (shoe) and 4 (spoon) | | | | | | 47 | 65 | 69 | 65 | 95 | | | | | | | | | |
| 1, 2, 3, and 4 | | | | | | | | | | | 81 | | | | | | | | |
| 5 (  ) and 6 (  ) | | | | | | | | | | | | | | | | | | | |
| 7 (  ) and 8 (  ) | | | | | | | | | | | | | | | | | | | |
| 5, 6, 7, and 8 | | | | | | | | | | | | | | | | | | | |
| 9 (  ) and 10 (  ) | | | | | | | | | | | | | | | | | | | |
| 11 (  ) and 12 (  ) | | | | | | | | | | | | | | | | | | | |
| 9, 10, 11, and 12 | | | | | | | | | | | | | | | | | | | |
| 13 (  ) and 14 (  ) | | | | | | | | | | | | | | | | | | | |
| 15 (  ) and 16 (  ) | | | | | | | | | | | | | | | | | | | |
| 13, 14, 15, and 16 | | | | | | | | | | | | | | | | | | | |
| Skill Test | 19 | | | | | | | | | | | | | | | | | | |
| Date | 2-25-75 | | | | | | | | | | | | | | | | | | |

*This sample summary data sheet indicates criterion performance (80% or better correct responses) was achieved in session 5 for objects 1 and 2 (ball and cup); criterion performance for the second pair or objects (shoe and spoon) was reached in session 10; and criterion performance for all four objects trained together (see example scoring sheet) was achieved in session 11. The student responded correctly to 19% of the objects in the pretraining skill test (see example skill test scoring sheet). In accordance with the training instructions in Step 1, the language trainer would next readminister the skill test, following the criterion performance (81%) in session 11 where all four objects were trained together. If the student failed to pass the skill test, training would proceed with objects 5 and 6, etc. However, criterion performance on the second skill test would enable the student to advance to Step 2.

# Index

AAMD scale, *see* American Association on
    Mental Deficiency Adaptive
    Behavior Scale
Abortion, therapeutic, 270
Accident prevention, during pregnancy,
    244–245
*Action with Persons and Things,* in
    Language Development Program,
    305, 309, 319
Adaptive behavior, defined, 184
Adjunctive services, in comprehensive
    intervention, 28–29
Advancing of pupils, rules for, 231
Age-related factors
    parenting and, 242–243
    in study program, 93–94
American Association on Mental
    Deficiency, 111–112
American Association on Mental Deficiency
    Adaptive Behavior Scale, 183–186,
    235
American Medical Association, 243
Amniocentesis, 270
Antecedent arrangement, in skill domains,
    296–297
Application, in learning process, 26
Arkansas Department of Social and
    Rehabilitation Services, 195–196
Art pinpoints, 80–81
Assessment, educational, *see* Educational
    assessment; Performance
    measurement
*Attitudes Towards the Retarded,* 12
Auditory discrimination, in severely/
    profoundly handicapped, 126

Battered child syndrome, 243
Bayley Scales of Input Development, 235
Behavioral change, technology and, 19–21

Behavioral technology
    principles of, 19
    teaching methods and, 19–20
Behavior counts, in performance
    measurement, 215–216
Behavior specification, in performance
    measurement, 219
Biofeedback data, potential of, 262–263
Blind children, "retreat" by, 257
Bureau of Education for the Handicapped,
    262, 273, 297

Cain–Levine Social Competency Scale,
    182–183
Calyer–Azusa Scales, 235
Camelot Behavior Checklist, 189–192, 235
Cardination, in programs for handicapped,
    8–11, 98
"Celeration" statement, in performance
    measurement, 235
Changed attitudes, need for, 4–5
Child abuse, parenting and, 243–244
Children's Hospital, Boston, 250
*Christmas in Purgatory* (Blatt), 4
*Closer Look Report,* 11
Cognitive development, intervention and,
    288
Communication
    Development Pinpoints and, 55–70
    intervention and, 288–290
    language deficits in, 55–57
    language structures and, 57–59
Community, intervention strategies within,
    267–273
Community Living, in language
    development program, 305–306
Competency checklists, in curriculum for
    severely/profoundly handicapped,
    125–149

Comprehensive intervention
  adjunctive services in, 28–29
  appropriate curriculum in, 27–28
  components for, 21–30
  cueing in, 25
  defined, 21
  developmental framework for, 22–23
  early and continuous nature of, 23–24
  imitation in, 24–25
  objective evaluation of, 30
  prompting in, 25
  shaping in, 24
  systematic instructional procedures in,
    24–27
Constructive strategy, for severely/
    profoundly handicapped, 287–297
Corrective strategy, for severely/profoundly
    handicapped, 281–288
Counting procedures, in performance
    measurement, 229–230
Cover Card, 282
Critical outcome determination
  accuracy in, 219–220
  endurance, latency, and duration in, 221
  in performance measurement, 219–221
  proficiency in, 220–221
Cues and cueing
  as instructional procedure, 25
  teaching the use of, 258–259
Curriculum
  in comprehensive intervention, 27–28
  for severely/profoundly handicapped,
    115–116, 124–149
Curriculum materials
  development and dissemination of, 27
  structuring of, 27–28
Curriculum planning, for severely/
    profoundly handicapped, 114–115

Dade County Public Schools, 281
Data Card, 286
Data collection
  counting, timing, and recording of,
    229–230
  formulation of, 226–227
Data collection form, in performance
    measurement, 222
Data collection planning
  critical outcomes in, 219–221
  in performance measurement, 218–230
  specifying behavior in, 219
Data collection specification, in
    performance measurement, 226–227

Denver Developmental Screening Test, 235
Dependency, "fading out" of, 259
Developmental Disabilities Technical
    Assistance Systems National Public
    Awareness Task Force, 269
Developmental Pinpoints
  see also Study program
  checklists and inventories in, 36
  classroom implementation of, 38
  communication in, 55–70
  defined, 37
  eye readiness in, 41–43
  fine motor overview in, 41–48
  format of, 37
  general overview of studies in, 92–100
  gross-motor pinpoints in, 48–55
  guidelines for use of, 38–39
  for language acquisition, 60–61
  leisure time activities and, 79–81
  motor skills in, 39–55
  movements involving hands in, 41, 43–48
  in premath, 90–91
  prewriting in, 88–90
  readiness in, 101–106
  reinforcement activities in, 106–108
  in selected studies, 91–92
  self-help skills in, 70–75
  social interaction skills in, 75–79
Disease, parenting and, 243
Down's syndrome, 242, 270
Dressing, by severely/profoundly
    handicapped, 135–138, 261–262
Drug abuse, parenting and, 241–242
Duration, in performance measurement, 218

Early and continuous intervention
  constructive strategy and, 287–297
  vs. institutionalization, 239
  parents and children in, 249–253
  prevention and, 239–249
Early stimulation, importance of, 245–247
Educable child, defined, 209
Educational assessment
  defined, 179
  AAMD Adaptive Behavior Scale in,
    183–186
  Balthazar Scales of Adaptive Behavior in,
    186–189
  Caine-Levine Social Competency Scale
    in, 182–183
  Camelot Behavioral Checklist in, 189–192
  Portage Project Checklist in, 192
  TARC Assessment System in, 193–205

Vineland Social Maturity Scale in,
    180–182
Educational Encounter Report, 122
Educational goals, in TARC System, 193
Educational intervention, *see* Intervention
Educational Testing Service, 262
Educator
    *see also* Teacher
    as disseminator, 264
    as evaluation facilitator, 263–264
    as "generalist," 260
    goals and general strategies of, 254–259
    as intervention specialist, 253–254
    public awareness of, 263–264
    as researcher, 261–263
    "tool skills" teaching of, 255–256
    as trainer of parents and other
        interventionists, 261
    "whole child" and, 260
Evaluation facilitator, educator as, 263–264
*Exceptional Children*, 8
Experimental Education Unit, University of
    Washington, 235
Expressive language pinpoints, 65–70
Eye readiness, in Development Pinpoints,
    41–43

Feedback
    dissemination and, 264
    from systems, 262–263
Feeding and drinking, by severely/
    profoundly handicapped, 132–135
Field testing, of pretest package in
    prototypic model, 168–173
Fine-motor competency, in severely/
    profoundly handicapped, 130–132
Florida State Department of Education, 281
Formative evaluation, vs. normative, 210
Foster Grandparent Program, 271
Frequency, in performance measurement,
    217

Genetic counseling, as preventive measure,
    248–249
Geographic locations, in study program,
    92–93
Grey Panthers, 12
Gross-motor pinpoints, 48–55
Gunzberg Behaviour Scales, 235

Handicapped child
    *see also* Moderately handicapped child;
        Severely/profoundly handicapped

aid to families of, 13
chronic health problems of, 28–29
curriculum materials for, 27–28
developmental patterns for, 35–109
"fading out" of dependency in, 259
foster parenting of, 13
learning capacity of, 18
parents of, 251–253
parents and family as adjunctive
    personnel for, 29
programming guidelines for, 35–109
as self-manager, 259
support system for family of, 23
Handicapped infant, prevention of
    secondary handicaps in, 251
*see also* Parenting
Handicapped persons
    *see also* Severely/profoundly
        handicapped
    changed attitudes toward, 4–5
    community acceptance of, 11–13
    inadequate services to, 9
    public apathy toward, 4
Happenings chart, for severely/profoundly
    handicapped, 123–124
Head Start, 9
"Human resources," teaching of, 258

Imitation, as instructional procedure, 24–25
Infant
    complex visual and auditory
        discriminations by, 246
    early stimulation of, 245–247
    handicapped, 251
    sensory deprivation in, 246–247
Infant, Toddler, and Pre-School Research
    and Intervention Project, 303
Information, matching services and needs
    in, 271
Information gaps, types of, 269–2$0
Initial field test, for pretest package in
    prototypic model of instructional
    materials, 168–171
Institutionalization, vs. early and
    continuous intervention, 239
Instructional materials
    *see also* Lattice system
    prototypic model for, 155–176
    teachers' willingness to evaluate, 175
Instructional Objectives, in TARC
    Assessment System, 202–204
Instructional procedures
    application in, 26

Instructional procedures (*continued*)
in comprehensive intervention, 24–27
differentiation in, 26
primary reinforcer in, 25–26
Instructional programs
prerequisite knowledge for, 156
prototypic model for, 156–175
Interdisciplinary work, 9–11
Intervention
within community and society, 267–272
comprehensive, *see* Comprehensive
intervention
coordination of service, training, and
research in, 272
earliest, 239–249
early and continuous, *see* Early and
continuous intervention
educator's role in, 253–254
information dissemination and, 269–271
need for, 23
sensorimotor stages and, 289
for severely/profoundly handicapped,
277–298
I.Q.
in early and continuous intervention, 250
early stimulation and, 247
of severely/profoundly handicapped,
111–112
Item data, in performance measurement,
214–215

Kansas, University of, 304–305
Kansas Neurological Institute, 195,
204–205, 304
Key-word classification system, in TARC
Assessment System, 204–205

Language acquisition, generative theory of,
59–60
*Language Acquisition Program for the
Severely Retarded* (Kent), 303
Language deficits, in severely handicapped
population, 55–57
Language development
expressive language overview in, 65
normal, 59–61
receptive language overview in, 62–65
in severely/profoundly handicapped,
144–147
Language Development Program
Guess, Sailor and Baer form of, 304–309
illustration of, 312–318
instructions in, 310

preliminary results in, 318–320
programming for generalization in,
311–318
scoring sheets for, 322–324
sequence of training steps in, 306–307
for severely handicapped child, 301–323
stimulus materials needed in, 309–310
structure of training steps in, 309–318
three-term relations in, 302–303
training goal in, 309
Language structures
language acquisition and, 57–59
at phonological level, 57–58
at semantic level, 58–59
at syntactic level, 58–59
Latency, in performance measurement, 217
Lattice developed, in lattice system,
165–166
Lattice system
cell compartments in, 162
construction of, 158–166
defined, 157–158
en route objections in, 162–164
entry behaviors in, 161, 165
lattice developed in, 165–166
modifications to, 166
prerequisite knowledge in, 158–160
in prototypic model of instruction
materials, 157–166
ridgeline in, 162
rules for, 163
for sensorimotor period, 290
sequence in, 162
"shoes tied" in, 167
skills analysis in, 161
skills hierarchy in, 162
skills identification in, 160–161
stepladder format in, 163
subgoals in, 164–165
subject matter in, 160
task analysis in, 160
terminal goals in, 163–165
testing and evaluating in, 165
Learning capacity, limitations on, 18
Learning process, stages in, 6
Leisure time activities, Developmental
Pinpoints in, 79–81
Limited-response strategy, in performance
measurement, 225–226
Linguistic development, intervention and,
288
*see also* Language development;
Language Development Program

Mailman Center for Child Development, 281, 288, 297
Maternal nutrition, parenting and, 241
Math related topics, in study program, 99–100
Mental age, reading readiness and, 82–83
Mental retardation, prevention of, 239–249
   see also Parenting; Retardation; Severely/profoundly retarded
Miami, University of, 288
Mimosa collage program, 257
Moderately handicapped child, 6–7
   see also Handicapped child
Mother's age, mental retardation and, 242–243
Mother's nutrition, mental retardation and, 241
Motor development, in severely/profoundly handicapped, 128–130
Motor sequence, definitions of terms in, 41
Motor skills, Developmental Pinpoints for, 39–55
Multidisciplinary effects, 9
Music pinpoints, 80

Nasal hygiene, in severely/profoundly handicapped, 139–140
National Association of State Directors of Special Education, 273
National Center for Child Abuse and Neglect, 243
National Institute of Mental Health, 183
Numerical identification, in study program, 99

Office of Child Development, Bureau of Education for Handicapped Collaborative Projects, 9
Oral hygiene, in severely/profoundly handicapped, 140–141
Ordination, in study program, 98–99

Parallel play, 9
Parent(s)
   in constructive strategy approach, 288
   educator as trainer of, 261
   of handicapped child, 251–253
   as intervention specialists, 257–258
   "mourning" of handicapped child by, 251–252
   role of in early and continuous intervention, 249–252

Parenting
   accident prevention and, 244–245
   age-related factors in, 242–243
   child abuse and neglect in, 243–244
   disease and, 243
   drug ingestion and drug abuse in, 241–242
   early stimulation of infant in, 245–247
   education for, 240–247
   maternal nutrition in, 241
   prenatal care in, 244
   problems of, 240–247
Parent-professional partnership, 8
Parent training programs, for severely/ profoundly handicapped children, 279
   see also Parenting
Parsons (Kansas) State Hospital and Training Center, 183, 205
Patience, exercise and teaching of, 259
Perceptual cognitive competency, in severely/profoundly handicapped, 147–149
Percent data, in performance measurement, 216
Performance measurement, 209–236
   advancing children to new tasks in, 231
   behavior counts in, 215–216
   binary data in, 214
   counting, timing, and recording procedures in, 229–230
   data collection in, 214, 222–230
   data collection planning in, 218–230
   data collection specification in, 226–227
   data decision rules in, 230–235
   data types in, 213–218
   duration in, 218
   formative classroom type, 211–213
   formative vs. summative, 210–211
   frequency in, 217
   item data in, 214–215
   latency in, 217
   limited-response strategy in, 225–226
   objective specification in, 221
   percent data in, 216
   rate of change or "celeration" in, 235
   ratings scales in, 212
   rules for evaluation of progress toward objective, 232–233
   standard data procedures in, 211
   summative data in, 235
   teaching strategies in, 221–226
   trials to criterion in, 218
   visual display in, 233–235

Personal/social behavior skills, teaching of, 256–258
*Persons and Things*, in Language Development Program, 305, 309, 312–313, 318–319
Pinpoint, defined, 37
Pinpointing, in program development, 38
    *see also* Developmental Pinpoints
POER (Problem Oriented Educational Record), 282
Portage Project Checklist, 192, 235
*Possession, Color, Size, Relation, and Morphological Grammar*, in Language Development Program, 305, 309
Precautionary Card, 282–284
Precision teaching, 37
    *see also* Educator; Teacher; Teaching strategies
Pregnancy
    accident prevention during, 244–245
    age-related aspects of, 242
    termination of, 243
    Developmental Pinpoints in, 90–91
Premath overview, 102–106
Premath pinpoints, 103–106
Prenatal care, parenting and, 244
Prereading, Developmental Pinpoints in, 81–88
Prereading overview, 87
Prereading pinpoints, 88
Prerequisite knowledge, in lattice system, 158–160
Prerequisite knowledge, in skills acquisition, 156
Prescriptive planning skill, for severely/ profoundly handicapped, 121–122
Pretest package
    final field testing in, 173
    initial field testing and, 168–171
    program format in, 168
    in prototypic model, 166–174
    secondary field testing in, 171–173
Prevention
    *see also* Parenting
    as earliest form of intervention, 239–249
    educator as evaluator of, 263–264
    genetic counseling in, 248–249
Prewriting, Developmental Pinpoints in, 88–90
Prewriting pinpoints, 89–90
Primary reinforcer, in skill acquisition and maintenance, 25–26

Problem Oriented Educational Record, 282
Problem Survey Card, 284
Professional, training of, 10
Profoundly handicapped
    *see also* Severely/profoundly handicapped
    characteristics of, 112
    comprehensive services for, 17–30
    educational programming for, 111–154
    institutionalizing of, 113, 239
    model community programs for, 20–21
Program Conclusion Card, 287
Program development, pinpointing in, 38
Program Implementation Card, 286
Program Monitoring Card, 285
Program Overview Card, 284–285
Program Plan Card, 285–286
Project MESH, Parsons State Hospital, 205
Prototypic model
    child and teacher data statements in, 175
    instructional program development in, 173–175
    lattice system in, 157–166
    pretest package and, 166–174
    primary decisions in, 156–157
    teacher error and feedback in, 172
Public awareness, educator's role in, 263–264

Rate of change, in performance measurement, 235
Readiness
    defined, 83–84
    Developmental Pinpoints in, 85–87
    other factors associated with, 100
    for severely/profoundly handicapped, 116
Readiness pinpoints, format of, 101–106
Reading readiness
    defined, 83–84
    factors relating to, 85
    history of concept, 81–83
Receptive language overview, 62–65
Recording procedures, in performance measurement, 229–230
Registry system, 10
Reinforcement
    auditory, 107
    gustatory, 107
    olfactory, 107
    proprioceptive, 107
    in skill acquisition, 25
    tactual-kinesthetic, 107
    visual, 107

Reinforcement activities, Developmental Pinpoints in, 106–108
Research, educator's role in, 261–263
Research background, in studies program, 94–95
Rote counting, in studies program, 95–96
Rubella epidemic, effects of, 243

Secondary field test, shoe tie program in, 169–170
Self-care development, in severely/profoundly handicapped, 132–144
Self-Extended Control, in Language Development Program, 307
Self-help skills, in Development Pinpoints, 70–75
Self-help skills pinpoints, 71–75
Sensorimotor period, mapping of, 290
Sensorimotor stages, intervention and, 289
Sensorimotor training, theoretical framework for, 292–293
Sensory deprivation, in infant, 246–247
Sensory development, for severely/profoundly handicapped, 125–128
Sequence, in study program, 99
Sequenced Inventory of Communication Development, 235
Set size, in study program, 96–97
Severely handicapped child
    see also Handicapped child; Severely/profoundly handicapped
    adjunctive services for, 28–29
    basic life skills of, 155
    behavioral technology for, 19
    "care" for, 267
    comprehensive services for, 17–30
    defined, 180
    dietary problems of, 29
    educational assessment for, 179–207
    future work with, 3–14
    language acquisition by, 57–59
    language deficits in, 55–57
    model community programs for, 20–21
    prototypic model of instructional materials for, 155–176
    social adjustment for, 75–79
    teaching methods for, 19–20
    as uneducable, 8
Severely handicapped infants
    early and continuous intervention for, 239–273
    interdisciplinary preparation for work with, 264–265

Severely/profoundly handicapped
    auditory discrimination in, 126
    card programs for, 281–287
    charting and behavior evaluation for, 117
    constructive strategy for, 287–297
    corrective strategy for, 281–287
    cost of care for, 267
    curriculum chart for, 117–119
    curriculum planning for, 114–115
    demand for resources for, 278
    dressing by, 135–138, 261–262
    Educational Encounter Report for, 120–122
    educator's goals and strategies for, 254–259
    educator's shaping of responses in, 255
    feeding and drinking by, 132–135
    fine-motor competency in, 130–132
    Guess, Sailor, and Baer language development program for, 304–309
    happenings chart for, 123–124
    "human resources" teaching for, 258
    individual prescriptive planning sheet for, 120–122
    instructional objectives for, 116
    intense and frequent stimuli for, 254
    intervention approaches for, 280–297
    intervention strategies for, 277–298
    language development in, 144–147
    language development programs for, 301–323
    life-encompassing service plans for, 279
    motor development in, 128–130
    nasal hygiene of, 139–140
    oral hygiene in, 140–141
    parent training programs for, 240–247, 279
    perceptual cognitive competency in, 147–149
    personal/social behavior skills for, 256–258
    program implementation for, 279
    readiness in, 116
    recognizing and reinforcing approximations for, 255
    self-care development in, 132–144
    sensory development of, 125–128
    skills retained by, 294–296
    tactile discrimination in, 125
    toileting of, 141–144
    toilet training chart for, 123
    "tool skills" essential for, 255–256
    training for work with, 265–266
    training system for, 294

Severely/profoundly handicapped
(*continued*)
    visual discrimination in, 127
    vocational skill training programs for, 279
    washing and bathing by, 138–139
Severely retarded
    *see also* Severely/profoundly
        handicapped
    characteristics of, 112
    defined, 111–112
    educational programming for, 111–154
    institutionalizing of, 113, 239
Shaping, as instructional procedure, 24
Shoe tie program, in prototypic instructional
        model, 167, 169–170, 175
Skill acquisition
    *see also* Prototypic model
    differentiation in, 26
    lattice system in, 160–161
    prerequisite knowledge in, 156
    vs. skill maintenance, 25
    vs. skill mastery, 6–7
Skill Acquisition Program Bibliography,
        191–192
Skill domains, antecedent arrangement in,
        296–297
Skill generalization, 26
Skill reinforcement, 25
Skills hierarchy, sequence in, 162
Social adjustment, for severely
        handicapped, 75
Social behavior skills, for severely/
        profoundly handicapped, 256–258
Social interaction pinpoints, 77–79
Social interaction skills, in Developmental
        Pinpoints, 75–79
Social worker, role of, 252–253
Society, intervention strategies within,
        267–272
Socioeconomic status, in study program, 93
Speech retardation, in severely
        handicapped, 56
    *see also* Language development
Standardized Test Data Card, 284

Study program
    age and, 93–94
    background of research in, 94–95
    cardination in, 98
    Developmental Pinpoints and, *see*
        Developmental Pinpoints
    geographic locations in, 92

math-related topics in, 99–100
numerical identification in, 99
ordination in, 98–99
rote counting in, 95–96
sequence in, 99
set size in, 96–97
socioeconomic status and, 93
Systematic instruction, need for, 5–8
Systems, feedback from, 262–263

Tactile discrimination, in severely/
        profoundly handicapped, 125
TARC (Topeka Association for Retarded
        Citizens) Assessment Inventory,
        194–196
TARC Assessment System, 193–205, 235
    assessment stage in, 194–196
    curriculum selection in, 204–205
    instructional objectives in, 203–204
    formulating instructional objectives in
        202–204
    profiling stage in, 196–201
TARC Profile data, 198–201
Teacher
    *see also* Educator; Instructional
        materials; Teaching (*adj.*)
    application and, 26–27
    developmental projects for, 37–109
    human resources use and, 258
    programming problems of, 35
    in prototypic model of instructional
        program, 175
    use of cues and, 258–259
Teacher error, in prototypic skills model,
        172
Teaching fads, 7
Teaching strategies, selection of in
        performance measurement, 221–226
Terminal goal, in lattice system, 163
Three-term relationships, in language
        development, 302–303
*Time*, 12
Timing procedures, in performance
        measurement, 229–230
"Titicut Follies," 4
Toileting, of severely/profoundly
        handicapped, 141–144
Toilet training chart, 123
Topeka Association for Retarded Citizens,
        193
    *see also* TARC Assessment System
*Trainer Correction Procedure*, in Language

Development Program, 314
Training
    educator's role in, 264–266
    interdisciplinary preparation for, 264–265
    research and, 272–273
Trials to criterion, in performance
    measurement, 218

University-Affiliated Facilities, 252–253

Velcro fasteners, in self-dressing skills,
    261–262
Very young handicapped children, early and
    continuous intervention for, 231–273
    see also Handicapped child; Handicapped
        infant; Severely/profoundly
        handicapped
Vineland Social Maturity Scale, 180–182
Vineland Training School, 180
Visual discrimination, in severely/

profoundly handicapped, 127
Visual display, in performance
    measurement, 233–235

Want-object-label, in Language
    Development Programs, 316–318
Washing and bathing, by severely/
    profoundly handicapped, 138–139
Washington State, education-for-all
    legislation in, 268–269
Washington University Experimental
    Education Unit, 235
"Whole child"
    care program for, 252
    global skills for, 260
Willowbrook (Rivera), 4
Wisconsin, University of, 247

Yakima Valley School, 18

# CONTRIBUTORS

DONALD M. BAER, Ph.D., Professor, Bureau of Child Research, Department of Human Development, University of Kansas, Lawrence, Kansas 66045

DIANE BRICKER, PhD., Associate Professor of Pediatrics and Educational Psychology; Administrator, The Debbie School, Mailman Center for Child Development, University of Miami, P. O. Box 520006, Biscayne Annex, Miami, Florida 33152

WILLIAM BRICKER, Ph.D., Professor of Pediatrics and Educational Psychology, The Debbie School, Mailman Center for Child Development, University of Miami, P. O. Box 520006, Biscayne Annex, Miami, Florida 33152

MARILYN COHEN, Ph.D., Program Coordinator—Elementary and Secondary Training, Experimental Educational Unit, WJ-10, CDMRC, University of Washington, Seattle, Washington 98195

LAURA DENNISON, M.A., Training Coordinator, Debbie School, Mailman Center for Child Development, University of Miami, P. O. Box 520006, Biscayne Annex, Miami, Florida 33152

VALENTINE DMITRIEV, M.Ed., Educator III, Coordinator of the Down's Syndrome Programs, College of Education, and Experimental Education Unit, WJ-10, Child Development and Mental Retardation Center*, University of Washington, Seattle, Washington 98195

EUGENE EDGAR, Ph.D., Associate Professor of Education, Experimental Education Unit, WJ-10, CDMRC, University of Washington, Seattle, Washington 98195

DALE GENTRY, Ph.D., Lecturer and Principal, Experimental Education Unit, WJ-10, CDMRC, University of Washington, Seattle, Washington 98195

*Hereafter referred to as CDMRC.

PAM GROSS, M.A., Assistant Program Coordinator—Elementary and Secondary Training, Experimental Education Unit, WJ-10, CDMRC, University of Washington, Seattle, Washington 98195

DOUG GUESS, Ed.D., Associate Professor, Department of Special Education, University of Kansas, Lawrence, Kansas

NORRIS G. HARING, Ed.D., Director, Experimental Education Unit, Child Development and Mental Retardation Center, University of Washington, Seattle, Washington 98105

ALICE HAYDEN, Ph.D., Director, Model Preschool Center for Handicapped Children, Experimental Education Unit, WJ-10, CDMRC, University of Washington, Seattle, Washington 98195

R. DON HORNER, Project Coordinator, Professional Training Program Development Unit, Department of Special Education, University of Kansas, Lawrence, Kansas 66045

RICHARD IACINO, M.A., Program Coordinator, Debbie School, Mailman Center for Child Development, University of Miami, P. O. Box 520006, Biscayne Annex, Miami, Florida 33152

BILL KEOGH, M.S., Research Associate, Kansas Neurological Institute, 3107 West 21st Street, Topeka, Kansas 66604

DONALD MEYERS, Program Director, Pennsylvania Department of Education, 123 Forster Street, Harrisburg, Pennsylvania 17102

GAEL D. McGINNESS, M.A., Research Information Specialist III and Educator II, Experimental Education Unit, WJ-10, CDMRC, University of Washington, Seattle, Washington 98195

CONNIE G. PIOUS, B.A., Research Publications Editor and Information Specialist, Experimental Education Unit, WJ-10, CDMRC, University of Washington, Seattle, Washington 98195.

WAYNE SAILOR, Associate Professor, Department of Special Education, San Francisco State University, San Francisco, California

DR. DEBORAH D. SMITH, Special Education, Kennedy Center, Peabody College, Nashville, Tennessee 37203

DR. JAMES O. SMITH, Special Education, Kennedy Center, Peabody College, Nashville, Tennessee 37203

ELLEN SOMERTON, Program Director, Pennsylvania Training Model, Pennsylvania Department of Education, Bureau of Special and Compensatory Education, Division of Special Education, 123 Forster Street, Harrisburg, Pennsylvania 17102